The Essential Guide to Open Source Flash Development

Chris Allen
Wade Arnold
Aral Balkan
Nicolas Cannasse
John Grden
Moses Gunesch
Marc Hughes
R. Jon MacDonald
Andy Zupko

an Apress® company

The Essential Guide to Open Source Flash Development

Credits

Lead Editor
Ben Renow-Clarke

Production Editor
Laura Esterman

Technical Reviewer
Christophe Herreman

Compositor
Dina Quan

Editorial Board
Clay Andres, Steve Anglin, Ewan Buckingham,
Tony Campbell, Gary Cornell, Jonathan Gennick,
Matthew Moodie, Joseph Ottinger, Jeffrey Pepper,
Frank Pohlmann, Ben Renow-Clarke,
Dominic Shakeshaft, Matt Wade, Tom Welsh

Proofreader
April Eddy

Indexer
Becky Hornyak

Project Manager
Kylie Johnston

Artist
April Milne

Copy Editor
Kim Wimpsett

Interior and Cover Designer
Kurt Krames

Associate Production Director
Kari Brooks-Copony

Manufacturing Director
Tom Debolski

For my dear, wonderful parents, Haluk and Mehlika Balkan. Thank you for a lifetime of unconditional love and support. Thank you for believing in me. Thank you for teaching me that I can do anything I set my mind to. I am forever in your debt.
—*Aral Balkan*

To Airi.
—*Nicolas Cannasse*

A glass raised to Winsor McCay—the original animator and one of America's greatest talents.
—*Moses Gunesch*

To my wife, Jess, for putting up with me, and to the open source community, for constantly amazing me.
—*Marc Hughes*

To my family and friends who provide constant encouragement and support even though I often take on much more work than our relationships should allow.
—*R. Jon MacDonald*

CONTENTS AT A GLANCE

CONTENTS

ABOUT THE AUTHORS

With extensive experience developing for the Flash Platform and Java, **Chris Allen** is a leader in the open source Flash community. Over the past eight years he has been a software architect and developer for various companies including Cambridge Technology Partners, Mass General Hospital, and Scholastic. Chris is currently the president and CEO of Infrared5, a consulting firm built around services for the open source Red5 server, and he is the co-project manager and a Java developer for the open source Red5 project.

Wade Arnold is the CEO of T8DESIGN, which is a rich media and application firm located in Cedar Falls, Iowa. Wade is responsible for strategic planning and product development as well as for creating an exciting and rewarding corporate environment. Wade has been selected to be a speaker at several national software development and security conferences. He has an active dialogue with Adobe and actively participates in prerelease beta development of Flash, Flex, and AIR, and he is passionately involved in open source Flash/Flex development and aligns T8DESIGN behind these initiatives. Wade is the lead developer of AMFPHP and the open source implementation of Flash Remoting. Wade has a degree in computer science emphasizing intelligent systems and an MBA from the University of Iowa. T8DESIGN works with hundreds of community banks and medium to enterprise customers including Nike, McDonald's, John Deere, AT&T, Lindsay Corporation, Best Buy, and the Department of Defense.

Aral Balkan is a Flash Platform veteran and overall Internet junkie. Oh, and this year he's producing the world's first large-scale online web conference, Singularity.

Aral cofounded and coordinates OSFlash.org, authored the pattern-based ActionScript framework Arp, and created the SWX data format, SWX RPC, and SWX PHP. His latest open source project is the GAE SWF Project, providing Flash and Flex developers with knowledge and tools to build Rich Internet Applications on Google App Engine.

Aral is a published author and has contributed to several books and magazine articles. Specifically, he is the author of the *Adobe Flex 2 QuickStart Guide* and *Flex 3 QuickStart Guide* and has authored six courses on Flash, Flex, ActionScript, and open source development.

Aral is a regular speaker at international conferences including Macworld, FlashForward, d.construct, FITC, Wizards of OS, and Adobe MAX.

Nicolas Cannasse is one of the cofounders of OSFlash.org and the creator of the MTASC compiler. He is also the CTO at Motion-Twin, a French independent game studio making web games in Flash. For the past two years, he has been working on haXe, an open source programming language for the Web, capable of compiling to Flash but also to JavaScript and the server side.

With more than eight years of experience in working with Flash technology, **John Grden** is the creator of the Xray debugger, FLEXible (an MXML editor), and the FLASC compiler GUI, and he is a core member and contributor on the Papervision3D project. John also started the Red5 open source server project and is the co-project manager along with Chris Allen. John has also served as the director of Flash Platform for BLITZ and was the senior Flash developer with Zing.com. John currently lives near Houston, Texas, and works as a senior software developer for Infrared5.

Moses Gunesch has spent a decade teaching and working with ActionScript, inspired early on by Flash phenomena like Flight404.com, Remedi Project, Praystation, Second Story, Deconcept, Natzke.com, Yugop.com, and Robert Penner. MosesSupposes.com is currently based in Brooklyn, where Moses can be found architecting large-scale web applications for advertising clients and startup ventures (between tasty slices of New York pizza). His current interest in social networking design is rooted in having cofounded the popular GotoAndPlay.net group in his hometown of Portland, Oregon, in 2001—a hub for Flash, 3D, and graphic design professionals and host to its own digital film festival. Moses established himself as a leading figure in animation systems for ActionScript with his popular Fuse Kit. Fuse has now been used in more than 60 countries, as well as in many top advertising agencies and award-winning websites. Moses strives to continue contributing valuable ideas to the ActionScript community via open source.

Marc Hughes is the manager of software engineering at Tom Snyder Productions, an educational software publisher in Watertown, Massachusetts. While there, he's worked on several large educational applications including FASTT Math and TimeLiner XE. Outside of his day job, Marc wrote AgileAgenda (http://www.agileagenda.com), an AIR/Flex-based project-scheduling application that won the Best in Show award of Adobe's AIR Developer Derby in October 2007. He's also authored several useful Flex-based open source projects, including a popular library called ObjectHandles that allows users to move and resize components inside a Flex application. His open source projects, as well as his blog, can be found at http://www.rogue-development.com.

A certified Adobe Flash and web developer, **R. Jon MacDonald** offers a wealth of expertise in development, design, usability, and visual communication. Over the course of nine years, Jon has honed his skills through a multitude of experiences.

Jon works with household brands, advertising agencies, and talented designers and developers across the country through JonnyMac Design, the interactive collective he started, as well as XPLANE, a consulting and design firm that drives business results by clarifying complex information through visual communications.

His portfolio and blog can be found at http://www.jonnymac.com.

With more than seven years development experience, **Andy Zupko** has extensive knowledge of object-oriented programming and the Flash framework. Originally a developer of COM servers for medical imaging systems and custom RIAs, he has recently shifted his focus to the development of front-end UIs, combining math and visuals to create rich environments that enhance user experience. He is a senior software engineer for Infrared5 and a core member of the Papervision3D team.

ABOUT THE TECHNICAL REVIEWER

Christophe Herreman is a software architect and developer living in Belgium. He mainly focuses on Flex-based Rich Internet Applications and likes to philosophize about object-oriented development. He is an active open source contributor and the author and lead developer of the Prana Framework (http://www.pranaframework.org). He has also been involved in other projects such as AS2lib, AMFPHP, and ARP.

You can find him blogging at http://www.herrodius.com.

ACKNOWLEDGMENTS

I would like to thank my wife and business partner, Rebecca Allen, for supporting me while I'm trying to do too much. I would also like to thank everyone on the Red5 team for doing their parts to make Red5 a reality. Some of those guys include John Grden, Luke Hubbard, Joachim Bauch, Dominick Accattato, Paul Gregoire, Steven Gong, and Thijs Triemstra. It's also worth mentioning a word of gratitude to conference organizers Shawn Pucknell, Stewart McBride, and John Davey for seeing the potential and interest in Red5 and being willing to take a chance on letting us present on our technology before it was the thing to do. Others who deserve mention are Keith Peters, Sam Agesilas, Todd Anderson, Jon Valliere, Andy Zupko, Richard Blakely, Jerry Chabolla, and Paul Blakely. Then of course there's the whole team at friends of ED that made this book possible: Chris Mills, Ben Renow-Clarke, Pete Aylward, Kylie Johnston, Kim Wimpsett, and the rest. Thanks!

Chris Allen

I would like to thank the community of developers who continue to push what is capable online. Your questions and inspirational projects are what keep me working into the late hours to push what is possible. To Dr. Gray and Dr. Wallingford, thank you for teaching me how to *think* computer science. For allowing me to start working on computers from an early age when the rest of the world could not even access a PC, thank you, Mom and Dad; in addition to resources, thanks for aiding in the development of my perseverance. And most important, thanks to my amazing wife, Shannon, who not only puts up with but supports my dreams. Bushel and a peck, Shannon, David, and #2!

Wade Arnold

I want to thank the open source Flash community: every day I learn from you, I get inspired by the amazing things you do, and I feel honored to count so many of you among my friends. You make a difference every day by sharing your knowledge and your passion with others. You are the soul of Flash.

Aral Balkan

I'd like to thank Aral for being a good friend and allowing me to help out way back when we were creating new OS projects by hand and for giving us a place to park these awesome ideas! Without Aral, we wouldn't have a community like we do now—that's a fact. Also, I don't know where I'd be without Chris Allen—he has been a great friend, has been an awesome mentor, and has really made an impact on my Flash life. I couldn't have gotten this far without him. I *have* to say thanks to Luke Hubbard, Joachim Bauch, Steven Gong, and Dominick Accattato for having the backbones to jump in on Red5 from day one and make it happen! That comprises the "original 6" that was known back in the day when Red5 first breathed life. I have to give thanks for my family as well: Linda, Riley, and Luke (yes, I named my son after Luke Skywalker—get used to it). Because of them, I was able to do these projects and succeed, and they're the coolest fans I could ever ask for. I love them dearly. And mostly, I want to thank God for all the blessings he's given me; by saving me from either myself or calamity altogether, he's always been by my side, and I'm most grateful for His patience, peace, and help in my life. Rock on.

John Grden

I would like to thank my parents, whose foresight to put a Commodore 64/128 in my bedroom as a child provided me with the start to a wonderful means of turning a passion into a living. Thanks to Aral Balkan for providing me with this opportunity and trusting me to do right by his project. Thanks to all of my co-workers, past and present, who have influenced and aided in my growth as a developer. Finally, thanks to the amazing Flash Platform community—without such an active and open community, projects like those included in this book would not exist.

R. Jon MacDonald

INTRODUCTION

Welcome to *The Essential Guide to Open Source Flash Development*. The concept of "open source" has been around for a while now, and most people are familiar with its meaning, but how does that relate to Adobe Flash, which is a traditionally closed platform? When people talk about open source Flash, they can mean any number of things—an ActionScript library, a code editor, a new messaging format—what's important is that the project extends or supports Flash and follows the open source methodology. One of the leading lights in the open source Flash world is Aral Balkan, and he put together the OSFlash.org website that brought together all of the existing disparate open source Flash projects into one focused community. This community blossomed to produce some incredible projects that not only expanded the possibilities of what Flash can do but also completely altered people's perceptions of what Flash meant as a tool and how SWF files could be created.

This book is a collection of some of the best of those projects. We've collected projects that run the whole gamut of the open source Flash world so you can get an idea of just what sort of power is available to you. Alongside the project-specific chapters, we've also gone into a lot of detail on how these projects can be integrated to make a full open source SWF workflow or how you can pick and choose the projects that you want to use to expand your existing workflow. After all, it's one thing to experiment with these projects at home, but their real use is to empower your current workflow to make Flash a bigger, better, faster, and more fun field to work within.

Adobe has also started an open source initiative (see `http://opensource.adobe.com`) that already has some pretty exciting projects as part of it and is sure to see even more in the future. This is great news for the open source Flash community. With Adobe's dedication to opening up its platform and more and more users becoming involved in open source projects, the future looks pretty rosy for open source Flash development. There hasn't been a better time than now to dive in.

Layout conventions

To keep this book as clear and easy to follow as possible, the following text conventions are used throughout.

Important words or concepts are normally highlighted on the first appearance in **bold type**.

Code is presented in `fixed-width font`.

New or changed code is normally presented in **`bold fixed-width font`**.

Pseudo-code and variable input are written in *italic fixed-width font*.

Menu commands are written in the form Menu ➤ Submenu ➤ Submenu.

Where we want to draw your attention to something, we've highlighted it like this:

> *Ahem, don't say I didn't warn you.*

Sometimes code won't fit on a single line in a book. Where this happens, we use an arrow like this: ➡.

```
This is a very, very long section of code that should be written all on ➡
the same line without a break.
```

Chapter 1

INTRODUCING THE WORLD OF OPEN SOURCE FLASH

by Aral Balkan

I was eight years old when my father brought home our first computer. It was an 8MHz IBM XT PC compatible with a four-color CGA display, a whopping 640KB of RAM, and a 20MB hard drive. I quickly tired of playing the few games available at the time—Alley Cat, Moonbugs, Dig Dug—and began leafing through the BASIC manual that came with the computer to write my own games.

Source code, especially in those days, was everywhere. Most computer magazines had pages and pages of code—games, utilities, what have you. Commercial software was in its infancy, and you were as likely to copy a listing from a magazine as you were to find an application to buy.

So, I learned BASIC by copying source code written and shared by others. I dabbled in Logo. I wrote games and even a primitive word processor to keep myself amused. When I started to outgrow BASIC, I moved on to Pascal and C and briefly flirted with Prolog.

That was 23 years ago.

Many years later, I would find that programming knowledge invaluable when a company called Macromedia released a version of a web animation application called Flash with a scripting language called ActionScript.

Today, software is something most people buy in a box off a shelf (or download from the Web) and you'd be hard-pressed to find source code listings in computer magazines, but there is more readily available source code in the world than ever before thanks to the astronomic rise in popularity of the open source software movement.

Open source software is software for which the source code is freely available. But that's not its only defining characteristic. In fact, the Open Source Initiative lists ten criteria that an approved open source license must meet.

> *You can read the Open Source Initiative's definition of* open source *at* `http://opensource.org/docs/osd`.

The *sprit* of open source is the free sharing of knowledge. The ultimate goal is to create high-quality software by practicing an open and transparent development process that is subject to peer review. These types of definitions, however, are dry, academic statements that cannot capture the character or spice of a thing. So, let's get back to the story.

When I first started dabbling in ActionScript in the days of Flash 4 and Flash 5, I learned an invaluable amount from the knowledge shared by members of the Flash community. Flash pioneers such as Branden Hall, Sam Wan, Ted Patrick, Joshua Davis, Jared Tarbell, Ralf Bokelberg, Keith Peters, Colin Moock, Peter Hall, Charlie Cordova, and Jesse Warden taught me invaluable lessons by sharing their code, their time, and their perspectives with me and the rest of the community on their blogs and on lists such as the seminal FlashCoders.

All this is to say that the Flash Platform, from its earliest days, has always been about sharing and community. In the beginning, open source on the Flash Platform was limited to sharing source code, the binary FLA files used by the Flash IDE, and (later) the ActionScript files and classes. In 2004, Nicolas Cannasse released an open source ActionScript 2 compiler called Motion-Twin ActionScript 2 Compiler (MTASC), and the character of open source on the Flash Platform was changed forever.

Having an open source compiler meant that developers on the Flash Platform were not limited to just sharing Flash code but could create their own open source development tools. The release of swfmill, an XML-to-SWF compiler, allowed developers to add assets to their Flash applications. This was followed by the creation of a fully open source development stack for the Flash Platform called AMES. AMES stands for "ASDT, Apache, MTASC, Eclipse, swfmill"—the four open source tools that compose it. ActionScript Development Tool (ASDT) is an Eclipse plug-in for developing ActionScript code. It was the first development environment for ActionScript that gave Flash developers the professional-quality tools (such as language intelligence) that the primitive code editor in the Flash IDE did not provide.

AMES influenced the creation of the commercial Flash Development Tool (FDT) and later provided healthy competition for the Flex team at Adobe, spurring Adobe to improve its own Flex Builder. Alongside AMES, other development tools such as FlashDevelop also surfaced at this time and are still going strong.

Development tools aside, open source frameworks such as Arp, Cairngorm, and PureMVC make it easier for developers to work in teams and build scalable web applications on the Flash Platform, regardless of whether they are using open source tools, the Flash IDE, or Flex.

The birth of OSFlash.org, a hub where open source developers could meet, plan, and build their projects, coincided with the "tipping point" in open source development that was spurred on by the release of MTASC and swfmill. OSFlash became an incubator that led to the creation of new open source software on the Flash platform. I remember the days when Red5 was nothing more than an idea voiced by John Grden on the OSFlash mailing list! What's most special about OSFlash for me is that it led to the formation of lasting friendships, companies, and even a rock group!

Fast-forwarding to the present day, some of the most exciting technologies on the Flash Platform are open source. These include Papervision3D, the simple and powerful 3D library that made 3D feasible on the Flash Platform; Red5, the open source server that handles streaming audio and video and real-time shared objects; SWX, the native data format for the Flash Platform; and, with Flex 3, the Flex SDK, including the Flex compilers, as open sourced by Adobe.

You will read about many of these technologies, and others, in the rest of this book, many times from the actual authors and contributors to the projects. The contribution of the open source community to the Flash Platform has been and continues to be immense. And what a lovely community it is too. Open source is about sharing knowledge and furthering the state of the art. I hope that this book helps you start on your own journey of knowledge. And once you're ready, I hope that you too share what you have learned, and the wonderful things you have created, with others. You can start getting involved today by joining OSFlash's mailing list and saying "hi."

Today, we stand on the brink of a web application revolution with Google's recent announcement of Google App Engine, a massively scalable, integrated development and deployment platform that perfectly complements the toolsets—both open and closed source—that we have on the Flash Platform. This is truly an exciting time to be creating web applications, and the tools and servers you will be reading about in this book are at the cutting edge of web technologies today.

Welcome to the revolution. Welcome to open source Flash. I hope you enjoy the journey!

The following links should help you get started on your journey in the world of open source Flash. Remember that you can almost always find information about an open source Flash project by going to http://osflash.org/<project name> *(for example,* http://osflash.org/papervision3d*).*

- *OSFlash*: http://osflash.org
- *OSFlash Mailing List*: http://osflash.org/mailman/listinfo/osflash_osflash.org
- *The GAE SWF Project*: http://gaeswf.appspot.com
- *Google App Engine*: http://code.google.com/appengine/
- *Papervision3D*: http://osflash.org/papervision3d
- *Red5*: http://osflash.org/red5
- *SWFAddress*: http://www.asual.com/swfaddress/
- *PyAMF*: http://pyamf.org/
- *Fuse*: http://osflash.org/fuse/
- *GoASAP*: http://osflash.org/goasap/
- *SWX*: http://swxformat.org
- *AMFPHP*: http://www.amfphp.org/
- *MTASC*: http://mtasc.org
- *swfmill*: http://osflash.org/swfmill
- *AMES*: http://osflash.org/ames
- *FlashDevelop*: http://osflash.org/flashdevelop
- *ASDT*: http://osflash.org/asdt
- *PureMVC*: http://puremvc.org/
- *Arp*: http://osflash.org/arp
- *Cairngorm*: http://labs.adobe.com/wiki/index.php/Cairngorm

Chapter 2

EXPLORING OPEN SOURCE FLASH: WHAT'S AVAILABLE

by Marc Hughes

In this chapter, you will get a brief introduction to some of the open source tools that are available, including both the projects covered in the rest of the book and some other noteworthy projects worth checking out on your own. We'll cover three major categories of tools:

- Development tools
- Libraries and toolkits
- Back-end, server-side technologies

These tools come from two major sources: the general open source community, which is often centered on the OSFlash.org website, and the open source initiatives that originated at Adobe to help further the Flash Platform. In this chapter, we'll look at the tools broken down by these two main contributors.

Community open source initiatives

"Community" open source projects constitute the projects contributed by individuals and companies unrelated to Adobe. Many of these started as internal company or personal projects that grew to the point where an open source development model could benefit both the people using the projects and the projects themselves.

Development tools

When doing Flash development, most people think of working in Adobe's Flash IDE. The tools covered in the following sections represent an alternate workflow when writing ActionScript code and integrating it with assets from designers. These are compilers, development environments, and other useful Flash development tools.

MTASC

The Motion-Twin ActionScript 2 Compiler (MTASC) written by Nicolas Cannasse is the cornerstone of open source ActionScript 2 development. It acts as a full compiler and linker for ActionScript 2 projects and is able to create SWFs from your source code. It's capable of compiling large amounts of code quickly, far exceeding the capabilities of the default compiler that comes with the Flash Platform.

Besides mimicking the functionality of the default Adobe compiler (MMC), MTASC introduces a few features to help aid good development practices. The first of these is preventing variables from being doubly declared in a function. For example, the following code will compile under MMC but will not compile under MTASC:

```
function test()
{
  var i = 5;
  if( true ) {
    for( var i = 0 ; i < 10 ; i++ ) { /* do something */ }
  }
}
```

Under the Flash runtime, there is only function-level scoping of variables. So, the for loop modifies the same variable that was declared before it, which leads to a common source of bugs. MTASC identifies these situations, and the compile will fail.

MTASC also doesn't allow local function definitions. This provides an extra layer of compile-time checking for parentheses closure. MTASC does support anonymous inner functions assigned to a variable.

In MTASC, you can replace the default trace() method with a method you write. This allows you to implement extended logging capabilities, redirect the output to other locations, or ignore it altogether. You'll learn more about this in Chapters 4 and 5 of this book.

For more information about MTASC and to download it, visit the project website at http://www.mtasc.org/.

ASDT

Eclipse is an open source development environment originally written for Java development. It has since been extended to work with a variety of languages from C++ to PHP. The ActionScript Development Tool (ASDT) is an Eclipse plug-in that brings ActionScript development to the Eclipse platform.

ASDT provides features such as the following:

- Code completion
- Code folding
- Code navigator and exploration tools
- Compilation using MTASC
- Syntax checking
- Syntax highlighting
- Code templates

Chapters 3 and 4 of this book go into detail about how to set up and use an ASDT-based development workflow. You can find out more about Eclipse at http://www.eclipse.org/. Information about ASDT is available at http://aseclipseplugin.sourceforge.net/.

FlashDevelop

FlashDevelop is a Windows-only alternative to the Eclipse and ASDT environment. It supports ActionScript 2 and 3 development and supports many of the same features as ASDT, including the following:

- Code completion
- Code folding
- Code navigator and exploration tools
- Compilation using MTASC or the Flex SDK
- Syntax checking
- Syntax highlighting
- Code templates
- Version control system integration

In addition, FlashDevelop has a plug-in architecture to support additional features including support for other languages such as haXe.

Chapters 3 and 4 cover using FlashDevelop, and you can read more about it on the FlashDevelop website at http://www.flashdevelop.org.

haXe development tools

haXe is a modern, high-level programming language targeting web technologies originally written by the same author of MTASC, Nicolas Cannasse. Like ActionScript, haXe can target Flash Player. Unlike ActionScript, it can also target a JavaScript or Neko runtime environment. Neko is a native system runtime environment (much like a Java JRE) that allows you to run haXe programs on a local system. It's oftentimes used for server-side development.

Being able to target multiple types of runtimes means you can write your application in a single language. You can greatly reduce your development time by sharing code between your Flash application, your server-side back-end, and the JavaScript pages on your site. Many of the standard API calls for all three environments have been generalized in the haXe standard library, allowing a high degree of reuse between environments.

The haXe syntax is similar to ActionScript and should be easy for a veteran Flash developer to pick up. Chapter 9 of this book gives you a primer of the haXe programming language to get you started writing haXe-based applications.

You can learn more about haXe from the project website at http://www.haxe.org/.

swfmill

MTASC, the Flex SDK, and the haXe compiler all provide mechanisms for converting source code into compiled SWFs. swfmill provides a mechanism for compiling raw art assets into a SWF. Using swfmill, you can create SWFs that contain bundles of art assets or fonts. swfmill is capable of putting those assets into a library for use by ActionScript or, alternatively, placing an object directly on the viewable stage. swfmill is capable of pulling assets from the following:

- Other SWF files
- Compiled SWC files (component libraries)
- PNG and JPEG images
- SVG graphics (imported as vector graphics)
- TrueType fonts

Once you create an asset SWF with swfmill, you can use MTASC to inject compiled ActionScript code into that SWF to provide an end-to-end development solution capable of replacing Adobe's Flash IDE.

You can learn more about swfmill in Chapter 4 and from the project website at http://www.swfmill.org/.

SWFObject

SWFObject is a set of JavaScript libraries and best practices for embedding Flash content into an HTML page. It provides features such as the following:

- Flash plug-in version detection
- Flash plug-in upgrades using the autoupdate feature
- Support for a wide variety of web browsers and operating systems
- Standards-compliant markup
- Graceful fallback when embedding techniques fail, including allowing you to specify alternative content
- A workaround for the "click to activate" functionality in the Internet Explorer and Opera browsers

Chapters 6 and 11 of this book talk more about SWFObject and provide several examples. You can also learn more from the SWFObject websites at http://blog.deconcept.com/swfobject/ and http://code.google.com/p/swfobject/.

Ant

Ant is a general-purpose Java-based build tool. Ant is meant to work alongside your ASDT builds, not to replace it.

As projects get more complex, the process of gathering components from different teams and assembling them becomes more and more complicated. Building through ANT allows you to maintain the integrity of your build cycle so you can be guaranteed that each build is made in the same repeatable way.

Imagine a situation where you are doing the ActionScript development, a designer down the hall is making the art assets for your project, and a web design firm in Turkey is creating the web pages in which your application will be embedded. Fully creating a new build might involve several steps:

1. Copying files from your designer to the correct location in your build tree
2. Downloading new content from the web design firm
3. Actually building your application
4. Copying your application, plus all that content, to a staging server
5. At some later time, publishing everything to a live production server

Few things in software development are more frustrating then tracking down bugs that were caused by a missed step in the build cycle. By creating an automated build script, you'll both make your life easier throughout the project and be able to guarantee a completely repeatable build process. Using Ant provides several advantages over using ASDT to make this easier:

- You can copy, delete, and move both files and directories.
- You can deploy your application over FTP, WebDav, or SSH.
- You can invoke other build tools, such as swfmill, automatically.
- You can create a build environment that others, who may not be using ASDT or FlashDevelop, can use.
- You can integrate build scripts into automated build environments.

You'll learn how to set up and use Ant in Chapters 3 and 4. Chapter 6 will revisit the topic by showing how to extend your Ant scripts to deploy your applications.

Sprouts

Although not covered in this book, Sprouts is a new open source project aimed at making it easier to set up and maintain a Flash development environment. Sprouts is capable of creating and managing the configuration of ActionScript 2, ActionScript 3, and Flex-based projects.

You can learn more about Sprouts at the Sprouts website (http://www.projectsprouts.org/).

Libraries and toolkits

A large part of the effort put in by the open source community is in producing various libraries or toolkits to make development easier. In this book, we'll be looking at a few of those including Fuse Kit and Papervision 3D. Besides these, there are many more; you can find a list of a few of them at the end of this chapter.

Fuse Kit

Fuse Kit, often referred to simply as Fuse, is a development library by Moses Gunesch that combines a tweening engine and sequencer to provide a powerful code-based animation solution for Action-Script 2 development. Using Fuse you can easily set up complex sets of animations without the need of callback functions, timers, or extensive calls to the Tween class.

The tweening engine allows you to animate all of the usual Flash properties (such as changing the x coordinate of an object to move it across the screen), plus all other properties of an object, and it even includes filter tweening.

The sequencer allows you to set up chains, or **fuses**, of tweens to create complex animation effects that are timed and sequenced with each other.

To give an idea of the power of Fuse, here is a simple example from the Fuse Kit documentation that moves a MovieClip in a rounded square.

```
var f:Fuse = new Fuse( { _x:'100', controlY:'-50' },
{ _y:'100', controlX:'50' },
{ _x:'-100', controlY:'50' },
{ _y:'-100', controlX:'-50' });
f.target = box_mc;
f.start();
```

This example shows off the simplified syntax of the tweening engine, and the first four lines represent the movement of an object in four different directions. The sequencer kicks in by executing each of these tweens sequentially without the need for the developer to determine when each part of the animation should start or stop.

You can learn more about Fuse in Chapter 10 of this book or from the project website at http://www.mosessupposes.com/Fuse/.

Papervision3D

Papervision3D is a full-featured 3D rendering engine for Flash Player. The core Papervision3D development team consists of Carlos Ulloa, John Grden, Ralph Hauwert, Tim Knip, and Andy Zupko. Using Papervision3D you can create simple 3D effects such as rotating planes or cubes or complex fully interactive 3D environments. Versions are available for both ActionScript 2 and ActionScript 3 depending on your needs.

You can read more about Papervision3D in Chapter 12 of this book, on its website at http://papervision3d.org/, or in the Papervision3D blog at http://blog.papervision3d.org/. To download the latest release from the Google Code repository, visit http://code.google.com/p/papervision3d/.

Screenweaver HX

Screenweaver HX is a desktop application deployment option for Flash applications originally created by Edwin Van Rijkom and Nicolas Cannasse. Screenweaver HX is largely written in haXe and runs in the Neko runtime environment. Using Screenweaver HX, you can host the Flash plug-in in a window and load SWFs created with either ActionScript or haXe (or any other technology capable of creating SWFs). Using this technology, you can create desktop applications in Flash that have access to local resources, such as read/write access to files, and also leverage all the capabilities of the Flash Platform. Chapter 6 of this book presents an example of how to deploy a desktop application using Screenweaver HX.

You can find out additional information or download Screenweaver HX from `http://www.screenweaver.org/`.

Server-side technologies

Much of the focus on Flash development is focused on the visual front-ends, but the server back-end can be just as tricky to get right. In the following sections, we'll explore two open source technologies—AMFPHP, SWX, and Red5—that help to create robust and scalable back-end solutions with a minimum amount of effort.

AMFPHP

The Action Message Format (AMF) is a binary data exchange format optimized for the Flash Platform. AMFPHP is one server-side implementation of this format and is the oldest of the three server-side solutions we'll be covering. AMFPHP provides Remote Procedure Call (RPC) functionality allowing Flash applications to call server-side functions. In addition to supporting AMF, it can communicate via JavaScript Object Notation (JSON) and XML-RPC. These last two options open the possibility of talking to AMFPHP using client-side technologies other than Flash.

AMFPHP allows you to focus on the domain-specific logic of your application instead of worrying about the transport mechanisms used to send data back and forth between the server and client. It's designed to be a lightweight and unobtrusive solution that is applicable to a wide variety of development approaches.

As the name implies, AMFPHP is written in PHP, allowing it to be used on a wide variety of inexpensive web hosting environments. It doesn't require any special PHP extensions. Anyone with knowledge of PHP should be able to quickly learn how to develop an AMFPHP application.

Chapter 7 of this book goes into detail about AMFPHP. You can also find out more information from the project website at `http://www.amfphp.org/`.

Red5

Red5 is an open source project focused on delivering a full Flash remoting development environment. Like AMFPHP, it provides RPC functionality over AMF. Unlike AMFPHP, it also provides streaming media and server-side shared object support.

Video and audio media can be streamed to the client, replicating much of the functionality of the Flash Media Server (FMS). Video or audio can also be recorded from the client's webcam and microphone and sent back to the server for further processing or distribution.

Shared remote objects give Flash clients a way to keep data synchronized across different clients and give them a mechanism to push data from the server to the client. Some example applications using this functionality might include a real-time chat room or a multiplayer video game.

Red5 is a Java-based server with stand-alone and J2EE-hosted versions. It's built on standard Java technologies such as Spring, Mina, and Jetty.

You can read more about Red5 at the official Red5 website at http://www.red5.org/ or in Chapters 13 and 14 of this book.

SWX

SWX is a relatively new server-side technology by Aral Balkan. It uses the SWF format for data exchange, which provides a few significant advantages over other transport mechanisms:

- Support for Flash Lite development
- Natively understood by Flash Player for a minimum of processing time
- Extremely easy to use

SWX provides an RPC mechanism allowing Flash to directly make calls into the server. Unlike AMFPHP or Red5, there are several server-side implementations of SWX:

- *SWX PHP*: http://swxformat.org/documentation/swx-php/
- *SWX Ruby*: http://swxruby.org/
- *SWX Java*: http://www.swxjava.org/

An example of using SWX from Flash follows:

```
loader.serviceClass = "Flickr";
loader.method = "swxPhotosGetRecent";
loader.debug = true;
loader.loadMovie("http://swxformat.org/php/swx.php", "GET");
```

This example downloads the 100 most recent Flickr photos and comes from an example that Aral Balkan has been distributing on small cards that measure less than $1^1/_2$ inch by $2^3/_4$ inches. That's how easy SWX is!

You can read more about SWX in Chapter 8 of this book or on the project website at http://www.swxformat.org.

Adobe open source initiatives

In recent years, Adobe has recognized the benefits of the open source development model for several of its projects and has launched a website dedicated to open source at http://opensource.adobe.com/. This includes the Flex 3 SDK development toolkit, the BlazeDS server-side solution, and several ActionScript 3–based libraries.

Flex 3 SDK

The Flex 3 SDK package is Adobe's official development environment for ActionScript 3 development using the Flex framework and targeting Flash Player 9 and newer. In April 2007 Adobe announced its intention to make the entire Flex SDK open source. Since then, Adobe has made the SDK publicly available for free, with the full source to the framework code including access to the source code of all the tools (compiler, debugger, and so on) and the framework. Adobe has also made the bug-tracking system open to the public.

You can currently find more information at the following locations:

- *The Flex 3 SDK*: http://opensource.adobe.com/wiki/display/flexsdk/Flex+SDK

- *The Flex bug-tracking database*: http://bugs.adobe.com/flex/

> *Although the core SDK is open source, Flex Builder is not part of Adobe's open source initiative and will remain a commercial product. Likewise, its Flash authoring environment remains a commercial endeavor.*
>
> *There is also a set of additional charting components that come exclusively with Flex Builder Professional, which is also not part of the open source initiative.*

BlazeDS

BlazeDS is a Java-based server solution offering real-time communication services for the Flash Platform. It consists of three major components:

- A remoting service to access server-side methods and objects

- A messaging service for a publish/subscribe messaging support

- A proxy service to allow Flash applications to access types of data not usually allowed under the Flash security sandbox

BlazeDS can be installed on a J2EE-based server or run stand-alone using the BlazeDS turnkey server. You can find both deployment options, as well as access to the source code, at the BlazeDS website (http://opensource.adobe.com/wiki/display/blazeds/BlazeDS).

ActionScript 3 libraries

In addition to the large, officially funded projects at Adobe, several ActionScript libraries are written and maintained by Adobe staff members. Some of those libraries include the following:

- as3ebaylib is a library for accessing eBay's XML API through ActionScript. You can find it at http://code.google.com/p/as3ebaylib/.

- as3corelib is a collection of classes and utilities that make ActionScript development easier. You can find it at http://code.google.com/p/as3corelib/.

- as3flexunitlib is a unit testing framework for Flex development. See Chapter 5 of this book for additional information. You can find it at http://code.google.com/p/as3flexunitlib/.

- as3odeolib is an ActionScript library for retrieving podcasts from the Odeo service. You can find it at http://code.google.com/p/as3odeolib/.

- as3youtubelib is a library for accessing the YouTube data API. You can find it at http://code.google.com/p/as3youtubelib/.

- as3syndicationlib provides a single interface for dealing with RSS and Atom feeds. You can find it at http://code.google.com/p/as3syndicationlib/.

- as3flickrlib is a library for consuming the Flickr API. You can find it at http://code.google.com/p/as3flickrlib/.

- as3mapprlib provides access to the Mappr API that combines Flickr and geo-tagged information. You can find it at http://code.google.com/p/as3mapprlib/.

- Cairngorm is a framework for developing Flex-based rich Internet applications. You can find it at http://labs.adobe.com/wiki/index.php/Cairngorm.

And many more . . .

As you've seen in this chapter, a lot of open source projects are available for Flash development. The rest of this book looks at a few of those projects. But the best thing about open source Flash is that new projects are starting all the time. Visit Flash community blogs, read the OSFlash mailing list, and do the occasional Google search since you never know what useful and amazing projects you'll find.

We'll end this chapter with a list of a few projects not covered in this book that are still worth checking out:

- AlivePDF is an ActionScript library to generate PDFs. You can find it at http://alivepdf.org/.

- ARP is a lightweight development framework. You can find it at http://osflash.org/projects/arp.

- AsWing is a GUI framework and set of ActionScript components. You can find it at http://www.aswing.org/.

- Degrafa is a Flex library for creating a drawing API in MXML. You can find it at http://www.degrafa.com/.

- FlexLib is a set of Flex-based components ranging from an animated fire effect to a full schedule display framework. You can find it at http://code.google.com/p/flexlib/.

- GoASAP is a lightweight framework for building ActionScript 3 animation tools. Its main contributor is Moses Gunesch, also the author of Fuse. You can find it at http://www.goasap.org/.

- ObjectHandles is a Flex library that helps you build an interface to allow users to move and resize objects on the screen. You can find it at http://www.rogue-development.com/objectHandles.html.

- Pulse Particle System is a general-purpose particle library that includes an interactive particle explorer to help you create visual particle effects. You can find it at http://www.rogue-development.com/pulseParticles.html.

- Sandy is an ActionScript 2/ActionScript 3 3D rendering engine. You can find it at http://www.flashsandy.org/.

- Several projects are located at the Spicefactory website (http://spicefactory.org/). These include Spicelib, a library for task management, reflection, and logging; Parsley, an Inversion of Control (IoC) container, MVC framework, and localization utility; and Cinnamon, an ActionScript 3/Java remoting solution.

- Prana is an application framework centered around an IoC container. You can find it at http://www.pranaframework.org/.

- Tweener is an ActionScript 3 tweening engine usually used to create both simple and complex animations. You can find it at http://code.google.com/p/tweener/.

Chapter 3

PREPARING AN OPEN SOURCE WORKFLOW

by Marc Hughes

This chapter covers the following:

- Installing the tools necessary for Flash development
- Setting those tools up so they best work with each other
- Creating a simple sample project with those tools
- Exploring some alternative workflows

In previous chapters, we described some of the tools available for open source Flash development. It's time for you to install those tools and configure them to work together.

Many tools for open source Flash development exist. By combining different combinations of those tools, you can make hundreds of different development workflows, and different workflows will work better or worse for different developers. I will briefly describe two alternative workflows here. One will use ASDT and Eclipse, and the other will use FlashDevelop.

Before reading on, it may be helpful to download the accompanying material for this chapter from the friends of ED website (http://www.friendsofed.com). Once you've done that, extract the contents, and locate the Chapter 3 directory. It contains samples that will be referenced throughout the rest of this chapter.

ActionScript 3 development

Developing applications at the most basic level involves editing source code files, combining the files into a project, and then compiling your project. To edit ActionScript, you will learn how to install and use FlashDevelop and ASDT. Depending on your choice of ActionScript 2 or ActionScript 3 development, you will use either MTASC or the Flex SDK as your compiler. Beyond the pure basics of development, installing standard libraries of code and debugging tools are also covered in the following workflows.

There are some great options for a developer wanting to use open source tools to do ActionScript 3 development. Some of those tools, such as the Flex SDK or the Java JDK, come from large, established companies. Still others, such as FlashDevelop and MTASC, come from small independent groups of developers.

Introducing the Flex SDK

Adobe has made a significant leap into the open source world by completely open sourcing its entire Flex SDK. This includes the ActionScript and MXML compilers, a debugger, and the ActionScript libraries that make up the core Flex framework.

The Flex SDK is made available under the open source Mozilla Public License (MPL) and is available for download from Adobe's website free of charge. This gives you a very liberal license to use it to create your own open source or commercial applications.

Flex is a term developers usually associate with a specific way of writing applications using the Flex framework. If you're looking to create non-Flex applications, don't let the name Flex SDK scare you. By using this SDK, it's possible both to create Flex-based applications and to create Flash applications not based on that framework.

> *Adobe publishes a product called Flex Builder, which is a fully integrated Eclipse and ActionScript 3 development environment with many of the tools you need to create Flex-based applications. The Flex SDK is included in that product, but you can also get it separately for free as I'll show how to do later in this chapter.*
>
> *When communicating with others, it's important to remember that oftentimes people may use the term* Flex *to refer to Flex Builder and not just the SDK.*

Installing the Java JDK

It may seem odd that the first step in the installation of a Flash development environment is to install the Java Development Kit (JDK), but the reason for this is that the Flex compilers and debuggers are written in Java. Because of this, you must have a Java Runtime Environment (JRE) installed for Flex, but since other components later in the chapter require the full JDK, we'll go over the installation of that. Some other tools that require Java include Ant and the Red5 server (see Chapters 13 and 14 for information on Red5).

Many systems have a version of Java installed by default, so before attempting to install, you should check to see whether a Java JDK is already installed and, if so, what version it is. Open a command prompt, and enter the command java -version to check your installed version. If you receive a "command not found" error, you most likely don't currently have Java installed. If you do have Java installed, make sure you have version 1.5 or higher.

> There are two types of Java downloads. The JRE contains all the files necessary to run Java-based applications. Unless you're planning on developing Java-based software, that's sufficient for this and the next chapter. If you're planning on trying Red5 (see Chapters 13 and 14), you'll have to install the full JDK, which allows you to write Java-based applications.

If you don't have a JRE installed or if you have a version previous to 1.5, you will need to install a fresh copy. We recommend getting the latest version of the full JDK (JDK 6 Update 5 as of the writing of this book).

Installing the JDK on Windows or Linux

Follow these steps to install the JDK on Windows or Linux:

1. Open a web browser to http://java.sun.com/javase/downloads/index.jsp.
2. Click the Download button next to the option for the JDK.
3. Choose the appropriate installation package for your system, and download it. Under Windows, you have the option for an offline install or an online install. If you will be connected to the Internet for the entire time while you install the software, choosing the online version can often save you time since it will download only the components you want to install.
4. Install the file you downloaded. On Windows, run the executable, and follow the directions. On Linux, use your system's package manager utility to install the software.

Installing the JDK on OS X

OS X comes with a Java JDK installed by default. If you have an outdated version, you can upgrade using the standard OS X software update mechanism. First, connect to the Internet. Then select the Software Update option from your Apple menu. A dialog box listing all the available updates will appear. Find the Java 1.6 option, make sure the check mark next to it is enabled, and click the Install button at the bottom of the window. OS X will download and install the update for you.

Installing the Flex SDK

You can download the Flex SDK for your platform from Adobe's website. Point your web browser at http://opensource.adobe.com/wiki/display/flexsdk/Downloads, and follow the Free Adobe Flex 3 SDK link.

The Flex SDK comes packaged as a single ZIP file containing the necessary files for all the platforms it supports. Download this file, and uncompress it to a location on your hard drive. The examples in this and the next chapter place it in a directory called flex3sdk inside a directory named FlashTools in

21

the root of your drive for Windows, or in your user directory for OS X and Linux (C:\FlashTools\ flex3sdk on Windows or ~/FlashTools/flex3sdk on OS X/Linux).

After extracting the archive, add the bin directory to your system search path. If you're using Windows and the recommended paths, this would be C:\FlashTools\flex3sdk\bin, whereas if you're using Linux or OS X, the path would be ~/FlashTools/flex3sdk/bin. The next sections show how to modify your system's PATH variable if you're unsure how.

Configuring your system's search path

Your system's PATH variable tells your computer where to search for executable programs. If you are on Windows, follow these steps to modify your PATH variable:

1. Right-click the My Computer icon, and select Properties.
2. Click the Advanced tab.
3. Click the Environmental Variables button; you should see a window similar to Figure 3-1.
4. Find the entry for Path in the System Variables section, and select it.
5. Click the Edit button, and a window to edit the value will appear.
6. Prepend the value with the path to your Flex SDK compiler followed by a semicolon. If you used the recommended path, you would enter **C:\FlashTools\flex3sdk\bin;** at the beginning of the path.
7. Click OK. Verify the path looks like Figure 3-1.

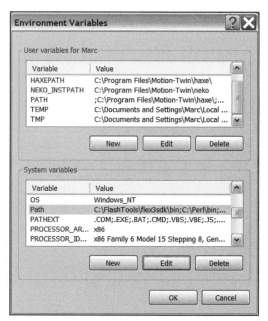

Figure 3-1. The Environment Variables dialog box on Windows XP. Notice the PATH variable has been modified to include the flex3sdk directory.

Modifying your PATH variable on OS X or Linux can vary greatly depending on what shell you use. The default shell on OS X and many Linux distributions is Bash. If you are using Bash, you can edit a file in your home directory called .bashrc. In that file, add a line similar to the following:

```
export PATH=$PATH:~/FlashTools/flex3sdk/bin
```

This tells Bash to append the directory called ~/FlashTools/flex3sdk/bin to the end of the PATH variable. If you are using a shell other than Bash, please consult the documentation that comes with that shell.

Testing your installation

After installing the Flex SDK, you can test that everything is working correctly by opening a command prompt (terminal on OS X) and issuing the compc command. You should receive output similar to the following:

```
C:\>compc
Adobe Compc (Flex Component Compiler)
Version 3.0.0 build 477
Copyright (c) 2004-2007 Adobe Systems, Inc. All rights reserved.

Use 'compc -help' for information about using the command line.
```

If you get a "command not found" or some other error, review the installation instructions, and make sure you set your PATH variable correctly.

Installing FlashDevelop

For this section, I'll be using FlashDevelop as the IDE to show how to edit and compile ActionScript code. FlashDevelop is Windows-only since it requires the Microsoft .NET 2.0 runtime. If you're using OS X or Linux, you should take a look at FDT, which is mentioned in the "ActionScript 2 Development" section of this chapter since it is also capable of creating ActionScript 3 applications.

To install FlashDevelop, first download and install the .NET runtime from the Microsoft website (http://www.microsoft.com). To find the download link, perform a search for *Microsoft .NET Framework Version 2.0 Redistributable*.

After you have installed the .NET runtime, you're ready to install FlashDevelop. To find the latest download, go to the FlashDevelop website (http://www.flashdevelop.org), and click the Releases link. FlashDevelop regularly releases versions, so it's up to you to choose whether you want to get the latest, possibly buggy, beta version or go with a slightly older but more stable officially released version. After downloading, a standard installation wizard will guide you through the rest of the process.

Once you've installed the Flex SDK and FlashDevelop, you'll need to configure a few settings. Launch FlashDevelop. Select the Tools ➤ Program Settings menu option, and a dialog box such as Figure 3-2 will appear.

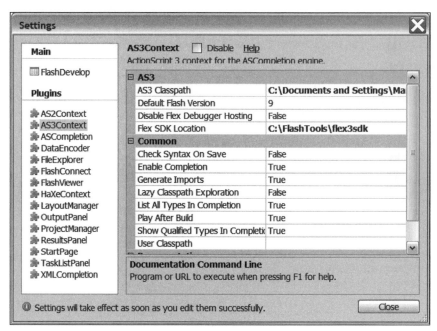

Figure 3-2. The Settings dialog box of FlashDevelop

In this dialog box, find the Flex SDK Location entry under AS3Context, and set the directory where you unpacked your Flex SDK. With that done, you're ready to start using FlashDevelop to create ActionScript 3 projects.

Creating a sample application

In this section, I will show how to create a simple sample application; you will learn how to set up and compile a project from FlashDevelop.

To begin, select the Project ➤ New Project menu option, which will cause the New Project dialog box to be displayed (see Figure 3-3). Select Empty Project under the ActionScript 3 heading, which will create a standard Flash ActionScript 3 project. If you were developing a Flex or an AIR application, you would see options for those environments as well. In Chapter 4, you'll be creating an application to view recipes. So, let's give this a name of **RecipeViewer** by typing that into the Name field. To keep things organized, also enter a directory name of **RecipeViewer**, and then click the OK button.

Once you have a new project created, you select the Project panel on the right side of your screen. Right-click in that panel, and select Add ➤ New Class. This will open a dialog box asking for a name for the new class. Enter **RecipeViewer.as** in that dialog box, and click the OK button. A new ActionScript file will be created.

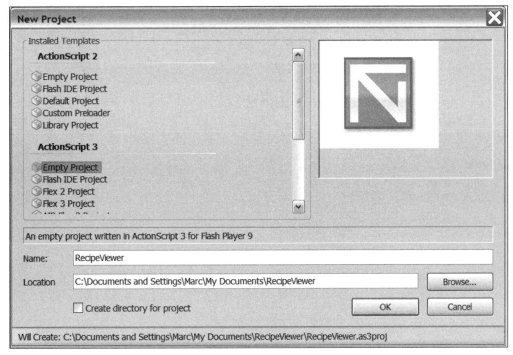

Figure 3-3. The FlashDevelop New Project dialog box

Modify the generated class in the following ways:

1. Add a SWF metatag before the class to specify the properties of the resulting Flash application.

2. Add extends Sprite to the class definition. This will let the class act as the default object in an ActionScript 3 Flash application.

3. Add code in the constructor to create a TextField, assign some text to it, and add it to the display list.

The resulting class should resemble the following:

```
package
{
  import flash.display.Sprite;
  import flash.text.TextField;

  [SWF(backgroundColor="#eeeeff", frameRate="60", width="500", ➥
  height="350")]
  public class RecipeViewer extends Sprite {
```

```
      public function RecipeViewer()
      {
        var tf:TextField = new TextField();
        tf.text = "Hello World";
        addChild(tf);
      }
    }
  }
```

You now have all the code necessary for your simple test application. To run it, you must first right-click the file in the Project panel and select Always Compile. If the file isn't appearing in your list, select the Show Hidden Items toolbar option. After you do that, select the Project ➤ Properties menu option, and a dialog box like Figure 3-4 will appear.

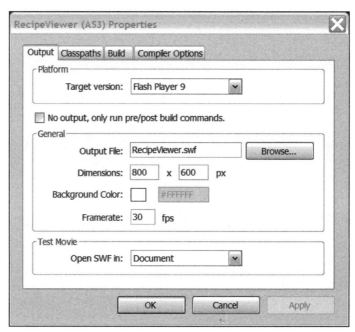

Figure 3-4. The project properties panel in FlashDevelop

Type a file name for the resulting compiled application in the Output File field, and click the OK button. Pressing F5 or clicking the blue triangle play icon in the toolbar will cause your application to be compiled, and the resulting output will be displayed in FlashDevelop (see Figure 3-5).

Now that you can create and run an ActionScript 3 project, you're ready for other topics in this book, such as creating an Ant build script, using some ActionScript 3–based libraries such as Papervision3D, or writing client-server applications using a technology such as Red5.

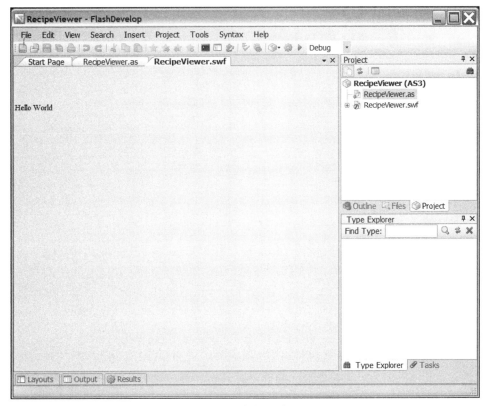

Figure 3-5. The final sample application running in FlashDevelop

ActionScript 2 development

You've already seen how to use FlashDevelop to create ActionScript 3 projects; you can also use FlashDevelop to create ActionScript 2. In the following sections, we will show a different workflow commonly called AMES because it consists of **A**SDT, **A**pache, **M**TASC, **E**clipse, and **s**wfmill.

Installing MTASC

Installing MTASC is a simple matter of downloading and unpacking it:

1. Download a precompiled binary from the download section of the MTASC website (http://www.mtasc.org). At the time of writing, the latest version of MTASC was 1.13.

2. Unpack the archive to a suitable location. On my Windows system, I have installed MTASC in a folder I created named FlashTools in the root of my C: drive. This means the mtasc.exe executable is located at C:\FlashTools\mtasc-1.13\mtasc.exe. When working on OS X or Linux, I usually create the FlashTools folder in my user directory.

3. After extracting the archive, add the mtasc directory to your system's search path. (See the earlier "Configuring your system's search path" section for help with this.)

Testing your installation

After installing MTASC, open a command prompt, and issue the command mtasc. You should receive output similar to the following:

```
C:\>mtasc
Motion-Twin ActionScript2 Compiler 1.13 - (c)2004-2007 Motion-Twin
 Usage : mtasc.exe [options] <files...>
 Options :
  -pack <path> : compile all files in target package
  -cp <paths> : add classpath
  -v : turn on verbose mode
  -strict : turn on strict mode
  -infer : turn on local variables inference
  -wimp : turn on warnings for unused imports
  -msvc : use MSVC style errors
  -mx : use precompiled mx package
  -swf <file> : swf file to update
  -out <file> : swf output file
  -keep : does not remove AS2 classes from input SWF
  -frame <frame> : export into target frame (must exist in the swf)
  -main : enable main entry point
  -header <header> : specify header format 'width:height:fps'
  -group : group classes into a single clip
  -exclude <file> : exclude classes listed in file
  -version : change SWF version (6,7,8,...)
  -trace <function> : specify a TRACE function
  -help  Display this list of options
  --help  Display this list of options
```

If you get a "command not found" or some other error, review the installation instructions, making sure you set your PATH variable correctly.

Installing an IDE

One of the most important, and certainly the most visible, components of a development environment is the integrated development environment (IDE). This usually consists of a code editor, file management functions, and integration with a compiler. In the following sections, I'll explain how to install Eclipse as your IDE.

> *In this book we use the term* Flash IDE *to refer to the product that Adobe publishes called Flash (Flash MX 2004, Flash 8, Flash CS3, and so on). Don't be confused by our use of the term* IDE *here, because we're not referring to the Flash IDE.*

Installing Eclipse

As a Flash developer, I find myself wearing many hats. One day I might need to edit PHP and manipulate a database, while the next I do nothing but ActionScript. One of the greatest benefits of the Eclipse platform is that it has plug-ins for almost every language imaginable. There's a plug-in for XML, a plug-in for PHP, yet another plug-in for Ruby, and of course a plug-in for ActionScript. Beyond simple code editing, there are plug-ins to connect to databases, to build UML models, and to connect to version control systems. While the variety of plug-ins is a great benefit of the platform, it can also be a nightmare since tracking down the correct plug-ins and getting them to play nicely with each other can be difficult.

Luckily, there's help from a group of software developers whose goal is to make Eclipse installation easy. They can be found at the website Easy Eclipse (http://www.easyeclipse.org). They have several distributions of Eclipse aimed at web developers with editions for Windows, Mac OS X, and Linux. I usually choose the Easy Eclipse for LAMP package because it includes most of the functionality I use on a day-to-day basis. If you do other types of development, you may want to take a look at the other options listed on the website.

Downloading and Installing Easy Eclipse

To download and install Easy Eclipse for LAMP, follow these steps:

1. Download your desired distribution from the Easy Eclipse website (http://www.easyeclipse.org/site/distributions/index.html).

2. Launch the installer. You will be presented with a standard installation wizard, as shown in Figure 3-6.

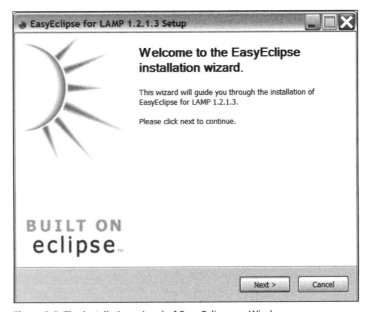

Figure 3-6. The installation wizard of Easy Eclipse on Windows

3. Click the Next button, and answer the remaining prompts to complete the installation. You can either leave the defaults or customize where your project workspace will be created.

> *Some people dislike Easy Eclipse because it tends to lag behind the official Eclipse version or because it comes with too many plug-ins. If you prefer to download a more bare-bones or bleeding-edge distribution of Eclipse, you can get it from the official Eclipse website (*http://www.eclipse.org*).*

Installing Eclipse plug-ins

Eclipse, by itself, is not well suited for ActionScript development. To really make it shine, you need to install an ActionScript plug-in. There are currently two options: a fully open source solution called ASDT and a commercial plug-in called FDT. Both offer similar functionality of editing ActionScript, maintaining projects, and compiling applications from within Eclipse. At the time of this writing, ASDT does not support ActionScript 3, whereas FDT does. Table 3-1 compares ASDT and FDT.

Table 3-1. Comparison of ASDT and FDT

FDT	ASDT
ActionScript 2 and 3 support	ActionScript 2 support
Code completion	Code completion
Code folding	Code folding
Compile using MTASC	Compile using MTASC
Full on-the-fly syntax checking	Syntax checking on file save; only the first error is displayed
Free for open source development	Free for all development
Commercial software	Open source software
299.00 € (euros) price for commercial development	
Automatic import statements	
ActionScript 3 support	
30-day free trial available	

While deciding which plug-in to use, you may want to install them both to give them a try. In my experience, it is not a good idea to install them both in Eclipse at the same time. Make sure to uninstall your first option before installing your second.

In this chapter, I'll describe how to install both plug-ins. However, after that, the focus will be on ASDT, since it is the open source solution of the two. It may seem odd that we mention FDT at all. The reason behind this is that FDT is a much more polished product, and it offers free licenses to open source developers. The feature list of the two plug-ins seems similar, but that doesn't capture the fact that many of the features simply work better in FDT. Many developers who have the ability to choose between the two pick FDT over ASDT. Much of the information regarding ASDT development is also directly applicable to development in an FDT environment.

Installing ASDT

Installing Eclipse plug-ins is easy through Eclipse's software update feature. You can install ASDT through this mechanism by following these steps:

1. Launch Eclipse.
2. Select the Help ➤ Software Updates ➤ Find and Install menu option. A dialog box entitled Install/Update will appear.
3. Select the Search for new features to install radio button, and click the Next button.
4. Click the New Remote Site button. This will display a dialog box that allows you to enter information about where to find the ASDT Eclipse plug-in.
5. In that dialog box, enter **ASDT** in the Name field, and enter **http://aseclipseplugin.sourceforge. net/updates/** in the URL field, as shown in Figure 3-7. Click the OK button to close the dialog box.

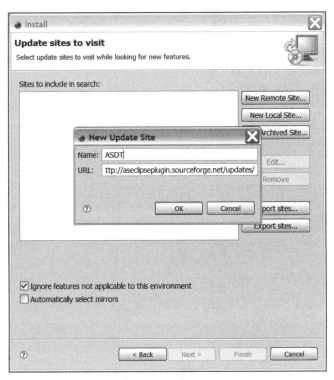

Figure 3-7. Configuring Eclipse to install ASDT

6. Make sure that only the entry for ASDT is checked, and click the Finish button. Eclipse will now download a list of available updates. Once that is complete, you will be presented with a new dialog box to choose which updates to install.

7. Select the ASDT option, and click the Next button.

8. Progress through the rest of the installation wizard until the Finish button is made available, making sure to accept the license agreement.

9. Click the Finish button. Eclipse will now download the plug-in. After all files are downloaded, you will be presented with a dialog box to confirm your installation options.

10. Click the Install All button.

11. When prompted, restart Eclipse.

To configure the plug-in, you can select the Window ➤ Preferences menu option. Then select the ActionScript 2 entry from the tree on the left. The default options are suitable for most users. However, we suggest making sure that the Use separate source and output folders option is enabled.

Installing FDT

The installation process for FDT is nearly identical to the installation for ASDT. The only significant change is typing **FDT** in the Name field and **http://fdt.powerflasher.com/update** in the URL field of step 5.

Once installed, you will be able to use FDT for 30 days for trial purposes. If you intend on using FDT long term, you have two options:

- Buy a commercial software development license from http://fdt.powerflasher.com/.
- Apply for an open source developer's license. Follow the instructions posted at http://fdt. powerflasher.com/forum/viewtopic.php?t=139.

To configure FDT, select the Window ➤ Preferences menu option. Then select the FDT entry from the tree on the left. You must make sure to properly set two settings. The first is the location of your core libraries, which is a reference to the standard set of Flash libraries. To edit this setting, choose the Core Libraries option under the FDT heading. Using the Add button, create two entries: one named std8 that points to the std8 directory in your MTASC installation and one named std that points to the std directory in your MTASC installation. Once completed, make sure std8 is checked. This will enable the necessary classes for ActionScript 2 development targeting Flash Player 8 or newer. When completed, your dialog box should look similar to Figure 3-8.

After you set up your core libraries, you need to tell FDT where to find the MTASC compiler. You do this by setting the Location of mtasc.exe option under the Tools ➤ MTASC heading.

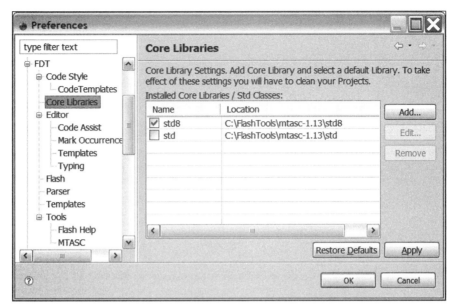

Figure 3-8. The FDT configuration dialog box after setting up your core libraries

Installing ActionScript 2 libraries

Third-party libraries are what make open source Flash development so attractive. There are a myriad of libraries out there to do all sorts of useful things. The installation of most libraries simply consists of downloading the source and extracting it to a location where your project can find it. Some libraries will require you to pick out a subdirectory from the archive or to create a directory structure. Since you're likely to use the same set of libraries across many of your projects, it's convenient to create a central repository that all your projects can pull from.

I usually have a directory on my computer called `projects` with subdirectories under that for each project I work on. Choose a location on your computer, and create a `projects` directory. Inside that directory create a `lib` directory to store all your third-party libraries. Once you've done that, download the following libraries, and extract them into your `lib` directory.

For your convenience, you can also find copies of all the libraries mentioned in this chapter in the `Chapter3\lib` directory of the downloadable material that accompanies this book. Although downloading each from its original source may give you more up-to-date versions, simply copying the entire `lib` directory can be a way to quickly start developing.

> The commercial Flash authoring environments by Adobe come with a set of classes called the V2 components. These components are not open source, and the license governing them does not allow distribution. This is a significant issue for open source Flash developers because developers who are used to using the tools from Adobe often take it for granted that these classes will be available. This is also a great benefit to open source developers since the V2 components are generally regarded as a less than optimal solution.
>
> One of the open source libraries we want to showcase is Fuse. However, two classes from the V2 components are used in Fuse. We will be replacing those classes with open source alternatives, but that does introduce an extra step in setting up our ideal open source workflow.

Installing Delegate

The Delegate class written by Steve Webster provides a replacement for Adobe's implementation of its class with the same name that comes with the V2 components. He has published the source for his Delegate class at the URL http://dynamicflash.com/classes/Delegate.as.

To install it, download that file into a com\dynamicflash\utils directory inside your lib directory.

Installing GDispatcher

The GDispatcher class by Grant Skinner replaces the EventDispatcher class from the V2 components. You can download it from http://www.gskinner.com/blog/assets/GDispatcher.as.zip.

To install it, download and then extract the GDispatcher.as file into a com\gskinner\events directory that you create inside your lib directory.

Installing Fuse

Fuse is a library maintained by Moses Gunesch for easily creating animations in Flash applications. You can download it from http://www.mosessupposes.com/Fuse/.

Once you have downloaded the archive, extract it to a temporary location on your hard drive. Find the com directory from that temporary location, and copy it to the lib directory that you've already created.

As previously mentioned, Fuse uses two classes from the V2 components that must be replaced by their open source counterparts that you have just installed. Open the Fuse.as file located in the com\mosesSupposes\fuse directory. At the top of the file, replace the following lines:

```
import mx.utils.Delegate;
import mx.events.EventDispatcher;
```

with the following lines:

```
import com.dynamicflash.utils.Delegate;
import com.gskinner.events.GDispatcher;
```

Then, further down around line 550 in the file in the Fuse() function, replace the following line:

```
EventDispatcher.initialize(this);
```

with the following line:

```
GDispatcher.initialize(this);
```

The version of Fuse included in the downloadable materials with this book has already been modified in this way.

After installing these libraries, you should have a directory structure similar to the following:

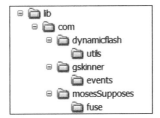

Creating a project

Now that you have Eclipse and MTASC set up, let's take a break from installations and try some of our new tools. In Chapter 4, we'll be creating an application to view recipes with. Let's start creating the structure for that project.

If you haven't taken my earlier advice of a projects directory while installing libraries, now is a good time to create a directory to hold your projects. Once you've decided where your projects should be located, launch Eclipse. Select the File ➤ New ➤ Project menu option, and the New Project Wizard will be displayed. Select New ActionScript Project from the ActionScript submenu, and click Next.

Figure 3-9 shows the ActionScript Project dialog box after configuring it for our new project. Project Name is how this project will be referred to in the Eclipse environment. The Location represents where on your computer the files for this project should be stored. By specifying Separate source and output folders, you're instructing Eclipse to separate your source code from the compiled output. Once you have made those changes, click the Next button.

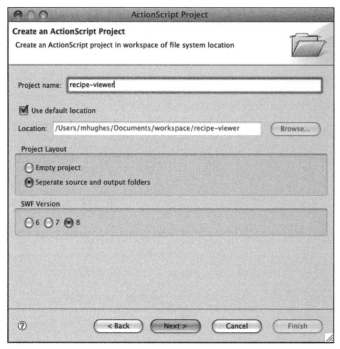

Figure 3-9. The new ActionScript Project dialog box after making the necessary modifications for the recipe viewer application

The next dialog box allows you to configure the location of your source code folders. By default, a src folder should be there. The only thing you must do is tell Eclipse where any additional folders that contain source code you need might be. If you followed my suggestion of putting all your libraries in a lib directory, you can now add that directory by clicking the Add Linked Folder button. Specify **lib** as the name and the correct path to the lib directory in the window that pops up. Once completed, you should see a dialog box similar to Figure 3-10. You can now click the Finish button to complete the project creation. Eclipse should prompt you to ask whether you want to switch to the ActionScript 2 development perspective; answer Yes.

If you're familiar with Flash development using the Flash IDE, you're probably now looking for a frame on a timeline as an entry point for the application. The MTASC compiler has no notion of timelines. Although that may seem startling to a long-time Flash developer at first, it's actually one of the great benefits to this style of development. It allows you to completely separate your code from the graphical assets you or other designers make.

Instead of a timeline, MTASC looks for a static function called main in a class you specify as the launching point of the application. Let's create a simple "Hello World" example that uses our Fuse library we have already installed.

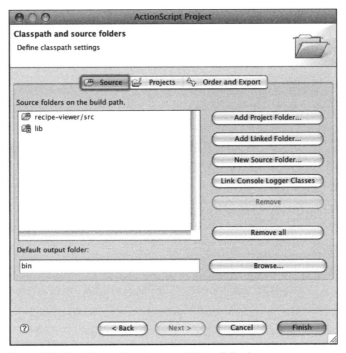

Figure 3-10. The Classpath and source folders dialog box

Creating your first ActionScript class

To create your first ActionScript class, follow these steps:

1. On the left side of your workspace, you should see an area called the Navigator (see Figure 3-11). Select the src directory by clicking it.

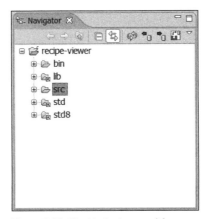

Figure 3-11. The Navigator panel from within Eclipse after creating the recipe viewer project

2. Select the File ➤ New ➤ New ActionScript Class menu option. As a shortcut, there is also a button that looks like a green circle with a white letter *C* on the toolbar that performs this function. The New ActionScript Class dialog box will be displayed.

3. Enter **com.friendsofed.recipeviewer** in the Package field and **RecipeViewer** in the Name field. Your dialog box should now look like Figure 3-12.

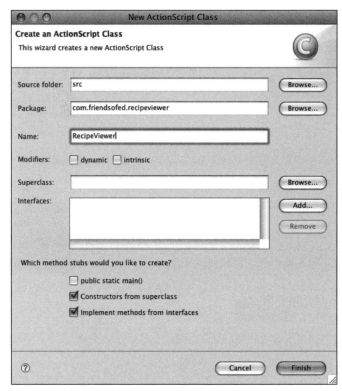

Figure 3-12. The New ActionScript Class dialog box after making the appropriate modifications for the initial class

4. Click the Finish button. Your class will be created and shown to you in your code editor.

You now need to create a new method within that class to actually do something. Let's create a text field and give it the text "Hello World." Since this is a Flash application, let's make it a little flashier and add a little animation to make it scroll in from the bottom and bounce when it hits the top. To perform this animation, I will use Fuse. Don't be intimidated by the Fuse syntax for now. You can read more about Fuse in Chapter 10. Enter the following code into your newly created class:

```
class com.friendsofed.recipeviewer.RecipeViewer
{
  public static function main(base:MovieClip) : Void
  {
    ZigoEngine.simpleSetup(FuseItem,PennerEasing);
```

```
        var tf:TextField=base.createTextField("testField",1,50,10,200,200);
        tf.text = "Hello World.";

        var f:Fuse = new Fuse();
        f.push({target:tf, start_y:1000, y:50,  duration:3});
        f.start();
    }
}
```

After you've entered that code, save the file. ASDT will recognize that you've added the static main method and add it to a list of files to compile. While it's doing that, it needs to know some information about the SWF you want to create and will automatically prompt you with a dialog box like Figure 3-13.

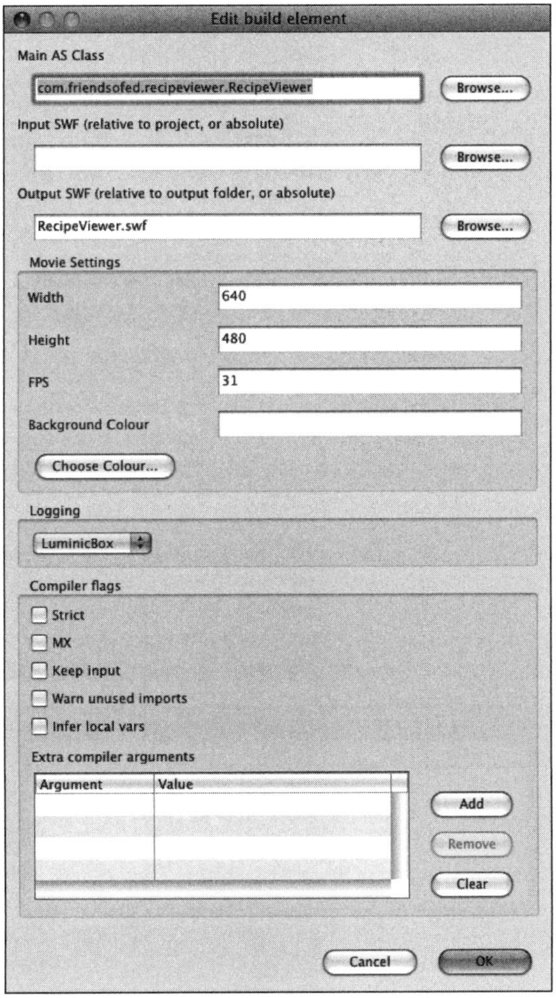

Figure 3-13. The SWF build options

ASDT will immediately attempt to compile your class but will fail because you have forgotten to import some of the external classes you've used. The code ZigoEngine.simpleSetup should be underlined in red indicating a problem. In addition, there should be a red *X* icon in the margin to the left, and a line has been added to your Problems panel below your code editor. Forgetting to import classes is a common mistake. To fix it, add an import line at the beginning of your class. As you type, notice that ASDT gives you contextual help and code completions. ASDT, in contrast to FDT, can detect only the first error in an ActionScript class, so if there were multiple errors, the next one would have been highlighted after you fixed the first error and saved the file. The complete class should be as follows:

```
import com.mosesSupposes.fuse.*;

class com.friendsofed.recipeviewer.RecipeViewer
{
  public static function main(base:MovieClip) : Void
  {
    ZigoEngine.simpleSetup(FuseItem,PennerEasing);

    var tf:TextField = base.createTextField("testField",1,50,10,200,200);
    tf.text = "Hello World!";

    var f:Fuse = new Fuse();
    f.push({target:tf, start_y:1000, y:50,  duration:3});
    f.start();
  }
}
```

Once there are no additional errors, your Problems panel below your code editor should be empty. This means your application has been successfully built and is ready to be run. Open the bin directory in the Navigator panel, and double-click the RecipeViewer.swf file. It should open and be run in a new subwindow of Eclipse. I oftentimes drag the SWF panel to the right of my code window so I can see them both side by side. Whenever I save my ActionScript code, the class is automatically compiled and restarted in that window.

You previously saw that ASDT automatically attempts to compile classes with a static main method. But how does it associate an output SWF file name with the class that generates it? Internally, ASDT added your class to a list of ActionScript 2 build targets. You can access that list at any time by right-clicking the project name in the Navigator panel on the left and choosing Properties. Then select the AS2 Builder option; you should now be looking at a dialog box like Figure 3-14. Notice that ASDT is compiling the class to the RecipeViewer.swf output file. Since you previously selected the option to separate your source and output directories, this will be created in the bin directory of your project. You can now close this dialog box by clicking the OK button.

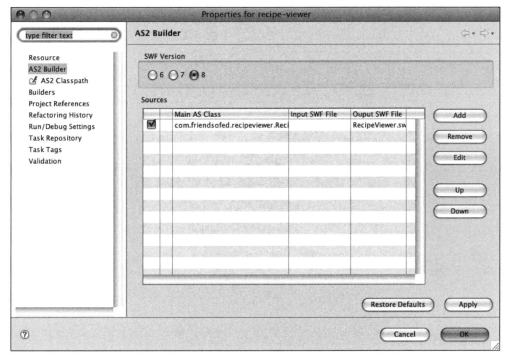

Figure 3-14. ASDT automatically recognizes new classes with static main methods and creates new AS2 Builder targets for them.

Common components

Besides the compilers and development environments, several open source tools can aid both ActionScript 2 and ActionScript 3 developers.

Installing swfmill

swfmill is a tool to create multimedia assets for use by a Flash application. You can install swfmill by going to the swfmill home page (http://swfmill.org/) and downloading a binary distribution for your platform. Extract the archive you downloaded into the FlashTools directory you previously created, and add that directory to your system's search path in the same way you added MTASC to your path.

After you've completed the installation, running the command swfmill from a terminal or command shell should output version and usage information:

```
> swfmill
swfmill 0.2.12
    XML-based SWF (Shockwave Flash) processing tool

usage: swfmill [<options>] <command>
...
```

In Chapter 4 you'll learn how to integrate swfmill into your build process to create asset SWF files during build time.

Installing Xray

Xray will give you several tools to help debug your application. You need to install two pieces of Xray. The first is the connector, which consists of a small bit of code you compile into your application. The other piece is the Xray interface that has a UI you can interact with.

The Xray interface allows you to inspect the running application in real time. It also provides the display of logging information from your application. To accomplish this, it makes a local connection to the Xray connector that you embed in your application.

Installing the ActionScript 3 connector

To install the ActionScript 3 Xray connector, download the package labeled Xray AS3 SWC for Flex3 logging and inspection from the Xray Google Code repository (http://code.google.com/p/osflash-xray/downloads/list). You can use this package for both Flex and Flash development.

Next, add this SWC to your mxmlc compilation. If you're using FlashDevelop, you can go to Project ➤ Properties, click the Compiler Options tab, and then click the ... button next to the SWC Libraries option. This will cause a new dialog box to open, allowing you to specify additional libraries to include. Type the path and name of the Xray SWC there. If you saved the SWC to your lib directory, you would enter **C:\FlashTools\lib\Xray.swc** on Windows or **~/FlashTools/lib/Xray.swc** on OS X.

Once that's done, you can add the import for the Flex2Xray class to your main ActionScript class, create a variable, and instantiate a Flex2Xray object. Assuming this instantiation doesn't throw any exceptions, you should now have a working Xray connector in your application:

```
import com.blitzagency.xray.inspector.flex2.Flex2Xray;
private var xray:Flex2Xray;
xray = new Flex2Xray();
```

If you want to use the Xray logging functionality in your application, you'll also want to create an XrayLog object. Don't forget to import the XrayLog class:

```
private var log:XrayLog = new XrayLog();
```

Installing the ActionScript 2 connector

To install the ActionScript 2 Xray connector, download the package labeled Xray AS2 Logger classes and Mtasc Utilities with samples from the Xray Google Code repository (http://code.google.com/p/osflash-xray/downloads/list). Extract the archive to a temporary location on your hard drive. Copy the classes/com directory to the lib directory you previously set up (see "Installing ActionScript 2 libraries"). Copy the xrayConnector-XXXX.swf file to the bin directory inside your project. You'll have to copy this SWF to the bin directory of every project you create, so make sure to keep a copy handy between projects; we suggest keeping an extra copy in your FlashTools directory.

If you're using the Flash IDE for development, installing the connector is even easier. Just download the package labeled Latest component package for AS2. *It contains an MXP file, so if you double-click it, the Flash Extensions Manager should recognize it and install it for you. Then, to use the connector, just drop the Xray connector component onto the stage of your project.*

You need to configure two major pieces of Xray to use all the features. One is the execute connection, which allows you to inspect and modify the objects of the running SWF. The other is the logger connection, which will redirect your log statements to the Xray window.

Configuring the execute connection

The execute connection is enabled by adding a few lines of code to your application. Xray comes with a utility class called XrayLoader that loads the connector SWF you previously installed. To use it, you need to make several changes to your code.

Modifying the code for the Xray execute connection

Follow these steps to modify the code for the Xray execute connection:

1. Extract most of the functionality of the code from the static main() method to a new startApp() method.

2. Add a private member variable representing the base MovieClip.

3. Create a constructor that takes a MovieClip as a parameter. In that constructor, set the base clip.

4. In the constructor, set up two event listeners on XrayLoader to call startApp() after either a successful load or a failed load. You do the same thing on fail or load so you can later deploy your application without the Xray connector, and it will still work.

5. Also in the constructor, add a call to XrayLoader to load the connector SWF. Make sure to specify the exact SWF name of your connector because you may have a newer version than what was available at the time of this writing. The second parameter specifies the base MovieClip to use. The third parameter specifies whether to display the FPS meter.

```
import com.mosesSupposes.fuse.ZigoEngine;
import com.mosesSupposes.fuse.FuseItem;
import com.mosesSupposes.fuse.PennerEasing;
import com.mosesSupposes.fuse.Fuse;
import com.blitzagency.xray.util.XrayLoader;
import com.dynamicflash.utils.Delegate;
import com.mosesSupposes.fuse.Shortcuts;
class com.friendsofed.recipeviewer.RecipeViewer
{
    private var baseClip:MovieClip;
```

```
public static function main(base:MovieClip) : Void
{
  var app:RecipeViewer = new RecipeViewer(base);
}

public function RecipeViewer(base:MovieClip)
{
  baseClip = base;
  XrayLoader.addEventListener( XrayLoader.LOADCOMPLETE, this,"startApp");
  XrayLoader.addEventListener( XrayLoader.LOADERROR, this,"startApp");
  XrayLoader.loadConnector("xrayConnector_1.6.3.swf",base,true);
}

public function startApp() : Void
{

  ZigoEngine.simpleSetup(Shortcuts,FuseItem,PennerEasing);

  var tf:TextField = baseClip.createTextField("testField",1,50,10,
                                                   200,200);

  tf.text = "Hello World.";

  var f:Fuse = new Fuse();
  f.push({target:tf, start_y:1000, y:0,  duration:6,
             ease:"easeOutBounce"});
  f.start();
}
}
```

Configuring the logger connection

If you've configured the execute connection, you already have some of the logger connection functionality enabled. You can create a log variable of type XrayLogger in your class:

```
private var log:XrayLogger = new XrayLogger();
```

Then you can use the debug(), warn(), and so on, methods to display debug information. The other mechanism of logging requires you to change an MTASC compile option. To set that up, follow these steps:

1. In Eclipse, right-click your project, and select Properties.
2. Select the AS2 Builder option on the left.
3. Select the RecipeViewer builder from the grid, and click the Edit button.
4. In the Trace Function field, enter **com.blitzagency.xray.util.MtascUtility.trace**.
5. Click the OK button to accept your change.

You can now use the two methods of logging in your code. To test them, add a `log.debug()` line and a `trace()` line to your `startApp()` method:

```
import com.mosesSupposes.fuse.ZigoEngine;

import com.mosesSupposes.fuse.FuseItem;
import com.mosesSupposes.fuse.PennerEasing;
import com.mosesSupposes.fuse.Fuse;
import com.blitzagency.xray.util.XrayLoader;
import com.blitzagency.xray.logger.*;
import com.dynamicflash.utils.Delegate;
import com.mosesSupposes.fuse.Shortcuts;
class com.friendsofed.recipeviewer.RecipeViewer
{
    private var baseClip:MovieClip;
    private var log:XrayLogger = new XrayLogger();

  public static function main(base:MovieClip) : Void
  {
    var app:RecipeViewer = new RecipeViewer(base);
  }

  public function RecipeViewer(base:MovieClip)
  {
      baseClip = base;
      XrayLoader.addEventListener( XrayLoader.LOADCOMPLETE, this,"startApp");
      XrayLoader.addEventListener( XrayLoader.LOADERROR, this,"startApp");
      XrayLoader.loadConnector("xrayConnector_1.6.3.swf",base,true);
  }

  public function startApp() : Void
  {
      log.debug("this is a log message using log.debug()");
      trace("this is a log message using trace()");

      ZigoEngine.simpleSetup(Shortcuts,FuseItem,PennerEasing);

     var tf:TextField = baseClip.createTextField("testField",1,50,10,
                                                      200,200);
    tf.text = "Hello World.";

    var f:Fuse = new Fuse();
     f.push({target:tf, start_y:1000, y:0,  duration:6,
               ease:"easeOutBounce"});
    f.start();
  }
}
```

Once you've done that, you can begin watching log output in the Xray interface. The next section of this chapter explains how to get that working. After that, run your application. You should see some debugging information appear in the Output panel, as shown in Figure 3-15. Notice that your trace() call added a method name and line, whereas the log.debug() call didn't. This is because MTASC adds that extra information for trace().

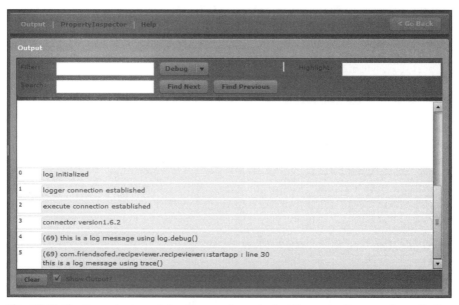

Figure 3-15. The Xray output panel showing some log output while running the example application

Using the AS3 XrayLogger class

The previous example had you installing the connectors for an ActionScript 2–based project. There is a similar API available for ActionScript 3–based projects. The only significant difference is there is no trace redirect support on the Flex 3 SDK compiler. This means you must use the XrayLog class from Xray to get logging output to the Xray window.

To do that, create a new XrayLog variable and then call the debug, warn, or error methods of that new object to invoke the different logging levels. A modified version of the previous "Hello World" example to use XrayLog follows:

```
package {
    import com.blitzagency.xray.inspector.Xray;
    import com.blitzagency.xray.logger.XrayLog;
    import com.blitzagency.xray.logger.XrayLogger;
    import flash.display.Sprite;
    import flash.text.TextField;
```

```
          [SWF(backgroundColor="#eeeeff", frameRate="60", width="500", ↪
            height="350")]
          public class RecipeViewer extends Sprite
          {
            protected var xray:Xray = new Xray();
            protected var log:XrayLoggeryLog = new XrayLog();

            public function RecipeViewer()
            {
              var tf:TextField = new TextField();
              tf.text = "Hello World";
              addChild(tf);

              log.debug("This is a debug message");
            }
          }
        }
```

Installing the Xray interface

You can download the Xray Interface from the Xray website (http://osflash.org/xray). The Xray interface is packaged in two different formats:

- *Web-based Flex2 Interface (requires Flash Player 9)*: This is the simplest option to quickly get up and running since there is nothing to install. To use it, just click the link and allow the interface to open in your browser. You must have the Flash Player 9 plug-in already installed. This option is useful for quick tests, but if you're using Xray often, it's likely more convenient to install a copy of the interface locally on your computer.

- *SWF only*: Oddly enough, the SWF-only package contains just the SWF that makes up the Xray interface. You can run it either in the stand-alone Flash Player or in a web browser.

Installing a web server

Installing a web server to test your Flash application locally on your development machine can save time and aggravation later when it comes time to deploy to your website for real. Properly setting up a web server with all the necessary libraries, add-ins, and configuration options can be a lengthy process. The people at Apache Friends have put together a project called XAMPP that makes installing a development web server easy. Apache Friends has versions available for Windows, Mac OS X, and Linux. Simply visit the website (http://www.apachefriends.org/en/xampp.html) and download the installer for your operating system. From there it's a simple installation wizard to get your web environment up and running. When running the installer, make sure to install the Apache web server, any Apache modules you might want (like PHP), and the MySQL database server.

Once you've installed XAMPP, you can launch the XAMPP Control Panel (see Figure 3-16) to start the services you've installed. Once you start the Apache web server, you should be able to point your browser at http://localhost/ to view pages served from it.

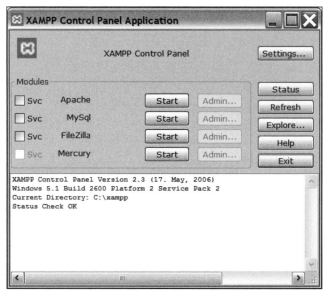

Figure 3-16. The XAMPP Control Panel is used to start and stop your development web server.

XAMPP is a great way to quickly get a development environment up and running. However, it is not suitable for production websites. Installing and setting up a public-facing web server with scalability and security in mind are beyond the scope of this book.

MAMP (Macintosh, Apache, MySQL, PHP) is another popular choice for a development environment on Mac OS X. You can find out more about it at http://www.mamp.info.

Installing Ant

To install Ant, download the binary distribution from the Ant website (http://ant.apache.org), and extract the files in the archive to a location on your computer. Then, add the bin directory from that archive to your system search path. At this point, issuing the command ant in a terminal or command shell will run Ant, and it should complain about a missing build.xml file.

Ant, like Eclipse and FlashDevelop, has many different libraries that can be plugged into it to perform different functions.

The functionality to compile ActionScript 2–based Flash applications using MTASC is achieved through the as2ant library that can be downloaded from the as2lib website (http://www.as2lib.org).

To install as2ant, download the archive from the website, and extract it to a temporary location on your hard drive. Then copy the as2ant.jar file to the lib directory inside your Ant installation.

If you will be doing ActionScript 3 development, you can get the Flex Ant tasks from the Adobe Labs project at `http://labs.adobe.com/wiki/index.php/Flex_Ant_Tasks`. Download the ZIP file linked on that page, and copy it either to your project directory or to a directory you can share across projects.

You now have a working stand-alone version of Ant.

If you're developing using Eclipse, you should be aware that it also ships with a stripped-down version of Ant. To avoid problems that may arise from installation differences between the two, you should configure Eclipse to use your stand-alone version of Ant. To do this, select the Window ➤ Preferences menu option. Then select the Ant ➤ Runtime option on the left. Finally, click the Ant Home button, and select the directory you installed Ant to from the resulting dialog box.

Using FlashDevelop to create an ActionScript 3 build script

Now that you have Ant installed, you need to create a build script that defines the actions that Ant should perform to complete a build of your application. From the FlashDevelop menu, select the File ➤ New ➤ XML Document option. A new file will open in the editor. Save this file with a name of `build.xml`. Once you've done that, you can begin writing your build script by entering the following code into the file.

The project tag is the starting point for an Ant-based project:

```
<project name="RecipeViewer" basedir="." default="compile">
```

The taskdef tag tells Ant where to find the Flex tasks you have downloaded. The file `flexTasks.tasks` contains definitions of the available tasks, and the `classpath` attribute should point to the JAR file you downloaded.

```
<taskdef resource="flexTasks.tasks" classpath="lib/flexTasks.jar" />
```

The following line creates a new property called FLEX_HOME and assigns a value to it that points to the Flex SDK. Make sure to enter the directory to the SDK on your machine.

```
<property name="FLEX_HOME" value="C:/FlashTools/flex3sdk"/>
```

Ant projects are broken up into a series of targets. Each target generally performs a different action such as compiling a piece of an application or copying files to an output destination. This `target` tag will be the only one for now, and it will hold the commands to compile the RecipeViewer application. Notice the `project` tag before it specifies a default target. That default target will be run when Ant is executed without any arguments.

```
<target name="compile"
        description="Compile the RecipeViewer application">
```

The `mxmlc` tag invokes the `mxmlc` compiler that ships with the Flex SDK. This compiler is capable of compiling ActionScript 3 or MXML files. You also specify that the compiler should use the Xray library; if you had other libraries that you use, you could add them as additional `include` tags. After the `mxmlc` tag, you must close the `target` and `project` tags to create well-formed XML.

```
    <mxmlc file="RecipeViewer.as">
        <load-config filename="${FLEX_HOME}/frameworks/flex-config.xml"/>
        <source-path path-element="${FLEX_HOME}/frameworks"/>
        <compiler.include-libraries dir="." append="true">
          <include name="Xray_Flex2_Library_v0.5.swc" />
        </compiler.include-libraries>
        </mxmlc>
    </target>
</project>
```

Once you've written your build script, you can open a command prompt, change into your project directory, and issue the command ant. If everything works correctly, you should see the following output and have a new RecipeViewer.swf file:

```
C:\projects\RecipeViewer>ant
Buildfile: build.xml

compile:
     [mxmlc] Loading configuration file➡
      C:\FlashTools\flex3sdk\frameworks\flex-config.xml
     [mxmlc] C:\Documents and Settings\Marc\RecipeViewer\➡
         RecipeViewer.swf (144175 bytes)

BUILD SUCCESSFUL
Total time: 3 seconds
```

If you double-click the RecipeViewer.swf file in your Windows Explorer or OS X Finder, the Flash movie should launch in your default viewer, and the words "Hello World" should be displayed.

Using Eclipse to create an ActionScript 2 build script

Let's create a build script that will build the ActionScript 2 sample application and then copy the resulting SWF to your testing web server:

1. Select your project in the Eclipse Navigator panel.
2. Create a build.xml file in your project directory. Select the File ➤ New ➤ Other menu option. Then select XML, and click the OK button. In the next dialog box, select Create XML from scratch. Finally, enter the name **build.xml**, and click the Finish button.
3. Enter the following code into that file.

The project tag is the starting point for an Ant project:

```
    <project name="RecipeViewer">
```

The taskdef tag tells Ant about any custom tasks you want to use. This line registers the mtasc task with the org.as2lib.ant.Mtasc class you recently installed:

```
    <taskdef name="mtasc" classname="org.as2lib.ant.Mtasc" />
```

Property tags are used to keep the configuration of a project in a central location. Here, you set up the location of several directories that will be required later in the Ant script. To use a property, you use a ${property name} notation, as you will see.

```
<property name="mtasc" location="C:/FlashTools/mtasc-1.12/mtasc" />
<property name="deploy.dir" location="C:/xampp/htdocs" />
<property name="lib.dir" location="../lib" />
<property name="src.dir" location="src" />
```

Ant partitions units of work into targets. Here, you create a target called build that will compile the application:

```
<target name="build">
    <mkdir dir="builds" />
      <mtasc mtasc="${mtasc}"
       version="8"
       main="true"
       header="800:600:30"
       src="com/friendsofed/recipeviewer/RecipeViewer.as"
       classpath="${src.dir} ; ${lib.dir}"
       swf="builds/RecipeViewer.swf"
       trace="com.blitzagency.xray.util.MtascUtility.trace" />
</target>
```

Before you compile, you use the mkdir task to assure that the builds directory exists. To do the actual compiling, you use the mtasc Ant task. The mtasc property points to the location of the compiler. version represents the Flash Player version to compile for. The main property tells MTASC that it should look for the static main() method that you created when it starts the application. The classpath property lets MTASC know where to look for source files. The swf property tells MTASC where to place its finished file. And lastly, the trace property tells MTASC to use Xray for the logging mechanism.

The buildAndCopy target is meant to build your application and then copy it to your webserver directory. By adding the depends="build" attribute, Ant understands that it must complete the build target before running this one. This target then simply makes sure the deployment location exists and copies the files from the builds directory there.

```
<target name="buildAndCopy" depends="build">
    <mkdir dir="${deploy.dir}/recipe_viewer" />
    <copy todir="${deploy.dir}/recipe_viewer" >
      <fileset dir="builds" />
    </copy>
  </target>
</project>
```

Once you have made the script, open a terminal or command shell, and change to your projects directory. Issue the command ant buildAndCopy, and your application will be compiled and copied to the webserver directory. The output should look something like this:

```
C:\projects\recipe-viewer>ant buildAndCopy
Buildfile: build.xml

build:
    [mtasc] Compiling 2 source files.
    [mtasc] C:\FlashTools\mtasc-1.12\mtasc -swf C:\projects\personal\OS
    F-Book\workspace\recipe-viewer\builds\RecipeViewer.swf -header 800
    :600:30 -trace com.blitzagency.xray.util.MtascUtility.trace -version 8 -c
    p C:\projects\personal\OSF-Book\workspace\recipe-viewer\src -cp C:\
    projects\personal\OSF-Book\workspace\lib -main com\blitzagency\xra
    y\util\MtascUtility.as com\friendsofed\recipeviewer\RecipeViewer.as

buildAndCopy:
    [mkdir] Created dir: C:\xampp\htdocs\recipe_viewer
    [copy] Copying 2 files to C:\xampp\htdocs\recipe_viewer

BUILD SUCCESSFUL
Total time: 1 seconds
```

The important line to look for is BUILD SUCCESSFUL. If your web server is running, you should now be able to view your application by pointing a web browser at http://localhost/recipe_viewer/ RecipeViewer.swf.

Displaying the Eclipse Ant view

There is an easier way to run your build script than going to the command line and executing Ant. Eclipse has a special view just for this purpose.

1. In Eclipse, select the Window ➤ Show View ➤ Other menu option. A dialog box listing all the available Eclipse views will appear.

2. Select the Ant view, and click the OK button. A new panel called Ant will be displayed underneath your code editor.

3. Drag your build.xml file from the Navigator to the Ant panel. When you are done, it should like Figure 3-17.

Figure 3-17. The Eclipse Ant panel displaying the build script

You've successfully installed an open source Flash development workflow! Just double-click the buildAndCopy target to execute it and then open a web browser to http://localhost/ recipe_viewer/RecipeViewer.swf to see the completed application (see Figure 3-18).

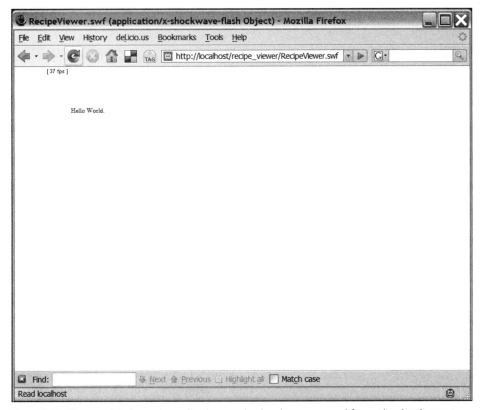

Figure 3-18. The completed sample application running in a browser served from a local web server

In this chapter, you set up both an ActionScript 2 and an ActionScript 3 project using two different sets of tools and workflows. You also saw how to use some other tools such as Xray and Ant. In the next chapter, you'll build on this knowledge to create more involved applications. You'll also explore how to use the open source tools to more efficiently develop Flash-based applications. In Chapter 5, you'll learn more about debugging applications using Xray, and in Chapter 6 you'll learn more about Ant and how to use it in your release and deployment process.

Chapter 4

USING AN OPEN SOURCE WORKFLOW

by Marc Hughes

This chapter covers the following:

- Using open source tools to create an application
- Effectively using graphical assets given to you by a designer
- Working efficiently with other developers on the same project

In the previous chapter, you set up the open source tools necessary to create a Flash application. In this chapter, you will see how to use those tools to create an application for a hypothetical website that allows you to view recipes online. While doing that, you will concentrate on those tools and explore some of the useful features they provide. You will also see how to create a smooth workflow between multiple people working on a single project.

The sample application you'll create will read in an XML file that lists details about several recipes. It will then display a list of recipes with a quick preview of the currently selected recipe. When the user clicks a More Details button, the full recipe will be displayed. You'll create three versions of this application in this chapter: an ActionScript 3 Flash-based application, an ActionScript 3 Flex-based application, and lastly an ActionScript 2 Flash-based version.

Getting assets from designers

Flash development is often very user-interface-centric, which oftentimes means creating visually pleasing graphical assets. It is a rare person who can cross both worlds of development and design. As you'll see from the examples later in this chapter, I am not one of those people. I rely on the artistic ability of the designer I'm working with to make things that look good. During my Flash development career, I've worked with two main types of designers.

The first type of designers includes those who are used to working in the Flash IDE environment. They can both create static art and work with the timeline to create animations. With a little guidance, they can set up their work in a way that completely relieves me of having to modify it. This might mean sticking to some simple naming conventions or adding unique instance names to objects they create.

The other type of designers includes those who focus completely on the visual experience and expect me to take their work and somehow transform it into something functional. They might work in the Flash IDE but are equally as likely to work in Adobe Illustrator, in Adobe Photoshop, or in any other graphically oriented environment.

> *Although this book focuses on open source development tools, there are some great open source design tools. Some of those tools include the following:*
>
> - *Paint.NET*: http://www.getpaint.net/
> - *GIMP*: http://www.gimp.org/
> - *Blender*: http://www.blender.org/

In the next section, you'll learn how to work with designers who can deliver a SWF with a logical structure and naming scheme. Later in this chapter, you will learn how to use swfmill to transform simple graphics into a more complex SWF structure.

Integrating SWFs from designers

When working with designers who are capable of delivering content to you that's ready to use, a short planning session before the work starts can save you countless hours later in the development cycle. During this planning session, you should come up with a way to organize the artwork and a simple set of naming conventions to use both within the art and for the names of the art files.

The first step in this planning session might be to create a quick wireframe that contains the different elements that will be present in the interface. The wireframe should try to identify the different components of the UI, without specifying how they will look. A simple wireframe for the recipe-viewing application in this chapter might look like this:

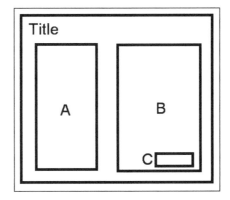

The next step is to decide what the different pieces are and how to organize them. For the sample wireframe shown here, you might create the following guidelines:

- The artwork will be delivered as assets in a SWF.

- "Title" will be a static text element entirely under the control of the designer.

- The section labeled "A" will be used for a list of recipe names. The designer will create a MovieClip with an instance name of recipeList_mc that will live on the stage in the Flash IDE. The developer will programmatically populate it with text fields.

- The section labeled "B" will be used for some details about the currently selected recipe. It will be a MovieClip with an instance name of recipeDetails_mc. Within this MovieClip, there will be the following elements:

  - A TextField named prepTime_txt that should be filled in with the amount of prep time that the recipe requires

  - A TextField named description_txt that should be filled in with a short description of the currently selected recipe

  - A Button ("C") with an instance name of details_btn that should trigger the display of the details of the currently selected recipe

> *For those of you not familiar with the Flash IDE or the ActionScript API, MovieClip, TextField, and Button are all native constructs in the Flash environment. The designer can easily create these using the IDE, and the developer can manipulate them through ActionScript (as you'll see later in this chapter).*

After a wireframe is made and a set of conventions is created, the designer is free to go off and create the content. At the same time, the developer is free to begin developing the component without waiting for the designer to finish. This sort of parallel development can help cut development time.

By coming up with this list of guidelines, it gives the designer great flexibility in the look of the application. If he decides to change the layout by putting "A" above "B" instead of next to it, or if he decides to completely rework the artwork and color scheme, he's free to do so at any point in the development cycle without involving the developer, as long as the same logical structure is followed.

At this point, it's often helpful for either the designer or the developer to quickly mock up the interface in the Flash IDE so both have something to work from. See Figure 4-1 for a mock-up of the example interface.

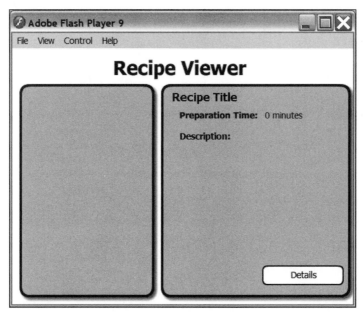

Figure 4-1. The developer-made mocked-up interface for the Recipe Viewer application

After you have the assets delivered from the designer, the method to integrate those assets is a little bit different depending on whether you're doing ActionScript 3 development with the Flex SDK or doing ActionScript 2 development using MTASC as your compiler. Later in this chapter I'll go over both of these scenarios.

Creating some data

The first step to displaying some useful information is to create that information. Since you're building a recipe-viewing application, you need to come up with a list of recipes. You'll hold the list in an XML file to make it easy to parse out the different parts.

Creating the XML file

Create a new file called recipes.xml in your project folder. Then add a couple of your favorite recipes to it in the following format:

```
<recipes>
  <recipe preptime="15 Minutes">
    <name>Smores</name>
    <description>
      Smores are a favorite camp-time
```

```
          treat consisting of a melted marshmallow
          sandwiched between two graham crackers
          and a piece of chocolate.
        </description>
        <ingredients>
          <ingredient>1 Marshmallow</ingredient>
          <ingredient>1 Chunk of chocolate </ingredient>
          <ingredient>1 Graham cracker, broken in two pieces</ingredient>
        </ingredients>
        <directions>
          Roast marshmallow over an open fire until toasty.
          Put chunk of chocolate on graham cracker.
          Place marshmallow on top of chocolate chunk, cover with
          other piece of graham cracker.
        </directions>
      </recipe>
      <recipe preptime="10 Minutes">
        <name>Peanut Butter and Jelly</name>
        <description>
          The peanut butter and jelly sandwich (or PB&amp;J) is a classic
          lunchtime food.
        </description>
        <ingredients>
          <ingredient>2 slices of bread</ingredient>
          <ingredient>2oz. Peanut Butter </ingredient>
          <ingredient>1oz. Jelly</ingredient>
        </ingredients>
        <directions>
          Spread peanut butter on one slice of bread.  Spread
          jelly on the other.  Press slices of bread together,
          cut in half.
        </directions>
      </recipe>
    </recipes>
```

> *Both FlashDevelop and Eclipse allow you to create and edit XML documents. In FlashDevelop, select the* File ➤ New ➤ XML Document *menu option. Depending on how your Eclipse environment is set up, you might find an identical menu option, or you may have to select* File ➤ New ➤ Other *and choose* XML *from the resulting dialog box.*

With an XML data file and some sample mock assets, you're ready to start developing the recipe-viewing application. Alternatively, you can get a copy of this data file in this book's downloadable content in Chapter 4's directory.

By using an XML file like this, you could later swap out a static XML file with the results from a web service that either you or another developer creates.

ActionScript 3 development

There are two significantly different workflows for ActionScript 3 development. One uses a Flash-based development model with Sprites, MovieClips, and so on. The other follows a Flex-based model using the Flex components that are often declared in MXML files in addition to ActionScript files. Using FlashDevelop to accomplish both of those workflows is described in the following sections. If you're using OS X or Linux, you should be aware that it's also possible to do ActionScript 3 development using FDT. If you're interested in that, the later "ActionScript 2 development" section closely mimics what you will see in that environment.

Creating a Flash application with FlashDevelop

If you followed along in Chapter 3, you should have a sample FlashDevelop project that you can start with for this chapter. If you don't, you can create a new FlashDevelop project from scratch or copy the one provided in the downloadable archive for this book from the friends of ED website.

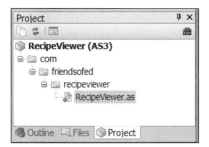

Figure 4-2. The modified package structure of the Recipe Viewer sample application

To better organize the application, you'll make one small change to the sample application from Chapter 3. Specifically, you'll put the main application class in a package structure called com.friendsofed.recipeviewer. To do this, create three new directories named com, friendsofed, and recipeviewer within each other by right-clicking in the FlashDevelop Project panel and selecting Add ➤ New Folder. Once that's done, move the RecipeViewer.as file into that newly created directory. The final file layout should resemble Figure 4-2. After doing that, update the package line at the top of the class to reflect the new structure:

```
package com.friendsofed.recipeviewer
```

Entering the code

To begin the new development for this project, you'll add a new data object class to represent a single recipe. While you're making that, let's add the ability to parse out a single recipe XML node to the values in that class.

Right-click the recipeviewer folder in your Project panel, and select Add ➤ New Class. Give the file a name of Recipe.as, and enter the following code:

```
package com.friendsofed.recipeviewer
{
  import com.blitzagency.xray.logger.XrayLog;
  public class Recipe
  {
    public var prepTime:String = "";
    public var name:String = "";
    public var description:String = "";
    public var ingredients:Array = [];
    public var directions:String = "";
    protected var log:XrayLog = new XrayLog();
```

```
      public function Recipe( xml:XML ) : void
      {
        log.debug("new Recipe " + arguments );
        prepTime = xml.@preptime;
        name = xml.name;
        description = xml.description;
        directions = xml.directions;
        for each ( var ingredient:XML in xml..ingredient )
        {
          ingredients.push( ingredient.toString() );
        }
      }
    }
  }
```

This class has several public variables to hold some details about a single recipe. The constructor takes an XML node and is capable of parsing a single <recipe> node from the sample file using E4X. The following is example input that it can parse from the XML format:

```
<recipe preptime="10 Minutes">
    <name>Peanut Butter and Jelly</name>
    <description>
      The peanut butter and jelly sandwich (or PB&amp;J) is a classic
      lunchtime food.
    </description>
    <ingredients>
      <ingredient>2 slices of bread</ingredient>
      <ingredient>2oz. Peanut Butter </ingredient>
      <ingredient>1oz. Jelly</ingredient>
    </ingredients>
    <directions>
      Spread peanut butter on one slice of bread.  Spread
      jelly on the other.  Press slices of bread together,
      cut in half.
    </directions>
</recipe>
```

While typing your code, you may notice a small pop-up list sometimes appears (see Figure 4-3). This is a context-aware code completion mechanism of FlashDevelop that you can access at any time by pressing Ctrl+spacebar. You can continue typing your code and ignore it, or you can use the up/down arrows on your keyboard to select one of the suggested completions and then press Enter to use it. Pressing the Escape key will cause the window to close if it's obscuring a part of the code you want to view.

Figure 4-3. The FlashDevelop context-aware completion list

FlashDevelop also has code-folding capabilities. In the far-left margin of the text editor are a series of small boxes with minus signs in them. Clicking these will collapse the visible portion of the code, hiding the block-level element that was represented by that box. This allows you to hide the code of a class, function, or control structure (if, for, while, and so on) so you can see the "big picture."

In the code you entered, notice the use of the XrayLog object. This allows you to redirect logging output to the Xray interface. You can learn more about how to use Xray for logging in Chapter 5.

Later, during development, you'll also need to be able to access the ingredient list as a formatted string, so while you're writing this class, let's add a quick helper method that will concatenate all the ingredients, one per line, into a string:

```
public function getIngredientList() : String
{
  return ingredients.join("\n");
}
```

Next, create a new class in the recipeviewer folder called RecipeXMLLoader, and enter the following code. This will allow you to load and parse the XML data file you previously created.

```
package com.friendsofed.recipeviewer
{
    import com.blitzagency.xray.logger.XrayLog;
    import flash.events.Event;
    import flash.events.EventDispatcher;
    import flash.net.URLLoader;
    import flash.net.URLRequest;

    public class RecipeXMLLoader extends EventDispatcher
    {
        protected var xml:XML;
        protected var recipes:Array = [];
        protected var log:XrayLog = new XrayLog();

        public function RecipeXMLLoader(url:String)
        {
            super(this);
            log.debug("RecipeXMLLoader() - " + arguments);
            var loader:URLLoader = new URLLoader();
            loader.addEventListener( Event.COMPLETE, onLoadXML );
            loader.dataFormat = "e4x";
            loader.load( new URLRequest(url) );
            log.debug("Loading XML");
        }

        protected function onLoadXML( e:Event ) : void
        {
            log.debug("onLoadXML() - " + arguments);
            var loader:URLLoader = e.target as URLLoader;
            xml = new XML(loader.data);
```

```
        for each (var recipe:XML in xml..recipe )
        {
          recipes.push( new Recipe(recipe) );
          dispatchEvent( new Event(Event.COMPLETE) );
        }
    }

    public function getRecipes() : Array
    { return recipes; }
  }
}
```

While entering in this class, try to take advantage of FlashDevelop's snippets feature. **Snippets** are small chunks of commonly used code that can be inserted into your file quickly. They help reduce the amount of typing you need to do. To use the snippets feature, press Ctrl+B. A pop-up menu will appear with the available snippets. Select one using the keyboard and then press Enter. This will insert a block of code into your file. For instance, the function snippet inserts the following code:

```
function () {

  }
```

This also places your cursor just to the left of the parentheses, allowing you to type a new function name. There are many premade snippets; to view them, select the Tools ➤ General Tools ➤ Snippet Editor menu option. This will display the Snippet Editor dialog box, as shown in Figure 4-4. Along the top of that dialog box are tabs for the different languages for which FlashDevelop has snippets.

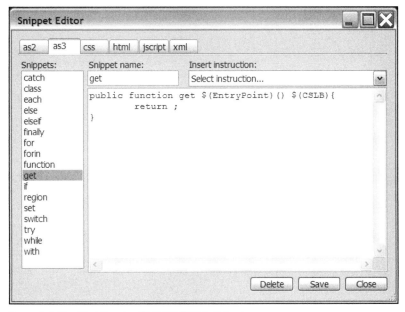

Figure 4-4. The FlashDevelop Snippet Editor dialog box

Besides viewing the available snippets, you can also create your own in the Snippet Editor dialog box by entering a new name for your snippet and the code that you want to appear when the snippet is selected, and then clicking the Save button. Snippets can contain special variables like $(EntryPoint) in the previous example. The $(EntryPoint) variable tells FlashDevelop where to place the cursor when the snippet is inserted. You can find other variables and what they mean in the Insert instruction pull-down menu.

After you've created the RecipeXMLLoader class, you can fill out the rest of your RecipeViewer class. Open the RecipeViewer.as file, and modify it as follows:

```
package com.friendsofed.recipeviewer
{
  import com.blitzagency.xray.inspector.Xray;
  import flash.display.MovieClip;
  import flash.display.SimpleButton;
  import flash.display.Sprite;
  import flash.events.Event;
  import flash.events.EventDispatcher;
  import flash.events.MouseEvent;
  import flash.text.TextField;
  import mx.controls.Button;


  [SWF(backgroundColor = "#eeeeff", frameRate = "60", width = "550", ➥
    height = "400")]
```

Add a SWF metatag before the class declaration. Metatags are specified in ActionScript 3 with bracket notation. The SWF metatag defines properties for the size, frame rate, and background color of the exported Flash application.

```
public class RecipeViewer extends MovieClip
{
  [Embed(source='/RecipeViewerArtAssets.swf',symbol="RecipeViewerUI")]
  protected var recipeViewerAssetClass:Class;
```

Next, add a new variable in your class declaration, and embed a mocked-up RecipeViewerAssets.swf file. The Embed metatag causes the Flex compiler to embed an asset into the application and make it available using the variable declared after it. Here you're using it to learn how to embed the RecipeViewerUI symbol from a SWF provided to you by a designer or other source. You can also embed graphic files in JPEG, GIF, or PNG format if your designers prefer to work with tools that output those formats.

The download for this book comes with a sample RecipeViewerArtAssets.swf file that you can use for this chapter. Simply copy that file into your project directory so that FlashDevelop and the Flex compiler can find it.

Next, modify the RecipeViewer constructor, as shown here:

```
        protected var recipeViewerAsset:Sprite;

        protected var prepTime:TextField;
        protected var recipeDescription:TextField;
        protected var detailsButton:SimpleButton;
        protected var recipeList:MovieClip;
        protected var xray:Xray = new Xray();
        protected var recipeXml:RecipeXMLLoader;
        protected var selectedRecipe:int = 0;
        protected var menuOptions:Array = [];


        public function RecipeViewer()
        {
          addChild(xray);
          recipeViewerAsset = new recipeViewerAssetClass();

          addChild(recipeViewerAsset);
          recipeList = recipeViewerAsset.getChildByName("recipeList_mc")
                              as MovieClip;

          var detailsMc:MovieClip = recipeViewerAsset.getChildByName ➥
                              ("recipeDetails_mc") as MovieClip;
          prepTime = detailsMc.prepTime_txt;
          recipeDescription = detailsMc.description_txt;
          detailsButton = detailsMc.details_btn;

          prepTime.text = "";
          recipeDescription.text = "";
          detailsButton.addEventListener( MouseEvent.CLICK,
                                                    onDetailsClick );

          recipeXml = new RecipeXMLLoader( "recipes.xml" );
          recipeXml.addEventListener( Event.COMPLETE, onXmlLoad );
        }
```

This assigns various parts of the UI to variables that you can access later and starts the loading of the XML file that contains the recipe data. The constructor also sets up a click handler, so when a user clicks the Details button, the onDetailsClick method is called.

Next, create a new onXmlLoad method, as shown here:

```
        protected function onXmlLoad( e:Event ) : void
        {
          displayMenu();
          displayRecipe();
        }
```

This serves as an event handler and is called once the XML file is loaded into the application. When that's complete, you want to set up the menu of available recipes and display the first one in the list, so let's call two methods to do that. The code for those new methods follows:

```
protected function displayMenu() : void
{
  var y:int = 20;
  for each (var recipe:Recipe in recipeXml.getRecipes() )
  {
    var tf:TextField = new TextField();
    tf.text = recipe.name;
    recipeList.addChild( tf );
    tf.x = 10;
    tf.y = y;
    tf.width = 200;
    tf.selectable = false;
    y += 12;
    tf.addEventListener( MouseEvent.CLICK, onItemClick );
    tf.addEventListener( MouseEvent.MOUSE_OVER, onItemOver );
    tf.addEventListener( MouseEvent.MOUSE_OUT, onItemOut );
    menuOptions.push(tf);
  }
}
```

The displayMenu method dynamically creates a TextField object for each recipe that was loaded. It sets three mouse event handlers to handle clicking and changing the color of the text when the mouse hovers over or out of the recipe label.

Next, write the code for those three mouse event handlers:

```
protected function onItemOver(event:MouseEvent) : void
{
  (event.target as TextField).textColor = 0x005500;
}
protected function onItemOut(event:MouseEvent) : void
{
  (event.target as TextField).textColor = 0x000000;
}
protected function onItemClick(event:MouseEvent) : void
{
  var tf:TextField = event.target as TextField;
  var recipeIndex:int = menuOptions.indexOf(tf);
  if ( recipeIndex == -1 ) { return ; }
  selectedRecipe = recipeIndex;
  displayRecipe();
}
```

The onItemOver and onItemOut methods handle changing the color of the text as the user hovers over the field. When an item is clicked in the menu, the onItemClick method will display the new recipe in the right-side panel of the UI using the displayRecipe() method.

Finish up this class with the following code:

```
protected function displayRecipe() : void
{
  var recipe:Recipe = recipeXml.getRecipes()[ selectedRecipe ];
  prepTime.text = recipe.prepTime;
   recipeDescription.htmlText = recipe.name + "<br/>" +
                                            recipe.description;
}
protected function onDetailsClick( event:MouseEvent ) : void
{
  // TODO: display the details.
}
  }
}
```

The displayRecipe method takes care of actually showing the recipe in the panel on the right. It uses the prepTime and recipeDescription variables that you set up in the constructor of the class. You also created a blank onDetailsClick event handler to take care of a click on the Details button; you'll finish that later in this chapter.

Building the application

The source code for a simple version of the project is now complete. If you haven't already, make sure your recipes.xml file is in your FlashDevelop project directory. To build from within FlashDevelop, there are a couple things you need to set up first.

First, you need to tell FlashDevelop where to find your Flex 3 SDK. Select the Tools ➤ Program Settings menu option. From there, select the AS3Context option from the left. A dialog box will appear with various options about ActionScript 3 development. Make sure to set your Flex SDK location. Click the Close button when you're done.

If you had any ActionScript 3 libraries you planned on using in your project, you could select Tools ➤ Global Classpaths and then specify them in the dialog box that is displayed. You don't have any other libraries for this project, so close the dialog box when you're done.

Next, right-click your project from the panel on the right, and select Properties. Select the Compiler Options tab, scroll to the bottom, and turn Use Network Services to false. This option controls the security sandbox when running SWFs locally on your computer. If you want to access local files (such as recipes.xml), you must turn this off. This setting has no effect when running remotely over the Internet. After you've completed this, close the dialog box.

You should be now be able to press F5 in FlashDevelop or select the Project ➤ Test Movie menu option to launch your new application. If everything goes correctly, you should see the application running in FlashDevelop, as shown in Figure 4-5.

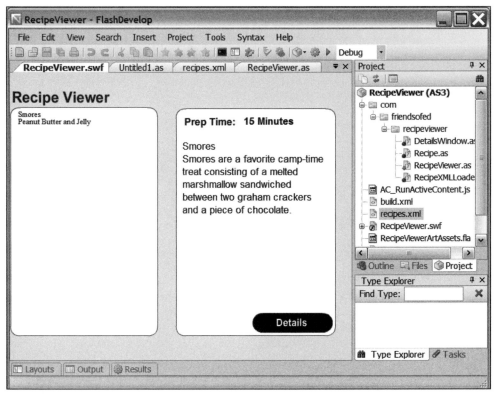

Figure 4-5. The resulting Recipe Viewer application running from inside FlashDevelop

The last thing to do is make the Details button active. You want to have a new window pop up when the button is clicked with a list of ingredients and directions to make the recipe. To accomplish this, create a DetailsWindow class with the following code. This will embed a second graphical asset from the SWF file with two components on it, a text field (details_txt) and a button (close_btn).

```
package com.friendsofed.recipeviewer {
    import flash.display.MovieClip;
    import flash.display.SimpleButton;
    import flash.display.Sprite;
    import flash.events.MouseEvent;
    import flash.text.TextField;

    public class DetailsWindow extends Sprite
    {
        [Embed(source='/RecipeViewerArtAssets.swf',symbol="DetailsWindow")]
        protected var windowAssetClass:Class;
        protected var window:Sprite;
        protected var details:TextField;
        protected var closeButton:SimpleButton;
```

```
public function DetailsWindow(message:String)
{
  window = new windowAssetClass();
  addChild(window);

  details = window.getChildByName("details_txt") as TextField;
  closeButton = window.getChildByName("close_btn") as SimpleButton;
  details.text = message;
  closeButton.addEventListener( MouseEvent.CLICK, onCloseClick );
}

protected function onCloseClick(event:MouseEvent) : void
{
  parent.removeChild(this);
}
    }
  }
```

Then modify your onDetailsClick event handler to create a message to display and to show your newly created window class with that message:

```
protected function onDetailsClick( event:MouseEvent ) : void
{
  var recipe:Recipe = recipeXml.getRecipes()[ selectedRecipe ];
   var window:DetailsWindow = new DetailsWindow(
                             recipe.getIngredientList() +
                             "\n\n" + recipe.directions);
  addChild(window);
  window.x = width / 2 - window.width / 2;
  window.y = 50;
}
```

Once this is done, you can build your application, choose a recipe from the left, and click the Details button to view the instructions to make the recipe, as shown in Figure 4-6. If this had been a real application, you would probably want to make sure the elements behind the "window" weren't active while the window was open.

Now that you've seen how to use FlashDevelop to build a simple application, you'll learn how to use Ant to help streamline the release process.

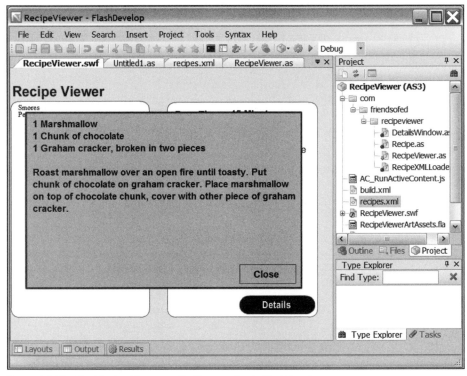

Figure 4-6. The final Recipe Viewer application running in FlashDevelop

Building with Ant

Building the application through FlashDevelop is an easy way to quickly test things, but creating an Ant script to share with others or to integrate into larger build systems can be a great benefit.

In Chapter 3 you created a simple Ant build script for the sample application. The only change you need to make to that is to include the new com.friendsofed.recipeviewer package structure that you set up earlier in the chapter. The full build script is listed here with the changed line in bold:

```
<project name="RecipeViewer" basedir="." default="compile">
  <taskdef resource="flexTasks.tasks" classpath="lib/flexTasks.jar" />
  <property name="FLEX_HOME" value="C:/FlashTools/flex3sdk"/>
  <target name="compile"
      description="Compile the RecipeViewer application">
    <mxmlc file="com/friendsofed/recipeviewer/RecipeViewer.as">
      <load-config filename="${FLEX_HOME}/frameworks/flex-config.xml"/>
      <source-path path-element="${FLEX_HOME}/frameworks"/>
      <compiler.include-libraries dir="." append="true">
        <include name="Xray_Flex2_Library_v0.5.swc" />
      </compiler.include-libraries>
    </mxmlc>
  </target>
</project>
```

If you don't have a sample build script from Chapter 3, you can create a new build script from scratch using the File ➤ New ➤ XML Document menu option. Enter a build script similar to the previous listing.

You can use this Ant target to build the application in a predictable, repeatable way at any time. This is useful when multiple developers are all working on the same project to assure that there is a version of the project that everyone can compile. Having a repeatable build method is also crucial to maintaining a certain degree of release quality.

Creating a Flex application with FlashDevelop

FlashDevelop gives the Windows-based open source Flash developer an excellent development platform for Flex-based applications. In this section, you will make a similarly functioning Recipe Viewer application as the Flash version earlier in this chapter, but this time you'll use a Flex style of development.

If you are on OS X or Linux, you can follow along in this chapter. Just replace FlashDevelop with a text editor of your choice. Although you won't get the contextual help or be able to run the application from your editor, you can edit the code, create the Ant script, and build the application.

The user interface for a Flex-based application is usually laid out in MXML files. That MXML can be skinned by a designer through several different methods, but this is outside the scope of this book. To learn more about skinning Flex applications, consult the Flex SDK documentation.

Creating the project

To begin, create a new project by selecting the Project ➤ New Project menu option. A dialog box like Figure 4-7 will appear. Select the Flex 3 Project option, type a new name for the project, and select an empty destination directory for where you want to save it.

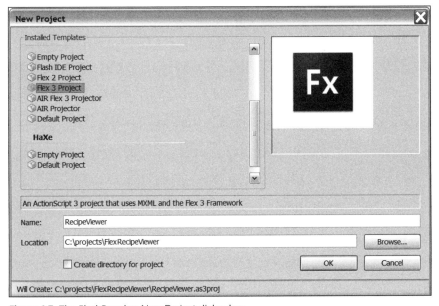

Figure 4-7. The FlashDevelop New Project dialog box

When you've completed that, click the OK button. FlashDevelop will create your project with a
Main.mxml file and a Main.as class to hold your code. Upon opening Main.mxml, your environment
should resemble Figure 4-8.

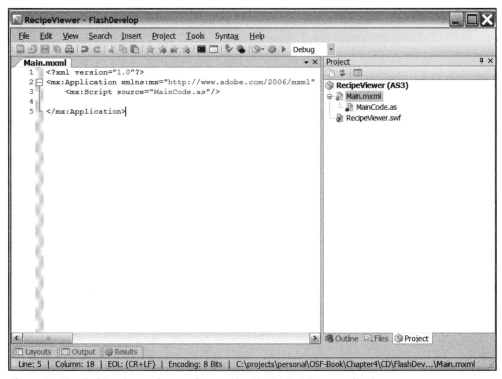

Figure 4-8. The FlashDevelop workspace after creating the Recipe Viewer application

Entering the code

To see some Flex-style development and to quickly move through this part of the chapter, you will use
some basic MXML to lay out the interface. The interface will consist of a window with a ViewStack on
it. On the ViewStack will be two Canvas objects that represent the two main UI states of the application. Within each of those will be the various Labels, TextAreas, and Buttons that make up the interface. In Main.mxml, enter the following code to define that interface:

```
<?xml version="1.0"?>
<mx:Application xmlns:mx="http://www.adobe.com/2006/mxml"
               layout="absolute"
               creationComplete="onCreationComplete()">
    <mx:Script source="MainCode.as"/>
    <mx:TitleWindow
        layout="absolute"
        title="Recipe Viewer"
        left="10" top="10" bottom="10" right="10">
        <mx:ViewStack id="viewstack1" top="0" left="0" right="0" bottom="0">
```

```
<mx:Canvas width="100%" height="100%">
  <mx:List left="10" top="10" bottom="10" id="recipeList" />
  <mx:Label x="180" y="10" text="recipeTitle" fontSize="20"
              width="397"/>
  <mx:Label x="202" y="49" text="Preparation time:"
              fontWeight="bold"/>
  <mx:Label x="313" y="49" text="recipePrepTime" width="264"/>
  <mx:TextArea right="10" left="180" top="87" bottom="48"
                id="recipeDescription"/>
  <mx:Button x="528" y="394" bottom="10" right="10"
    label="Details" click="onViewDetailsClick()"/>
</mx:Canvas>
<mx:Canvas width="100%" height="100%">
  <mx:Label x="6" y="6" text="Recipe Details" fontSize="20"
              fontWeight="bold"/>
  <mx:Label x="29" y="45" text="Label" id="recipeTitle"
              fontSize="20" width="495"/>
  <mx:TextArea right="10" left="10" top="84" bottom="43"
                id="recipeDirections"/>
  <mx:Button x="528" y="402" bottom="10" right="10" label="Close"
              click="onCloseClick()"/>
</mx:Canvas>
      </mx:ViewStack>
    </mx:TitleWindow>
  </mx:Application>
```

Similarly to editing ActionScript files, while typing the MXML code FlashDevelop gives you features such as code folding and completion. Folding is accomplished by the same sort of [+/-] control in the left margin, and code completion is accomplished by pressing Ctrl+spacebar on the keyboard. Figure 4-9 shows both these features while editing MXML.

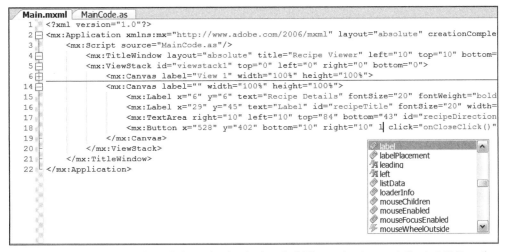

Figure 4-9. As in ActionScript files, FlashDevelop has both code folding and code completion in MXML; notice that the <mx:Canvas> tag at line 6 is folded.

The Flex SDK gives a great capability called **data binding** that will allow you to create this version of the Recipe Viewer application much more quickly than the ActionScript 3 version earlier in this chapter. To take advantage of this, create an HTTPService object just below your `<script>` tag in your .mxml file like so:

```
<mx:HTTPService id="recipeXml" url="recipes.xml" result="onXmlLoad()"/>
```

Next, set the List control's dataProvider and labelField properties to bind it to the HTTPService object:

```
<mx:List left="10" top="10" bottom="10" id="recipeList"
       change="onListChange()"
       dataProvider="{recipeXml.lastResult..recipe}"
       labelField="name"
       />
```

Setting the dataProvider property to recipeXml.lastResult..recipe uses E4X notation to parse the XML and find all the recipe tags. Now, when the HTTPService object loads the XML, the List control will automatically search for all the recipe nodes and use the XML name tag as the label to display.

Once that is done, you can bind the Label and TextArea controls to the List control using the following similar syntax:

```
<mx:Label x="180" y="10" text="{recipeList.selectedItem.name}"
                fontSize="20" width="397"/>
<mx:Label x="202" y="49" text="Preparation time:" fontWeight="bold"/>
<mx:Label x="313" y="49" text="{recipeList.selectedItem.@preptime}"
                width="264"/>
<mx:TextArea right="10" text="{recipeList.selectedItem.description}"
       left="180" top="87" bottom="48" id="recipeDescription"/>
...
<mx:Label x="6" y="6" text="Recipe Details" fontSize="20"
                fontWeight="bold"/>
<mx:Label x="29" y="45" text="{recipeList.selectedItem.name}"
       id="recipeTitle" fontSize="20" width="495"/>
<mx:TextArea right="10" left="10" top="84" bottom="43"
                        id="recipeDirections"/>
```

Now, when the currently selected item in the List control changes, all of those labels will automatically update to the correct data through binding.

In the previous code, several methods are referenced as event handlers, such as the onXmlLoad method:

```
<mx:HTTPService id="recipeXml" url="recipes.xml" result="onXmlLoad()"/>
```

If you open the MainCode.as file, you can now enter the code for those methods. When the application is fully created, you will want to activate the HTTPService object and load the results. This is done on the onCreationComple method.

```
private function onCreationComplete():void
{
    recipeXml.send();
}
```

Once the XML has been loaded, you need to set the first item as selected and fire off the onListChange method:

```
private function onXmlLoad() : void
{
    recipeList.selectedIndex = 0;
    onListChange();
}
```

You may have already noticed, but you did not set the recipe direction's TextArea through binding. This is because it should incorporate both the ingredients and the directions. The onListChange method will do exactly this:

```
private function onListChange() : void
{
  var ingredientList:String = "";
  for each (var ingredient:XML in recipeList.selectedItem..ingredient)
  {
    ingredientList = ingredientList + ingredient + "\n";
  }

    recipeDirections.text = ingredientList + recipeList.selectedItem.directions;
}
```

The last thing to do is switch between the two different UI views. You had set up two buttons with two click handlers to accomplish this. All they need to do is switch the ViewStack between the two Canvas objects.

```
private function onViewDetailsClick():void
{
    mainStack.selectedIndex = 1;
}
```

```
private function onCloseClick():void
{
    mainStack.selectedIndex = 0;
}
```

This simple MXML-based application performs all of the vital features as the ActionScript version, such as displaying a list of recipes and allowing the user to select one, but in a significantly less amount of code. In the following sections, you'll look at how to build and manage it.

Building the application

In the "Creating a Flash application with FlashDevelop" section, you reviewed how to set up your project options to enable building from within FlashDevelop.

From the FlashDevelop toolbar, change the pull-down menu on the right from Debug to Release. Now, press F5, or select the Project ➤ Test Movie menu option. This will build the application and launch it in your web browser. You should now be looking at a fully working Recipe Viewer application, as shown in Figure 4-10.

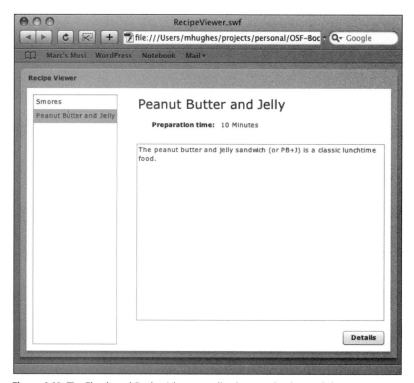

Figure 4-10. The Flex-based Recipe Viewer application running in a web browser

Building with Ant

The build script for the Flex-based application is nearly identical to the ActionScript 3 Flash-based version. The only change necessary is to point the compiler to the main `.mxml` file instead of the main ActionScript file:

```
<project name="RecipeViewer" basedir="." default="compile">
  <taskdef resource="flexTasks.tasks" classpath="lib/flexTasks.jar" />
  <property name="FLEX_HOME" value="C:/FlashTools/flex3sdk"/>
  <target name="compile"
     description="Compile the RecipeViewer application">
    <mxmlc file="main.mxml">
```

```
            <load-config filename="${FLEX_HOME}/frameworks/flex-config.xml"/>
            <source-path path-element="${FLEX_HOME}/frameworks"/>
            <compiler.include-libraries dir="." append="true">
              <include name="Xray_Flex2_Library_v0.5.swc" />
            </compiler.include-libraries>
        </mxmlc>
      </target>
    </project>
```

Upon issuing the same build command of ant buildAndCopy, you should see output similar to the following:

```
>ant
Buildfile: build.xml
build:
    [mxmlc] C:\FlashTools\flex3sdk\bin\mxmlc.exe Main.mxml -as3 ➥
-output bin/RecipeViewer.swf
      [mxmlc] Loading configuration file C:\FlashTools\flex3sdk\ ➥
frameworks\flex-config.xml
    [mxmlc] bin/RecipeViewer.swf (254697 bytes)

BUILD SUCCESSFUL
Total time: 4 seconds
```

You've now seen how to create two different types of ActionScript 3 applications using FlashDevelop and the Flex SDK. The rest of this chapter will focus on using open source tools to create an ActionScript 2–based project.

ActionScript 2 development

ActionScript 2 has been around a lot longer than ActionScript 3, and the tools to support it are often-times more mature or complete because of that. This section of the chapter will walk you through using Eclipse, ASDT, Ant, and swfmill to create an application.

Once you have an art asset from the designer in the form of a SWF to work with, you have two options for how to use it in an ActionScript 2–based application:

- You could compile your code directly into the SWF from the designer. This will give you the benefit of a less complex application to write and a slightly faster download time.
- You could compile your application into a separate SWF and load it at runtime. This gives the benefit that you can easily swap out art assets without rebuilding your application.

For the main application's art asset, we will use the first option. Later in this chapter, I will show you how to use the other option. However, the method of generating the SWF does not dictate how you must load it, and either way will work.

When I talk about compiling your code directly into the SWF delivered from the designer, I'm not talking about the way the Flash IDE works. In that environment, the developer would open the .fla file and add code and publish from there. In this scheme, the designer is the only one who works in the Flash IDE, publishing a SWF and handing it off. The developer then writes the code in Eclipse and compiles it into the SWF from the designer using MTASC. This removes issues with the traditional Flash development workflow where multiple people want to modify the same binary .fla file at the same time during development.

Adding the asset to your project

In Chapter 3, you set up Eclipse and ASDT and created a new Recipe Viewer ActionScript 2 project. If you followed along, you can launch Eclipse and open that project. If not, you can download a file from the friends of ED website that contains a completed project from Chapter 3 and import it into Eclipse using the File ➤ Import ➤ General ➤ Existing Project into Workspace menu option.

Now, create a new folder in your project by right-clicking the project name and selecting New ➤ Other; a dialog box will appear. From this dialog box, select the Folder option under the General section. Name the folder Assets, and click the Finish button. Now, copy the mocked-up SWF I talked about earlier in the chapter into that directory. You can find a copy of that SWF in the Chapter4\Assets folder of the downloadable file for this book from the friends of ED website. Once you've done this, you should have a directory structure similar to Figure 4-11 in your Eclipse Navigator.

Figure 4-11. The Eclipse Navigator after adding your asset to the project

Modifying the build process

You've already seen an Ant build script for the ActionScript 3 version of the program, and you've also created a simple ActionScript 2 build script in Chapter 3. The only significant difference between the ActionScript 3 build script and the script for the ActionScript 2 version of the Recipe Viewer application is the method of compiling. Whereas you used the mxmlc task before, you will use the MTASC task here.

If you have a build.xml file from Chapter 3, you can use that as a base for this section. If not, you can either get a copy from this book's downloadable archive or type the following by hand:

```
<project name="RecipeViewer">
<taskdef name="mtasc" classname="org.as2lib.ant.Mtasc" />
<property name="mtasc" location="C:/FlashTools/mtasc-1.12/mtasc" />
<property name="deploy.dir" location="C:/xampp/htdocs" />
<property name="lib.dir" location="../lib" />
<property name="src.dir" location="src" />
 <target name="build">
   <mkdir dir="builds" />
   <mtasc mtasc="${mtasc}"
           version="8"
           main="true"
           header="800:600:30"
           src="com/friendsofed/recipeviewer/RecipeViewer.as"
           classpath="${src.dir} ; ${lib.dir}"
           SWF="builds/RecipeViewer.SWF"
           trace="com.blitzagency.xray.util.MtascUtility.trace" />
  </target>
  <target name="buildAndCopy" depends="build">
   <mkdir dir="${deploy.dir}/recipe_viewer" />
     <copy todir="${deploy.dir}/recipe_viewer" >
   <fileset dir="builds" />
  </copy>
  </target>
</project>
```

For a detailed explanation of this build script, consult Chapter 3.

Right now, the MTASC compiler doesn't know anything about the art asset you've added. You need to tell it how to build the application and use RecipeViewer.swf as a base. To do this, you need to edit the build target in the build script so it looks like the following:

```
<target name="build">
  <mkdir dir="bin" />
  <mtasc mtasc="${mtasc}"
    version="8"
    main="true"
    src="com/friendsofed/recipeviewer/RecipeViewer.as"
    classpath="${src.dir} ; ${lib.dir}"
    swf="assets/RecipeViewer.swf"
    out="bin/RecipeViewer.swf"
    trace="com.blitzagency.xray.util.MtascUtility.trace" />
</target>
```

You made the following modifications:

1. First, you removed the header="800:600:30" parameter. This is required only when you want MTASC to create the SWF from scratch. Now, the dimensions and frame rate of the resulting SWF will be taken from the mocked-up RecipeViewer.swf.

2. Then you modified the SWF line and pointed it to the premade SWF file. This is the file that will be read in when building.

3. Lastly, you added an out parameter. This specifies where the resulting SWF should be placed.

If you now execute the build task, you should get output similar to the following:

```
Buildfile: C:\projects\workspace\recipe-viewer\build.xml
build:
    [mtasc] Compiling 2 source files.
    [mtasc] C:\FlashTools\mtasc-1.12\mtasc -swf C:\projects\workspace\
recipe-viewer\assets\RecipeViewer.swf -out C:\projects\personal\
OSF-Book\workspace\recipe-viewer\bin\RecipeViewer.swf -trace
com.blitzagency.xray.util.MtascUtility.trace -version 8 -cp
C:\projects\personal\OSF-Book\workspace\recipe-viewer\src -cp
C:\projects\personal\OSF-Book\workspace\lib -main
com\blitzagency\xray\util\MtascUtility.as com\friendsofed\recipeviewer
\RecipeViewer.as

BUILD SUCCESSFUL
Total time: 500 milliseconds
```

If you now double-click RecipeViewer.swf inside your bin folder, the application will launch. It should look exactly like the mocked-up interface (Figure 4-1) with the addition of a small FPS meter from Xray.

As you can see, the graphics from the input SWF appear, but your code was also run (evidenced by the Xray meter appearing). What happened is MTASC compiled your code and then embedded it within a copy of the RecipeViewer.swf file. In this manner, you can inject code into static SWF content.

Reading a list of recipes

Now that you have some graphical elements loading with your code, it's time to make it do something useful. The first step is to add support for reading a list of recipes from an XML file and storing the results, and that's what you'll do over the next several sections.

Copying the input file

First you need to set up your build script so that it will copy your XML file to a location that the application will be able to find when it runs. So, open your build.xml file, and find the buildAndCopy target. Add a <copy> command to copy recipes.xml to your bin directory. Your resulting buildAndCopy target should look like the following:

```
<target name="buildAndCopy" depends="build">
  <copy todir="bin" >
    <fileset file="assets/recipe.xml" />
  </copy>
```

```
    <mkdir dir="${deploy.dir}/recipe_viewer" />
    <copy todir="${deploy.dir}/recipe_viewer" >
      <fileset dir="builds" />
    </copy>
  </target>
```

Although it may be easier to simply create the XML file in the bin directory in the first place, this is a bad practice. You should consider anything in the bin directory as temporary and eligible to be deleted between builds. By using Ant to copy the XML file, you also open the possibility of retrieving it from a remote location through FTP, HTTP, or even a version control system, allowing content producers to author it outside your development environment.

> *When dealing with static XML files in a project, especially when those files are created by others, it can be helpful to create an XML schema to validate the document. By doing this, you can help to eliminate a source of bugs and save time in the long run. If you want to do this, you can use the* xmlvalidate *Ant task to automatically validate the XML when you build your application. You can read more about* xmlvalidate *at the Ant website:*
>
> http://ant.apache.org/manual/OptionalTasks/xmlvalidate.html

Create a Recipe class

Before you load that XML file, you need somewhere to store the information. Let's create a class called Recipe to keep the various attributes associated with a recipe.

Create the Recipe class

1. Right-click the recipeviewer directory in the Eclipse Navigator, and select New ➤ ActionScript Class.

2. Enter a class name of **Recipe**. Make sure the package is correctly set to com.friendsofed. recipeviewer.

3. Click the Finish button.

A new ActionScript file called Recipe.as will be displayed in the main text edit window. You'll need to know the preparation time, name, description, ingredient list, and directions to make the recipe. Create private variables to hold the various pieces of data.

```
class com.friendsofed.recipeviewer.Recipe
{
  private var prepTime:Number;
  private var name:String;
  private var description:String;
  private var directions:String;
  private var ingredientList:Array;
}
```

Now, let's use an ASDT feature to generate some getter and setter functions for all the members except ingredientList. For ingredientList, you will just automatically generate a getter function. To do this, select the Source ➤ Generate Getters and Setters menu option. A dialog box like Figure 4-12 will appear. Select the check boxes to select the methods you want to generate, and click the OK button.

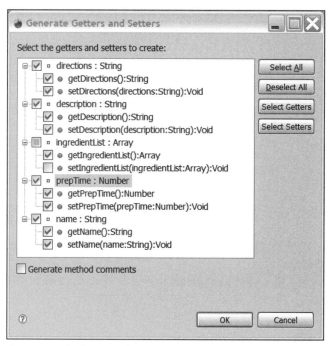

Figure 4-12. The Generate Getters and Setters dialog box is used to automatically create some boilerplate methods.

Once you do that, the following nine methods will be generated for you:

```
public function getPrepTime():Number {
  return prepTime;
}

public function setPrepTime(prepTime:Number):Void {
  this.prepTime = prepTime;
}

public function getDescription():String {
  return description;
}

public function setDescription(description:String):Void {
  this.description = description;
}
```

```
public function getIngredientList():Array {
  return ingredientList;
}

public function getDirections():String {
  return directions;
}

public function setDirections(directions:String):Void {
  this.directions = directions;
}

public function getName():String {
  return name;
}

public function setName(name:String):Void {
  this.name = name;
}
```

To handle ingredients, initialize the ingredientList array in the constructor, and create an addIngredient method:

```
public function Recipe()
{
  ingredientList = new Array();
}
public function addIngredient( ingredient:String ) : void
{
  ingredientList.push( ingredient );
}
```

Now save the file and make sure there are no syntax errors in your Problems panel at the bottom of Eclipse that may have been caused by a typo or other error.

Load the XML file

Now that you have a class to hold the details of a recipe, you need to add functionality to load an XML file. While creating this class, let's explore the ASDT templates feature. First, create a new class named RecipeXMLLoader. Let's make this class a Singleton so only a single object of this type ever exists. Instead of writing the code to do that, you will use the template functionality of ASDT. First, delete all the code in the file. Then type **sing**. Press Ctrl+spacebar to invoke the template functionality. You should now have code similar to the following:

```
class com.friendsofed.recipeviewer.RecipeXMLLoader
{
  private static var instance : RecipeXMLLoader;
```

```
/**
 * @return singleton instance of RecipeXMLLoader
 */
public static function getInstance() : RecipeXMLLoader
{
  if (instance == null)
    instance = new RecipeXMLLoader();
    return instance;
  }
}

private function RecipeXMLLoader()
{
}
}
```

As you can see, code templates can make writing large amounts of boilerplate code very easy. To understand what happened when you invoked the code template, you should open the Window ➤ Preferences menu. From the left panel, select ActionScript2 ➤ Editor ➤ Templates; you will see a dialog box similar to Figure 4-13.

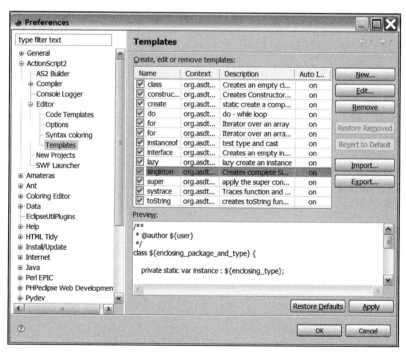

Figure 4-13. The ASDT Templates dialog box

When you press Ctrl+spacebar in the code editor after a word or word fragment, the Name column of the templates is searched for a match. In this case, there was a single match called *singleton*. ASDT then copied the template code into your source file and replaced template variables (the ${text} pieces) with the appropriate pieces of data. Besides the templates that come with ASDT, you can also create your own. Let's create one for writing a public method signature.

Creating a custom template

Creating a custom template makes it available to you when pressing Ctrl+spacebar in the ActionScript editor of ASDT. You can add that custom template to ASDT with the following steps:

1. Click the New button in the Templates dialog box.
2. You want to create a template for a public method, so let's give it a name of pubmeth.
3. In the description field, type **A public method signature**.
4. Type the following code into the Pattern field, and then click the OK button:

```
public function ${methName} () : ${methType}
{
  ${cursor}
}
```

While you type in the pattern, you will notice a pop-up menu appears whenever you press the dollar symbol ($). In this pop-up is a list of premade variables from which you can choose. As you can see, you inserted the ${cursor} variable. This will move the cursor position to that spot when the template is done executing.

You can also create your own custom variables like you did with methName and methType. Custom variables act as placeholders for text when you use the template. When you insert a template, Eclipse will allow you to enter text for each variable that will be replaced in the template. Every occurrence of the same custom variable will be replaced with the same text. Although the simple example contained each variable only once, you could have used them multiple times like so:

```
// ${methName} was an automatically generated method
public function ${methName} () : ${methType}
{
  ${cursor}
}
```

This would cause a comment to appear before the method that contained the name of the method. Since you used ${methName} in multiple locations, you'd have to type it in only once when using the template.

To use this template, exit the template dialog box and return to the RecipeXMLLoader.as file. Position your cursor in the class, but outside of any other method. Type **pubmeth**, and press Ctrl+spacebar. The code from your template will appear. Your first custom variable (methName) will be highlighted. You can type a method name that will overwrite the variable; let's use loadXML. Then press the Tab key. The cursor will advance to the methType variable, and you can type the method type. For this example, let's use Void. After entering the type, you can press the Tab key one more time, and the cursor will be positioned inside the method body, ready for you to type in the body of the method.

Now that you know how to use templates, finish the RecipeXMLLoader class by filling in the following code:

```
class com.friendsofed.recipeviewer.RecipeXMLLoader
{
  public static var XML_LOADED_EVENT:String = "xmlLoadedEvent";
  private static var instance : RecipeXMLLoader;

  public function dispatchEvent() {}
  public function addEventListener() {}
  private var xml:XML;

  public static function getInstance() : RecipeXMLLoader
  {
    if (instance == null)
      instance = new RecipeXMLLoader();
    return instance;
  }

  public function loadXML () : Void
  {
    xml = new XML();
    xml.onLoad = Delegate.create(this, onXMLLoaded );
    xml.ignoreWhite = true;
    xml.load("recipes.xml");
  }

  private function onXMLLoaded(success:Boolean) : Void
  {
    if( success )
    {
      dispatchEvent( {type:XML_LOADED_EVENT , target:this} );
    {
    else
    {
        trace("Could not load XML");
    }
  }

  private function RecipeXMLLoader()
  {
    GDispatcher.initialize(this);
  }

  public function getXml():XML
  {
    return xml;
  }
}
```

If you are familiar with ActionScript, most of the preceding code should be familiar. The event dispatching functionality that uses the GDispatcher class may be new to you, so some explanation is in order.

These lines define two empty methods that will be filled in by GDispatcher in the constructor:

```
public function dispatchEvent() {}
public function addEventListener() {}
```

When the GDispatcher.initialize(this) call is made, those methods are dynamically replaced by code in the GDispatcher class. The modified dispatchEvent method is then used by this class in the onXMLLoaded method:

```
dispatchEvent( {type:XML_LOADED_EVENT , target:this} );
```

This call causes an event of type XML_LOADED_EVENT to be dispatched to any other objects listening for it. Later in this chapter you will use the addEventListener method to add an event listener from the RecipeViewer class.

> To load the XML, you used the XML.load() method. Although it's easy to use here, when loading different types of assets in the same application, the syntax for each is slightly different and can become confusing quickly. There is an open source project called Fling (http://osflash.org/fling) that contains utility methods for loading any type of content over the network in a consistent manner.

Create an XML parser

Once the XML file has been loaded, you need to parse the details and put it in a form you can more easily use. To do this, create a class named RecipeXMLParser with the following code that loops through an XML object and creates an array of Recipe objects.

The parseXml method will take a chunk of XML and return an array of Recipe objects:

```
class com.friendsofed.recipeviewer.RecipeXMLParser
{
  public static function parseXml( xml:XML ) : Array
  {
```

Next, loop through the XML, getting each recipe node, and create a recipe object to hold the results in. Since preptime is stored as an attribute of the recipe XML node, you also set that here:

```
var rv:Array = new Array();
var recipes:XMLNode = xml.childNodes[0];
for( var i:Number = 0 ; i < recipes.childNodes.length ; i++)
{
  var recipeNode:XMLNode = recipes.childNodes[i];
  var recipe = new Recipe();
  recipe.setPrepTime(recipeNode.attributes.preptime);
```

Next, you loop through the recipe's child nodes, and you parse each child node, determine what type it is, and set the appropriate property on the recipe object. Since ingredients are more complex, you separate the parsing of them into a new function called parseIngredients.

```
for(var j:Number = 0 ; j < recipeNode.childNodes.length ; j++ )
{
  var node:XMLNode = recipeNode.childNodes[j];
  switch( node.nodeName )
  {
    case "name": recipe.setName( node.firstChild ); break;
     case "description": recipe.setDescription( node.firstChild );
                            break;
    case "directions":  recipe.setDirections( node.firstChild );
                            break;
    case "ingredients": parseIngredients(node, recipe); break;
  }
}
```

After each recipe is parsed, you add it to the array. At the end of processing, you return the list of recipes:

```
    rv.push(recipe);
  }
  return rv;
}
```

Lastly, you add the parseIngredients method, which will loop through the list of ingredients and add them to the recipe:

```
private static function parseIngredients(node:XMLNode, recipe:Recipe)
{
  for( var i:Number = 0 ; i < node.childNodes.length ; i++)
  {
    var ingredient:String = node.childNodes[i].firstChild;
    recipe.addIngredient( ingredient );
  }
}
}
```

While writing this class, remember to take advantage of some of the Eclipse/ASDT features. If you used code folding to collapse the parseXml method, the display in Eclipse will look like the following:

```
RecipeXMLParser.as

import com.friendsofed.recipeviewer.*;

class com.friendsofed.recipeviewer.RecipeXMLParser
{
  public static function parseXml( xml:XML ) : Array

  private static function parseIngredients(node:XMLNode, recipe:Recipe) : Void
  {
    for( var i:Number = 0 ; i < node.childNodes.length ; i++)
    {
      var ingredient:String = node.childNodes[i].firstChild.toString();
      recipe.addIngredient( ingredient );
    }
  }
}
```

The code for the parseXml method is still there; it's just hidden from view to make it easier to find other parts of the class. You can mouse over the circle with a plus sign in it to get a tooltip of the hidden code, or you can click it to reexpand the code. Classes, methods, import statements, and comments can all be collapsed.

Bringing it all together

Once the ability to read in and parse the XML data file is done, it's time to add code in the RecipeViewer class to tie it all together. For the first step, add two private variables to store information about the recipes and the currently selected recipe:

```
private var recipes:Array = [];
private var selectedRecipe:Number = 0;
```

Next, add some variables that will represent the various onscreen MovieClips and TextFields:

```
private var recipeList_mc:MovieClip;
private var recipeDetails_mc:MovieClip;
private var recipeTitle_txt:TextField;
private var prepTime_txt:TextField;
private var description_txt:TextField;
```

In the constructor, initialize those references:

```
public function RecipeViewer(base:MovieClip)
{
  baseClip = base;
  recipeList_mc = baseClip.recipeList_mc;
  recipeDetails_mc = baseClip.recipeDetails_mc;
  recipeTitle_txt = recipeDetails_mc.recipeTitle_txt;
  prepTime_txt = recipeDetails_mc.prepTime_txt;
  description_txt = recipeDetails_mc.description_txt;
  ...
```

Later in the application, you could have accessed these onscreen components through code such as this:

```
baseClip.recipeDetails_mc.recipeTitle_txt.text
```

However, by doing that, the compiler doesn't know what types recipeDetails_mc and recipeTitle_txt are until runtime. By explicitly declaring variables, you get type checking during compile and context help while editing.

Now, you need to update the display with details from your recipe. While writing the next bit of code, press Ctrl+spacebar after typing the pieces in bold to get a code completion pop-up. This code completion is part of the context-sensitive help you gain by explicitly declaring variables.

```
private function updateDisplay() : Void
{
  var recipe:Recipe = recipes[selectedRecipe];
  recipeTitle_txt.text = recipe.getName();
  prepTime_txt.text = String(recipe.getPrepTime());
  description_txt.text = recipe.getDescription();
}

private function updateIndex() : Void
{
  for( var i:Number = 0 ; i < recipes.length ; i++)
  {
    var recipe:Recipe = recipes[i];
    var tmp:MovieClip = recipeList_mc.createEmptyMovieClip("recipeSpot"
                                  + i,
                                  recipeList_mc.getNextHighestDepth());
    tmp._x = 5;
    tmp._y = 5 + i*15;
    var tf:TextField = tmp.createTextField("recipeIndex" + i,
                                  tmp.getNextHighestDepth(), 0, 0,
                                  200,18 );
    tf.text = recipe.getName();
    tmp.onRelease = Delegate.create(this, onClick, [i]);
  }
}
```

The updateDisplay method populates the four text fields with data from the currently selected recipe. The updateIndex method creates a list of recipes the user can click. To do this, it creates a MovieClip and assigns a method to the onRelease property. It then adds a TextField to that MovieClip and updates it with the recipe name. Since you're using the open source Delegate class from Steve Webster, you can supply additional parameters that will be passed to the onClick method. The third parameter to Delegate.create is an array of parameters to pass. As you can see, you've set it to [i], which will pass the index of the recipe to the onClick method.

```
private function onClick(index:Number) : Void
{
  selectedRecipe = index;
  updateDisplay();
}
```

The next step is to create and invoke the XML loader at application startup. Modify the startApp method to add this:

```
public function startApp() : Void
{
  var loader:RecipeXMLLoader = RecipeXMLLoader.getInstance();
   loader.addEventListener(RecipeXMLLoader.XML_LOADED_EVENT,
                                   Delegate.create(this, onXmlLoaded) );
  loader.loadXML();
}
```

Here, you're using the addEventListener to create a new event listener on the loader. As discussed previously, this functionality comes from the GDispatcher class. You've set the event to be dispatched to a method called onXmlLoaded, so that's the next thing to write.

```
private function onXmlLoaded() : Void
{
  var xml:XML = RecipeXMLLoader.getInstance().getXml();
  recipes = RecipeXMLParser.parseXml(xml);
  updateIndex();
  updateDisplay();
}
```

After adding that code, run Ant to build and then run your new SWF to see the output like Figure 4-14. Clicking the recipe titles on the left will switch the view on the right between them.

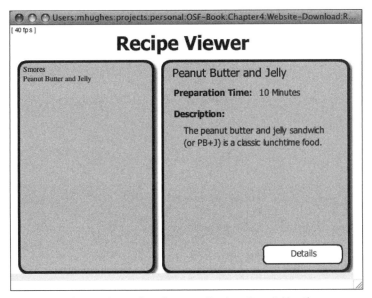

Figure 4-14. The running Recipe Viewer application after clicking the Peanut Butter and Jelly option

Viewing the recipe details

In the previous section, you created a simple recipe viewer that displays a list of recipes and their descriptions. In this section, you will add a details screen for viewing the directions and ingredient list. While doing this, you will learn how to integrate graphical assets given to you from a designer who does not work in the Flash IDE.

When you were developing `RecipeViewer.swf`, you compiled your code directly into it. In this section, you will also add to that code and make it load the new content at runtime to see a different mechanism for pulling in content.

Creating the RecipeDetails.swf file

Imagine a scenario where a designer gives you four graphical assets to represent a window in PNG format. Those assets consist of a background image and three images to represent different states of a Close button. You can find sample images in this book's downloadable materials; copy those files to your assets directory.

Once you have the raw assets, you need to create a SWF containing them. To create that SWF, you will use swfmill. You should have installed swfmill in Chapter 3. If you haven't, please review and complete the installation.

swfmill reads an XML file that describes the SWF you want to create. It can import graphics, sounds, and fonts and can generate a single SWF from them. To start, create a new XML file called `recipe_details_swf.xml` in your assets folder. Once done, you should have a directory structure like Figure 4-15.

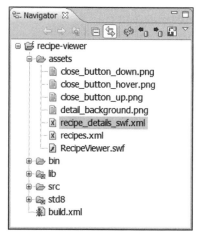

Figure 4-15. The directory structure after adding the necessary files for the recipe details window

swfmill has two dialects of XML input. The first is the "simple" format, which we'll use here and, as the name implies, is the easier of the two to write. The other, "lower-level" format gives a much higher amount of control over the generated SWF but at the cost of additional complexity.

Edit the `recipe_details_swf.xml` file, and add the following code.

The following tells swfmill to create a SWF that is 550×400 pixels with a frame rate of 31 frames per second, and it sets the background color to white (hex code #ffffff). Next, you want to create a new frame in the SWF and add some items to the library.

```
<movie width="550" height="400" framerate="31">
  <background color="#ffffff"/>
```

The following tells swfmill to import the four graphics into the library as MovieClips and assign unique IDs to each. The ID can be used as a library identifier from ActionScript. You can also place them directly on the stage through swfmill, which is the approach you will take a bit later in the file. But before that, create a new MovieClip that will represent all the states of the Close button.

```
<frame>
  <library>
    <clip id="background" import="assets/detail_background.png"/>
    <clip id="close_up" import="assets/close_button_up.png"/>
    <clip id="close_hover" import="assets/close_button_hover.png"/>
    <clip id="close_down" import="assets/close_button_down.png"/>
```

This section of code created a new empty MovieClip with an ID of closeButton. It then created a single frame within it and placed three of the previously imported button graphics within it. The id field of the `<place>` tag represents a library identifier. The name field represents the instance name of the MovieClip that will be available to your ActionScript code.

```
<clip id="closeButton">
  <frame>
    <place id="close_up" name="Up" depth="1"/>
    <place id="close_hover" name="Over" depth="2"/>
    <place id="close_down" name="Down" depth="3"/>
  </frame>
</clip>
```

Enter the following code to finish the swfmill definition file:

```
  </library>
    <place id="background" name="detailBackground_mc" x="0" y="0"
              depth="1"/>
    <place id="closeButton" name="closeButton_mc" x="390" y="325"
              depth="2"/>
  </frame>
</movie>
```

This code ends the library definition and then actually places two objects on the stage. It places the background at position 0,0 and the Close button at 390,325. With the given depths, the button will appear in front of the background like you would expect. To build your SWF, execute the following command from your project directory:

```
swfmill simple assets\recipe_details_swf.xml RecipeDetails.swf
```

93

The simple parameter tells swfmill to use its simple XML syntax. Then you specify the input XML file and lastly the output SWF.

Now, open the RecipeDetails.swf file. You should see the same output as Figure 4-16.

Figure 4-16. The RecipeDetails.swf as generated by swfmill

Updating the build script

Now that you can generate RecipeDetails.swf, you will learn how to automate the process in the Ant build script. The first step is to define the swfmill task in the build script. This task comes with the as2lib Ant tasks, so you should already have the necessary files installed. Add the swfmill taskdef line to the top of your build script:

```
<project name="RecipeViewer">
  <taskdef name="mtasc" classname="org.as2lib.ant.Mtasc" />
  <taskdef name="swfmill" classname="org.as2lib.ant.Swfmill" />
```

Next, create a new property that tells Ant where to find the swfmill executable:

```
<property name="swfmill" location="C:/FlashTools/swfmill/swfmill" />
```

Lastly, add a call to swfmill to your build target:

```
<target name="build">
  <mkdir dir="builds" />
   <swfmill src="assets/recipe_details_swf.xml"
        dest="bin/RecipeDetails.swf" cmd="simple"/>
  <mtasc mtasc="${mtasc}"
```

```
                version="8"
                main="true"
                src="com/friendsofed/recipeviewer/RecipeViewer.as"
                classpath="${src.dir} ; ${lib.dir}"
                swf="assets/RecipeViewer.swf"
                out="bin/RecipeViewer.swf"
                trace="com.blitzagency.xray.util.MtascUtility.trace"
                />
        </target>
```

Now, when you execute Ant, both RecipeDetails.swf and RecipeViewer.swf will be created in your bin directory.

Loading RecipeDetails.swf

In this section, you will add code to the Recipe Viewer application to load and display the details window. To load the new SWF, first create a private variable to store a reference to it:

```
        private var details_mc:MovieClip;
```

Next, add the following code to your startApp method:

```
        details_mc = baseClip.createEmptyMovieClip("detailsClip",
                                        baseClip.getNextHighestDepth());
        details_mc._y = baseClip._height;
        details_mc.loadMovie("RecipeDetails.swfSWF");
```

This creates an empty MovieClip and then loads the RecipeViewer.swf file into it. We also set the y coordinate so it will not appear over the current graphics. This is a quick hack to get you something functional; in a real application, it would be best to use a MovieClipLoader to load the external SWF. Then you could add an event listener that upon loading would set the visible property to false. Using a MovieClipLoader would also allow you to detect a failed load.

Displaying the recipe details

To display the recipe detail window, create a new class called RecipeDetails. This class will contain the logic to display the recipe details dialog box:

```
        class com.friendsofed.recipeviewer.RecipeDetails
        {
```

In that class, add three member variables: one to represent the base dialog box, one to represent the Close button, and one to represent the text you want to display:

```
        private var base_mc:MovieClip;
        private var close_mc:MovieClip;
        private var detail_txt:TextField;
```

95

If you recall, when you made the Close button in swfmill, you created a MovieClip with three child clips inside it that represented the three states of the button. You will have to add some code to manage those states. Let's start with a method named showButtonState to display the different states:

```
private function showButtonState(over:Boolean, up:Boolean,
                                               down:Boolean) : Void
{
  close_mc.Over._visible = over;
  close_mc.Up._visible = up;
  close_mc.Down._visible = down;
}
```

Next, create four methods that will handle the mouse input from the user. In each of them you will change the state of the button. In the mouse release method you will also hide the recipe details dialog box.

```
public function closeRelease() : Void
{
  base_mc._visible = false;
  showButtonState(false,true,false);
}
private function closePress() : Void
{
  showButtonState(false,false,true);
}

private function closeRollOver() : Void
{
  showButtonState(true,false,false);
}

private function closeRollOut() : Void
{
  showButtonState(false,true,false);
}
```

Once that is done, you can write a constructor that brings those pieces together:

```
public function RecipeDetails(baseClip:MovieClip)
{
  base_mc = baseClip;
  close_mc = base_mc.closeButton_mc;

  base_mc.createTextField("detail_txt",10,45,60,440,250);

  detail_txt = base_mc.detail_txt;
  detail_txt.wordWrap = true;
  detail_txt.selectable = false;
  detail_txt.html = true;
```

```
            close_mc.onRollOver = Delegate.create(this,closeRollOver);
            close_mc.onRollOut = Delegate.create(this,closeRollOut);
            close_mc.onPress  = Delegate.create(this, closePress);
            close_mc.onRelease  = Delegate.create(this, closeRelease);
            showButtonState(false,true,false);
        }
```

The last step is writing a public method that will populate the text field and display the dialog box:

```
        public function showRecipe(recipe:Recipe) : Void
        {
          detail_txt.text = "" + recipe.getName() + "\n\n" +
                    recipe.getIngredientList().join("\n") + "\n\n" +
                    recipe.getDirections();
          showButtonState(false,false,true);
          base_mc._y = 0;
          base_mc._visible = true;
        }
```

In RecipeViewer.swf, there is a button labeled Details that has been unused up until now. To display the details, edit the RecipeViewer, class and add a reference to the button. While you're editing that part of the file, also create a new private variable of type RecipeDetails.

```
        private var details:RecipeDetails;
        private var details_btn:Button;
```

Next, add code to your RecipeViewer constructor to initialize that variable and set up an onRelease event handler:

```
        public function RecipeViewer(base:MovieClip)
        {
          baseClip = base;

          recipeList_mc = baseClip.recipeList_mc;
          recipeDetails_mc = baseClip.recipeDetails_mc;
          recipeTitle_txt = recipeDetails_mc.recipeTitle_txt;
          prepTime_txt = recipeDetails_mc.prepTime_txt;
          description_txt = recipeDetails_mc.description_txt;
          details_btn = recipeDetails_mc.details_btn;
          details_btn.onRelease = Delegate.create(this, onDetailsClick );

          XrayLoader.addEventListener( XrayLoader.LOADCOMPLETE, this,
                                              "startApp");
          XrayLoader.addEventListener( XrayLoader.LOADERROR, this,"startApp");
          XrayLoader.loadConnector("xrayConnector_1.6.3.swf",base,true);
        }
```

Lastly, write the onDetailsClick method so it initializes the details object and calls the showRecipe method:

```
private function onDetailsClick() : Void
{
  if( ! details )
  {
    details = new RecipeDetails( details_mc );
  }
  details.showRecipe(recipes[selectedRecipe]);
}
```

Now, run the Ant script to build and run your RecipeViewer.swf. A list of recipes should be loaded. If you click one of them, the description of the recipe will appear on the right. If you then click the Details button, the ingredients and directions will be displayed to you like Figure 4-17.

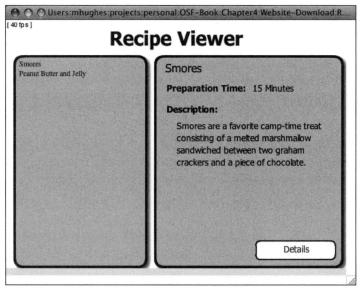

Figure 4-17. The finished Recipe Viewer application displaying the details for the Smores recipe

You have now seen two methods of getting assets from designers and two methods of integrating those assets into an ActionScript 2–based project. You have also learned about some of the features ASDT and Eclipse have to make development easier. It should now be possible for you to leverage this basic knowledge to build more complex and sophisticated applications.

In this chapter, you learned how to create both an ActionScript 2 and an ActionScript 3 application using completely free, open source tools. You used FlashDevelop to create an ActionScript 3 Flash-based and an ActionScript 3 Flex-based application, and then you used Eclipse and ASDT to make an ActionScript 2 Flash-based application. In later chapters of this book, you will expand this application and learn how to use additional open source tools for optimizing, testing, and deploying it. You will also learn details about several open source ActionScript libraries available to you.

Chapter 5

TESTING AND DEBUGGING

by Marc Hughes

This chapter covers the following:

- Writing and using unit tests for ActionScript 2 and ActionScript 3 development
- Using advanced logging techniques in Xray
- Using Xray to debug applications
- Using Xray to find performance bottlenecks

Testing and debugging are topics much too broad to cover in a single book, let alone in a single chapter of a book. In this chapter, I will focus on three open source projects that can aid you in these tasks. Those projects are AsUnit, FlexUnit, and Xray. AsUnit and FlexUnit provide a framework for unit testing. Xray provides a mechanism for logging and runtime inspection of a SWF.

Unit testing

Before I get into the details of AsUnit and FlexUnit, you may find it helpful to understand what a unit test is. **Unit tests** are small tests written in code by the developer to verify pieces of a program are working correctly independently of other parts of the application. Usually, these tests are automated and run at various points in the development cycle (such as before every build or after every version control submission).

A simple unit test might be written as follows:

```
class MyUnitTest
{
  public static function main(base:MovieClip) : Void
  {
    var value:Number = myClass.myMethod( 5 );
    if( value != 10 )
    {
      trace('Unit Test Failed!');
    }
  }
}
```

In this fictional example, the method called myMethod is expected to return 10 when it's passed the value of 5. The test runs the method, checks the return value, and traces out an error if something goes wrong. You could continue in this manner, adding more and more tests and methods to test. But managing a large body of tests like this can quickly become a maintenance nightmare. Luckily, there are open source libraries to make writing and maintaining unit tests easy. Later in this chapter, I will show you how to use AsUnit for ActionScript 2 development and FlexUnit for ActionScript 3 development. If you find yourself doing both ActionScript 2 and ActionScript 3 development and you want to learn only a single library, it's helpful to know that AsUnit also has ActionScript 3 support.

Many people believe these tests should be written before the development of the code they're meant to test in a process often called **test-driven development**. By adequately defining the functionality that a piece of code must implement, the developer gains a deeper understanding of what and how it should be implemented. It also provides a solid benchmark for determining whether a chunk of code is working correctly.

Test cases, suites, and runners

There are a lot of unit testing frameworks out there covering just about every language one could write a computer program in. Some popular packages include JUnit for Java, Boost for C++, and NUnit for C#. Many of the unit testing frameworks either are direct ports or have strong influences from Java's JUnit. Because of this, they have a common organizational structure consisting of test runners, test suites, and test cases. Both AsUnit and FlexUnit follow this organizational model.

Test case

A **test case** is a group of individual tests that are generally related. Depending on the size of your application, you might choose to have a single test case, a test case for each class, or a separate test case per package that you want to test. For very detailed tests, it's even possible to have multiple test cases for a single class. In both AsUnit and FlexUnit, a test case is a class with each individual test represented by a method in that class. Some pseudocode for a test case might look like this:

```
class MyTestCase
{
  public function test1()
  {
    Perform the test...
```

```
        Report any errors.
      }
      public function test 2() { ... }
      public function test 3() { ... }
    }
```

Test suite

A **test suite** is a grouping of test cases. It makes organizing similar test cases into logical chunks easier.
In most unit test frameworks, a test suite is just a special kind of a test case that implements the same
interface. Some pseudocode for a test suite follows:

```
    public class MyTestSuite
    {
      public function MyTestSuite()
      {
        Add test MyTestCase1
        Add test MyTestCase2
      }
      public function runTests()
      {
        For each test case
        {
          Run the test case
        }
      }
    }
```

Test runner

The **test runner** is the entry point for a set of unit tests. If you were using MTASC, it would contain
your main() method, or if you were using the Flash IDE, it might be the first frame of your initial timeline. The purpose of the runner is to initialize any test suites you may have and then run through and
execute each suite. Some pseudocode for a test runner might look like this:

```
    public class MyTestRunner
    {
      public static function main()
      {
        Add test suite MyTestSuite1
        Add test suite MyTestSuite2
        Create user interface
        For each test suite
          Run the test suite
          Update the user interface with progress & status
      }
    }
```

Structuring tests

This three-tiered layering of the testing structure may seem like overkill, but it gives a great amount of flexibility. The following example shows how a developer might structure tests and take advantage of some of this flexibility.

1. The developer creates a test case for every class in the project he wants to test.

2. He creates three test suites:

   a. One of these suites contains only a single test case that represents the piece of the application on which the developer is currently working. He updates this suite whenever he moves on to another part of the application, which gives him a quick way to see whether his current work is good.

   b. The second suite contains all the test cases that require a connection to a server.

   c. The third suite contains all the test cases that do not require a connection to a server. This allows him to run these tests whenever he wants without having to worry about maintaining the latest version of any server software (which another developer might be responsible for).

3. He creates three test runners:

   a. The first will contain only the first test suite.

   b. The second will contain the second and third test suites.

   c. The last will contain only the third test suite.

If you refer to Figure 5-1, it becomes obvious which test cases will be run for each test runner that is executed. In this example, the developer might use Test Runner 1 often to quickly test what he's working on at the moment. Test Runner 2 might be used right before a full build of the software to make sure all the components are working well together. Test Runner 3 might be run on a schedule or as a response to version control activity to make sure all the non-networked code is functioning correctly.

> *Segregating tests by networked/not networked is only one example of an organizational structure for your tests. Creating test suites that are grouped by functional area or by the developer responsible are other examples. Since a test case can be in multiple suites, you're not limited to a single grouping. You could have test suites for both networked status and developer responsible and then select which suites to run in your test runners.*

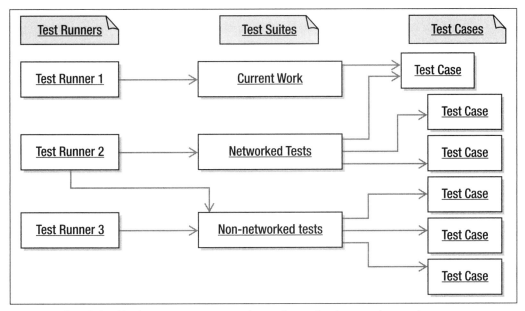

Figure 5-1. The relationships between test runners, suites, and cases for the example scenario

Creating *n*-tiered testing hierarchies

In both AsUnit and FlexUnit, a test suite is also a test case. This means a suite can be added to another suite to create complex trees of test cases, as shown in the following illustration.

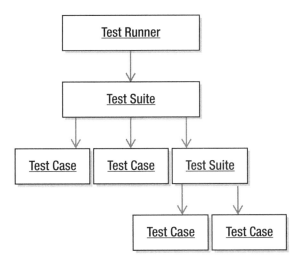

As you can see, the first test suite contains two test cases, plus another suite. That suite can then contain other cases or even other suites. This allows you to have a complex hierarchy of test cases.

Both FlexUnit and AsUnit provide all the features previously mentioned. They can manage complex hierarchies of tests, report the status of tests, and help you organize your code. In the next few sections, we'll explain how to actually use those frameworks to write some unit tests.

Getting started with AsUnit

To install AsUnit, head over to the AsUnit web page at http://www.asunit.com. Download the "Framework" package from midway down the page. This includes AsUnit sources for old ActionScript 2 applications, for newer ActionScript 2 applications (Flash 7, 8, and 9 only), and for ActionScript 3 applications. Once you've downloaded the file, extract it to a temporary location. Since I'm focusing on the ActionScript 2 support in this section, copy the contents of your AS25 folder from the temporary location to a location your compiler can find. If you've followed along in Chapters 3 and 4 for setting up your workflow, the lib directory you created is a good choice. If you haven't, simply placing it in your project folder will work equally well.

> In this section, you chose the AS25 directory from the AsUnit package. This contains the code for the ActionScript 2 testing environment focused on development for Flash Player version 7 and newer. The AS2 directory contains the source for testing applications that require Flash Player version 6 and newer. The AS3 directory contains the ActionScript 3 sources suitable for Flash or Flex development.

Now that you have AsUnit installed, you need something to test. In previous chapters, you were working on a website to view recipes. In such a website, it might be useful to have routines to convert units of measure. Let's create a simple UnitConverter class with two methods for changing pounds to ounces and tablespoons to teaspoons:

```
class com.friendsofed.recipeviewer.UnitConverter
{
  public static function poundsToOunces( pounds:Number ) : Number
  {
    return pounds * 13;
  }

  public static function tablespoonToTeaspoon( tbs:Number ) : Number
  {
    return tbs * 3;
  }
}
```

Since these methods are so simple, it makes sense to write them before the unit tests. For more complicated methods, it's oftentimes easier to write stub functions that return dummy data and then write your unit tests. Then, you can use those unit tests to execute the code you're working on in an isolated manner.

I intentionally made a mistake in the poundsToOunces method to help illustrate the benefits of using a unit test in the following sections. There are really 16 ounces to a pound, and not 13. We'll fix this in a moment.

An overview of key AsUnit classes

These are the three main classes in AsUnit you will use on a regular basis:

- asunit.framework.TestCase: This is the base class for each test case. You can extend this to create a new test case.
- asunit.framework.TestSuite: This class can combine a set of test cases into a suite. As mentioned, it descends from TestCase, so you can also add a TestSuite object to a test suite.
- asunit.textui.TestRunner: This is a basic test runner that can run one or more test suites.

You can learn more about these classes by browsing through their source code. In the next few sections, you'll be using them to create your sample unit testing framework.

Creating an AsUnit test case

Now that you have something to test, let's create an AsUnit test case. First, import the class you want to test and the TestCase class from the AsUnit framework:

```
import asunit.framework.TestCase;
import com.friendsofed.recipeviewer.UnitConverter;
```

Now, create a new class called ConverterTest; for this example, I'll show how to create it in the com.friendsofed.unittests package. If you choose to do this, make sure to put the class in an appropriate directory structure. This class should extend the TestCase class. The TestCase class takes a string in the constructor that represents the name of the method to test, so also create a constructor in your class that calls that.

```
class com.friendsofed.unittests.ConverterTest extends TestCase
{

  public function ConverterTest(testMethod:String)
  {
    super(testMethod);
  }
```

Next, create a method to test the poundsToOunces method. AsUnit automatically looks for methods that begin with the word test as valid tests to run. Let's call this method testPoundsToOunces:

```
public function testPoundsToOunces():Void
{
```

Inside this method is where the real testing begins. The TestCase class defines a series of "assert" methods to make testing easy. These include the following:

- assertEquals: Tests whether two objects are equal
- assertSame: Tests whether two objects are the same object
- assertNull: Tests whether a value is null
- assertNotNull: Tests whether a value is not null
- assertUndefined: Tests whether a value is undefined
- assertNotUndefined: Tests whether a value is not undefined
- assertTrue: Tests whether a value is true
- assertFalse: Tests whether a value is false

The first parameter to all of these methods is a message to be displayed if the test fails. Then assertEquals and assertSame take two parameters; the others take a single parameter. When the method is run, it evaluates its parameters, decides whether the test passes or fails, and reports on any failures. For example, a call to assertTrue("This will always fail", false); will always cause the message "This will always fail" to be displayed when the test is run because its second parameter is not true. A call to assetEquals("These aren't equal", a, b) will cause the message "These aren't equal" to appear depending on whether the variables a and b are equal.

For the testPoundsToOunces test, use the assertEquals method, and feed in some set values and expected results as follows:

```
assertEquals("UnitConverter failed for poundsToOunces(1)", ➡
    16,UnitConverter.poundsToOunces(1));

assertEquals("UnitConverter failed for poundsToOunces(3)", ➡
    48,UnitConverter.poundsToOunces(3));

assertEquals("UnitConverter failed for poundsToOunces(5)", ➡
    80,UnitConverter.poundsToOunces(5));

assertEquals("UnitConverter failed for poundsToOunces(0)", ➡
    0,UnitConverter.poundsToOunces(0));

}
```

In these examples, you're passing in an expected return value and then calling the method. Since you're using assetEquals, the test will pass if the two values are the same and fail if they aren't. You'll create a similar test method for the UnitConverter.tablespoonToTeaspoon method:

```
public function testTablespoonToTeaspoon():Void
{
    assertEquals("UnitConverter failed for tablespoonToTeaspoon(1)", ➡
    3,UnitConverter.tablespoonToTeaspoon(1));

    assertEquals("UnitConverter failed for tablespoonToTeaspoon(3)", ➡
    9,UnitConverter.tablespoonToTeaspoon(3));
```

```
    assertEquals("UnitConverter failed for tablespoonToTeaspoon(5)", ➡
    15,UnitConverter.tablespoonToTeaspoon(5));

    assertEquals("UnitConverter failed for tablespoonToTeaspoon(0)", ➡
    0,UnitConverter.tablespoonToTeaspoon(0));
  }
}
```

You now have a valid test case that you can use for the rest of the project to verify that the UnitConverter class works correctly and to identify any regressions that might occur during the course of development.

Creating an AsUnit test suite

Next, you need to create a test suite for the test case to be run from. In this example, the sample suite will have only a single test case in it. In a real-world application, you would probably have many test cases to add. To create the test suite, you extend the TestSuite class and add an instance of the ConverterTest class to it in the constructor:

```
import asunit.framework.TestSuite;
import com.friendsofed.unittests.ConverterTest;

class com.friendsofed.unittests.RecipeTests extends TestSuite
{
  public function RecipeTests()
  {
    super();
    addTest( new ConverterTest() );
  }
}
```

If you had other test cases to be added to this suite, you could have called addTest() multiple times, once for each case.

It is also possible to create test suites using composition instead of inheritance. To use this method, you would instantiate a TestSuite object and call addTest on it with your tests:

```
var suite:TestSuite = new TestSuite();
suite.addTest( new ConverterTest() );
```

Which of these two methods you choose is a matter of preference and style. For the rest of the chapter, I'll be assuming the inheritance model.

Creating an AsUnit test runner

The last piece to build for an AsUnit test is the runner that you can launch and that will handle running and reporting the status of the unit tests. In this example, we'll use MTASC to compile a new SWF from code. If you're using the Flash IDE, the same code should work, but instead of placing it in a new class's main() method, you can place it in the Actions panel of your first frame on the timeline.

To make the test runner, create a new class that extends from TestRunner. Add a static main() method to the class that instantiates it. Lastly, in the constructor of the class call, add the start() method with a class reference to your test suite.

```
import asunit.textui.TestRunner;
import com.friendsofed.unittests.RecipeTests;

class com.friendsofed.unittests.RecipeTester extends TestRunner
{
  public static function main()
  {
    var runner = new RecipeTester();
  }

  public function RecipeTester()
  {
    start(RecipeTests);
  }
}
```

To compile your unit tests, you can either call MTASC from the command line or add it to your Ant build script. A sample command line to build this application is as follows:

```
mtasc.exe -out RecipeViewer.swf -main ➥
    com/friendsofed/unittests/RecipeTester
```

After building the unit tests, you can run them in your browser or the stand-alone Flash Player.

Figure 5-2 shows some sample output from AsUnit for our example unit tests. As a quick visual reference, at the very bottom of the test runner, AsUnit displays a red bar if any of the tests fail and a green bar when all of the tests succeed. In the AsUnit output, you can see that the test runner attempted to run two tests (Tests run: 2) and one of them failed (Failures: 1). If there had been any fatal application errors, they would have been reported in the Errors section. Above that, you can see the specific test that failed and the error message that goes along with it. If you look at the code for the example test, you'll see this line:

```
assertEquals("UnitConverter failed for poundsToOunces(1)", ➥
    16,UnitConverter.poundsToOunces(1));
```

Notice that the message that you passed as the first parameter is displayed in the test output.

AsUnit, like most unit testing frameworks, stops the test at the first failure it finds. So if you had more test cases to try, you'd have to resolve any errors before you could progress to them.

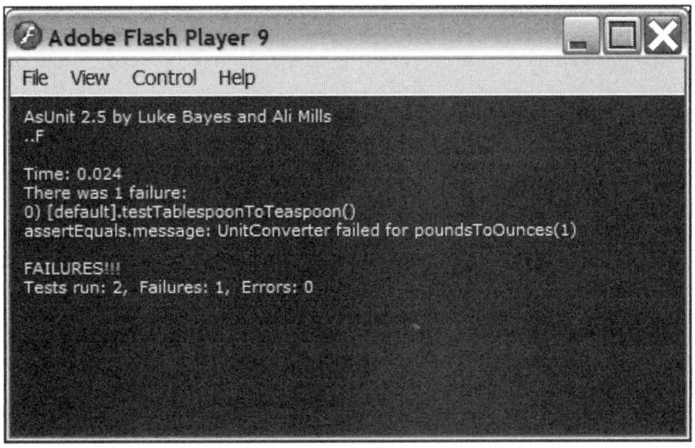

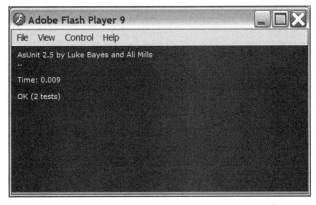

Figure 5-2. After running the unit tests, you can see that one of them has failed.

To fix the failure, you can edit the UnitConverter.poundsToOunces method and change the 13 to 16 in this line:

```
return pounds * 13;
```

After making the fix and rebuilding the application, the output from the successful unit tests will resemble Figure 5-3.

Figure 5-3. The successful results from the unit tests after fixing any errors

After you've written your first unit test for a project, adding more becomes easier since you don't always have to re-create the test suites or runners.

Getting started with FlexUnit

FlexUnit is a unit testing framework originally written by Adobe that is aimed at ActionScript 3 development. It is now hosted as an open source project on Google Code at this URL: http://code. google.com/p/as3flexunitlib/.

To use FlexUnit, download the archive from the URL and extract it to your computer. Then, in your project, add flexunit.swc to your compiler library options.

Adding flexunit.swc to Flex Builder

To add FlexUnit to a Flex Builder project, first right-click your project and then select Properties. Click the Flex Build Path option on the left, and a dialog box similar to Figure 5-4 will appear. Click the Library Path tab, click the Add SWC button, and select the flexunit.swc file.

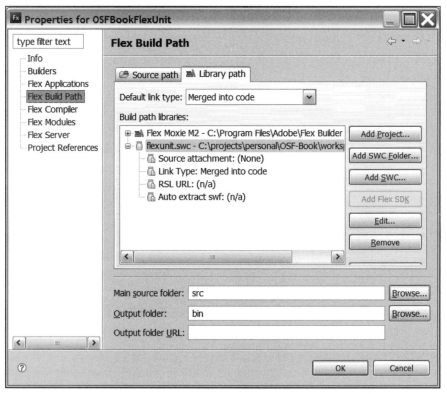

Figure 5-4. The Flex Builder project properties dialog box showing how to add flexunit.swc to your project

Adding flexunit.swc to FlashDevelop

The process for adding a SWC to FlashDevelop is similar to adding one to Flex Builder. First, right-click your project and select Properties. Next, click the Compiler Options tab. A dialog box like Figure 5-5 will be displayed. In this dialog box, click the ... button corresponding with the SWC Libraries option, and add the full path to flexunit.swc in the prompt.

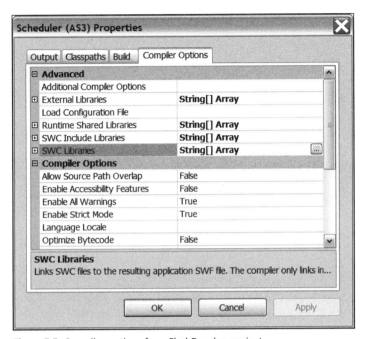

Figure 5-5. Compiler options for a FlashDevelop project

Adding flexunit.swc to your Ant-based build script

In Chapter 4, you saw how to build an ActionScript 3 project using an Ant script. To add a SWC using this method, you must add an include tag as a child to the mxmlc tag. A modified version from the example in Chapter 4 follows:

```
<mxmlc compiler="${mxmlc}"
  mainclass="Main.mxml"
  as3="true"
    output="bin/RecipeViewer.swf"
  benchmark="false">
<include name="flexunit.swc" />
</mxmlc>
</target>
```

If you had other library SWCs to add, you would have multiple include tags, with one for each library.

Creating the FlexUnit example

The FlexUnit API is similar to the AsUnit API. To help illustrate the similarities, I'll show how to write tests for an ActionScript 3 version of the UnitConverter class you used in the AsUnit section. Since the example class and the classes to test it are so similar to the ActionScript 2/AsUnit versions, I won't be spending a lot of time reexplaining them.

```
package com.friendsofed.recipeviewer
{
  public class UnitConverter
  {
    public static function poundsToOunces( pounds:Number ) : Number
    {
      return pounds * 13;
    }
    public static function tablespoonToTeaspoon( tablespoons:Number ) ➥
                                                              : Number
    {
      return tablespoons * 3;
    }
  }
}
```

Notice that I introduced the same error of 13 ounces to a pound instead of 16 as in the previous section.

Creating the FlexUnit test case

Like with AsUnit, the test cases are contained in classes that descend from a base TestCase class in the FlexUnit framework. Each test is contained within a method with a test prefix. FlexUnit also uses an identical syntax for the assert calls, with one exception. The assertSame method from AsUnit is called assertStrictlyEquals in FlexUnit.

The following listing shows the ConverterTest class with two test methods:

```
package com.friendsofed.unittests
{
  import flexunit.framework.TestCase;
  import com.friendsofed.recipeviewer.UnitConverter;

  public class ConverterTest extends TestCase
  {
    public function ConverterTest(methodName:String=null)
    {
      super(methodName);
    }
    public function testPoundsToOunces() : void
    {
```

```
        assertEquals("UnitConverter failed for poundsToOunces(1)", ➥
          16,UnitConverter.poundsToOunces(1));
        assertEquals("UnitConverter failed for poundsToOunces(3)", ➥
          48,UnitConverter.poundsToOunces(3));
        assertEquals("UnitConverter failed for poundsToOunces(0)", ➥
          0,UnitConverter.poundsToOunces(0));
      }
      public function testTablespoonToTeaspoon():void
      {
        assertEquals("UnitConverter failed for tablespoonToTeaspoon(1)", ➥
          3,UnitConverter.tablespoonToTeaspoon(1));
        assertEquals("UnitConverter failed for tablespoonToTeaspoon(3)", ➥
          9,UnitConverter.tablespoonToTeaspoon(3));
        assertEquals("UnitConverter failed for tablespoonToTeaspoon(0)", ➥
          0,UnitConverter.tablespoonToTeaspoon(0));
      }
    }
  }
}
```

Creating the FlexUnit test suite

Test suites in FlexUnit are classes that descend from the flexunit.framework.TestSuite class. The
following is a listing for a simple suite:

```
package com.friendsofed.unittests
{
  import flexunit.framework.TestSuite;
  public class RecipeTests extends TestSuite
  {
    public function RecipeTests(param:Object=null)
    {
      super(param);
      addTestSuite( ConverterTest );
    }
  }
}
```

This class simply extends the TestSuite class and adds a TestCase in its constructor. Like with AsUnit,
you could also have created the suite through composition using code like the following:

```
var suite:TestSuite = new TestSuite();
suite.addTestSuite( ConverterTest );
```

The style you use is a matter of preference. I like the inheritance model since you then have a suite
class that knows all the information it needs to run a set of tests.

Creating the FlexUnit test runner

FlexUnit has a graphical test runner that shows the current status of running tests as well as the status of any completed tests. First, create a new MXML application that descends from the normal Flex Application class. Add an event listener for the `creationComplete` event that you will use to execute the unit tests.

```
<?xml version="1.0" encoding="utf-8"?>
<mx:Application xmlns:mx="http://www.adobe.com/2006/mxml"
      layout="absolute"
      xmlns:flexui="flexunit.flexui.*"
      creationComplete="onCreationComplete()"
    >
```

Next, instantiate a TestRunnerBase that will represent the onscreen status of the unit tests. Notice you also set up an XML namespace of `flexui` in the previous Application tag:

```
<flexui:TestRunnerBase id="testRunner" width="100%" height="100%" />
```

Finally, create a script block and add the onCreationComplete method that you referenced in the creationComplete event handler. In that method, add code to create your test suite and start the tests.

```
<mx:Script>
    <![CDATA[
      import com.friendsofed.unittests.RecipeTests;

      private function onCreationComplete() : void
      {
        var tests:RecipeTests = new RecipeTests();
        testRunner.test = tests;
        testRunner.startTest();
      }
    ]]>
  </mx:Script>
</mx:Application>
```

You should now be able to compile your unit test application and execute the resulting SWF. Since I intentionally made an error in the UnitConverter test, you should see output similar to Figure 5-6. In it, you can see that one of the unit tests has failed. Along with that information, you can see the expected value (16) vs. the actual reported value (13). A full stack trace is provided so you can find the class, function, and line on which the test failed. FlexUnit also stops the test on the first failure it finds, so if you had more tests after the failure, they're not run until you fix the first problem.

Figure 5-6. FlexUnit displaying an error in the UnitConverter class

If you were to fix the UnitConverter test, recompile it, and run it again, the resulting output would resemble Figure 5-7.

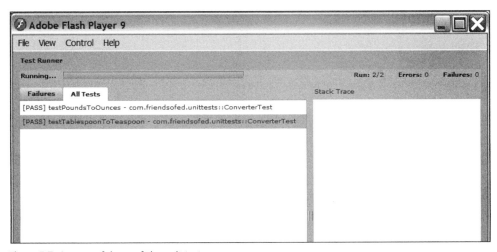

Figure 5-7. A successful run of the unit tests

Asynchronous testing

Many times in a Flash-based application, the operations you want to test are not synchronous. You might start a download, and at some later time either the response will be returned or a failure is reported. This type of testing is difficult to fit into the assert methods previously mentioned. Luckily, both AsUnit and FlexUnit have another trick up their sleeves, the addAsync method.

The addAsync method creates a delegate to an event handler with a timeout value. If the timeout happens before the handler is called, the unit test fails. If the event is broadcast within the timeout, the unit testing framework cancels the timeout and runs the intended event handler. Although that might sound confusing, here's an example to illustrate how it works.

> *The following example is written for ActionScript 3 using FlexUnit. However, the syntax/usage is nearly identical to the ActionScript 3 version of AsUnit, and it is similar to the ActionScript 2 varieties of AsUnit.*

Imagine a class that you might use in the Recipe Viewer application that downloads an XML file, parses it, and then dispatches an event signifying that it's done. That class might resemble this:

```
package
{
  public class XmlDownloader extends EventDispatcher
  {
    public var successful:Boolean = false;

    public function downloadXml() : void
    {
      var loader:URLLoader = new URLLoader();
      var request:URLRequest = new URLRequest("recipes.xml");
      loader.addEventListener(Event.COMPLETE, onComplete );
      loader.load(request);
    }
    public function onComplete(event:Event) : void
    {
      // Do something with the XML
      successful = true;
      dispatchEvent(new Event("xmlLoaded"));
    }
  }
}
```

Obviously, a real-world example would likely do some more processing once the XML was loaded. It would probably even dispatch some kind of failed event if something went wrong. But this simple example is good enough to show off the addAsync method.

A test case for the sample class follows:

```
public class DownloaderTest extends TestCase
{
  public function DownloaderTest(methodName:String=null)
  {
    super(methodName);
  }
  public function testLoader() : void
  {
    var loader:XmlDownloader = new XmlDownloader();
    loader.addEventListener("xmlLoaded", addAsync( onLoaded, 2000 ) );
    loader.downloadXml();
  }
  protected function onLoaded(event:Event) : void
  {
     assertTrue("Received event from wrong type", ➡
                    event.target is XmlDownloader);
    var loader:XmlDownloader = event.target as XmlDownloader;
    assertTrue("Xmldownloader was not successful", loader.successful );
  }
}
```

Notice that you added an event listener to the XmlDownloader object but use the addAsync method instead of just specifying the event handler. This created a delegate to the onLoaded method with a timeout of two seconds (2000 milliseconds). At the two-second mark, if the xmlLoaded event hasn't been broadcast, the unit test immediately fails. But, if the xmlLoaded event is broadcast before the two-second limit, it gets passed to an internal FlexUnit method that was created by the addAsync call. This method cancels the timer and then runs the real event listener (onLoaded in this example). The real event listener can then perform any tests it needs to on the result returned to it.

If you're using FlexUnit, you can pass additional parameters to the event handler by specifying them in the addAsync call. For example, you could modify the previous test as such:

```
loader.addEventListener("xmlLoaded", addAsync(onLoaded, 2000 , loader));
```

Then, the event handler would be expecting two parameters, and the beginning of it could be rewritten as follows:

```
protected function onLoaded(event:Event, originalLoader:XmlDownloader) ➡
  : void
{
  assertTrue("Received event from wrong object",
                  event.target ==  originalLoader );
```

You could pass parameters for any other reason as well. For instance, you might have a single event handler for a large number of tests, and you could specify the "correct" result through that second parameter.

Further reading

In the previous sections of this chapter, you learned how to set up, organize, and execute some simple unit tests using two open source frameworks. Both of those frameworks have additional documentation included in their downloads that you can use to learn more about specific features of either framework.

You can read about news and best practices about AsUnit and unit testing in general from Luke Bayes' blog at http://www.asserttrue.com/.

You can keep up-to-date on FlexUnit at the project's Google Code site at http://code.google.com/p/as3flexunitlib/.

Using Xray as a debug tool

In Chapter 3 you learned how to install Xray. In the rest of this chapter, you will learn how to use some of its features to aid you in testing and debugging an application. The information in this section is equally applicable to ActionScript 3 and ActionScript 2 development because the user interface for both is the same and the programming API is very similar.

Using Xray to log effectively

By default, when you launch the Xray interface, the Output panel as shown in Figure 5-8 opens on the right side. This is where the logging information from your application will appear.

Like many other logging frameworks, Xray has the concept of **logging levels**. When you're viewing the output in Xray, you can select a level to view. When you do this, you see any messages that happen at that level as well as any messages at higher priorities. The levels and what they traditionally have meant, in order of priority (from lowest to highest), are as follows:

- *Debug*: Debug is generally used for messages that only the developer working on the application might care about. An example is a developer wanting to see the value of a variable at a certain point in time.
- *Info*: Info is used for messages that are generated during the normal usage of the application. An example is to note the successful completion of a downloaded file.
- *Warn*: Warn is used for messages that indicate some recoverable error has occurred. An example is to note that a file has failed to download, but the application is going to automatically retry.
- *Error*: Error is used for messages that indicate a significant error has occurred that was not recoverable but doesn't immediately end execution. An example is when a file has failed to download and no further attempts will be made, but that file wasn't strictly needed to continue (maybe just a broken image link will appear).
- *Fatal*: These are errors that prevent the application from proceeding any further. A good example is the failure of a file download that was critical to the successful completion of the application.

Figure 5-8. The Xray output panel showing some logging information

You can switch what level to view logging at in the Xray interface by changing the Filter combo box. When you choose a level, you will see any log messages generated at that level or higher. So, for example, if you chose to view logging at the Warn level, you will see the logging messages generated at the levels of Warn, Error, and Fatal. Selecting the Debug level allows you to see all log messages.

There are several ways to direct logging output to the Xray interface, each with varying degrees of extra information that gets passed with the logging call.

The most complete method of logging is to use Xray's MTASC trace replacement in combination with the XrayLog class. This method of logging will give you the class and method the log call came from, the line number, and the logging level at which it occurred. You can read about how to set up the trace replacement in Chapter 3. This was the method used to generate the logging information shown in Figure 5-8. An example of this type of logging follows:

```
var log:XrayLog = new XrayLog();
trace( log.info("Log Message") );
```

Perhaps the simplest way to log is to use Xray's MTASC trace replacement by itself. Using this method, you get all the benefits of the previous option except for the use of logging levels; all messages will be sent at the Debug level. When using this method, you use trace() just like you would if you weren't using Xray, and the log messages will be forwarded to the Xray Output panel.

```
trace( "Log Message" );
```

The third way to log is using the XrayLogger class. Using this method, you get logging levels. You can optionally pass a parameter to the XrayLogger constructor and also receive the class name in your log output.

```
var logger:XrayLogger = new XrayLogger(this);
logger.info("Log Message");
```

> *Since there is no* trace() *redirection available in ActionScript 3 development, only the third option of logging is available to the ActionScript 3 developer who wants to use Xray.*

You've already read about how to filter the Xray log using debug levels in the Output panel, but there is another filtering option available to you. In the filtering section of the Output panel is a text field. When you enter text in this field, only log items containing that text will be displayed in the Output panel. The other log items will continue to exist, so you can later remove the filter and see all of the items. If you're using a logging mechanism that provides the package and class names, you can filter by these names to quickly narrow down to the messages you care about.

To the right of the filtering section is a Highlight text field. If you enter text in this field, any log items that contain that text will be highlighted in green. This is useful if you want to watch for a specific log message without turning all the others off. Both filters and highlights search in a case-insensitive manner.

Filtering and highlighting are meant to be used in a real-time manner. You can update them at any time and view the resulting output. But sometimes, you might want to methodically search through the output to find all occurrences of a phrase. The Search section of the Output panel will let you do this by searching forward or backward through the log output.

When logging, you're not limited to displaying simple strings. All of the previous logging options take an additional parameter. In that parameter you can specify any ActionScript object. All of the properties of that object will be displayed in the Output panel. As an example, the following code:

```
var logger:XrayLogger = new XrayLogger();
 var sampleObject:Object = { question:"What is the answer?", answer:42 };
logger.info( "Our sample object equals: " , sampleObject );
```

results in this output:

```
(246) Our sample object equals:
question: What is the answer?
Answer: 42
```

You can output any type of object, including arrays. For example, the output from this code:

```
var logger:XrayLogger = new XrayLogger();
var a:Array = [1,3,5,7,"nine",11];
logger.info( "Array equals: " , a );
```

results in the following output:

```
(247) Array equals:
5: 11
4: nine
3: 7
2: 5
1: 3
0: 1
```

Notice that arrays get printed out backward. This is because of the way Xray internally traverses objects.

Be careful when using this feature, because Xray will recursively log all the objects you specify. If you have a complex set of MovieClips on your stage doing something like this:

```
logger.info( "Everything" , _level0 );
```

then it could take several minutes for all the output to be sent to the Xray interface since thousands of lines are sent as Xray traverses all the children of every MovieClip on the stage.

Using the Xray Property Inspector

Besides logging, Xray has the ability to inspect and modify properties of a running SWF. To use this Property Inspector, you must have already set up your project to use the Xray execute connection. For ActionScript 3–based projects, you can simply create a variable of type com.blitzagency.xray. inspector.flex2.Flex2Xray and instantiate it. For ActionScript 2–based projects, you'll need to use XrayLoader to load the Xray connector into your application. Refer to Chapter 3 for instructions on getting this working.

Figure 5-9 shows the Xray Property Inspector in use. Specific features of this interface will be explained in detail in the upcoming sections of this chapter.

Figure 5-9. The Xray interface showing a listing of objects on the stage to the left and a list of properties of the selected object (detailsClip) on the right

Taking a snapshot

The Xray Property Inspector works on a loose concept of a snapshot. To begin using it, you select a root node to look at and click the Go button to take a snapshot. Xray then traverses all the children of the node you specified and presents you with an object tree you can navigate. By default, the root node is set for _level0, which in most applications should give you a complete inventory of onscreen objects. Figure 5-9 shows the _level0 tree from the Recipe Viewer application in Chapter 4. As you can see, all of the MovieClip, TextField, and Button objects we constructed in that example are visible there. I call it a "loose concept of a snapshot" because the individual properties that you view are updated every time you select a new node in the object tree.

Besides viewing _level0, you can also take a snapshot at _global to view anything in the global namespace, or you can type in a path to an object to view only it and its children. For instance, if you typed the value of **_level0.recipeDetails_mc** into the text field and clicked the Go button, you would see an object tree as shown in Figure 5-10. For more complex applications, this can help narrow down the list to only the objects you care about.

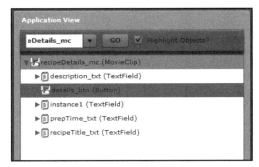

Figure 5-10. The object tree of the Recipe Viewer application when a snapshot of _level0. recipeDetails_mc was taken

There is a check box next to the Go button labeled Highlight Objects. If this option is selected, then objects in your running application will have a yellow outline drawn around them as you mouse over them in the Xray interface. This lets you quickly identify onscreen objects with their representation in the Xray interface.

> *Sometimes, you may want to look at a SWF given to you before integrating it into your project. Assuming you're working on an ActionScript 3–based SWF, you can use the XRayViewer application to load the SWF, and then you can view its details through the Xray interface. For more information on XRayViewer, visit* http://www. rogue-development.com/xrayviewer.xml.

Modifying values

As you click objects in the object tree, the properties of that object are loaded in the Property Inspector. From the Property Inspector, you can see and modify any value of Number, String, or Boolean type. To modify a value, click it. If the value is a Boolean, it will be toggled to the opposite value. If the value is a String or Number, a new input field at the top of the Property Inspector will be shown, allowing you to change it.

Changes in the Property Inspector immediately take effect in your application. If you set a MovieClip's _visible property from false to true, you will immediately see the clip appear onscreen (assuming it's not obscured by other content).

If you want to modify a value that isn't a Number, String, or Boolean, then you can use the runtime execution of ActionScript feature described later this chapter.

Inspecting nonvisual objects

Since Xray allows you to inspect the _global namespace, you can use it to inspect values of any object at runtime. To do so, add a line such as this in your code:

```
_global.debugObject = { debug:"My Debug Object" };
```

Then, any objects you want to inspect in any part of your application can have a reference added to that debug object. In the Recipe Viewer example from the previous chapter, you could add the debugObject object in the startApp method and then modify the onXmlLoaded method to add some properties to it:

```
public function startApp() : Void
{
  trace( log.info("Application started") );
  _global.debugObject = { debug:"My Debug Object" };

  var loader:RecipeXMLLoader = RecipeXMLLoader.getInstance();
   loader.addEventListener(RecipeXMLLoader.XML_LOADED_EVENT, ➡
Delegate.create(this, onXmlLoaded) );
  loader.loadXML();

  details_mc = baseClip.createEmptyMovieClip("detailsClip",➡
baseClip.getNextHighestDepth());
  details_mc._y = baseClip._height;
  details_mc.loadMovie("RecipeDetails.swf");
}
private function onXmlLoaded() : Void
{
  trace( log.info("XML Loaded") );
  var xml:XML = RecipeXMLLoader.getInstance().getXml();
  _global.debugObject.loadedXml = xml;
  recipes = RecipeXMLParser.parseXml(xml);
  _global.debugObject.parsedRecipes = recipes;
  updateIndex();
  updateDisplay();
}
```

After making these changes, you will be able to view the loaded XML and the parsed output from that XML in Xray, as shown in Figure 5-11. Since using this technique allows you to inspect any object, it can aid in debugging a wide variety of situations.

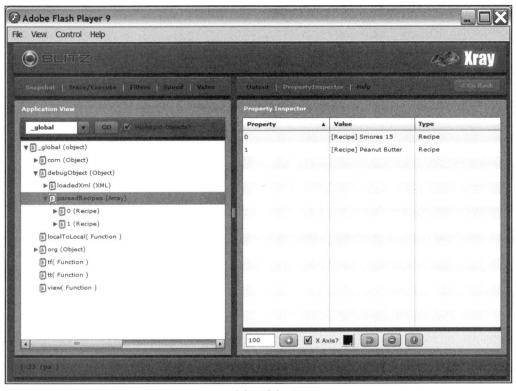

Figure 5-11. The Xray Property Inspector showing debugObject

Adding debugObject *to* _global *isn't strictly necessary. You could simply add the objects you want to view as a property of* _global *like so:*

```
_global.myXmlObject = xml;
```

However, this mechanism works only for complex objects. If you tried to assign a String to a property of _global, *it wouldn't show up in the Xray interface:*

```
_global.myString = "Hello World"; // This will not work
_global.debugObject.myString = "Hello World"; // This will work
```

By creating a debugObject, *you avoid this problem, and all of your debugging information will be conveniently grouped together.*

Executing ActionScript at runtime

Through Xray, you can execute any ActionScript code in your application's runtime environment. To access this functionality, choose the Trace/Execute panel on the left side of the Xray interface. A large text area will appear. Anything you type in that text area and hit Enter after will be executed by your application. Using this functionality, you can manipulate any property of an object, not just Numbers, Strings, and Boolean values that the Property Inspector allows you to edit. For example, typing the following code will remove any filters that were applied to a specific object onscreen:

```
_level0.recipeDetails_mc.filters = [  ];
```

Xray creates a special function in the global namespace called tt to handle many of its internal logging commands. You can use that function from the Trace/Execute panel to display complex content in the Output panel. If you were to execute the following code, the entire contents of the XML would be dumped to your Output panel:

```
_global.tt( _global.debugObject.loadedXml.toString() );
```

Using this, you can view values you hadn't previously added logging statements for in your application.

Finding performance bottlenecks

Flash Player can be fickle in what graphical operations will affect performance on any given platform the most. Finding performance-related bugs can be a difficult and time-consuming process. Xray aids in finding bugs related to graphical operations in two ways.

The first is the frames per second (FPS) meter that gives you a numeric scale of how well Flash Player is keeping up with the operations being asked of it. You can view this meter in the lower-left corner of the Xray interface and optionally from a text field in your running application. When this meter dips significantly below the published FPS rate of your SWF, some kind of performance problem is occurring.

To find what's causing the performance problem, you can selectively toggle the visible property of elements on the stage. When you cause the offending piece to become invisible, Flash Player will spend less time trying to render it, and your FPS rate should jump back up. Through a process of elimination you should be able to determine which pieces of your application are slowing it down the most. Once you've found where the problem occurs, you can start to diagnose what the cause of it is. To do this, use the Property Inspector to manipulate various properties of the object to find out what the root cause is. Oftentimes, filters or alpha transparency can be the cause of performance problems. From the Xray interface, you can try disabling either of these to find out whether that's the case.

In this chapter, you learned what a unit test is and how to use both AsUnit and FlexUnit to write those unit tests. You also experimented with Xray and saw how it can be used for both logging and exploring a running SWF. In the next chapter, you will look at some options for deploying a Flash-based application.

Chapter 6

DEPLOYING YOUR APPLICATION

by Marc Hughes

This chapter covers the following:

- Using the SWFObject project to embed your application in an HTML page
- Best practices for organizing and deploying web content
- Writing an Ant target to deploy your application
- Using Screenweaver to deploy a desktop application

This chapter covers the steps necessary to go from a compiled SWF to a web or desktop-based application that other people can use. I'll talk about HTML embedding techniques, discuss using Ant to transfer your files, and even look at a couple options to deploy your application without using the Web.

Embedding SWF content

On the Web, linking to a SWF directly is not a very attractive option. You can't control the content around the SWF or the title of the page in the browser title area. It's also difficult to add content that's friendly to search engines, and it's impossible to detect a Flash version or provide alternate content for people with special needs. For these reasons, most developers choose to embed their SWFs in an HTML page for their end users.

You can embed your SWF content into a web page in several ways, and each has different benefits. If you're using the Flash IDE and generate an HTML page while compiling, you'll get output similar to this:

```
<html xmlns="http://www.w3.org/1999/xhtml" xml:lang="en" lang="en">
<head>
<meta http-equiv="Content-Type" content="text/html; ➥
charset=iso-8859-1" />
<title>SoTemp</title>
<script language="javascript">AC_FL_RunContent = 0;</script>
<script src="AC_RunActiveContent.js" language="javascript"></script>
</head>
<body bgcolor="#ffffff">
<!--urls used in the movie-->
<!--text used in the movie-->
<!-- saved from url=(0013)about:internet -->
<script language="javascript">
  if (AC_FL_RunContent == 0) {
    alert("This page requires AC_RunActiveContent.js.");
  } else {
    AC_FL_RunContent(
      'codebase', 'http://download.macromedia.com/pub/ ➥
shockwave/cabs/flash/swflash.cab#version=9,0,0,0',
      'width', '550',
      'height', '400',
      'src', 'SoTemp',
      'quality', 'high',
      'pluginspage', 'http://www.macromedia.com/go/getflashplayer',
      'align', 'middle',
      'play', 'true',
      'loop', 'true',
      'scale', 'showall',
      'wmode', 'window',
      'devicefont', 'false',
      'id', 'SoTemp',
      'bgcolor', '#ffffff',
      'name', 'SoTemp',
      'menu', 'true',
      'allowFullScreen', 'false',
      'allowScriptAccess','sameDomain',
      'movie', 'SoTemp',
      'salign', ''
      ); //end AC code
  }
</script>
<noscript>
  <object
    classid="clsid:d27cdb6e-ae6d-11cf-96b8-444553540000"
    codebase="http://download.macromedia.com/pub/shockwave/ ➥
```

```
      cabs/flash/swflash.cab#version=9,0,0,0" width="550" height="400"
      id="SoTemp" align="middle">
   <param name="allowScriptAccess" value="sameDomain" />
   <param name="allowFullScreen" value="false" />
   <param name="movie" value="SoTemp.swf" />
   <param name="quality" value="high" />
   <param name="bgcolor" value="#ffffff" />
   <embed src="SoTemp.swf" quality="high"
      bgcolor="#ffffff" width="550" height="400"
      name="SoTemp" align="middle"
      allowScriptAccess="sameDomain"
      allowFullScreen="false" type="application/x-shockwave-flash"
      pluginspage="http://www.macromedia.com/go/getflashplayer" />
   </object>
 </noscript>
 </body>
 </html>
```

This uses some JavaScript to embed the content with an object tag as a fallback for when JavaScript isn't available. Although this code works most of the time, it lacks some of the advanced browser and plug-in detection that solutions such as SWFObject have.

Several other strategies for embedding Flash content have been introduced over the years, but most have some significant flaw ranging from a lack of browser support to breaking screen reader support. Many of these solutions have a "click to activate" restriction that requires you to click the Flash movie before it will activate on Internet Explorer 6+ or Opera 9 and newer.

Using SWFObject

Luckily, there is an open source project called SWFObject that solves most of these embedding problems. At the time of this writing, version 2.0 is the production-ready release; you can download it from http://code.google.com/p/swfobject/.

Even though 1.0 is still widely used today, I'll concentrate on version 2.0 in this chapter. Version 2.0 is a complete rewrite from the original SWFObject project, and up until recently was named SWFFix. At least one Adobe employee is helping to work on SWFObject, and it's expected to be used in official Adobe products at some point in the future. To do the embedding, SWFObject has two main methods of embedding Flash content into your web page.

The first option, called the **static** publishing method, is a fully standards-compliant take on things. This option relies on object tags to embed the content in most browsers, plus some JavaScript to work around flaws in some browsers. This is the more complex of the two methods, but it offers the most standards-compliant solution. However, it does suffer from the "click to activate" problem mentioned earlier.

The second option, called the **dynamic** publishing method, relies mainly on JavaScript to place the SWF in the web page. This option requires you to do a lot less but isn't 100 percent standards compliant and will fail if the user has JavaScript disabled in their browser. The biggest advantage to using this method is that the end user doesn't need to click the movie to activate it in Internet Explorer 6+ or Opera 9 and newer.

Installing SWFObject

Before going into the details of each method of using SWFObject, a quick primer on where to download the files from and where to put them is in order. You can download the latest SWFObject release from the Google Code repository at http://code.google.com/p/swfobject/. Click Downloads, and download the latest released version listed. Then uncompress the ZIP file, placing the files in the same folder as your SWF, and you're ready to start using it. Alternatively, you could set up a central location where all your Flash-based pages can retrieve the scripts from instead of having a copy of SWFObject for each page.

> Besides the main SWFObject download, you can grab several "generator" downloads as well. These are scripts that you can run (either in a web browser using the HTML version or as stand-alone with the AIR version) that ask you for a series of inputs. After filling in those inputs, the generator will give you the required output in a convenient form that you can simply cut and paste into your web page.

SWFObject static publishing method

This method of embedding Flash content is the most complete and standards compliant and is the version most likely to work for any user. An example of this method follows, with the important details explained afterward:

```
<!DOCTYPE html PUBLIC "-//W3C//DTD XHTML 1.0 Strict//EN"
    "http://www.w3.org/TR/xhtml1/DTD/xhtml1-strict.dtd">
<html xmlns="http://www.w3.org/1999/xhtml" lang="en" xml:lang="en">
  <head>
    <title>Recipe Viewer</title>
    <meta http-equiv="Content-Type"
      content="text/html; charset=iso-8859-1" />
    <script type="text/javascript" src="swfobject.js"></script>
    <script type="text/javascript">
      swfobject.registerObject("recipeViewerMovie", "9.0.0",
      "expressInstall.swf");
    </script>
  </head>
<body>
  <div>
    <object id="recipeViewerMovie"
      classid="clsid:D27CDB6E-AE6D-11cf-96B8-444553540000"
      width="800" height="600" >
    <param name="movie" value="recipeViewer.swf" />
      <!--[if !IE]>-->
        <object type="application/x-shockwave-flash"
          data="recipeViewer.swf" width="800" height="600">
      <!--<![endif]-->
```

```
          <a href="http://www.adobe.com/go/getflashplayer">
            Get Adobe Flash
          </a>
          <!--[if !IE]>-->
          </object>
          <!--<![endif]-->
      </object>
    </div>
  </body>
</html>
```

Most of the elements in this example are the same each time you use SWFObject. There are a few important elements to change. You should change the following line to match your minimum version of the Flash plug-in required as well as specifying the node ID of where the SWF should be placed:

```
swfobject.registerObject("recipeViewerMovie", "9.0.0",  ➥
"expressInstall.swf");
```

The node ID should be the same as the id attribute of the first object tag, as shown here:

```
<object id="recipeViewerMovie"
```

The SWF file name, as well as the width and height of the movie, must be repeated in two separate object tags. The first is for Internet Explorer, and the second is for most other browsers.

```
<object id="recipeViewerMovie"
        classid="clsid:D27CDB6E-AE6D-11cf-96B8-444553540000"
        width="500" height="300">
<!--[if !IE]>-->
  <object type="application/x-shockwave-flash"
   data="recipeViewer.swf" width="800" height="600">
<!--<![endif]-->
```

Finally, you should place some sort of fallback content within the inner object tag for people who don't have the required version of Flash. You could provide a link to a location to download the Flash plug-in, or you could provide a text-only version of the content that the SWF would have displayed.

```
<a href="http://www.adobe.com/go/getflashplayer">
        Get Adobe Flash
  </a>
```

You may have noticed a reference to the expressinstall.swf file in the JavaScript call to SWFObject. This enables the Express Install functionality of the Flash plug-in to automatically update itself if the required version of the plug-in isn't installed on the user's system. The end user will see an installation dialog box requesting them to upgrade by clicking a button in place of your SWF. When it's complete, the page should reload, and your expected content will be displayed.

135

SWFObject dynamic publishing method

The second way of using SWFObject is to allow the JavaScript functions to replace part of your page with the required content to display your SWF. An example of using it this way follows, with explanations afterward:

```
<!DOCTYPE html PUBLIC "-//W3C//DTD XHTML 1.0 Strict//EN" ➡
"http://www.w3.org/TR/xhtml1/DTD/xhtml1-strict.dtd">
<html xmlns="http://www.w3.org/1999/xhtml" lang="en" xml:lang="en">
  <head>
  <title></title>
  <meta http-equiv="Content-Type"
    content="text/html; charset=iso-8859-1" />
   <script type="text/javascript" src="swfobject.js"></script>
   <script type="text/javascript">
       var flashvars = {};
       var params = {};
       var attributes = {};
       attributes.id = "recipeViewerMovie";
       swfobject.embedSWF("recipeViewer.swf",
               "myAlternativeContent",
               "800", "600", "9.0.0", "expressInstall.swf",
               flashvars, params, attributes);
   </script>
  </head>
  <body>
    <div id="myAlternativeContent">
      <a href="http://www.adobe.com/go/getflashplayer">
      Get Adobe Flash
      </a>
    </div>
  </body>
</html>
```

As you can see, this method results in terser code that is easier to read. As mentioned, the biggest drawback to this method is its failure to work with browsers whose JavaScript is disabled, and its biggest benefit is that the movie will be active and available without the user clicking it. The two important sections are as follows:

```
<div id="myAlternativeContent">
        <a href="http://www.adobe.com/go/getflashplayer">
          Get Adobe Flash
        </a>
</div>
```

The previous section represents the place on the page that will be swapped out and replaced by your SWF. Like the previous method, you can specify alternative content that will be displayed in case something goes wrong and the SWF can't be shown to the user.

```
swfobject.embedSWF("recipeViewer.swf",
            "myAlternativeContent",
            "800", "600", "9.0.0", "expressInstall.swf",
            flashvars, params, attributes);
```

This JavaScript does the heavy lifting of actually specifying what to replace. In it you specify the following:

- `"recipeViewer.swf"`: The file name of your SWF
- `"myAlternativeContent"`: The ID of the div tag to replace
- `"800"`, `"600"`: The dimensions of the file
- `"9.0.0"`: The minimum version of the Flash plug-in
- `"expressInstall.swf"`: The location to expressInstall.swf
- `flashvars`, `params`, `attributes`: The FlashVars, parameters, and attributes that should be passed to Flash Player

As mentioned, the content for both of these methods can either be manually coded or generated using one of the SWFObject generators. Which method you choose will largely be a decision about whether you value fully standards-compliant markup that doesn't require JavaScript or a solution that doesn't force some users to click the embedded movie first.

Staging strategies

It's often a good idea to stage your web rollouts from a development environment to a staging (or testing) server and then finally to your production web server. Performing this three-stage process will help you identify problems before the files reach your production web server.

If you've followed along in previous chapters, you should already have an Ant script that can compile your application and copy it to your development web server. If you don't, you can refer to Chapter 3 to learn how to install XAMPP as a development server; in Chapter 4, you'll find out how to use Ant to build and copy your files to that server.

The Ant script from Chapter 4 currently copies the application files directly to the development server. To roll out the files to the staging and production web servers, I'll first show how to copy the necessary files to a temporary location and then transfer all the files from that location to the server(s). This way, you can avoid any temporary or old files that you don't want to transfer. In the following diagram, you can see how your files move from your development workspace to a staging directory and then can be transferred to your staging or production web server.

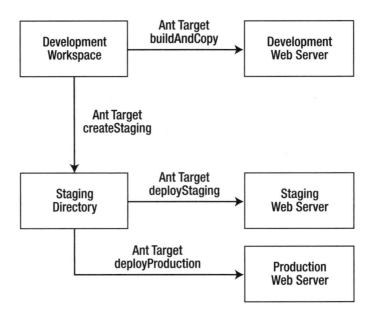

To extend your Ant script, let's first create the three new targets referenced in the diagram. Open your build.xml file, and add the lines in bold:

```
<project name="RecipeViewer-FD">
  <taskdef name="mxmlc" classname="org.flex2ant.Mxmlc" />
  <property name="deploy.dir" location="C:/xampp/htdocs" />
  <property name="mxmlc" value="C:\FlashTools\flex2sdk\bin\mxmlc.exe" />

  <target name="createStaging" depends="build" >
  </target>

  <target name="deployStaging">
  </target>

  <target name="deployProduction">
  </target>

  <target name="build">
    <mkdir dir="bin" />

    <mxmlc compiler="${mxmlc}"
           mainclass="Main.mxml"
           as3="true"
           output="bin/RecipeViewer.swf"/>

  </target>
```

```
    <target name="buildAndCopy" depends="build">
      <copy todir="bin" >
        <fileset file="recipes.xml" />
      </copy>
      <mkdir dir="${deploy.dir}/recipe_viewer" />
        <copy todir="${deploy.dir}/recipe_viewer" >
          <fileset dir="bin" />
        </copy>
    </target>
  </project>
```

The createStaging target should contain all the logic necessary to retrieve and copy the necessary files to the staging directory. It will likely involve copying files from your development workspace, but it might also retrieve assets from other locations.

Imagine you're working with a designer who sits across the room. You might want to copy art assets from a file share. Or maybe your designer is on the other side of the globe. If they can place their files on a web or FTP server, you can grab those through Ant as well.

A sample createStaging target follows. It illustrates how to copy your local files, how to copy files from another location, and how to download a file from a web server. Here's the code in full; I'll run through it in detail after the code:

```
    <target name="createStaging" depends="build" >
      <delete dir="staging" />
      <mkdir dir="staging" />
      <copy todir="staging">
        <fileset dir="bin" />
      </copy>

      <copy todir="staging">
        <fileset dir="/location/to/fileserver/designerfiles" />
      </copy>

      <get dest="staging" src="http://someothersite/logo.png"/>

    </target>
```

OK, let's see what the code does. Before copying files, it's a good idea to remove files from the previous copy so you don't inadvertently get old files on your server. The first line in the target accomplishes this:

```
    <delete dir="staging" />
```

The next lines create the destination directory and copy files from your local development workspace to it:

```
    <mkdir dir="staging" />
    <copy todir="staging">
      <fileset dir="bin" />
    </copy>
```

The next section copies files that may be located in another directory, perhaps a file share or drop-off location from a designer:

```
<copy todir="staging">
  <fileset dir="/location/to/fileserver/designerfiles" />
</copy>
```

The last section downloads a file from a web server and places it in the destination directory:

```
<get dest="staging" src="http://someothersite/logo.png"/>
```

To get a script working for your environment, all you have to do is swap in the locations for your files and run the following command:

```
ant createStaging
```

Alternatively, you could run Ant through Eclipse's Ant view. To get that view, select the Window ➤ Show View ➤ Other menu option. Then scroll down and select the Ant view. Once that opens in Eclipse, drag your build.xml file into that panel, and you should be able to run all your targets by double-clicking them.

Transferring your files

Using Ant, you have a few options for uploading files to your web server. You've already seen how the copy tag allows you to copy files to different directories. If you have a file share available to you on the web server, you can simply use this method to copy the files to the correct location. This is rarely practical, since most of the time you won't have access to a file share on your web server. You could also use the ftp task to transfer the files over the FTP protocol. This has the benefit of being usable on nearly any web hosting setup. However, it's not the most secure option, since your username and password are transmitted as clear text, and if it's possible for an attacker to snoop on your traffic, they can harvest this information. The last option is using SFTP or SCP over an SSH connection. This provides strong encryption and even implements some simple compression to help speed your transfer. I'll cover both options here.

Using Ant and FTP

Ant comes with an FTP task built in, but it's considered an "optional" task. What this means is you have to download some extra files into your Ant distribution to make it work. If you read the documentation on the Ant website at http://ant.apache.org/manual/OptionalTasks/ftp.html, you will see that it requires the following:

- A networking library called commons-net. You can download this library from http://commons.apache.org/net/.

- A regular expression library named jakarta-oro. You can download this library from http://jakarta.apache.org/oro/.

Download both of those libraries, unzip them, and place the .jar file in your ant/lib directory. Once you've done that, you can begin using the Ant FTP task. An example follows:

```
<ftp verbose="yes" passive="yes"
  remotedir="/www" server="www.yourserver.com"
  userid="ftp_login" password="ftp_password">
    <fileset dir="staging" />
</ftp>
```

The parameters to this command are as follows:

- verbose="yes": This tells Ant to issue a higher level of logging so you can see errors, warnings, or messages about current progress.

- passive="yes": This instructs Ant to use passive instead of active FTP transfers. Depending on the server you're connecting to, one option or the other might not be available.

- remotedir="/www": This tells Ant where to put the files on the remote server.

- server="www.yourserver.com": The server attribute specifies the host name of the server to connect to.

- userid="ftp_login" password="ftp_password": The userid and password attributes specify your login credentials to the remote server.

- <fileset dir="staging" />: The fileset tag (or multiple fileset tags) specifies what files to copy from the local machine.

In this example, we specified both the username and password, but you could have also specified those as parameters and placed the values in an external properties file like so:

```
<property file="build.properties"/>
<ftp verbose="yes" passive="yes"
  remotedir="/www" server="www.yourserver.com"
  userid="${ftp.username}" password="${ftp.password}">
    <fileset dir="staging" />
</ftp>
```

Then you could create a file called build.properties and place the following content inside it:

```
ftp.username=myUsername
ftp.password=myPassword
```

This gives you the benefit of not storing your username and password in the build.xml file, making it safe to share with others. But it still has the drawback of having your username and password in a file where anybody who uses your computer may find it.

If you don't like the idea of storing your password in a file on your computer, you can use the input task to cause Ant to prompt for it every time it's run:

```
<input message="Enter your FTP password." addproperty="ftp.password"  />
<ftp verbose="yes" passive="yes"
  remotedir="/www" server="www.yourserver.com"
  userid="myUsername" password="${ftp.password}">
    <fileset dir="staging" />
</ftp>
```

All the previous examples upload the entire site to the staging server. Oftentimes, you want to transfer only the files that have changed. The ftp task has a property called depends that will check the time stamp of the file on the server and compare it to the time stamp on your local copy and upload only the newer files. However, this method can be fragile, because the time of your local computer and the server might not be in sync. A better method is to use the modified subtag of the fileset tag. The first time the modified tag runs, it creates a file listing the checksums of all your files. A checksum is a short string automatically generated based on the content of a file. The next time the modified tag is encountered, those checksums are compared to the current checksums of your files to determine whether they've been modified and need to be re-sent. An example follows:

```
<input message="Enter your FTP password." addproperty="ftp.password" />
<ftp verbose="yes" passive="yes"
  remotedir="/www" server="www.yourserver.com"
  userid="myUsername" password="${ftp.password}">
    <fileset dir="staging">
      <modified>
        <param name="cache.cachefile" value="staging.cache"/>
      </modified>
    </fileset>
</ftp>
```

When using the modified tag, make sure to use a different cache file for each location you upload to. In this example, you want to upload to a staging and a production web server. If you were to use the same cache file for both and upload your files to the staging server, everything would work fine. But if you then tried to upload to the production server, no files would be transferred because the checksums in your cache would match the checksums of the file, making Ant think it had already sent those files. If you ever need to transmit all the files again, you can simply delete your .cache file, which will cause Ant to "forget" which files it sent. A full example of the deployStaging and deployProduction targets follows:

```
<target name="deployStaging">
  <input message="Enter your FTP password." addproperty="ftp.password"/>
  <ftp verbose="yes" passive="yes"
    remotedir="/www-staging" server="www.yourserver.com"
    userid="myUsername" password="${ftp.password}">
      <fileset dir="staging">
        <modified>
          <param name="cache.cachefile" value="staging.cache"/>
        </modified>
      </fileset>
  </ftp>
</target>

<target name="deployProduction">
  <input message="Enter your FTP password." addproperty="ftp.password"/>
  <ftp verbose="yes" passive="yes"
    remotedir="/www" server="www.yourserver.com"
    userid="myUsername" password="${ftp.password}">
      <fileset dir="staging">
        <modified>
```

```
            <param name="cache.cachefile" value="production.cache"/>
        </modified>
      </fileset>
    </ftp>
  </target>
```

Using Ant and SFTP/SCP

More and more web hosting companies are starting to support connections to the web server over a secure SSH connection. By using this type of connection, you can use either SFTP or SCP to copy your website files to the server. Like FTP, using either SCP or SFTP with Ant requires you to download and install an extra library. The required library is called JSch, and you can download it from http://www.jcraft.com/jsch/index.html. To install it, just download the jsch.jar file and place it in your ant/lib directory.

> *SCP and SFTP are similar protocols and can be used interchangeably most of the time. They both work over an encrypted SSH connection, and they both transmit files. When choosing which to use, keep these factors in mind. Secure Copy (SCP) is more widely available and is best when transmitting a few small files. Secure File Transfer Protocol (SFTP) isn't available as often but is optimized for big groups of larger files.*

To use either SCP or SFTP, you use the scp Ant tag. An example of SCP usage follows:

```
<scp trust="true" todir="username:password@yourServer.com:">
  <fileset dir="staging" />
</scp>
```

To use SFTP instead, simply add an sftp parameter:

```
<scp sftp="true" trust="true"
    todir="username:password@yourServer.com:">
  <fileset dir="staging" />
</scp>
```

You can employ all the methods you used in the FTP example to pass a username and password. You can also use the modified tag to send only those files that have changed. A full example of deployStaging and deployProduction using SCP follows:

```
<target name="deployStaging">
  <input message="Enter your SSH password." addproperty="ssh.password"/>
  <scp trust="true"
    todir="username:${ssh.password}@yourServer.com:/www-staging">
    <fileset dir="staging" >
      <modified>
        <param name="cache.cachefile" value="staging.cache"/>
      </modified>
    </fileset>
```

```
        </scp>
    </target>

    <target name="deployProduction">
        <input message="Enter your SSH password." addproperty="ssh.password"/>
        <scp trust="true"
          todir="username:${ssh.password}@yourServer.com:/www">
            <fileset dir="staging" >
                <modified>
                    <param name="cache.cachefile" value="production.cache"/>
                </modified>
            </fileset>
        </scp>
    </target>
```

As you can see, transferring files over SCP, SFTP, or FTP all have about the same complexity. Since both SCP and SFTP transmit your files and user credentials in a secure fashion, it's highly recommended that you choose one of those methods.

Executing commands on the server

If you are using one of the SSH-based methods for transferring files to the server, then you likely also have access to execute commands over SSH. You can accomplish this through Ant using the sshexec task. For instance, you could update the date/time stamp on a file called lastUpdated by executing the touch command like so:

```
<sshexec host="somehost"
    username="username"
    password="password"
    command="touch lastUpdated"/>
```

Using the sshexec tag, you can perform nearly any type of operation that you can while using the command line. Here are some ideas of things you may want to try:

- Back up your web space or database.
- Delete files that are no longer needed.
- Use image tools to periodically generate images based on some external input.
- Keep multiple servers all synchronized.

To find out the commands to perform these tasks, consult the documentation for the operating system that your web host uses.

> *Be careful when using* sshexec *since any command run through it is immediately executed on the server. You could accidentally modify or delete important files without any confirmation message.*

Excluding files

Sometimes you want to make sure some files aren't transferred to the web server. Usually, it's easiest to simply not include those files when copying them to your staging directory. But other times it's easier to exclude those files while transferring. Since the copy, ftp, and scp Ant tasks all use a fileset to determine which files to copy, you can use the excludes child of that to specify that some files shouldn't be copied. Extending the deployProduction target to exclude some common files that you don't want to transfer might look like this:

```
<target name="deployProduction">
  <input message="Enter your SSH password." addproperty="ssh.password"/>
  <scp trust="true"
    todir="username:${ssh.password}@yourServer.com:/www">
    <fileset dir="staging" >
      <modified>
        <param name="cache.cachefile" value="production.cache"/>
      </modified>
      <exclude name="*.fla"/>
      <exclude name="*.psd"/>
      <exclude name="*Thumbs.db"/>
    </fileset>
  </scp>
</target>
```

As you've see in this chapter, using Ant to publish files to your web server can standardize your release process, leading to fewer bugs and higher quality.

Deploying desktop applications

Most Flash development is focused around web-based applications, but there is a growing trend to use Flash for desktop applications as well. Two projects of late have been created to address this market. Adobe has produced a technology called Adobe Integrated Runtime (AIR) that allows Flash or HTML-based applications to be deployed to the desktop. Some components of AIR, including the ActionScript 3 compiler and the Flex library, have been open sourced by Adobe. Still, other components such as the AIR runtime remain a proprietary solution.

If you're looking for a fully open source desktop application solution, then Screenweaver is for you. It's a piece of software that acts as a bridge between the Neko virtual machine and the Flash browser plug-in. The Neko VM is the runtime environment used for haXe applications that run on the native machine. You can read more about haXe in Chapter 9.

To get started, there is a detailed tutorial for downloading and installing Screenweaver that you can access by clicking the Tutorials link on the Screenweaver website (http://screenweaver.org/).

How it works

Your desktop application will be split into two parts. A front-end, which generally contains the user facing part, and the back-end, which generally handles the I/O, window management, and any other non-UI functionality.

For the front-end, you write your Flash application and publish a SWF just like you normally would while working on a web-based project. This SWF either could be identical to a web-based version or could take advantage of some of the additional features that Screenweaver gives you.

To create the back-end, you write a small amount of loader code in haXe that will bootstrap your application. It will start up the Screenweaver subsystem, create a new OS window, load the Flash plug-in, and finally load your SWF into that window and allow the user to interact with it.

You can also allow the loaded SWF to access functionality defined in the back-end Screenweaver application. To do this, you define haXe methods on a haXe object and add that haXe object to a list of objects the Flash application is allowed to access.

The following sections will walk you through creating the Screenweaver loader and then adding some loader/application communication.

> *One of the benefits of Screenweaver is that you can write both your UI and back-end logic using the haXe programming language. In the example in this chapter, I'm assuming you're using ActionScript to create your front-end SWF. But you could also use haXe to create that SWF, allowing you to work in the same language and environment for both sides. Chapter 9 of this book focuses on haXe development.*

Creating the front-end SWF

Chapter 3 showed you how to create a simple "Hello, World" Flash application. This chapter will use a modified version of that to demonstrate Screenweaver; the source of that simple application follows:

```
package
{
  import flash.display.Sprite;
  import flash.text.TextField;

  [SWF(backgroundColor="#eeeeff", frameRate="60", ➥
width="800", height="600")]
  public class Example extends Sprite
  {
    public function Example()
    {
      var tf:TextField = new TextField();
      tf.text = "Hello World";
      addChild(tf);
    }
  }
}
```

As you can see, this is a very simple example that, when compiled, displays the words "Hello, World" in an 800×600 SWF. In a real-world Screenweaver application, you can create as complex an application as you do for the Web.

Creating the Screenweaver back-end

The back-end will handle loading the Flash plug-in, creating a window, and exposing any extra haXe functionality to the front-end that you need. To create it, using your favorite text editor, create a new file named App.hx. Enter the following code into that file:

```
class App
{
  static function main()
  {
    swhx.Application.init(9);
    var window = new swhx.Window("ExampleApplication",800,600);
    var server = new neko.net.RemotingServer();
    var flash = new swhx.Flash(window,server);
    flash.setAttribute("src","Example.swf");
    flash.start();
    window.show(true);
    swhx.Application.loop();
    swhx.Application.cleanup();
  }
}
```

An explanation of the source follows.

This calls the init() method on the Application class in the swhx package:

```
swhx.Application.init(9);
```

It initializes the Screenweaver system. During this initialization, Screenweaver searches the system for a compatible version of the Flash browser plug-in. The init() method has two optional parameters: a version number and a file location. If you specify a version number (such as 8 or 9), then that will cause Screenweaver to look only for Flash plug-ins meeting that version requirement. Since this example is trying to load an ActionScript 3–based SWF, we require version 9 of the plug-in. You can also optionally specify a path to the plug-in if you want to search for it in a nonstandard location.

If Screenweaver fails to find a suitable version of the Flash plug-in, then it will automatically attempt to download a version from Adobe's web server. If this happens, the plug-in will be saved in a file called flashplayer.bin in the same directory as your application.

This creates a new native system window that will host the Flash plug-in:

```
var window = new swhx.Window("ExampleApplication",800,600);
```

The Window constructor takes four parameters: a window title, the initial dimensions (width, height) of the window, and an optional set of flags that define how the window behaves. Those flags are all constants in the Window class and can be a combination of the following:

- WF_FULLSCREEN: Causes the window to take over the entire screen
- WF_TRANSPARENT: Causes the window to have transparency
- WF_DROPTARGET: Allows the window to participate in drag-and-drop operations
- WF_PLAIN: Provides a more lightweight chrome around the window
- WF_ALWAYS_ONTOP: Causes the window to appear on top of all other windows
- WF_NO_TASKBAR: Causes the application to not appear in the Windows taskbar

If you want, you can have multiple windows in a single application. One common use of that is to display a simple splash screen while your main application is loading. Let's look at the next line:

```
var server = new neko.net.RemotingServer();
```

A RemotingServer acts as the gateway for communication between the Flash application and the back-end code. You can learn more about this in later sections. The next few lines get things running:

```
var flash = new swhx.Flash(window,server);
flash.setAttribute("src","Example.swf");
flash.start();
```

This creates a new Flash virtual machine on the given window, using the given RemotingServer. It sets the source SWF location and starts up the Flash VM allowing your ActionScript in the SWF to begin executing. Onto the last lines:

```
window.show(true);
swhx.Application.loop();
swhx.Application.cleanup();
```

Finally, you display the window and start up the main event loop. The call to loop() will block until the window is closed or the application is closed through code. After that completes, the cleanup() call frees any memory that was being used by Screenweaver to run the Flash application.

Compiling the Screenweaver back-end

You use the haXe compiler to compile the App.hx file you just created into Neko bytecode that can be run by the Neko virtual machine. To compile the sample application, you would use the following command line:

```
haxe -neko app.n -main App -lib swhx -lib systools
```

The -neko app.n part tells the compiler to output a Neko-compatible file called app.n. The -main App lets the compiler know what class it should use as the main source file. The rest of the command line specifies two haXe libraries required for Screenweaver applications. When you issue this command, the compiler should silently return. If it displays any errors, check for typos or installation problems.

Once you've compiled the application, you can test it by running it directly through the Neko runtime by issuing the following command:

```
neko app
```

This should launch the Screenweaver application, which then creates a new window and loads your Example.swf into it to resemble Figure 6-1.

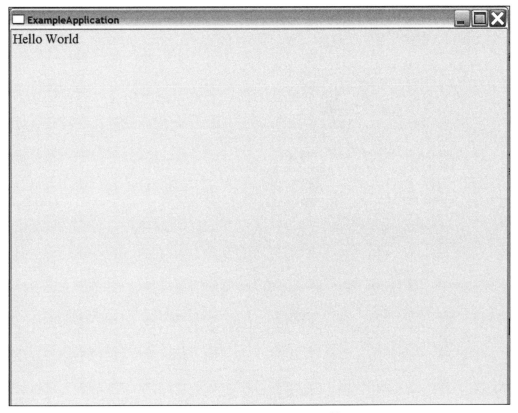

Figure 6-1. The example SWF running inside a native OS window created by Screenweaver

Interacting with the Screenweaver application from Flash

So far, all you've been doing is simply running a SWF. The only feature you've used that a simple projector doesn't give you is the ability to decide when and where the windows get created. The real power of Screenweaver is that it allows your Flash application to communicate with the underlying Screenweaver loader to execute functionality not provided by the ActionScript API. For instance, you might want to read or write to a file on the local file system.

If you remember from the simple example, you created a neko.net.RemotingServer object in the haXe code:

```
var server = new neko.net.RemotingServer();
```

The RemotingServer class provides a gateway from the Flash VM to your Screenweaver code. By adding classes to the RemotingServer, you make those classes available to the Flash VM. For instance, you could create a new method in the App class and add it to the Remoting server as such:

```
import neko.io.FileOutput;
import neko.io.File;
class App
{
  static function main()
  {
    swhx.Application.init(9);
    var window = new swhx.Window("ExampleApplication",800,600);
    var server = new neko.net.RemotingServer();
    server.addObject("App", App);
    var flash = new swhx.Flash(window,server);
    flash.setAttribute("src","Example.swf");
    flash.start();
    window.show(true);
    swhx.Application.loop();
    swhx.Application.cleanup();
  }

  public static function logText( msg:String )
  {
    var fi:FileOutput = File.append("log.txt", false);
    fi.writeBytes( msg + "\n",0 , msg.length + 1);
    fi.close();
  }
}
```

Here you created a new method called logText that takes a string and appends it to a file called log.txt. Then you added the App class to the RemotingServer object, giving it a name of App.

To call this from your ActionScript code, you need to use the Screenweaver ActionScript API. Assuming you've installed haXe and Screenweaver already, you can find a copy of this in the haxe\lib\swhx\1,1,2\api\actionscript\AS3 directory. Either copy it to your source directory or configure your ActionScript compiler to include it in the classpath. Once you've done this, you can modify your ActionScript code to use the API as so:

```
package
{
  import flash.display.Sprite;
  import flash.text.TextField;
  import swhx.Api;

  [SWF(backgroundColor="#eeeeff", frameRate="60", width="500", ➥
height="350")]
  public class Example extends Sprite
  {
    public function Example()
```

```
      {
        var tf:TextField = new TextField();
        Api.init(this);
        tf.text = "Hello World";
        addChild(tf);
        var date:Date = new Date();
        swhx.Api.call("Api.logText", "Hello World, the time is: " +
        date.toTimeString());
      }
    }
  }
```

The Api.init() call initializes the Flash/Screenweaver connection. The Api.call() line calls into the Neko runtime and runs the Api.logText method with the given parameter. If you now compile the Example.swf and App.n files and run the application, a new file named log.txt will be created with output similar to the following in it:

```
    Hello World, the time is: 16:07:14 GMT-0500
```

Using this method, you can take advantage of all that the haXe/Neko environment provides. See Chapter 9 for more ideas on how you could use this.

Distributing your desktop application

Requiring a user to execute a command line to run an application is usually not an acceptable solution. To solve this, Screenweaver comes with a precompiled boot loader that includes the Neko VM and required libraries to make Screenweaver work. You can find this in the haxe\lib\swhx\1,1,2\ tools directory.

To distribute your application, all you have to do is copy the files from that tools directory, your .swf, and your .n file to a directory. The tools directory includes executables for both Windows and OSX that will load your App.n file and launch your application. All you need to do is double-click that executable to launch the application. You can optionally rename the Windows executable and OSX bundle to reflect the name of your application.

In this chapter, you learned how to distribute a Flash application in both website and desktop scenarios. You looked at a staging strategy and the Ant script required to make that happen. You also looked at how you can distribute a desktop-based application using haXe and Screenweaver. In future chapters, you'll learn how to use open source tools and libraries to create more complex and interesting Flash applications that include features such as complex server communication and 3D graphics. In Chapter 9, you'll also learn more about haXe and find out techniques that could be applied to your Screenweaver back-end code.

Chapter 7

USING AMFPHP

by Wade Arnold

Connecting Flash and Flex applications to PHP gives your application access to PHP's robust open source server programming language and supporting frameworks. In this chapter, you will explore AMFPHP, which is an open source gateway for easily connecting your Flash Player–based application to PHP. With the experience you gain from this chapter, you will be ready to start adding server-side functionality to your projects. Get ready to leverage one of the most popular open source languages within your web experience.

Introducing AMFPHP

AMFPHP was designed to allow simple to complex data communication between the Flash Player client and PHP running on a server. AMFPHP is an open source project that implements Adobe's Action Messaging Format (AMF), which is the binary protocol that Flash Player uses to handle objects. AMFPHP is an alternative to Adobe's LiveCycle Data Services ES, BlazeDS, and Flash Remoting, with PHP as the endpoint rather than Java. AMFPHP allows a seamless connection between Flash Player and PHP classes. By leveraging the AMF protocol, AMFPHP doesn't require any additional client-side work in order to encode and decode data objects that are sent to and from the server. AMFPHP acts as a gateway to PHP and, through a process known as **serialization**, transforms the data types between ActionScript into PHP data types on incoming messages and then transforms the data back for returning data. In addition

153

to writing your own PHP classes with AMFPHP, you can leverage the extensive resources found in open source PHP classes, applications, and frameworks.

Generally, AMFPHP applications implement an *n*-tiered architecture. The following illustration depicts such an architecture, separated into a thin client/presentation tier (in Flash Player), a middle tier composed of AMFPHP and the business logic located in your PHP services, and a data tier that could be a combination of databases, SOAP services, and other data services that PHP can consume.

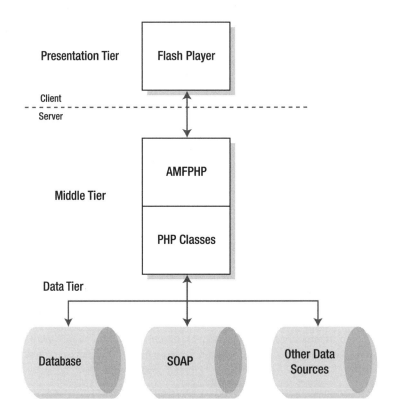

What are the benefits of AMF?

AMF is a binary file format representing a serialized ActionScript object. The AMF file type is used throughout Flash Player for data storage and data exchange. For example, in Flash Player, AMF is used in SharedObject, RemoteObject, LocalConnection, ByteArray, RTMP, and all RPC operations. Some of the benefits of AMF include the following:

- *File size*: AMF objects are very small and are compressed using zlib.

- *Fast serialization/deserialization*: AMF is transformed using native C code in Flash Player, making it very fast. AMF was designed to serialize and deserialize quickly under low memory and slower CPU conditions, making it perfect for the Web. AMF data is parsed directly into objects, meaning there is no lag for interpreting or parsing AMF, making the creation of objects complete in a single pass.

- *Native types and custom classes supported*: You can serialize any object in Flash Player with the only exception being DisplayObject. You can also map serialized objects back to custom class instances provided the custom class is in Flash Player when the AMF object is deserialized.

AMF 3, the default serialization for ActionScript 3, provides various advantages over AMF 0, which is used for ActionScript 1.0 and 2.0. AMF 3 sends data over the network more efficiently than AMF 0. AMF 3 supports sending int and uint objects as integers and supports data types that are available only in ActionScript 3, such as ByteArray, ArrayCollection, and IExternalizable. AMF 3 now utilizes zlib compression for faster transfer to the server. AMF is a generic term because it is accurate for both versions; however, the context of the application such as Flex or Flash CS3 implies AMF 3, whereas Flash 8 or Flash MX implies AMF 2 because AMF 3 did not exist then.

What are the benefits of using AMFPHP?

You will gain several benefits if you choose to use AMFPHP as your method of bringing server data into your Flash application. Some of these reasons could be more significant to your development team than other teams.

- It handles the conversion of data types between ActionScript and PHP.
- It can convert complex objects, and it supports class mapping.
- It allows you to make direct calls to server-side methods, which eliminates time spent developing parsers in Flash and PHP.
- AMF serialization is part of Flash Player, which decreases the code footprint and optimizes server communication.
- It is simple to start using on any web server that runs PHP 5.2.3 or newer.
- Services are "nonspecific" PHP classes that are portable without any code change.
- It easily separates the workload of ActionScript programmers from PHP programmers and lets each use best-of-breed tools for development.

The requirements for using AMFPHP in the examples

The following sections use ActionScript 3 and AMF 3 for the examples. I will be using Flash CS3 as the example IDE because it is the most common development environment for Flash applications. One of the joys of AMFPHP is that the services can be consumed by either Flash or Flex. The examples provided here are tailored toward showing how AMFPHP works, not at specific ways of using the Flash or Flex framework to consume services. Each of these examples is similar to how you would build them in Flex, and they use the same AMFPHP information. Later in the chapter, I will review how to connect to these same services in Flex but will focus on Flex and not the PHP service created in the Flash examples. Included in the chapter download file (at http://www.friendsofed.com) is the Flex version of the example, and you'll find plenty of comments throughout the code that will allow you to understand what each section does. For complex projects, I recommend you use a framework that implements the Service Locator design pattern. In Flash, you should use the ActionScript 3 Lightweight Remoting Framework (http://osflash.org/as3lrf) from Danny Patterson or SSR (http://osflash.org/projects/ssr). In Flex it is worth taking your time to understand Adobe's Cairngorm framework (http://labs.adobe.com/wiki/index.php/Cairngorm), because it is a great aid in developing scalable and maintainable applications.

Getting started

In the following sections, I'll show you how to install and configure AMFPHP. Then, since the best way to start learning a new technology is to start with the fundamentals, I'll show a working "Hello, World"-style example so you can make sure your installation is configured properly.

Installation requirements

AMFPHP runs on a web server with a PHP release newer than 5.2.3. AMFPHP does not require any special configuration to the PHP environment for it to perform. A PHP module called AMFEXT speeds up data communication, but this is an optional performance module.

AMFPHP does not require any special components or libraries in ActionScript 3. Everything that is necessary for AMF data communication is now part of the language, as opposed to ActionScript 2, which required the installation of the Flash remoting components. If you have a copy of Flash CS3 or Adobe Flex 2 or 3, you are ready to follow these examples.

Server configuration

With access to a PHP 5.2.3 (or newer) web server, installing AMFPHP is as fast as you can place the files on the server. Throughout the following examples, I will use http://localhost/ as the domain of your web server. For speed of development, I recommend that you configure your computer with a web server and PHP. If you have never configured a web server, I suggest you try Apache2TRIAD (http://www.apache2triad.net) or XAMPP (http://www.apachefirends.org), which is a packaged installation to get your own development environment running quickly. If you choose to use a remote server or use virtualization of another operating system, replace http://localhost/ with the URL to your own web server in each example.

The first thing to do is download AMFPHP 2.0 (or newer) from SourceForge (http://sourceforge.net/project/showfiles.php?group_id=72483).

Then create a project folder for the examples on your desktop or your preferred location, and unzip the download to reveal a folder called amfphp. This folder holds everything necessary to install the application, as shown in the following screenshot.

Transfer the amfphp folder into the document root of your web server. Many examples on the Web rename the amfphp folder to flashservices when they place the contents on the server. For simplicity's sake, I will keep it as amfphp in this example.

Now you need to create a cross-domain policy file so that Flash Player can alter the HTTP header when it connects to the AMFPHP service. Adding the following crossdomain.xml file to your website allows the sending and receiving of custom headers from Flash to your server. Please make sure you have a policy file in the document root of the web server on which to host your amfphp services. Add the following XML to a file called crossdomain.xml. Update the domain name to the name of the web server that hosts your SWF file.

```
<cross-domain-policy>
<!-- Place top level domain name -->
<allow-access-from domain="yourdomain.com" secure="false"/>
<allow-access-from domain="yourdomain.com" to-ports="80,443"/>
<allow-http-request-headers-from domain="yourdomain.com" headers="*" />
<!-- use if you need access from subdomains..domain.com -->
<allow-access-from domain="*.yourdomain.com" secure="false" />
<allow-access-from domain="*.yourdomain.com" to-ports="80,443" />
<allow-http-request-headers-from domain="*.yourdomain.com" ➥
    headers="*" />
</cross-domain-policy>
```

Testing the server installation

Using a web browser, load the gateway.php file in the folder you just uploaded. If you are developing locally, you can load http://localhost/amfphp/gateway.php. If the installation is working properly, you will see the following content in your web browser. Otherwise, you have a PHP configuration error on your server. Review the "Debugging" section later in this chapter if you do not see the following page.

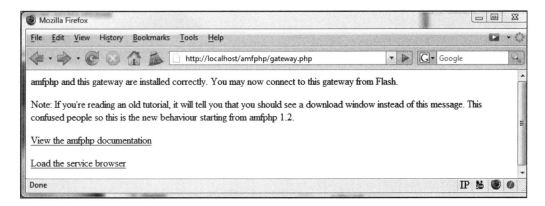

It's installed!

That's all there is to getting AMFPHP installed on your server. Next, I will show how to write your first remote service for ActionScript to consume.

Creating your first service

AMFPHP allows ActionScript to instantiate remote PHP classes. There is nothing unique about the class files that AMFPHP consumes, which makes them highly portable to other projects. As long as there are public methods in the class file, ActionScript will be able to use those methods.

The following example is a PHP class file called HelloWorld with a single public function called say. The method say takes a string as a parameter and then returns what was said with the day of the week.

```php
<?php
class HelloWorld {
  public function say($sMessage) {
  $date = getdate();
  return 'You said: ' . $sMessage .' on '.$date[weekday];
  }
}
?>
```

Open your favorite PHP text editor, and create the contents of the HelloWorld class. The file is also included in the chapter download file (http://www.friendsofed.com). Save the file as HelloWorld. php, and upload it to your web server into the amfphp/services/ folder to add the class to your AMFPHP installation. I always like to test new classes to make sure nothing is wrong with what was uploaded. Use a web browser, and go to http://localhost/amfphp/services/HelloWorld.php, where you should see a blank web page because the class ran properly and does not have any output. If you see errors, you will need to investigate what went wrong. Review the "Debugging" section later in this chapter if the server throws any errors.

Using the Service Browser tool

AMFPHP comes with a Flex-based Service Browser for testing services. This is a great tool to speed your PHP development and also ensure that everything on the server is working properly.

To access the Service Browser, go to http://localhost/amfphp/browser/index.php with a web browser that has Flash Player 9 or newer enabled. Before the Service Browser opens, you will be prompted to make some configuration choices, as shown in the following screenshot.

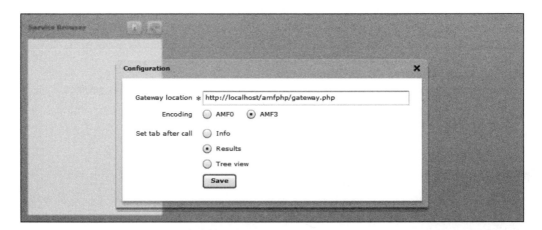

You do not need to change any of these selections. Click Save to access the Service Browser. On the left side, select HelloWorld. This is the file that you just created. Notice on the left that it has a list of methods and the inputs necessary to test the methods. You can test the service by typing anything into the sMessage input field and clicking Call.

The results from the service appear in the text area on the Results tab, as shown in the following screenshot. The Info tab shows how long it took to execute the command on the server.

At this point, you have a properly installed installation of AMFPHP and a working remoting service. The next step is to set up a simple connection from Flash.

Consuming HelloWorld

It's time to put the entire process together! I'll show how to create the UI elements in Flash first and then create a Main.as class file that will make the connection to AMFPHP and populate the UI components. Follow these steps:

1. Open Flash CS3, and create a new Flash file (ActionScript 3).
2. Save the document as HelloWorld.fla in a new folder.

3. Create a new ActionScript file by selecting File ➤ New ➤ ActionScript File.

4. Save the file, and name it Main.as.

5. Select the HelloWorld.fla tab to continue working on the interface.

6. In the Components window, drag a user interface TextInput component to the stage. This will be the input field for the text to be sent to the server.

7. Place the TextInput component in the top-left corner. In the Properties Inspector, give the component the instance name of server_txt, and change the Text property to AMFPHP is Easy.

8. Drag a Button component to the right of the server_txt component. Change the Button component's instance name to send_btn. Change the label of the Button component to send to server.

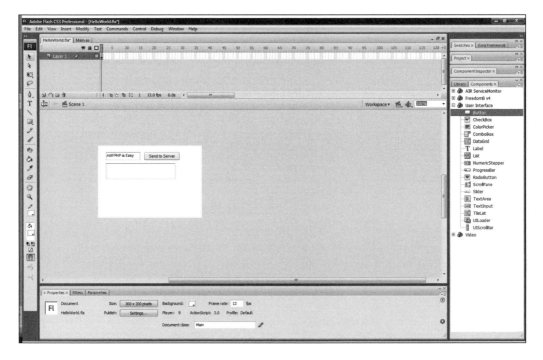

9. Drag a TextArea component to the stage below the server_txt component. Change the instance name to response_txt, and change the width of the TextArea to 200.

10. Select the stage by clicking it. This opens the stage Properties Inspector at the bottom of the Flash CS3 IDE.

11. Change the stage width to 300 and height to 200.

12. From the stage Properties Inspector, also change the Document class to Main. This links the Main.as ActionScript file with the user interface HelloWorld.fla.

13. When you are done, you should have a HelloWorld.fla file and a Main.as file located in a single folder. Your HelloWorld.fla file should look similar to the following screenshot.

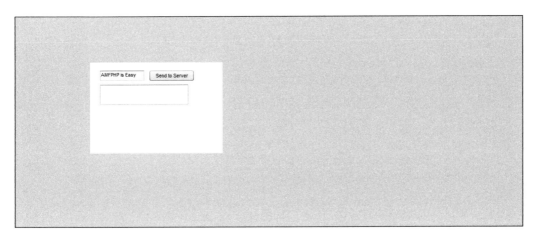

The HelloWorld logic

Open the Main.as tab in Flash to work on the class file. First you'll build the Main.as class file so that all the events are fully functional without the connection to the server. Then you will update the class with the remoting functionality.

```
Package {
  import flash.display.MovieClip;
  import fl.events.*;
  import flash.events.*;
  // Flash CS3 Document Class.
  public class Main extends MovieClip {
    public function Main() {
      // Event listner for buttons
      send_btn.addEventListener(MouseEvent.CLICK, sendData);
    }

    public function sendData(e:MouseEvent):void {
      // Get the data from the input field
      var params = server_txt.text;
      response_txt.text = 'Send '+server_txt.text+' to server)';
    }
  }
}
```

If you are new to ActionScript 3, the public class Main is executed as soon as the HelloWorld.fla document is run. This is called the **constructor**. The constructor adds an event listener for the send_btn component and tells it to use the sendData function whenever the button is clicked. The sendData method takes the input from the server_txt component and displays it in the response_txt component. It's very simple, so let's make it a little more complicated. I'll now show how to update the class so that you can send the data to the server and display the result. You first need to import two ActionScript libraries that perform the bulk of the work. The first is NetConnection, which acts like a bidirectional pipe between the client and the server. The second is a Responder object, which handles the return values from the server related to the success or failure of the call.

```
import flash.net.NetConnection;
import flash.net.Responder;
```

In the class, you need three variables to represent the NetConnection library, the Responder library, and the gateway URL to your AMFPHP installation:

```
private var gateway:String = "http://localhost/amfphp/gateway.php ";
private var connection:NetConnection;
private var responder:Responder;
```

In the Main constructor, create a Responder and a new connection to the AMFPHP gateway. The Responder defines two different methods for handling the response from the server. For simplicity I have called these onResult and onFault. You can call them whatever you want, but many examples use these method names.

```
responder = new Responder(onResult, onFault);
connection = new NetConnection;
connection.connect(gateway);
```

In the sendData function, you need to now send the data to the server. You need to add one more line that makes a call to HelloWorld, say in the AMFPHP services directory:

```
connection.call("HelloWorld.say", responder, params);
```

When you created the Responder variable, you defined onResult and onFault functions to handle the response from the server. You need to add the onResult function for the successful result from the server. A successful event handler is run every time the connection is handled properly to the server.

```
private function onResult(result:Object):void {
  response_txt.text = String(result);
}
```

The onFault function is called if there was an invalid response from the server. This happens when the PHP file errors out, when the URL to the server is invalid, when the remote service or method does not exist, or with any other connection-related issues.

```
private function onFault(fault:Object):void {
  response_txt.text = String(fault.description);
}
```

Adding the ActionScript to make the remoting connection is now complete. In review, you added the required variables to open a connection to the remote server, you defined what methods should be used when your application receives a response from the server, and finally you displayed the returned data to the user interface. Walk through the completed example one more time to make sure you understand it:

```
package {
  import flash.display.MovieClip;
  import fl.events.*;
  import flash.events.*;
  import flash.net.NetConnection;
  import flash.net.Responder;

  public class Main extends MovieClip {
    private var gateway:String = "http://localhost/amfphp/gateway.php";
    private var connection:NetConnection;
    private var responder:Responder;

    public function Main() {
      send_btn.addEventListener(MouseEvent.CLICK, sendData);
      responder = new Responder(onResult, onFault);
      connection = new NetConnection;
      connection.connect(gateway);
    }

    public function sendData(e:MouseEvent):void {
      // Get the data from the input field
      var params = server_txt.text;
      response_txt.text = 'Send '+server_txt.text+' to server)';
      connection.call("HelloWorld.say", responder, params);
    }

    private function onResult(result:Object):void {
      // Display the returned data in the textarea
      response_txt.text = String(result);
    }
    private function onFault(fault:Object):void {
      response_txt.text = String(fault.description);
    }
  }
}
```

Publish the HelloWorld.fla file to see your fully functional remoting application, as shown in the following screenshot.

The finished HelloWorld.fla, Main.as, and HelloWorld.php files are located in the download examples for this book.

Creating, reading, updating, and deleting with Flash and PHP

Most users turn to AMFPHP for a simple way to get database data in and out of their Flex or Flash application. The remaining examples in this chapter are built on a Product View mock application. Say you have a list of products located in a database to which you want to display, update, delete, and add new products. You will build upon this example with the end goal that you are capable of managing data from Flash. To start, I will walk you through how AMFPHP handles database connections and how it retrieves that data into a Flash DataGrid. After this example, you'll learn how to update from Flash to PHP the same data that you displayed in the first product example. Finally, I'll explain how to use class mapping to better organize the data on the client and the server. Each example builds on the last, so let's get started!

Building the database adapter

An impressive and time-saving feature of AMFPHP is its ease of returning a result set from a database query formatted for use in Flash or Flex. By default, AMFPHP investigates the resource being used to connect to the database. When you return a query, AMFPHP checks the resource type against a list of database adapters and then automatically converts the result into an ArrayCollection for AMF 3 and a RecordSet for AMF 0. As of the writing of this book, Flash CS3 does not support ArrayCollection objects, and therefore AMFPHP always returns a RecordSet unless the connection is a RemoteObject connection from Flex. The following database adapters are available in AMFPHP 2:

- MySQL
- SQLite
- PDO
- Zend::DB, including ZendDBTable_Rowset
- PHP Doctrine
- Postgres
- PEAR:DB
- ODBC
- MySQLi
- MS SQL
- Informix
- FrontBase
- ADODB
- Oracle: oci8

For testing purposes, you can now use the RecordSet class in AMFPHP. This enables you to test your application without having to connect to a database. Place the following code in one of your services, and it will return an ArrayCollection for AMF 3 or RecordSet for AMF 0:

```
function getCubes() {
  for ($i = 0; $i < 3; $i++) {
    $rows[] = array("val" => i, "cube" => i*i*i);
  }
  return new RecordSet($rows);
}
```

Testing the database connection

For the following examples, you will need a MySQL database to connect to. MySQL is a robust database that is easy to install and usually supported on web servers with PHP. Create a new database named products in MySQL. Use the create_product.sql file located in the chapter download file (http://www.friendsofed.com) to create the tables and insert the data necessary for the example. Run create products.sql against your MySQL products database to create the tables and insert the data necessary for the examples. To use the script from the command line, run mysql -u USERNAME -p PASSWORD products < create_products.sql. Replace USERNAME and PASSWORD with your own. Create a new PHP file called ProductService.php. This file will be used to connect to the product database and retrieve the data for Flash.

```
<?php
class ProductService {
  var $dbh;
  public function __construct() {
    $this->dbh = mysql_connect ("localhost", "amf_username", ➡
        "amf_password") ➡
or die ('I cannot connect to the database because: ' . mysql_error());
    mysql_select_db ("products");
  }
  function getProducts() {
    $sql = "SELECT * FROM Product";
    return mysql_query($sql);
  }
}
?>
```

Walking through the code, you can see that the database connection is created on line 5 in the class constructor. This makes sure the connection is available before any of the methods are called from Flash Player. The getProducts method is a simple query to select all the data from the products database and return it in a data set. Notice that there is nothing unique about the query. What is unique is that AMFPHP handles the return type, catches that it is a resource type of mysql, and converts the result into an ArrayCollection for AMF 3 connections or a ResultSet for AMF 0 connections. This makes it easy to start using the result in Flex or Flash.

Make sure you edit your ProductService.php database name, username, and password to what you used when you created the database, ran the create_products.sql script, and then uploaded the file to amfphp/services/ on your web server. As always, navigate in a web browser directly to the service (http://www.localhost/amfphp/services/ProductServices.php) to test it for any errors. If the script is unable to connect to the database, it should display an error when you go to the URL. If there is no error, open the AMFPHP browser to test the getProducts method. In a web browser, go to http://localhost/amfphp/browser/, and select ProductService from the left navigation. Select the Test tab, and select getProducts. Click the Call button to make the service call from the browser. The Results tab will show you the raw result from the query. Select the RecordSet view tab to see a Flex DataGrid populated with the ArrayCollection returned from AMFPHP. Everything is working perfectly on the server now, as shown in the following screenshot, so let's connect Flash to your new database service.

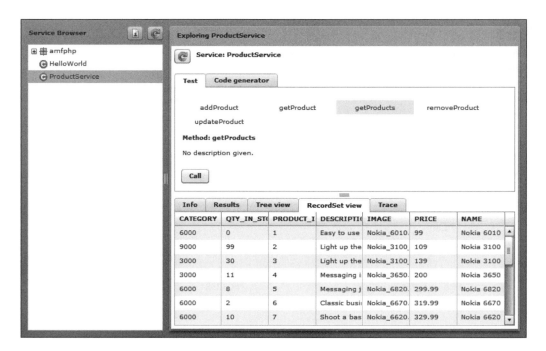

Integrating the database and Flash

It's time to connect the product view from Flash CS3 to the ProductService.php file you just created. You will start with populating a Flash user interface DataGrid component with the products data returned from the new ProductService class. You'll first set up a new Flash for a Product View user interface. Like the "Hello, World" example, you will then create a Main class that will make the connection to the server and bind the returned data to the user interface.

1. Open Flash CS3, and create a new Flash file (ActionScript 3).
2. Save the document as ProductView.fla in a new folder.
3. Create a new ActionScript file by selecting File ➤ New ➤ ActionScript File.
4. Save the file, and name it Main.as.
5. Select the ProductView.fla tab to continue working on the interface.
6. Change the stage width to 800 and height to 400.
7. From the Components window, drag a user interface DataGrid component to the stage. We will use the DataGrid component to show the results from the getProducts remote method.

8. Align the DataGrid in the top-left corner of the stage. Update the DataGrid's properties to have an instance name of products_dg and a width of 600 and height of 350.

9. Drag a Button component to the stage, and place it below the products_dg component. Update the properties of the Button component to have an instance name of getProducts_btn, and change its label to Get Products.

10. Select the stage by clicking it.

11. Change the Document class to Main, which links the Main.as ActionScript file with the HelloWorld.fla user interface.

12. Copy RecordSetDP.as from the examples folder into the same directory as your ProductView.fla file and your Main.as file. The RecordSetDP.as file will be imported into your Main.as class file to help in putting the returned data into the DataGrid.

The user interface on the stage is ready to consume the getProducts data. Now open the Main.as tab in Flash to work on the class file. The code you'll write for retrieving the data set from the ProductService is similar to the HelloWorld example. The main difference between the two examples is that we are now getting an ArrayCollection as a result rather than a String.

As of the writing of this book, Flash CS3 does not support ArrayCollection objects, although they are extensively used in ActionScript 3 in Flex. It is my assumption that Flash CS3 will eventually have this class, but until then I have provided a simple class called RecordSetDP that converts a RecordSet into a DataProvider. You can then apply the DataProvider directly to your DataGrid and instantly have your data update the DataGrid. Let's look at the Main.as file:

```
package {
  import flash.display.MovieClip;
  import fl.events.*;
  import flash.events.*;
  import flash.net.NetConnection;
  import flash.net.Responder;
  import RecordSetDP;

  public class Main extends MovieClip {
    private var gateway:String = "http://localhost/amfphp/gateway.php";
    private var connection:NetConnection;
    private var responder:Responder;

    public function Main() {
      getProducts_btn.addEventListener(MouseEvent.CLICK, sendData);
      responder = new Responder(onResult, onFault);
      connection = new NetConnection;
      connection.connect(gateway);
    }

    public function sendData(e:MouseEvent):void {
      connection.call("ProductService.getProducts", responder);
    }
```

```
        private function onResult(result:Object):void {
          products_dg.dataProvider = RecordSetDP.toDataProvider(result);
        }

        private function onFault(fault:Object):void {
          trace(String(fault.description));
        }
      }
    }
```

Your first reaction should be that not much has changed. You are right—there are only three little changes to make this work:

1. First, you import RecordSetDP, which needs to be in the same directory as your Main.as file. This class file will be used later to convert the result from the server into a DataProvider.

2. Second, you changed the server class from HelloWorld.say to ProductServices.getProducts in the sendData method. This change makes it so that Flash is now connecting to the new ProductService class rather than HelloWorld. You are also calling the getProducts method inside the ProductService class. This method was created to query all the data in the products table and return that data set.

3. Finally, you changed the onResult method to pass the result into RecordSetDP. toDataProvider, which returns a formatted DataProvider that is applied directly to the DataGrid on the stage. You can open the RecordSetDP and see that it is just looping through the result to format the data properly for a DataGrid DataProvider.

Run the application, and click the Get Products button. You now have a DataGrid populated from your remote MySQL table, as shown in the following screenshot.

NAME	QTY_IN_STOC	IMAGE	DESCRIPTION	CATEGORY	PRICE	PRODUCT_ID
Nokia 6010	0	Nokia_6010.gif	Easy to use w	6000	99	1
Nokia 3100 Blu	99	Nokia_3100_bl	Light up the nig	9000	109	2
Nokia 3100 Pin	30	Nokia_3100_pi	Light up the nig	3000	139	3
Nokia 3650	11	Nokia_3650.gif	Messaging is r	3000	200	4
Nokia 6820	8	Nokia_6820.gif	Messaging jus	6000	299.99	5
Nokia 6670	2	Nokia_6670.gif	Classic busine	6000	319.99	6
Nokia 6620	10	Nokia_6620.gif	Shoot a baske	6000	329.99	7
Nokia 3230 Silv	10	Nokia_3230_bl	Get creative w	3000	500	8
Nokia 3120	10	Nokia_3120.gif	Designed for b	3000	159.99	9
Nokia 3220	20	Nokia_3220.gif	The Nokia 322	3000	199	10
Nokia 6680	36	Nokia_6680.gif	The Nokia 668	6000	222	11
Nokia 6630	8	Nokia_6630.gif	The Nokia 663	6000	379	12
Nokia 7610 Bla	20	Nokia_7610_bl	The Nokia 761	7000	450	13
Nokia 7610 Wh	7	Nokia_7610_w	The Nokia 761	7000	4500	14
Nokia 6680	15	Nokia_6680.gif	The Nokia 668	6000	219	15
Nokia 9300	26	Nokia_9300_cl	The Nokia 930	9000	599	16

Get Products

Updating the product database

Now that you have retrieved a record set of data from the products database, you want to be able to manipulate that data before sending it back. The following example shows how to update, delete, and create products through the Flash interface. I will start by showing how to add methods to the ProductService.php file to allow for the new features. In the following sections, I will not be walking you through the step-by-step instructions to build the updated user interface because of the immense amount of repetitive changes.

I'm doing this so you can add buttons to evoke changes and add several input fields for altering data. Because of the amount of changes to the user interface, it's best to load up the ProductUpdate example from the chapter download file (http://www.friendsofed.com) into Flash to walk through this example.

Additional ProductService methods

You need to make three additions to ProductService to handle the new functionality. The new method removeProduct deletes a row based on a product ID, updateProduct makes updates to an existing row in the database, and finally addProduct creates a new row in the database. Here are the three new methods in full:

```
function removeProduct($Product_ID) {
  $sql = "DELETE FROM Product WHERE Product_ID='$Product_ID'";
  return mysql_query($sql);
}

function updateProduct($Product_ID,$Name,$Category,$Image, ➥
$Price, $Description, $Qty_In_Stock) {
  $sql = "UPDATE Product SET PRODUCT_ID='$Product_ID', ➥
NAME='$Name',CATEGORY='$Category',IMAGE='$Image', ➥
 PRICE='$Price', DESCRIPTION='$Description', ➥
 QTY_IN_STOCK='$Qty_In_Stock' WHERE➥
PRODUCT_ID=$Product_ID";
  return mysql_query($sql);
}

function addProduct($Name,$Category,$Image, $Price, $Description, ➥
$Qty_In_Stock) {
  $sql = "INSERT INTO Product (Name,Category,Image, Price, ➥
Description, Qty_In_Stock) VALUES ('$Name','$Category','$Image', ➥
'$Price', '$Description', '$Qty_In_Stock')";
  return mysql_query($sql);
}
```

Each of the three new methods uses a SQL statement and the mysql_query method to execute the SQL statement. You can define more complex functions by utilizing the same concepts to search, get products of a certain type, or get products greater than or less than a certain price. PHP is the optimal place to put your business logic because it is faster than the client computer, it is a controlled environment, and it protects your intelligence from being downloaded to each computer.

Before moving forward, update your `ProductService` with the new methods or upload the completed `ProductService.php` file from the `ProductUpdate` folder in the chapter download file. You can use the Service Browser to test these new methods.

Interface alterations to manipulate products

Open `ProductUpdate.fla` in the `ProductUpdate` folder in the chapter download file, and you will see that the interface has been updated to add several text areas and labels to the right side of the DataGrid. These will be used for updating the selected product content or just adding a new product. When you select a row out of the DataGrid, the input fields on the right side are populated with the associated data. The running application looks like the following screenshot.

Let's first walk through the data ActionScript code that is used to populate the input fields on the right side of `ProductUpdate.fla`. It is important to note that you are copying the data into the text input fields so that you are working with copies of the live data. All the data sent to the server for updates, deletions, and additions will be based on this copied data. The following is an updated `Main.as` file with all the functionality needed for the UI to work. After you look through the code, I will walk through the additions to enable the new functionality.

```
package {
    import flash.display.MovieClip;
    import fl.events.*;
    import flash.events.*;
    import flash.net.NetConnection;
    import flash.net.Responder;
    import RecordSetDP;

    public class Main extends MovieClip {
        private var gateway:String = ➥
"http://localhost/amfphp/gateway.php";
        private var connection:NetConnection;
```

```
private var responder:Responder;
private var refresh:Responder;
private var product_id:int;

public function Main() {
  getProducts_btn.addEventListener(MouseEvent.CLICK, sendData);
  update_btn.addEventListener(MouseEvent.CLICK, updateProduct);
  delete_btn.addEventListener(MouseEvent.CLICK, removeProduct);
  add_btn.addEventListener(MouseEvent.CLICK, addProduct);
  responder = new Responder(onResult, onFault);
  refresh = new Responder(refreshData, onFault);
  connection = new NetConnection;
  connection.connect(gateway);
  products_dg.addEventListener(Event.CHANGE, gridItemSelected);
  refreshData(true);
}

public function sendData(e:MouseEvent):void {
  refreshData(true);
}

private function refreshData(reload:Boolean):void {
  if (reload) {
    connection.call("ProductService.getProducts", responder);
  }
}

private function onResult(result:Object):void {
  products_dg.dataProvider = RecordSetDP.toDataProvider(result);
}

private function onFault(fault:Object):void {
  trace(String(fault.description));
}

private function gridItemSelected(e:Event):void {
  product_id = e.target.selectedItem.PRODUCT_ID
  name_txt.text = e.target.selectedItem.NAME;
  category_txt.text = e.target.selectedItem.CATEGORY;
  image_txt.text = e.target.selectedItem.IMAGE;
  price_txt.text = e.target.selectedItem.PRICE;
  desription_txt.text = e.target.selectedItem.DESCRIPTION;
  qty_txt.text = e.target.selectedItem.QTY_IN_STOCK;
}

private function getParams() {
  var param = new Object;
  param.PRODUCT_ID = product_id;
  param.NAME = name_txt.text;
```

171

```
            param.CATEGORY = category_txt.text;
            param.IMAGE = image_txt.text;
            param.PRICE = price_txt.text;
            param.DESCRIPTION = desription_txt.text;
            param.QTY = qty_txt.text;
            return param;
        }

    private function updateProduct(e:MouseEvent):void {
        var param:Object = getParams();
        connection.call("ProductService.updateProduct", refresh, ➡
param.PRODUCT_ID, param.NAME, param.CATEGORY, ➡
 param.IMAGE, param.PRICE, param.DESCRIPTION, ➡
param.QTY);
        }

    private function removeProduct(e:MouseEvent):void {
        var param:Object = getParams();
        connection.call("ProductService.removeProduct", refresh, ➡
param.PRODUCT_ID);
        }
    private function addProduct(e:MouseEvent):void {
        var param:Object = getParams();
        connection.call("ProductService.addProduct", refresh, ➡
 param.NAME, param.CATEGORY, param.IMAGE, param.PRICE, ➡
 param.DESCRIPTION, param.QTY);
        }
    }
}
```

The first place where you have updated the ProductUpdate Main.as file is when you added another Responder called refresh. The refresh Responder is used whenever you successfully update, delete, or add a new product to the database. The refresh Responder is instantiated in the constructor with the callback method refreshData to be used on a successful service call. The method refreshData takes a single Boolean parameter. In each of our new ProductService methods (removeProduct, updateProduct, and addProduct), you return true if the SQL statement is executed successfully. When this happens, you want to refresh the DataGrid with the new data. The refreshData method calls the ProductService getProducts method again to bring the user interface in sync with the changes to the server. I will talk more about the refresh Responder when I cover the three new service call methods in Main.as (updateProduct, deleteProduct, and addProduct).

In the Main method or class constructor, you have added three new event listeners for the three new buttons, update_btn, delete_btn, and add_btn. The buttons have assigned the functions updateProduct, deleteProduct, and addProduct, respectively, as the function to handle the click event fired when the button is selected. In addition to the button event handlers, an event handler for products_dg has been added to call the griditemSelected method whenever a row is selected in the DataGrid.

You have also added in the constructor a call to the refreshData method to populate the DataGrid as soon as the Flash file is loaded. As in the previous example, clicking the Get Products button still performs the same operation of refreshing the data in the DataGrid.

Let's look through some of these new methods to see what they do. The method gridItemSelected handles the event of someone clicking the DataGrid and selecting a product. The method takes the values in the DataGrid and assigns them to the associated text areas on the right side of the stage. It also populates the product_id variable, which is used to keep track of the currently selected product.

The method getParams is used to prepare any changes that have been made to the TextInput into an object to be sent to the server. This method will be used in all of the new features to the application to make sure it has the most recent data.

The next three methods make service calls to the ProductService class on the web server. These methods are called when their respective buttons are clicked. These three methods all use the refresh Responder to handle data returning from the server. Each one of the server methods returns a Boolean true when the update, delete, or add is executed on the database successfully. The true result from the server methods is checked in the Main.as refreshData, and if this is successful, getProducts is called again to update the interface.

- updateProduct is the first new feature to the application; it takes the data in the TextInput and sends it back to the ProductService.updateProduct method, which takes the variables and calls a SQL update on the product database. With each of these three methods, it is important to note that the order of the parameters must be the same as the order they are listed in their corresponding method in ProductService.php. Changing the order will result in the data being placed in the wrong field.

- removeProduct deletes from the database the currently selected product_id. For testing I recommend you first add a product and then delete it from the database.

- addProduct looks almost exactly like updateProduct except it does not send the product_id to the server. When the server tries to insert the new product into the database without a product_id, the database automatically increments the unique field and creates a new product_id.

Although I have covered a lot of functionality in a short time, you should be able to see that it is not difficult to implement a create, read, update, delete (CRUD) user interface in Flash with the help of AMFPHP. I recommend that you try to add some functionality to this base application. Some suggestions are to add validation to the TextInputs so that you can validate whether the data has changed on button submissions and also format some of the inputs. From the service side, try sorting the data in different ways when you call getProducts. You could even add a parameter for the way you want the returned data sorted. If you are ready to try to consume the same services in Flex, move on to the next tutorial, where you'll rebuild a similar user interface and use the same ProductService to access the database.

Connecting to HelloWorld with Flex

I made an assumption in this chapter that the typical Flex developer could take a little bit of information and apply all of the existing concepts to Flex. The biggest difference between Flash and Flex is that Flex has a fantastic class called RemoteObject. If you spend a lot of time in Flash, you will find yourself writing your own implementation of RemoteObject because it adds several useful utilities. In this section, I will walk you through the two examples from the previous section and show how to implement them in Flex. This will give you the basics that you need in order to get started. Make sure you review the supplied Flex examples.

Let's get started with AMFPHP in Flex Builder. Open Flex Builder, and start a new Basic Flex project, as shown in the following screenshot.

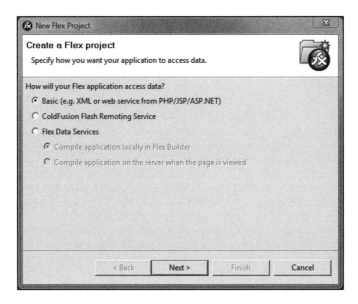

Name the Flex project product, and create it in your default workspace, as shown in the following screenshot. Click Finish to build the project.

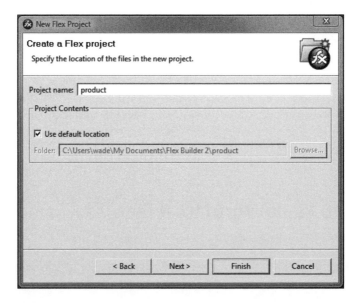

You should now have an open project called product in your Navigator panel. Right-click the product name, and select Properties. In the project's properties dialog box, go to the Flex Build Path menu, select the Library path tab, and be sure the rpc.swc file is added to your project's path, as shown in the following screenshot. Click OK to close the window.

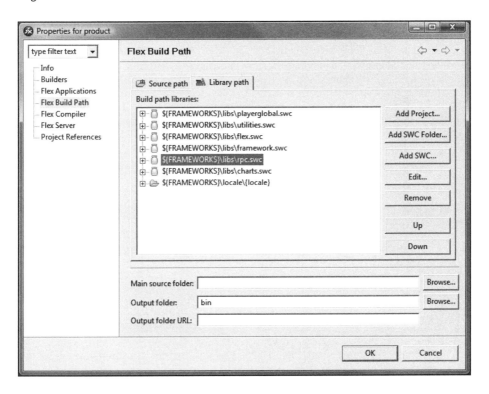

You now need to tell Flex which services configuration file to use for inspecting your remote methods. For this reason, create a new services-config.xml file in your Flex project's root folder. To do this, right-click the product project folder, and select New File, which will pop up a new window. Select the product folder, and then name the file services-config.xml. Finally, click Finish.

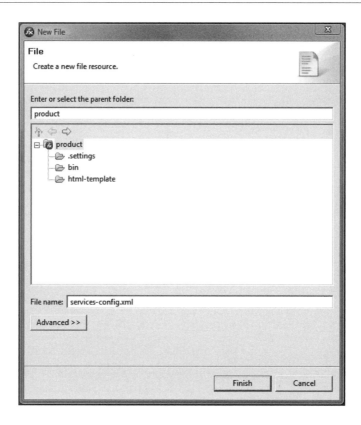

Flex has created the new services-config.xml file and has it open. Use the following example text for your services-config.xml file. Make sure you update your endpoint to match that of your testing server like you did in the Flash examples. Make sure you save the file.

```xml
<?xml version="1.0" encoding="UTF-8"?>
<services-config>
  <services>
    <service id="amfphp-flashremoting-service"➥
class="flex.messaging.services.RemotingService"➥
messageTypes="flex.messaging.messages.RemotingMessage">
      <destination id="amfphp">
        <channels>
          <channel ref="my-amfphp"/>
        </channels>
        <properties>
          <source>*</source>
        </properties>
      </destination>
    </service>
  </services>
  <channels>
```

```
        <channel-definition id="my-amfphp"➡
          class="mx.messaging.channels.AMFChannel">
          <endpoint uri="http://localhost/amfphp/gateway.php"➡
class="flex.messaging.endpoints.AMFEndpoint"/>
        </channel-definition>
      </channels>
    </services-config>
```

Now open your project's properties dialog box again by right-clicking the project folder in the Navigator panel and selecting Properties. From the properties pop-up menu, select Flex Compiler, and add the string -services "services-config.xml". Click Apply and then OK to return to update the option. What you have just done is told the Flex compiler to look to the services-config.xml file for runtime variables that will be used by the RemotingService class.

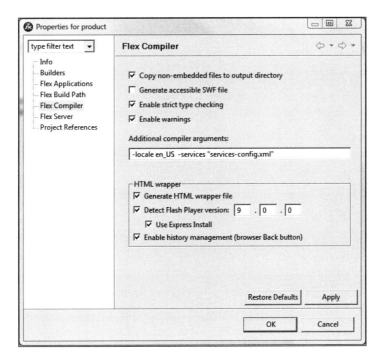

For this example, I'll show how to connect to the HelloWorld service that you created earlier in this chapter. Open the Source view of product.mxml, and add the following MXML code for defining the user interface:

```
<?xml version="1.0" encoding="utf-8"?>
<mx:Application xmlns:mx="http://www.adobe.com/2006/mxml"➡
layout="absolute">
  <mx:TextInput x="10" y="20" id="server_txt" text="AMFPHP is Easy"/>
  <mx:TextArea x="10" y="50" id="response_txt" width="278"/>
  <mx:Button x="178" y="20" label="Send to Server" id="send_btn"/>
</mx:Application>
```

177

As you can see, the interface is similar to what you created in Flash. As a reference, I have used the same variable names as in the first example. Run the application by clicking the green play button to see the interface (shown in the following screenshot).

You now need to add the code to handle your connection to AMFPHP. Return to the Source view of product.mxml, and add the following code:

```
<?xml version="1.0" encoding="utf-8"?>
<mx:Application xmlns:mx="http://www.adobe.com/2006/mxml"➥
layout="absolute">
 <mx:RemoteObject id="myservice" fault="faultHandler(event)"➥
showBusyCursor="true" source="HelloWorld"➥
destination="amfphp">
   <mx:method name="say" result="resultHandler(event)" />
 </mx:RemoteObject>
  <mx:Script>
    <![CDATA[
      import mx.managers.CursorManager;
      import mx.rpc.events.ResultEvent;
      import mx.rpc.events.FaultEvent;
      private function faultHandler(fault:FaultEvent):void
      {
        CursorManager.removeBusyCursor();
        trace("code:\n" + fault.fault.faultCode + "\n\nMessage:\n"➥
+ fault.fault.faultString + "\n\nDetail:\n"➥
+ fault.fault.faultDetail);
      }
      private function resultHandler(event:ResultEvent):void
      {
        response_txt.text = event.result.toString();
      }
    ]]>
  </mx:Script>
  <mx:TextInput x="10" y="20" id="server_txt" text="AMFPHP is Easy" />
  <mx:TextArea x="10" y="50" id="response_txt" width="278"/>
  <mx:Button x="178" y="20" label="Send to Server" id="send_btn"➥
click="myservice.say(server_txt.text)"/>
</mx:Application>
```

Looking through the MXML, the first new addition is the RemoteObject tag. RemoteObject is used in Flex to make the connection to the server. Let's look through the variables that are part of the RemoteObject tag:

- Id is the variable name that will be used throughout the rest of the application to reference this RemoteObject.

- Fault defines the method that should be used when there is an unsuccessful connection to the server or service.

- showBusyCursor changes the cursor to a busy icon while data is being sent to the remote server and is removed when data is returned to Flex, keeping the user from interacting with the application.

- Source is the name of the remote service for this RemoteObject ID.

- Destination is the same name as the destination name that you placed in the services-config.xml file. The Destination tag is what makes the connection to the config file so that RemoteObject can load its endpoint.

- On line 3, there is one mx:method tag that defines the name of the remote method and what local method should be executed when the result comes back from the server. We will see in the next example that there is an mx:method tag for every remote method. RemoteObject uses the NetConnection class but adds some functionality for developers. One of those features is used in this first tag called showBusyCursor. This automatically puts up the hourglass cursor when a remoting call is fired until Flex gets a response. This is a great way to keep users from clicking other buttons or hitting the Send to Server button multiple times.

In the Script section of the MXML code, you import the cursor manager and ResultEvent and FaultEvent to handle the data being returned from the AMF 3 call to AMFPHP. You have two methods, faultHandler and resultHandler, that were defined in the RemoteObject tags as the methods to handle results. faultHandler was defined as the method to be run for any fault that occurs with the myservice RemoteObject, and resultHandler was defined as the method to be run on the successful result of the HelloWorld.say method. I am just tracing out debugging information in faultHandler that will help if you are having difficulties without your server connection. On line 18 inside resultHandler, we are taking the event.result from the server, converting it to a String, and then applying that data to the text property of response_txt. This is what makes the result display.

The last thing that was added with this new MXML code was the click event on the send_btn. The click event references the myservices RemoteObject and calls the say method. It passes the text that was typed into the server_txt component.

Run the application again, and you now have your first Flex-to-AMFPHP connection! You now know that you have your Flex environment set up properly. In the next example, you'll build the CRUD interface for the product database in Flex.

Using Flex to update the product database

In this section, we will show how to create a Flex interface that consumes the `ProductService.php` file you created earlier. Let's start by creating a new MXML application by right-clicking the product folder and selecting New ➤ MXML Application. Name the new file `productUpdate`, as shown in the following screenshot.

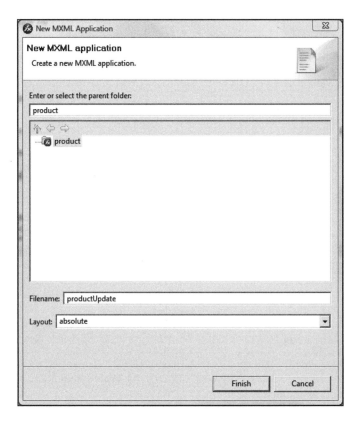

Right-click `productUpdate` in the Navigator panel, and select Set as Default Application. This tells Flex Builder to run this new file when you click the Run button in Flex Builder. To run the HelloWorld example again, you will need to change the default application back to `product.mxml`.

The following is the complete `productUpdate.mxml` file to populate a `DataGrid` with the `getProducts` remote method and update, remove, and add new products to the database. Copy the code into your `productUpdate.mxml` file, or copy and paste it from the chapter download file. Then scan through the code; after the code, I will walk you through the logic behind the functionality:

```
<?xml version="1.0" encoding="utf-8"?>
<mx:Application xmlns:mx="http://www.adobe.com/2006/mxml"➨
layout="absolute" backgroundColor="#FFFFFF">
  <mx:RemoteObject id="myservice" source="ProductService"➨
destination="amfphp" fault="faultHandler(event)" ➨
```

```
 showBusyCursor="true">
    <mx:method name="getProducts" result="getProductsHandler(event)" ➥
fault="faultHandler(event)" />
      <mx:method name="removeProduct"➥
result="refreshProductsHandler(event)" ➥
fault="faultHandler(event)" />
      <mx:method name="updateProduct"➥
 result="refreshProductsHandler(event)" ➥
fault="faultHandler(event)" />
      <mx:method name="addProduct"➥
result="refreshProductsHandler(event)" ➥
fault="faultHandler(event)" />
    </mx:RemoteObject>
    <mx:DataGrid x="10" y="10" width="381" id="products_dg"➥
change="changeHandler(event)" height="350">
      <mx:columns>
        <mx:DataGridColumn headerText="Name" dataField="NAME"/>
        <mx:DataGridColumn headerText="Category" dataField="CATEGORY"/>
        <mx:DataGridColumn headerText="Price" dataField="PRICE"/>
        <mx:DataGridColumn headerText="Qty" dataField="QTY_IN_STOCK"/>
      </mx:columns>
    </mx:DataGrid>
  <mx:Script>
  <![CDATA[
    import mx.rpc.events.ResultEvent;
    import mx.controls.Alert;
    import mx.rpc.events.FaultEvent;

    [Bindable]
    private var product:Object;

    private function faultHandler(fault:FaultEvent):void
    {
      Alert.show(fault.fault.faultString, ➥
fault.fault.faultCode.toString());
    }

    private function getProductsHandler(event:ResultEvent):void
    {
      products_dg.dataProvider = event.result;
    }

    private function refreshProductsHandler(event:ResultEvent):void {
      if (event.result) {
        myservice.getProducts();
      }
    }
```

```
      private function changeHandler(event:Event):void
      {
        product = DataGrid(event.target).selectedItem;
      }

      private function getParams():Object {
        var param:Object = new Object;
        param.PRODUCT_ID = product.PRODUCT_ID;
        param.NAME = product_name.text;
        param.CATEGORY = product_category.text;
        param.IMAGE = product_image.text;
        param.PRICE = product_price.text;
        param.DESCRIPTION = product_description.text;
        param.QTY = product_qty.text;
        return param;
      }

      private function updateProduct():void {
        var param:Object = getParams();
        myservice.updateProduct(param.PRODUCT_ID, param.NAME, ➥
param.CATEGORY, param.IMAGE, param.PRICE, ➥
param.DESCRIPTION, param.QTY);
   }

      private function removeProduct():void {
        var param:Object = getParams();
        myservice.removeProduct(param.PRODUCT_ID);
      }

      private function addProduct():void {
        var param:Object = getParams();
        myservice.addProduct(param.NAME, param.CATEGORY, ➥
param.IMAGE, param.PRICE, param.DESCRIPTION, ➥
param.QTY);
      }
  ]]>
  </mx:Script>
  <mx:Button x="10" y="368" label="Get Products"➥
click="myservice.getOperation('getProducts').send();"/>

  <mx:Form x="399" y="10" width="329" height="320">
  <mx:FormHeading label="Product Updater"  width="99"/>
    <mx:FormItem label="Name">
      <mx:TextInput id="product_name" text="{product.NAME}"➥
width="200"/>
    </mx:FormItem>
    <mx:FormItem label="Category">
      <mx:TextInput id="product_category" text="{product.CATEGORY}"➥
width="200"/>
```

```
        </mx:FormItem>
        <mx:FormItem label="Image">
          <mx:TextInput id="product_image" text="{product.IMAGE}"➥
width="200"/>
        </mx:FormItem>
        <mx:FormItem label="Price">
          <mx:TextInput id="product_price" text="{product.PRICE}"➥
width="200"/>
        </mx:FormItem>
        <mx:FormItem label="Qty">
          <mx:TextInput id="product_qty" text="{product.QTY_IN_STOCK}"➥
width="200"/>
        </mx:FormItem>
        <mx:FormItem label="Description">
          <mx:TextArea id="product_description"➥
text="{product.DESCRIPTION}" width="200" height="121"/>
        </mx:FormItem>
        </mx:Form>
        <mx:Button x="488" y="338" label="Update" click="updateProduct()"/>
        <mx:Button x="563" y="338" label="Remove" click="removeProduct()"/>
        <mx:Button x="644" y="338" label="Add" click="addProduct()"/>
</mx:Application>
```

Running the productUpdate.mxml file will launch the new Flex interface that resembles what you created in Flash. Flex is designed for this type of application and layout, so it is considerably easier to get a professional-looking interface. Run the application by clicking the green run button. Once the application is running, click the Get Products button to populate the DataGrid with the data from the getProducts remote method in ProductService.php. Select one of the products in the DataGrid, and it will populate the TextInputs to the right side of the interface, as shown in the following screenshot.

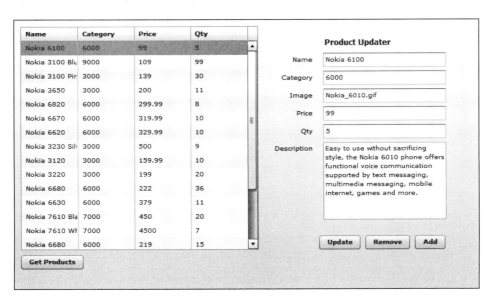

183

All of the buttons under the Product Update form are functional, so feel free to update some of the data, create a new product based on an existing product, or delete one of the products you created.

Let's walk through the MXML code together to understand what type of functionality you have added in order to make this application run properly. Let's start with the RemoteObject tag at the top of the application. Unlike the RemoteObject tag in the HelloWorld example, this code set has several method declarations. Each of the declarations is necessary so you can set a result-handler function for when the method is called.

The next tag is the DataGrid tag. In this example I have chosen to display only the name, category, price, and quantity fields from the result set. This cleans up the interface a little, and I have also given the columns easily readable header text labels. It is important that you notice the names of the dataField values for each column. These names have to match the DataProvider that we are going to apply to the DataGrid. The current values are the column names in the database.

The <![CDATA[tag breaks out of MXML and allows for ActionScript inline with the MXML. Starting with the ActionScript area, I have added an import for the alert component. This addition was required in the faultHandler function that now uses the alert component rather than just a simple trace statement.

I am using a meta tag called Bindable on the product object. This meta tag allows me to later bind values to this variable when the variable is changed. You will see that the TextInputs are bound to products and will update when the product variable updates. This is similar to how a DataProvider works on the DataGrid.

The following are the remaining methods in the Script section in order:

- faultHandler is the specified method by RemoteObject for handling when it cannot connect to the remote service.

- getProductsHandler is defined by RemoteObject to handle the successful result of the getProducts remote method call. The remote method returns an ArrayCollection, which you set directly against the DataGrid's DataProvider.

- refreshProductsHandler is defined by RemoteObject to handle the successful result of updateProduct, removeProduct, and addProduct. This method is similar to the refreshData method that you used in the Flash example. It checks to see whether the Boolean result set is true, which means the operation was successful, and then calls getproducts to sync the Flash interface with the current data on the server.

- changeHandler is a listener for the DataGrid. When something is selected in the DataGrid, this method is run, and it applies the column that was selected to the product object. Because product is bindable, it then updates the TextInputs if the data in product changes.

- getParams is the same as it was in the Flash example. This method is called before any update, add, or delete to the database to get the most current data from the TextInputs to be sent to the server.

- updateProduct is called from the Update button to send the changed data back to the server. This method uses the ID name of the RemoteObject myservice and then can call the remote method directly. removeProduct and addProduct work like this method and are called by their respective buttons.

If you scroll down to the TextInputs, you can see how you use {} to represent a bindable variable. You bind the person to the TextInput text property and the TextArea text property for the description field. These are automatically updated on every mouse click on the DataGrid.

The last piece of the puzzle is the click event on the buttons that explicitly call their corresponding functions to send data back to the server.

After walking through this code, you can see the similarities between the Flash example and the Flex example. You should also have a clear understanding of how RemoteObject works with multiple method calls and different handlers for their specific result sets. In the next, final tutorial section, you will review a simpler way to work with remote data in ActionScript 3.

Class mapping from PHP to ActionScript 3

Class mapping allows a remote PHP object to be mapped directly into an ActionScript object without having to construct code to iterate through the result to populate the class. This can save a lot of time, and it also has the advantage that you can use code completion in the editor because the ActionScript object is defined. Although the concept is technical, it actually can immensely simplify your code. In this example, you will use a traditional value object (VO) implementation. Value objects are usually accompanied by a data access object (DAO), but you'll continue to use ProductService.php as the data access object. I will talk more about VO and DAO when we get to the ProductService changes.

For a final example, you'll map a PHP class named ProductVO.php to an ActionScript 3 class named ProductVO.as. I'll start with the PHP services to show how you are going to return the ProductVO class.

The following code is the ProductVO.php file. Create a new file called ProductVO.php, and add the code to the file. Upload the file to your amfphp/services/vo/ folder on your web server. You will need to create the vo folder to place the file in. The vo folder is a special folder for AMFPHP in the services directory that does not have the reflection class run on it. If you had hundreds of VO files in the services directory, AMFPHP would try to parse them all when it is first loading.

```php
<?php
class ProductVO {
  var $productId;
  var $name;
  var $description;
  var $image;
  var $category;
  var $price;
  var $qtyInStock;
  // explicit actionscript package
  var $_explicitType = "ProductVO";
}
?>
```

This is a simple class that has all of the variables you would expect to see in a product class. There is no constructor because it is never used in the example. You can place business logic inside your VO if you want, but some OOP professionals will argue that this is not the proper usage of a VO.

What is unique and important about this class is the variable $_explicitType, which tells AMFPHP that this class has its equivalent package, ProductVO, in the calling Flash Player. If your ActionScript file is in a package, you can explicitly set the type in this string no matter the folder structure in PHP. For example, the following would map to an ActionScript equivalent class of com.friends.of.ed. ProductVO without moving the file on the server:

```
Var $_explicitType = "com.friends.of.ed.ProductVO";
```

The RemoteClass metadata tells Flex to which RemoteObject this class is associated (note that both classes must have the same structure; otherwise, Flex could not cast correctly the RemoteObject).

Creating the data access object

You need to update ProduceService.php to add a method for getting the ProductVO and populating the object. It is common to call the service that performs this function a ProductDAO.php file that has a getProduct method that returns ProductVOs. I highly recommend this naming convention for any application you are developing. However, for simplicity, you'll just add a getProductVO method to the ProductService.php file.

```php
<?php
require_once "./vo/ProductVO.php";

class ProductService {
  var $dbh;
  public function __construct() {
  $this->dbh = mysql_connect ("localhost", "amf_user ", "amf_password")➡
 or die ('I cannot connect to the database: ' . mysql_error());
  mysql_select_db ("t8edgec_product");

  /** Snip all other repeated methods **/

  function getProductVO() {
    $myProducts = array();
    $sql = "SELECT * FROM Product";
    $result = mysql_query($sql);
    while($row = mysql_fetch_array($result))
    {
      $product = new ProductVO();
      $product->productId = $row['PRODUCT_ID'];
      $product->name = $row['NAME'];
      $product->description = $row['DESCRIPTION'];
      $product->image = $row['IMAGE'];
      $product->category = $row['CATEGORY'];
      $product->price = $row['PRICE'];
      $product->qtyInStock = $row['QTY_IN_STOCK'];
      $myProducts[] = $product;
    }
    return $myProducts;
  }
}
?>
```

The addition of the ProductVO import at the beginning of the PHP file is required in order to instantiate the ProductVO class in ProductService.php. The additional function getProductsVO performs the same "select all rows" operation for the database query that the getProducts method performed. The addition is that you first create an array called myProducts. For each row that is returned from the database, you instantiate a new ProductVo and then add the new instance to the myProducts array. When you run out of rows, you return the array of ProductVOs for ActionScript to consume.

Displaying value objects in Flex

Although you have created the ProductVO on the server, you now need to make it in ActionScript 3 for the server object to be mapped to. Right-click the product project, and select New ➤ ActionScript File. Name the file ProductVO, and click Finish to see the new file. Copy the following code into the file to finish creating the class:

```
package
{
    [Bindable]
    [RemoteClass(alias="ProductVO")]
    public class ProductVO
    {
        public var productId:int;
        public var name:String;
        public var description:String;
        public var image:String;
        public var category:String;
        public var price:Number;
        public var qtyInStock:int;

        public function ProductVO()
        {
        }
    }
}
```

The class is syntactically equivalent to the PHP of the same name. The variable names are the same and need to be in the same case to work properly. There are two unique ActionScript 3 meta tags in this class. The first is bindable, which makes the class work like the bindable tag that you used in the previous example. The second tag is the RemoteClass tag, which defines what the remote server will call when the object comes in. It is mandatory that this tag and the $_explicitType value in PHP are the same.

Creating the application

To consume the ProductVO value object, you will need to create a new Flex application in the product project. Create a new MXML application by right-clicking the product folder and selecting New ➤ MXML Application. Name the new file productClassmap as you did when you created productUpdate. mxml. Remember to right-click productClassmap in the Navigator panel and select Set as Default Application to run it as the default application. The following is the code for productClassmap.mxml. For this example, I have removed the method calls and buttons for updating, deleting, and adding new products. This should make the tutorial simpler. At the end of the section, I will discuss how to implement those features. Let's look at the fully implemented ProductClassmap.mxml file:

```
<?xml version="1.0" encoding="utf-8"?>
<mx:Application xmlns:mx="http://www.adobe.com/2006/mxml"➥
layout="absolute" backgroundColor="#FFFFFF"➥
creationComplete="myservice.getProductVO()">
  <mx:RemoteObject id="myservice" source="ProductService"➥
destination="amfphp" fault="faultHandler(event)" ➥
showBusyCursor="true">
    <mx:method name="getProductVO" result="getProductsHandler(event)" ➥
fault="faultHandler(event)" />
  </mx:RemoteObject>
  <mx:DataGrid x="10" y="10" width="381" id="products_dg"➥
dataProvider="{dp}" change="changeHandler(event)" height="350">
    <mx:columns>
      <mx:DataGridColumn headerText="Name" dataField="name"/>
      <mx:DataGridColumn headerText="Category" dataField="category"/>
      <mx:DataGridColumn headerText="Price" dataField="price"/>
      <mx:DataGridColumn headerText="Qty" dataField="qtyInStock"/>
    </mx:columns>
  </mx:DataGrid>

 <mx:Script>
  <![CDATA[
  import mx.rpc.events.ResultEvent;
  import mx.controls.Alert;
  import mx.rpc.events.FaultEvent;
  import ProductVO;
  import mx.collections.ArrayCollection;
  import mx.utils.ArrayUtil;

   [Bindable]
  private var dp:ArrayCollection;

   [Bindable]
  private var product:ProductVO;


  private function faultHandler(fault:FaultEvent):void
  {
    Alert.show(fault.fault.faultString, ➥
fault.fault.faultCode.toString());
  }
```

```
        private function getProductsHandler(event:ResultEvent):void {
          dp = new ArrayCollection( ArrayUtil.toArray(event.result) );
        }

        private function changeHandler(event:Event):void
         {
          product = ProductVO(DataGrid(event.target).selectedItem);
        }

    ]]>
    </mx:Script>
    <mx:Button x="10" y="368" label="Get Products"➥
click="myservice.getProductVo(); "/>
    <mx:Form x="399" y="10" width="329" height="320">
      <mx:FormHeading label="Product Updater"  width="99"/>
      <mx:FormItem label="Name">
        <mx:TextInput id="product_name" text="{product.name}"➥
width="200"/>
      </mx:FormItem>
      <mx:FormItem label="Category">
          <mx:TextInput id="product_category" text="{product.category}"➥
width="200"/>
      </mx:FormItem>
      <mx:FormItem label="Image">
        <mx:TextInput id="product_image" text="{product.image}"➥
width="200"/>
        </mx:FormItem>
      <mx:FormItem label="Price">
          <mx:TextInput id="product_price" text="{product.price}"➥
width="200"/>
      </mx:FormItem>
      <mx:FormItem label="Qty">
          <mx:TextInput id="product_qty" text="{product.qtyInStock}"➥
width="200"/>
      </mx:FormItem>
      <mx:FormItem label="Description">
          <mx:TextArea id="product_description"➥
text="{product.description}" width="200" height="121"/>
      </mx:FormItem>
    </mx:Form>
</mx:Application>
```

When you run the application, it should look similar to the following screenshot.

So, what has changed in order to implement class mapping? For one, you were able to get rid of a lot of code in order to get the data into the application. But let's go from top to bottom to see what has changed. For starters, the RemoteObject now connects to ProductService getProductVO when the application starts. The DataGrid tag has been updated to have a bound DataProvider called DP, which will be used to populate the DataGrid in the getProductsHandler method. Also, in the DataGrid columns definition, you have changed the names of the dataFields to match the naming convention of the ProductsVO.as class file rather than the table names on the server. Inside the Script section of code, you start with three new imports (ProductVO, ArrayCollection, and ArrayUtil), which will be used later to display the returned data. There are now two Bindable objects: the first is the dp DataProvider that was also bound to the DataGrid, and the second is product, which will be a single instance of ProductVO. The faultHandler is the same as before utilizing the alert function. GetProductsHandler has been changed to convert the PHP array into an ArrayCollection. In the previous example, you already had an ArrayCollection because of AMFPHP's built-in casting of result sets. Once the result set is converted into an ArrayCollection, you update the DataProvider for the DataGrid. This will make the DataGrid populated with data. The changeHandler for the DataGrid has a subtle update that completes the class mapping. This is the part where we take the selected element in the ArrayCollection and map it to a ProductVO in Flex. The variable product is now an instance of ProductVO. Because of binding product to the TextInput, the data is now displayed on the right side of the user interface.

It is also possible to use class mapping from the Flash client to the server. To do this, you can create an array of productVOs and send them to the server. Then on the server you cast the array as a ProductVO. Sending class mapping back to the server does not have as many benefits as server to client. In closing, you can add the addProduct, updateProduct, and removeProduct methods back into this example easily because all the code will be the same as the previous example.

In this section, you have learned the basics of how to easily get complex objects back into ActionScript. Class mapping can greatly improve the rate at which you can produce functional code, and it aids in forcing the separation of the presentation tier from the data provider. Next, I will cover how to fix issues when you inevitably run into them.

Debugging

The following steps should allow you to figure out any issue with your AMFPHP application. Corrupt PHP installations, service errors, and client-side ActionScript errors are the three main areas you should focus on when trying to debug an AMFPHP application. By narrowing your efforts systematically through each of these areas, you will be able to quickly resolve issues and not waste time tracking something that is not broken.

Narrowing it down

If you follow these steps and are still confused, use the AMFPHP mailing list or forums hosted on SourceForge (http://sourceforge.net/projects/amfphp/), and review the examples. If you are able to get to step 3 with a simple HelloWorld.php example, I can assure you that AMFPHP is working properly. When you post to the mailing list or forum, please let us know how far you got in this process before you ran into issues.

1. With a web browser, go to the remoting URL: http://localhost/amfphp/gateway.php.

   The response should be as follows:

   amfphp and this gateway are installed correctly. *etc.....*

   If this is not the case, it is a corrupt PHP installation.

2. With a web browser, go to the URL of the service that is failing: http://localhost/amfphp/services/HelloWorld.php. If there is blank response, the PHP interpreter was able to compile the class. If not, it is a service error.

3. Test the same service through the AMFPHP Service Browser. Pass the parameters to the method, and you should get the expected result. If not, look into the PHP class to see why it is not handling your input, because you have a service error.

4. Use a proxy client such as Charles (http://www.xk72.com/charles/) or Service Capture (http://kevinlangdon.com/serviceCapture/) so that you can see all the traffic between Flash Player and the services. Make sure the requested data is being sent as you anticipated and that the result set is being returned as anticipated. This shows that the inputs and outputs are correct!

If you get through these four steps but you are still having problems, your issues are in the ActionScript. Review your code to make sure your inputs and outputs are correct. This is a good time to hard-code the input to the service call and trace all data that is returned from the service. For example, rather than the following dynamic code:

```
private function updateProduct():void {
  var param:Object = getParams();
  myservice.updateProduct(param.PRODUCT_ID, param.NAME, ➡
param.CATEGORY,param.IMAGE, param.PRICE, ➡
param.DESCRIPTION, param.QTY);
}
```

use static text to make the call:

```
private function updateProduct():void {
  //var param:Object = getParams();
  myservice.updateProduct(22,"iPhone", "Apple", "coverflow.png", ➥
600, "Be cooler if it ran Flash Player 9", 0);
}
```

Dealing with a corrupt PHP installation

Your services and Flash/Flex will not work if the PHP installation is corrupt or missing modules. The PHP requirements for the installation of AMFPHP are a minimal PHP install. However, PHP installations and upgrades can be botched, which inevitably stops your services. If PHP is not working properly, you will most commonly receive a 500 error when it tries to connect to one of the services. This is because PHP had a premature end-of-script error.

Try the following steps to debug the installation:

1. Check to make sure you have a current version of PHP installed. As of AMFPHP version 2.0, there is no longer support for PHP 4.4.*, and PHP 4 was discontinued at the end of 2007, so you will need to upgrade to PHP 5 for all future releases.

2. Check your version and modules installed by uploading a PHP info page into your web server's document root. A PHP info page is simply a PHP file with the following code:

```
<?php
  phpinfo();
?>
```

Open a web browser, and go to the uploaded file. You should see a similar page as the following screenshot with the version of PHP at the top.

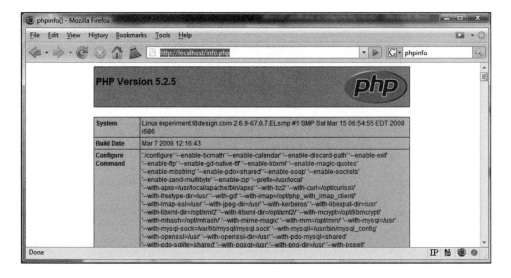

A PHP info page is critical for debugging the PHP installation and also your services. When you browse to your PHP info page, validate that it works. If it does, PHP is running but may not be configured right. If it does not, fix the PHP errors that the server throws.

3. The most common PHP installation errors are improper permissions set on folders/directories that PHP uses. AMFPHP requires the ability to create a session variable and access the tmp directory. To debug this issue, you will want to look at your PHP error logs for messages pertaining to why the script ended prematurely.

4. Use the HelloWorld example service to see whether AMFPHP is really not working or whether your services are not working. Refer to the installation process where you uploaded the HelloWorld.php file into the services directory, then went to the file in a web browser, and finally opened the service in AMFPHP's Service Browser. If you get the expected response from each test, you should start looking at your services.

Dealing with service errors

First accept that your code could have bugs under certain conditions. Old versions get uploaded, and services can stop working when administrators upgrade PHP without all the previous modules. With this in mind, it is critical to be able to isolate issues quickly.

1. It is best to debug PHP classes with PHP tools. Stop playing with AMFPHP, the browser, and your proxy tool, and get connected to the server!

2. When working on PHP, make sure you have error logging enabled. Add the ini_set values to the top of your class file if you do not have server-wide logging. Follow these steps to add logging to your PHP installation.

   Unless you have your own "dedicated" server, you are most probably sharing the same hardware with a few thousand other "virtual" domains. For this reason, it is all too natural that your hosting provider will deny you access to the systemwide php.ini file. Whatever value you enter there is going to affect all the virtual domains running on that machine! Production server administers usually have a similar view to changing php.ini values.

3. If you are not able to edit the php.ini file, you may still be able to get error logging working. In the gateway.php file located in your amfphp directory, add the following code right after the <?php at the start of the file:

```php
<?php
ini_set('display_errors','1');
ini_set('display_startup_errors','1');
error_reporting (E_ALL);
/* rest of file */
?>
```

4. You can then use a browser to go to the gateway.php page and in most cases see the error in the browser. If the gateway.php resolves and you still get errors when you call a service, you will need to use a debugging proxy in order to view the service errors. This may or may not work properly depending on your PHP installation because your administrator could disable your ability to do this.

   For more information on PHP debugging, walk through the great presentation at http://talks.php.net/show/debugging/.

5. Run the class in your services folder directly from a web browser by typing the entire path into the browser (http://localhost/amfphp/services/YourService.php). You should not receive any errors if the classes can be compiled by the PHP interpreter. If you do see errors, resolve them!

6. If you do not see any errors, you are dealing with a runtime error. Open the class file, and add an instantiation of the object to the bottom of the class in the same file. Call the method that failed in AMFPHP with the exact parameters you were trying to send to the remoting method from the AMFPHP Service Browser or your Flash application. In the following example, I instantiate the HelloWorld class and call the method say with the same data that you were sending from Flash in the examples. Adding the instantiation of the class will allow you to use a browser and go directly to the class URL to test the file. This does break AMFPHP, so make sure you remove it when you are done debugging.

```php
<?php
class HelloWorld
{
  public function say($sMessage)
  {
    $date = getdate();
    return 'You said: ' . $sMessage .' on '.$date[weekday];
  }
}
$myHelloWorld = new HelloWorld();
echo $myHelloWorld->say("AMFPHP is Easy");
?>
```

I highly recommend you use some kind of IDE that allows you to debug your PHP code quickly. I enjoy using the Eclipse PDT project (http://www.zend.com/en/community/pdt) because I can use one IDE for Flex, Flash, and PHP development. This toolkit has a debugger that makes the world a better place!

In the end, your services are just PHP classes. AMFPHP cannot help you write better PHP code. PHP best practices such as unit testing and development environments will only increase your chance of success.

Dealing with ActionScript errors

If you are looking at ActionScript, I assume you have made it through the first four steps of the "Narrowing it down" section and are still having issues. At this point, you are sure your services work fine in AMFPHP. ActionScript errors can be tricky to find. Little changes can create malformed data as inputs to the remote service such as removing bindings or a space before one of your dynamic variables. It is also easy to actually be receiving data from your service call but not handling it or displaying it. Your data can be returned in the ResultEvent, but you may have unknowingly nested the data. I always recommend having a dummy project that just has service calls to your remote methods handy for testing your services so that you are not lost in your own code. If you are using MVC, it is easy to place trace statements in your inputs and responses in your service locator.

1. Make sure you have a `NetStatusEvent` handler and a `SecurityErrorEvent` handler defined for the service you are calling. If you are getting errors, you can find them in these handlers.

2. Revert to a `HelloWorld` example. It is amazing how many people still use the wrong remoting URL or forget the `www` or `https`. Remember that your browser must be on the same URL as the `NetConnection` URL, or your service will not work.

3. Hard-code the input parameters that you used in testing your services into the service call. Also, trace the inputs at the service call to make sure they are what you meant to send. Are they the same? If this works, you need to track all your method calls and figure out why your inputs are corrupt.

4. Place a trace statement in the Responder method to make sure that it is being called when the client gets data back. If it is not, double-check that you have the right method name specified as the responder for your `NetConnection`.

5. If the method is being called, trace all the data that is being returned. Sometimes your service may not have been implemented in the way that you thought you would get the data back. Iterate through the returned object until you find the right data. You may need to update your return value in your service to return the data in the expected format.

Thanks . . .

In closing, I hope you are excited to utilize this great open source gateway to your PHP server framework for your future Flash Player–based applications. AMFPHP without question is one of the most efficient ways to send data to and from the server. I hope that these examples show that it is quick and easy from a developer perspective. Like all technologies and like most open source projects, AMFPHP is always being updated for additional functionality and efficiencies. I encourage you to visit `http://www.amfphp.net` and get involved in the mailing lists and forums available for support. If you are like me and fall in love with this framework, I encourage you to download the source code and start aiding this great community.

The AMFPHP project would not have been possible without the contributions of the following people:

- Alessandro Crugnola (documentation)
- Christophe Herreman (`MethodTable` class)
- John Cowen (documentation and programming on 0.9b)
- Justin Watkins (most of the programming on 1.0)
- Patrick Mineault (programming and documentation on 1.0)
- Thomas Craigen (beta testing and documentation on 0.9b & 1)
- Wade Arnold (programming and documentation on 2.0)
- Wolfgang Hamann (original AMF reverse engineering)

Chapter 8

WORKING WITH SWX: THE NATIVE DATA FORMAT FOR THE FLASH PLATFORM

by R. Jon MacDonald

SWX is the native data format for Flash. Data is wrapped inside a SWF shell (Figure 8-1), or the most native possible format on the Flash Platform. The SWF is then interpreted by Flash Player just like a SWF is compiled using the Flash IDE. The SWX format is a subset of the SWF format, just like JSON is a subset of JavaScript.

Figure 8-1. Datum, the SWX mascot/logo. He lives in a SWF shell.

For Flash developers, this means you can use Flash's loadMovie() method to load SWX data files, and that data is ready to use the moment it has loaded. There is no need to deserialize or massage the data in any way before using it, unlike XML where developers must parse using firstChild, lastChild, and so on, and then convert the text returned into native Flash objects. Instead, with SWX the data is stored in native Flash objects such as a String, a Number, or a generic object.

SWX is pronounced "swix."

The SWX philosophy: systemwide simplicity

A system is only as simple as its most complicated part. It's not enough to just simplify individual components and processes; you must also simplify the relationships and interactions between components and subprocesses. The philosophy of systemwide simplicity takes a wider approach to simplicity that involves understanding and supporting the entire user experience.

It is thus SWX's aim to make it as easy as humanly possible for Flash developers to start creating data-driven Flash applications from the moment they arrive on the SWX home page to the moment they first get data into Flash using SWX Remote Procedure Call (RPC).

In short, SWX is designed to provide Flash developers with a simple and enjoyable experience when building data-driven applications in Flash. The key words here are *simple*, *enjoyable*, and *experience*.

Simple

SWX is as simple as possible but no simpler. If something can be made simpler without sacrificing essential core functionality, it will be made simpler.

Enjoyable

The SWX tools aim to put a smile on your face, do the heavy lifting, provide a seamless experience, and be aesthetically pleasing so you'll be inspired to do the same in your applications.

Experience

These core tenets apply to the whole experience of SWX, not just the API or code base. That includes the website, documentation, and tools. The focus is to make it as easy as possible for you to get up and running with SWX from the moment you first visit the SWX website. This is called **systemwide simplicity**.

A common vocabulary

Before jumping into why the Flash community needs another data format (after all, there are already XML, AMF, and others), I'll define a common vocabulary for use throughout the rest of this chapter (see Table 8-1).

Table 8-1. Definitions for a Common Vocabulary

Term	Definition
SWX	Native data format for Flash. This is a subset of the SWF format. SWX SWFs are regular AVM 1* SWF files that are used to store data only.
SWX RPC	RPC protocol encoded in SWX format. The SWX RPC allows you to call methods on server-side classes and get the results returned in SWX format.

Term	Definition
SWX PHP	SWX RPC implementation in PHP. SWX PHP is the most common implementation of SWX RPC, but there are other implementations in various stages of development by the SWX community (Python, Ruby, J2EE, .NET, and so on). For the purposes of this chapter, all examples will be shown and discussed using SWX PHP.
SWX Tools	The SWX Service Explorer and SWX Data Analyzer. These tools come bundled with SWX PHP and will work with any future implementations of SWX RPC.
SWX AS	A high-level ActionScript library that handles the client-side queuing and execution of SWX RPC calls. Developers do not have to use the ActionScript library to work with SWX RPC because SWX is native to Flash, but the library does provide developers with useful functionality such as cross-domain access, queuing of data calls, and more.
SWX APIs	APIs for Flickr, Twitter, and so on. The SWX APIs are as important as the SWX data format and the SWX RPC, because they provide Flash developers with a very easy way to create mashups. Using the public SWX RPC gateway at http://swxformat.org, developers can use these APIs with ActionScript alone (no server-side programming is necessary).
Public SWX RPC gateway	Open SWX RPC endpoint. The public SWX RPC gateway is available for use at http://swxformat.org/php/swx.php, and all of the available services can be viewed using the SWX Service Explorer (http://swxformat.org/php/explorer/). You can use the public SWX APIs from this gateway in your own applications without having to write any server-side code whatsoever.

* ActionScript virtual machine, version 1 (AVM 1), is the code interpretation engine within Flash Player, which supports ActionScript versions 1 and 2. AVM 2 is found in Flash Player 9 and later and is required to interpret ActionScript 3 and later.

Why do you need a new data format?

When SWX was first released, there was a good amount of discussion about why a developer would need SWX. With all the other options for getting data into Flash, why should you use SWX? Aral Balkan, the founding developer of SWX, answered this on the SWX website by making the following points:

- Existing formats are non-native, are complicated, and require parsing and/or writing plumbing code such as XML (firstChild, lastChild), variable-encoded strings (LoadVars, loadVariables), Flash Remoting, and so on.

- SWX files have low processor overhead when parsed by Flash Player, because they are native SWF bytecode.

- SWX RPC is the only RPC solution for Flash Lite 2.0 and 2.1 (and thus for mobile Flash applications). Flash Remoting, such as AMFPHP, does not work with Flash Lite.

- Most important, SWX, being native, has inherent advantages such as cross-platform data exchange (via allowDomain support for SWF files), simplicity (no ActionScript library is necessary to use it, although there is a high-level library if you want to use it), and so on.

> *Aral continues:*
>
> *It's my first belief that every platform can benefit from a native data format that does not require parsing. The main advantage of SWX over other data formats and of SWX RPC over other RPC solutions is ease of use. I hope that this ease of use will spur a wealth of development of data-driven applications and mashups on the Flash Platform by developers who may traditionally have shied away from creating such applications because it was just too darn hard to do so.*

Supported platforms and technologies

Developers can make the server-side call to create (and the ActionScript call to retrieve data from) SWX SWF files with any version of Flash (6+), because they are simply SWF files.

> *If developing with ActionScript 3 for Flash Player 9 and AVM 2 (see the Table 8-1 footnote), you cannot simply load the SWF returned from SWX, because AVM 1 and AVM 2 SWF files cannot see within each other to read the encapsulated data. Until an update is developed for SWX by the open source community, you can load the data returned from SWX only into a SWF published for ActionScript 2.0/AVM 1.*

SWX PHP, the most popular current SWX RPC implementation, creates SWX files that are compatible with Flash Player 6+ and Flash Lite 2.0/2.1/3.0. Currently, SWX PHP does not support Flash 9/AVM 2, but it will eventually do so.

SWX AS, the SWX ActionScript 2.0 library, compiles on Flash 6+ and with MTASC. Future versions of SWX AS will also be developed in ActionScript 3, requiring Flash CS3 or Flex 2+ to compile.

Currently, you can use SWX to create applications that run on mobile phones (Flash Lite 2.0/2.1/3.0), the Nintendo Wii, Sony PlayStation 3, and devices such as the Nokia N800 Internet tablet and the Chumby.

You can also wrap SWX-based applications to create desktop versions using Adobe AIR by loading your completed AVM 1 SWF application into a Flash 9/AVM 2 SWF via the Loader class and loading the AVM 1 SWF just like any other external asset such as a JPG, PNG, or GIF. See `http://livedocs.adobe.com/flex/3/langref/flash/display/Loader.html` for more information.

How simple is SWX?

SWX is so simple that the instructions for getting data from SWX into Flash easily fit onto a Moo MiniCard (`http://moo.com/products/minicards.php`; see Figure 8-2).

Figure 8-2. Two SWX Moo MiniCards (both front and back views stacked on top of one another)

To get a list of the most recent 100 photos from Flickr into Flash, do the following:

1. Open the SWX Data Analyzer at `http://swxformat.org/php/analyzer/`.

2. In Flash, create a new FLA, and create a MovieClip on the stage. Give it an instance name of loader.

3. Write the following code on the main timeline frame that the loader MovieClip is on:

```
loader.serviceClass = "Flickr";
loader.method = "swxPhotosGetRecent";
loader.debug = true;
loader.loadMovie("http://swxformat.org/php/swx.php", "GET");
```

That's it! Test your movie and look in the SWX Data Analyzer to see the results being loaded into Flash from Flickr. That is how simple SWX is.

If you want to display the results from within Flash, create a long, single-line dynamic text field on the stage, and give it the instance name status. Add the following code to the timeline:

```
function onEnterFrame()
{
    status.text = loader.result.photo[0].src;
}
```

Initially, the status text field will display undefined until the data is loaded, and then it will display the URL of the first photo from the list of recent photos that is loaded from Flickr. Notice how you can access the results as native Flash objects the moment they are loaded. No deserialization or massaging of the data is necessary!

> *The Flash IDE will give you a security sandbox warning when you run the previous example, but the application will run correctly. This warning occurs because you are running the SWF in the Flash IDE. If you put the SWF file on the same domain as the SWX gateway, it will also work without requiring any further code. However, if you want to use the public SWX gateway and deploy your Flash applications to your own server, you must either manually call System.security.allowDomain or use the recommended fix, the SWX ActionScript library, as explained in the next section, "Diving deeper: SWX AS, SWX Service Explorer, SWX Data Analyzer."*

This example used the SWX public gateway (http://swxformat.org/php/swx.php), which you are welcome to use in your own applications to create mashups with the supported APIs (Flickr, Twitter, and more) without having to host or write any back-end code yourself.

Diving deeper: SWX AS, SWX Service Explorer, SWX Data Analyzer

As you just saw, SWX can be as simple as six lines of code. However, there is a more powerful and developer-friendly way to work with SWX: SWX AS, which is the ActionScript API.

SWX AS

The SWX AS library provides developers with useful functionality, such as cross-domain access, queuing of data calls, fault and timeout handlers, and more.

You can download the SWX AS package from the SWX website, and it is included with all SWX bundles, except for the deployment bundle (which includes only the server-side files necessary to run SWX PHP).

There are two additional tools provided with SWX on both a custom or local deployment and on the publicly hosted version located at http://www.swxformat.org that help to increase the simplicity of testing and debugging your applications: the SWX Service Explorer and the SWX Data Analyzer.

SWX Service Explorer

With the SWX Service Explorer, you can view and test your service classes without having to create your own Flash client. It does this by providing you with the means to call specific methods of your services and then by consuming the SWF returned and allowing you to inspect the data contained within that SWF.

In a custom or local deployment, you can find the SWX Service Explorer by clicking the thumbnail link on the SWX Start Page, which in most normal installations can be found at `http://localhost:8888/start.php`. You can also view the public installation of the Service Explorer available at `http://swxformat.org/php/explorer/`.

Once you load the Service Explorer, you will see that several PHP service classes are listed (see Figure 8-3). SWX PHP ships with several APIs preinstalled, including Flickr, Twitter, and many others. These APIs are also available for usage on the public gateway on the SWX website, making it easy to consume data from these services and create mashups.

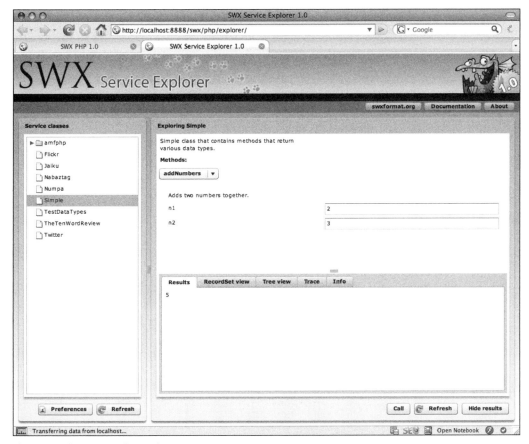

Figure 8-3. The SWX Service Explorer

SWX Data Analyzer

The SWX Data Analyzer (see Figure 8-4) is a debugging tool that shows you the SWX data that arrives inside your Flash movie. I'll discuss the Data Analyzer in more detail in the following examples.

In a custom or local deployment, you can find the SWX Data Analyzer by clicking the thumbnail link on the SWX Start Page, which in most normal installations can be found at http://localhost:8888/start.php. You can also view the public installation of the Data Analyzer available at http://swxformat.org/php/analyzer/.

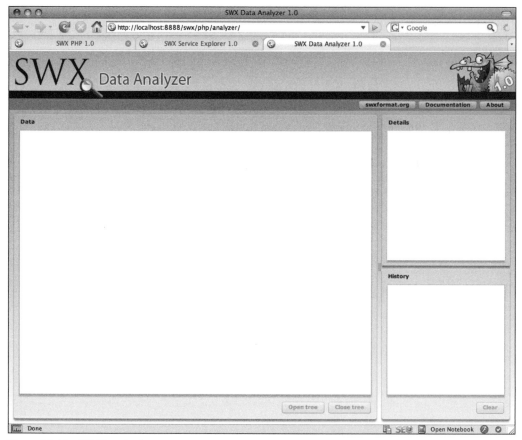

Figure 8-4. The SWX Data Analyzer

Installing SWX on your server

Before installing SWX PHP, you will need to have a web server running PHP on the machine on which you are installing it. SWX PHP is written in pure PHP, does not require any extensions, and runs under both PHP 4 and PHP 5. As such, it runs without problems on shared hosting accounts.

> *For the purposes of this chapter, we'll focus on SWX PHP. However, there are several other implementations of the SWX RPC gateway in various stages of development for languages such as Python, Ruby, J2EE, .NET, and more. Check the SWX website (http://www.swxformat.org) for more information.*

SWX PHP is a SWX RPC implementation in PHP. SWX PHP has a SWX RPC endpoint (called the **gateway**) and an assembler that creates and returns SWX files. Your service classes contain business logic only, meaning the assembly of the SWF that contains your data is handled for you. SWX PHP comes with service classes (APIs) for Flickr, Twitter, Ten Word Review, Nabaztag, and more, preinstalled as examples and/or ready-to-use services.

SWX PHP uses AMFPHP as a library, and as such, you can also utilize SWX PHP services via Flash Remoting, JSON, and XML-RPC. This means that you are not locked into using the SWX RPC, and you can switch easily between these various technologies if you want at any time.

SWX PHP comes with a plain-vanilla installer, so you can unzip it into your web folder on the server and be up and running. This is perfect for use on a hosted web server. However, if you want to run SWX locally and you do not have a web server and PHP installed, the following are some suggestions for getting a full-blown local web server with PHP installed as one package.

Mac OS X

If you're on a Mac running OS X, download and install the SWX PHP MAMP bundle available at http://swxformat.org/download. This will have you up and running with everything you need, including SWX.

Windows

Install WAMP, install XAMMP, or manually install a web server and PHP. WAMP is available at http://www.wampserver.com/en/. XAMMP is available at http://www.apachefriends.org/en/xampp.html.

Linux

Install XAMMP, or manually install a web server and PHP. XAMMP is available at http://www.apachefriends.org/en/xampp.html.

All platforms

Once you have installed a web server and PHP, download SWX PHP from http://swxformat.org/download, and unzip it into the web root of your server. Start your web server, and hit the web root in your browser to access the SWX PHP Start Page (see Figure 8-5).

> With the release of Flash Player 9.0.124, Adobe implemented additional security limitations, and as such, a properly configured crossdomain.xml file is required to allow full access to SWX. You can find more information, along with a link to an example crossdomain.xml file, at http://www.jonnymac.com/blog/2008/04/08/flash-player-90124-released-with-security-updates/.

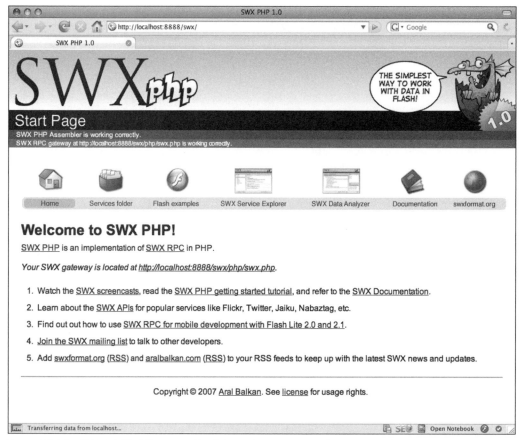

Figure 8-5. The SWX PHP Start Page provides links to documentation, the Service Explorer, and the Data Analyzer, and it runs a few tests to ensure your SWX RPC gateway is running correctly.

Writing your first custom service

Now that you have SWX PHP installed, let's create a simple custom service.

SWX is most useful when connected to data (either a database or an API), but for this example I'll show how to build a simple but complete web application with SWX PHP. You'll create both the client side and the server side of the application, and by the end of the following sections, you should have a clear conceptual understanding of how SWX PHP works.

The application you're building is a simple calculator that uses a server-side method to add two numbers together.

Creating the calculator service class in PHP

To start, you'll create a PHP service class. In SWX you place service classes in the php/services folder. Those classes are then available for testing with the SWX Service Explorer, as discussed earlier.

So, create a new file using your text editor of choice under php/services/, and call it Calculator. php. Add the following code to Calculator.php, and save the file:

```php
<?php
class Calculator
    {
        function addNumbers($n1, $n2)
        {
            return $n1 + $n2;
        }
    }
?>
```

This is a very simple server-side service class that has a single method called addNumbers(). This method takes two numbers as arguments and returns their sum.

> *Can you use a folder other than* /php/services *to hold your SWX PHP service classes?*
>
> *You sure can. All you need to do is change a setting in the SWX configuration file (swx_config.php). You can find the file in the* php *folder. In it, just change the* $servicesPath *variable to point to where your services are, relative to the SWX gateway.*

At this point, it would be nice if you could test the server-side method you just created without having to create a Flash client. The SWX Service Explorer lets you do just that.

Testing the calculator service with the SWX Service Explorer

Return to the SWX Service Explorer (or open it if you did not earlier), and you will see the Calculator class you just created.

Click it, and you will see the addNumbers() method. Enter two numbers in the $n1 and $n2 fields, and click the call button to test the method. You should then see the sum returned in the results area.

Consuming your calculator service in Flash

You've verified that your server-side service method is working correctly by using the SWX Service Explorer. Now let's call this method from Flash using SWX AS, the ActionScript API:

1. Open Flash, and create a new FLA (ActionScript 2). You can set the publish setting to Flash 7 or 8. Save your FLA in the flash/ folder (the one that has the org and com folders) before continuing. Or, add that folder to your ActionScript classpath in the Flash IDE and save your FLA anywhere.

207

2. On frame 1 of the new FLA, create a single-line dynamic text field instance, and give it the instance name status.

3. Create a new layer, and call it actions. On the actions layer, add the following code, being sure to update the gateway URL to match your own server settings:

```
import org.swxformat.SWX;

var swx:SWX = new SWX();
swx.gateway = "http://localhost:8888/php/swx.php";
swx.encoding = "GET";
swx.debug = true;

var callParameters:Object =
{
    serviceClass: "Calculator",
    method: "addNumbers",
    args: [35, 7],
    result: [this, resultHandler]
}

swx.call(callParameters);

function resultHandler(event:Object)
{
    status.text = event.result;
}
```

That's all the code you need to call the addNumbers method on the Calculator service class in PHP and pass it the numbers 35 and 7 as arguments. The swx.call() method calls the SWX gateway and passes to it any of the properties you set in your callParameters object. In this case, since you are sending a small number of arguments, you use the GET HTTP encoding method. You could just as easily have used POST by changing the encoding property to POST instead of GET.

Instead of putting call-related parameters directly into a MovieClip like you did with the Moo MiniCard example previously (and thus having to poll for the data using onEnterFrame()), you created a callParameters object and specified the serviceClass, method, and args properties.

Using SWX AS also allows you to specify **handlers**, which are functions that are called when certain actions occur with SWX, such as when data is returned or when the call times out.

Using a result handler

As you did previously, you can specify a result handler that will get called once the data has loaded. The result handler is set in the result property of the callParameters object, and it receives an event object as an argument. That event object has a result property that points to the loaded data.

Using a timeout handler

The SWX ActionScript library also provides an additional event listener: a timeout handler for your SWX instance to handle calls that take too long to return a result.

To set a timeout handler, modify your code to match the following:

```
import org.swxformat.SWX;

var swx:SWX = new SWX();
swx.gateway = "http://localhost:8888/php/swx.php";
swx.encoding = "GET";
swx.debug = true;
swx.timeout = 2;  // in seconds

var callParameters:Object =
{
    serviceClass: "Calculator",
    method: "addNumbers",
    args: [35, 7],
    result: [this, resultHandler],
    timeout: [this, timeoutHandler]
}

swx.call(callParameters);

function resultHandler(event:Object)
{
    status.text = event.result;
}

function timeoutHandler(event:Object)
{
    status.text = "Call timed out!";
}
```

The default timeout duration is 30 seconds, but you can override that, as shown earlier, where it's set to two seconds.

To make the call actually time out, modify the Calculator class in PHP too to make it sleep for ten seconds before returning the result. The Calculator class should now read as follows:

```
<?php
class Calculator
{
    function addNumbers($n1, $n2)
    {
        sleep(10); //make the call time out
        return $n1 + $n2;
    }
}
?>
```

Now test your Flash movie, and after two seconds, you should see the SWX call time out. Timed-out calls are canceled and will not trigger the result handler at any point in the future.

Using a fault handler

The SWX ActionScript library also provides one last event listener: a fault handler for handling errors during SWX RPC calls. To test the fault handler, modify your code to match the following:

```
import org.swxformat.SWX;

var swx:SWX = new SWX();
swx.gateway = "http://localhost:8888/php/swx.php";
swx.encoding = "GET";
swx.debug = true;
swx.timeout = 2;   // in seconds

var callParameters:Object =
{
    serviceClass: "Calculator",
    method: "addNumbers",
    args: [35, 7],
    result: [this, resultHandler],
    timeout: [this, timeoutHandler],
    fault: [this, faultHandler]
}

swx.call(callParameters);

function resultHandler(event:Object)
{
    status.text = event.result;
}

function timeoutHandler(event:Object)
{
    status.text = "Call timed out!";
}

function faultHandler(event:Object)
{
    status.text=event.fault.message;
}
```

You also need to modify your service so that it generates an error:

```
<?php
class Calculator
{
    function addNumbers($n1, $n2)
    {
        return $n3; //$n3 does not exist
    }
}
?>
```

Test your FLA, and you should get an error similar to the following in the status text field in Flash:

```
Error 8: Undefined variable: ➡
n3 in /htdocs/swx/php/services/Calculator.php, line 6
```

The fault handler also returns API-specific fault codes (for example, Flickr API error codes) back to Flash should they occur, making this useful for all APIs as well as custom classes.

At this point, you should have a clear understanding of how SWX PHP and the SWX ActionScript API work. In addition, you have all the knowledge you need to test and deploy your SWX applications.

With that in mind, let's take a moment to see what SWX is capable of when connected to a custom content management system (CMS) and when utilizing several custom service classes.

Case study: p.i.n.k. Spirits

SWX is capable of much more than just receiving an answer to a simple math equation as you did in the previous section. When deployed on your own server and combined with custom service classes, it can be used to develop a high-profile consumer site, such as the one JonnyMac Design (http://www.jonnymac.com) recently built for p.i.n.k. Spirits (see Figure 8-6).

Figure 8-6. The p.i.n.k. Spirits home page

The p.i.n.k. Spirits website (http://www.pinkspirits.com) uses a total of eight custom service classes, comprising forty-four custom methods.

Those methods each handle a specific task such as retrieving images and text for Flash to display throughout the site (see Figure 8-7) and interacting with Constant Contact (an e-mail newsletter service) to allow users to sign up for the p.i.n.k. Spirits newsletter (for more details or to download the open source Constant Contact service API, visit http://swxformat.org/159).

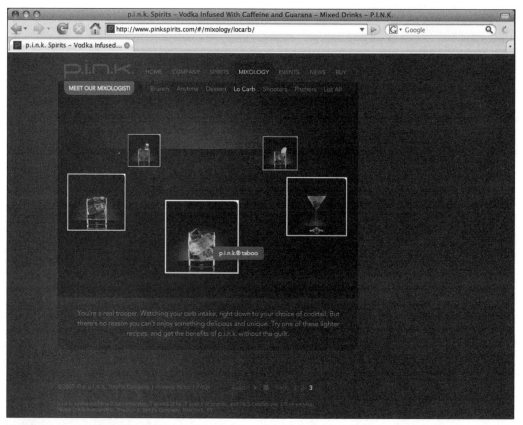

Figure 8-7. The p.i.n.k. Spirits mixology section, showing a few of the available drink recipes available to site visitors

However, the functionality I'd like to focus on is the product locator (see Figure 8-8), which you can view on the p.i.n.k. Spirits site at http://www.pinkspirits.com/#/buy/locate/. In the next section, I'll show how to use the same custom service written for the website and consume it in a Flash Lite application for mobile deployment.

So, I'll pause here so you can take a moment to review the p.i.n.k. Spirits site, especially the "find p.i.n.k." section at http://www.pinkspirits.com/#/buy/locate/. Once you have an understanding of how the product locator works from a user standpoint, continue to the next section where I'll discuss the specifics of the service and show how to create the Flash Lite application.

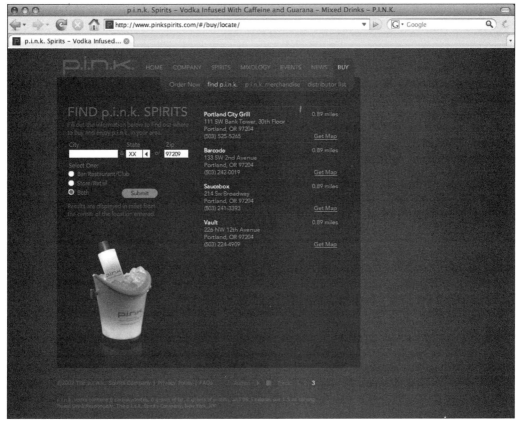

Figure 8-8. The p.i.n.k. Spirits product locator, where site visitors can search by city/state or ZIP code for restaurants/bars and retailers offering p.i.n.k. Spirits products

Project: utilizing a custom service in Flash Lite

While SWX makes developing and consuming custom back-ends for full Flash websites much easier and simpler to interface with, SWX really shines when used to develop for mobile phones and devices (see "Supported platforms and technologies" in this chapter for more information).

Goal: a product locator

In this section, I'll walk you through building a Flash Lite 3.0 application that will allow users to find the nearest restaurants/bars and retail locations selling the p.i.n.k. Sprits line of liquors using their Flash Lite–supported mobile phones.

Just like on the p.i.n.k. Spirits website in the earlier case study, the user will be able to enter a city and state or U.S. ZIP code, and the service will return the closest locations selling p.i.n.k. Spirits to the city/state or ZIP code entered. Note that this service will function only with U.S. cities, states, and ZIP codes.

213

The PHP service class

Because this chapter is focusing on SWX and not PHP and because the logic and database to set up a product locator is beyond the scope for this book, you won't be writing the necessary PHP service class. Instead, you will utilize the one already written that is currently being used on the p.i.n.k. Sprits website for the "find p.i.n.k." section. As is the case with all SWX service classes (APIs), the same service can be used for deployments of both Flash and Flash Lite projects.

The specific service class you will be using is entitled PinkBuy, and it contains a method called SearchLocations. SearchLocations handles all the logic of searching the ZIP code and p.i.n.k. Spirits locations database. It returns a native Array of objects for each location found matching the user entry, and it accepts four arguments, as shown in Table 8-2.

Table 8-2. Arguments Accepted by SearchLocations

Argument	Description
city	Data type: String. Optional. The city in which the user wants to locate the product. If a city argument is provided, a state argument must also be provided. If a city and state are provided, the zip argument can be left as an empty string.
state	Data type: String. Optional. The state in which the user wants to locate the product. If a state argument is provided, a city argument must also be provided. If a city and state are provided, the zip argument can be left as an empty string.
zip	Data type: Number. Optional. The five-digit U.S. ZIP code in which the user wants to locate the product. If a zip argument is provided, the city and state arguments can be left as empty strings.
type	Data type: String. Required. A String representing on-site or off-site consumption sales (in other words, a bar vs. a grocery store). Valid arguments are ON, OFF, and ON,OFF.

Downloading the SWX ActionScript library

The first step in building the Flash Lite application is to download the SWX ActionScript library, SWX AS. Visit http://www.swxformat.org/download, and click the Download SWX ActionScript Library link. Once you have downloaded the file, unzip and note the location of the new folder containing the necessary ActionScript libraries. For simplicity, this is also where you will save your Flash source file, or FLA.

Setting up the Flash Lite application FLA

To set up the Flash Lite application FLA, follow these steps:

1. Open Flash CS3 and create a new file, choosing Flash File (Mobile) as the type from the New Document window. This launches the Adobe Device Central window where you can choose the publish settings for your application.

2. For Player Version, choose Flash Lite 3.0; also set ActionScript Version to ActionScript 2.0. In the bottom of the Adobe Device Central window, check the Custom Size for All Selected Devices box (see Figure 8-9). You can leave the stage size set to the default of 176✕208, an appropriate safe area for viewing on the widest range of Flash Lite mobile phones.

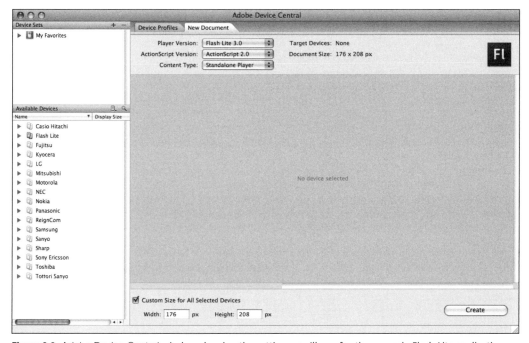

Figure 8-9. Adobe Device Central window showing the settings you'll use for the example Flash Lite application

3. Click Create, and you will be taken back to Flash CS3 with the stage all set up and ready to begin creating your application.

4. Save your FLA file into the same folder as the SWX ActionScript library files, which you previously noted. To avoid issues with the FLA finding the SWX ActionScript library files, be sure that the org folder is in the same folder as your FLA. If you want to store your FLA in a separate directory, you can alternatively add the folder containing the SWX ActionScript library to your FLA's classpath.

Establishing an initial service connection

To establish an initial service connection, follow these steps:

1. Create a second layer in your timeline, and name it actions. Lock the actions layer so it can contain code only. Label the other layer content. The content layer is where you'll put all your assets.

2. Create two keyframes on each layer. Frame 1 will be your search state; frame 2 will be your results state.

3. On the content layer of frame 1, create a dynamic text field across the width of the stage, and give it an instance name of status_txt. You'll use this text field to test your initial connection to your service on the p.i.n.k. Spirits web server.

4. On frame 1 of the actions layer, enter the following code.

First, import the necessary SWX ActionScript library and tell Flash to stop() on the current state until you tell it to go forward:

```
import org.swxformat.SWX;
stop();
```

Next, create an instance of the SWX ActionScript library and then set some of its properties, including the gateway URL, encoding type, and number of seconds to wait before timing out. Because you will not be sending large amounts of data to the service, GET encoding works well. The timeout should be set to 5 seconds, knowing that you are building a mobile application and the connection speeds will be slower than in the normal Flash Player.

```
var swx:SWX = new SWX();
swx.gateway = "http://www.pinkspirits.com/swx/php/swx.php";
swx.encoding = "GET";
swx.timeout = 5; // in seconds
```

Then, set up the callParameters object, which contains all the information you want to send to your service, as well as letting SWX know which additional options you want to use. As mentioned earlier, the service class you will be using is called PinkBuy, and the method you will be using is SearchLocations.

```
var callParameters:Object =
{
    serviceClass: "PinkBuy",
    method: "SearchLocations",
    args: ['','',97209,'ON,OFF'],
    result: [this, resultHandler],
    timeout: [this, timeoutHandler],
    fault: [this, faultHandler]
}
```

I have already discussed the arguments the SearchLocations method accepts (see Table 8-2). To test the initial connection to the SWX service class, you will hard-code the arguments. In this case, you are leaving the city and state arguments as empty strings, entering a known valid number for the zip argument, and setting ON,OFF as the type. For ease of use on mobile devices, you will not offer users a choice for type and will always set the type to the string ON,OFF.

You also set the result, timeout, and fault event handlers, assigning them a function to call when/if the events should occur.

Since you chose to define the result, timeout, and fault event handler options in the callParameters object, you must also define the functions that will be called when the events occur:

```
function resultHandler(event:Object)
{
    status_txt.text = event.result[0].account;
}

function timeoutHandler(event:Object)
{
    status_txt.text = "Call timed out!";
}

function faultHandler(event:Object)
{
    status_txt.text = event.fault.message;
}
```

In the resultHandler, you will set the status_txt text field to display the first result from the returned object. In the timeoutHandler, you will set status_txt to display a message letting you know the call has timed out. In the faultHandler, you will set status_txt to display the error message returned by SWX.

Once everything is set up for the call, you can make the call to the SWX service using the call() method of the SWX instance. The call() method accepts one parameter, the callParameters object:

```
swx.call(callParameters);
```

At this point, you are ready to test your service. Select Control ➤ Test Movie. The Adobe Device Central window will launch, and you will see the name of the first location returned from the SWX service for the ZIP code entered (97209 for Portland, Oregon), as shown in Figure 8-10.

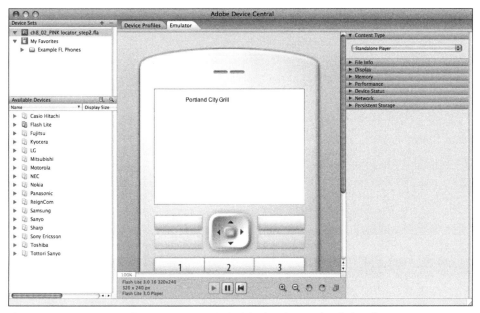

Figure 8-10. Adobe Device Central window with the initial testing results displayed

Notice how you did not have to do any complex parsing to retrieve your data? You simply needed to know what the property name of the returned object was that you wanted to access. No complex firstChild.node, lastChild.node XML parsing—the data was available in a native data format (in this case, an object) immediately after it was loaded into the Flash Lite application.

The PinkLocation method of the PinkBuy service returns several pieces of information about each location found matching the search parameters. Each of these pieces of information is stored as a property of an object, with each result being contained with its own object. Table 8-3 shows all the properties contained within each returned result object.

Table 8-3. Properties Included in Each Result Object Returned by PinkBuy.PinkLocation()

Property	Description
account	The name of the location, such as "Portland City Grill"
address	The physical street address of the location
city	The U.S. city of the location
state	The U.S. state of the location
zip	The five-digit U.S. ZIP code of the location
phone	The ten-digit phone number of the location
distance	The distance, in miles, from the center of the city/state or ZIP code entered to the location
type	Either ON or OFF, denoting whether on-site or off-site consumption sales are provided

Now that you have established an initial connection to your service, let's continue by building the assets you will need for the two states of the application, search and results.

Creating assets for search and results states

To create assets for search and results states, follow these steps:

1. Begin by creating three single-line input text fields with the border set to show around the text on the content layer of frame 1. To save on file size, you can use _sans as the font face. Arrange the text fields so they are stacked vertically on top of one another, adding a static text header above each one. The static text headers should read City, and State, and or ZIP.

2. For the top text field, assign it an instance name of city_txt, and set the maximum characters limit to 30. For the middle text field, assign it an instance name of state_txt, and allow only two maximum characters. Assign the bottom text field an instance name of zip_txt, and set the maximum characters limit to 5.

3. Next, you need to create a way for the user to submit the data to the service. Create a rectangle with rounded corners below the text fields. Select it, and hit F8 to create a MovieClip of the shape. Give the new MovieClip an instance name of submit_mc, and then double-click it to open it. Once inside the MovieClip, add a static text field over the rounded rectangle with the word *Submit*. Now double-click any unoccupied space on the stage to return to the main timeline.

At this point, frame 1 of your stage should look similar to Figure 8-11.

Figure 8-11. The Adobe Flash stage showing the application layout for the search state

You now have the initial state, or search state, completed. Click frame 2 of the content layer in the main timeline. On this frame, you'll build your results state.

4. Create two dynamic text fields on the stage, stacked on top of one another vertically. Assign an instance name of numResults_txt to the top text field, and set it to be a single line, with center text alignment. Again, to save file size, set the font face to _sans. You will use this text field to display the total number of results returned.

5. The bottom text field is where you will display the results returned from the SWX service class. Set this bottom text field to have an instance name of results_txt, to be multiline, to be HTML enabled, and to have left text alignment. Set the font face to _sans. You will want to resize the text field to have ample room to display about six or so lines of text while leaving enough room at the bottom of the stage for three buttons: Prev, New Search, and Next.

6. Below the bottom text field, add three new MovieClips similar to the submit_mc MovieClip you previously created for the search state. These three MovieClips should contain, from left to right, a static text field with the text Prev, New Search, and Next and should be lined up horizontally across the bottom of the stage. Assign instance names to the MovieClips—previous_mc, newSearch_mc, and next_mc—according to the text labels within them. These buttons will allow users to navigate between each of the results received from the PinkBuy service.

Frame 2 of your FLA should now look similar to Figure 8-12.

Figure 8-12. The Adobe Flash stage showing the application layout for the results state

Adding the functionality

Now that you have all your assets in place, you can begin adding the functionality to your application. Begin by selecting the actions layer of frame 1. To utilize the user input, you need to make some modifications to the ActionScript on this frame:

```
import org.swxformat.SWX;
stop();
var swx:SWX = new SWX();
swx.gateway = "http://www.pinkspirits.com/swx/php/swx.php";
swx.encoding = "GET";
swx.timeout = 5; // in seconds
```

You can leave all the initial SWX instance code as is, but you need to move the callParameters object, so delete it for now. In its place, add the following:

```
global.errorMsg = false;
global.SWXresults = "";
city_txt.text = "";
state_txt.text = "";
zip_txt.text = "";
```

Next, you are setting a couple of global variables to hold whether an error was returned and the results returned from SWX. You also clear the text fields in the event you are returning from the results state.

```
function resultHandler(event:Object)
{
    global.SWXresults = event.result;
    nextFrame();
}

function timeoutHandler(event:Object)
{
    global.errorMsg = true;
    nextFrame();
}
```

```
function faultHandler(event:Object)
{
    global.errorMsg = true;
    nextFrame();
}
```

The event handlers get a slight functionality change. They now assign values to your global variables and then move on to the results state so you can display any results or error messages.

```
submit_mc.onPress = function()

{
    swx.cancelAllCalls();

    var callParameters:Object =
    {
        serviceClass: "PinkBuy",
        method: "SearchLocations",
        args: [city_txt.text, state_txt.text, zip_txt.text,"ON,OFF"],
        result: [this, resultHandler],
        timeout: [this, timeoutHandler],
        fault: [this, faultHandler]
    }

    swx.call(callParameters);
}
```

Lastly, you need to create an onPress() event for the submit_mc MovieClip. Inside this function you call the cancelAllCalls() method of your SWX ActionScript library instance, which stops all current loads and resets the SWX instance to be ready for any additional calls. This helps to "clear the air," so to speak, and ensure that you can make another call should there have been a timeout or fault in the previous call. You have also moved the callParameters object into this function so that it is updated with the new user input when submit_mc is clicked. The arguments being passed into the SearchLocations method of PinkBuy have also been updated to accept the user input.

Next, you can now move on to your results state. On the actions layer of frame 2, add the following code:

```
stop();

var numResults:Number = SWXresults.length;
var currentResult:Number = 0;

if (errorMsg) {
    results_txt.text = "Error. Please try a new search.";
} else {
    if (SWXresults.length > 0) {
        numResults_txt.text = numResults.toString() + " locations found";
```

221

```
                    results_txt.htmlText = SWXresults[0].account + "<br />" + ➥
                    SWXresults[0].address + "<br />" + SWXresults[0].city + ➥
                    ", " + SWXresults[0].state + "<br />" + SWXresults[0].zip + ➥
                    "<br />" + SWXresults[0].phone + "<br />Distance: " + ➥
                    SWXresults[0].distance;
            } else {
                    numResults_txt.text = "0 locations found";results_txt.htmlText ➥
                    = "No results found, please try a new search.";
                    previous_btn.enabled = false;
                    next_btn.enabled = false;
            }
        }
```

Here you set up a couple of variables to determine the number of results returned (numResults) and to store the current result the user is viewing. Then you test to make sure you catch any errors that might be returned, and if there is an error, you display an error message in the results_txt text field. If no error was returned, you continue on to displaying the first result (if more than zero results were returned) or a message stating that no results were returned if that is the case. Refer to Table 8-3 for more information on the information (properties) included in the returned object.

```
        newSearch_mc.onPress = function() {
            prevFrame();
        }

        previous_mc.onPress = function() {
            if (currentResult > 0) {
                    currentResult--;
                    results_txt.htmlText=SWXresults[currentResult].account + ➥
                    "<br />" + SWXresults[currentResult].address + "<br />" + ➥
                    SWXresults[currentResult].city + ", " + ➥
                    SWXresults[currentResult].state + "   " + ➥
                    SWXresults[currentResult].zip + "<br />" + ➥
                    SWXresults[currentResult].phone + "<br />Distance: " + ➥
                    SWXresults[currentResult].distance + " mi";
            }
        }

        next_mc.onPress = function() {
            if (currentResult < numResults-1) {
                    currentResult++;
                    results_txt.htmlText = SWXresults[currentResult].account + ➥
                    "<br />" + SWXresults[currentResult].address + "<br />" + ➥
                    SWXresults[currentResult].city + ", " + ➥
                    SWXresults[currentResult].state + "   " + ➥
                    SWXresults[currentResult].zip + "<br />" + ➥
                    SWXresults[currentResult].phone + "<br />Distance: " + ➥
                    SWXresults[currentResult].distance + " mi";
            }
        }
```

Last, you set up the onPress() handlers for each of the navigation MovieClips. For newSearch_mc you just return the user to the previous frame and the search state. For previous_mc and next_mc, test the currently displayed result to ensure the previous or next result is within bounds of the number of results returned. If it is, you display the previous or next result to results_txt as an HTML string of text.

You are now ready to test your Flash Lite application. Select Control ➤ Test Movie. The Adobe Device Central window will launch, and you will be presented with the search state. Enter your U.S. ZIP code, or use **97209** as an example, and click the Search button using the mobile phone emulator keypad. Assuming you entered a valid U.S. ZIP code, you will be presented with the results state, similar to Figure 8-13.

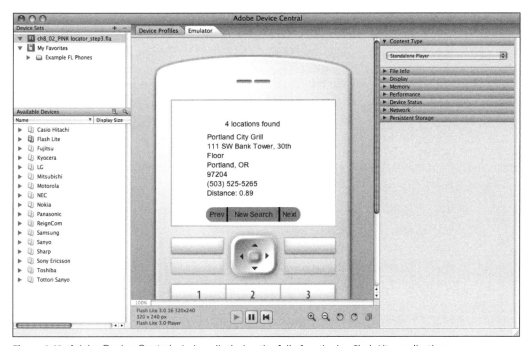

Figure 8-13. Adobe Device Central window displaying the fully functioning Flash Lite application

If more than one result is returned, try clicking the Prev and Next buttons to navigate through all the returned results.

That's it! You have now finished your first Flash Lite application using SWX.

You can continue to build out this example by adding some graphical elements such as the p.i.n.k. Spirits logo, and so on, or you can download the completed project with p.i.n.k. Spirits branding from http://www.friendsofed.com.

Getting more information

Now that you possess all of the knowledge you need to build your own SWX applications for the Web and for mobile devices, be sure to check out the SWX Showcase. Because SWX provides the ability to deploy to such a wide range of devices, the applications that developers are creating with SWX vary greatly as well, so there is always something interesting and new.

Visit http://swxformat.org/showcase/ to view a collection of projects completed with SWX and then take a look at the projects submitted to the SWX Contest held at the end of 2007 by visiting http://swxformat.org/contest/.

You can find more information about SWX on the project's website, http://www.swxformat.org, including detailed FAQs and "getting started" screencasts.

In addition, a great source of information is the SWX Mailing List on OSFlash (http://www.osflash.org). Developers can subscribe to this mailing list by visiting http://osflash.org/mailman/listinfo/swx_osflash.org. The list is fairly active, and the members usually return answers to posted questions within a matter of hours. You can also browse the SWX Mailing List archives for answers to previously asked questions.

SWX was conceived, was developed, and is currently maintained by Aral Balkan (http://aralbalkan.com/). A fair deal of the content for this chapter came from the documentation Aral wrote to support his creation. In general, SWX is licensed as an open source project and is free to use on both personal and commercial projects regardless if they are released as open or closed source. You can find more details at http://swxformat.org/documentation/#90.

Chapter 9

USING HAXE

by Nicolas Cannasse

haXe is a high-level programming language for web development. It can be compiled into `.js` files for JavaScript developers or into `.swf` files for Flash, and it also supports the Neko virtual machine. Before going into the details of haXe, I'll explain how it came to be and how it is related to the evolution of Flash, ActionScript, and some of the other open source Flash tools. Let's start then with a bit of history . . .

Flash for developers

Traditionally, Flash was a tool for designers, and programming was used for adding a little bit of "scripting" and interactivity to the different parts of a Flash project. That was ActionScript 1. But when programmers began using the language and some designers started digging deeper into ActionScript, they began building applications that even Macromedia[1] could not have envisioned: rich Internet applications, web games, complete content management systems, code-generated graphics . . . the list goes on. From the web developer perspective, Flash morphed from a tool for building ads and animations into a tool that could be used to increase the user experience on websites by doing things that were not possible in a traditional HTML-based website. Some of these Flash usages clearly went overboard (haven't we all seen complete Flash-based websites that no one is able to use correctly?). But the most important thing is that web developers learned from their mistakes and began using Flash in the right places where it had the greatest benefit for the end users.

---

1. Macromedia, the original company behind Flash, was later bought by Adobe.

So, with developers adopting Flash, the development tools were found to be wanting. This wasn't initially noticed, however, because most of the first Flash designers and developers were learning programming with ActionScript 1 and were happy with the available set of tools. But when developers with Java and PHP backgrounds started using Flash, they struggled with the IDE. Although they found some code-editing support in the Flash IDE, these developers were already used to their own powerful and customizable code editors or IDEs, and Flash was nowhere near as powerful or as easy to use.

What is nice when you are a programmer is that you can "scratch your own itch." Some external ActionScript editors were built at that time (such as the popular SEPY; http://osflash.org/sepy). These editors were customizable enough for developers to find themselves "at home" and ready to write code. By adding some "hacks" to be able to remotely run the Build command in the Flash IDE, programmers were then able to "compile and test" their code, just like they used to do with other programming languages.

Watching the interests of programmers using Flash and understanding the need for more developer support, Macromedia introduced ActionScript 2, an evolution of the original ActionScript language. ActionScript 2 maintains backward compatibility with ActionScript 1, with the additional ability to define classes in external .as files. In addition to classes, ActionScript 2 adds the possibility to specify optional types for variables and functions, and the compiler will check that these types are correctly matched by the actual program. This is a kind of optional Java-styled type system, which is widely known among programmers coming from other languages.

With the introduction of ActionScript 2, Flash developers were now able to build bigger applications faster, thanks to classes and types that ensure good coherency among all parts of the code, meaning fewer bugs occurring at runtime. Although ActionScript 1 was (and is) still used for small Flash projects, bigger projects profit from using a higher-level programming language.

Actually, ActionScript 2 was not an entirely new language; it just added syntax (classes) and rules (types) to ActionScript 1, so in the end ActionScript 2 code will be compiled into ActionScript 1 by the Flash IDE. Then that ActionScript 1 code will be turned into **bytecode** (binary low-level operations) that is stored in the final SWF file. The problem with ActionScript 2 was the time-to-test speed. With each compilation, the Flash IDE compiled all the classes, checked all the types, built all the graphical resources, compressed all the sounds, and did a lot of operations to build the final SWF file available for testing.

This required a lot of time, which increased with the size of the project—from a few seconds to sometimes several minutes spent building the SWF. And that had to be done every time you wanted to test your code! The Flash IDE added a cache system to speed up ActionScript 2 compilation, but it was found to be buggy and prevented users from seeing modifications being made until they cleared the ASO cache.

With long delays between each test, programming Flash at that time was not fun. Even the smallest change required you to wait, making you lose concentration and making the whole programming process painful.

The arrival of MTASC

In response to this, we created MTASC. MTASC was able to fix all these problems by taking a different approach to Flash compilation. Instead of having the compiler integrated into the Flash IDE, MTASC is a command-line compiler, which enables any developer to integrate it within an IDE. Instead of rebuilding the whole SWF for every compilation, MTASC just "updates" the SWF by replacing the old version of the code with the new one. With this single improvement, the whole team workflow for Flash projects changed.

Instead of having developers and designers working on the same FLA file, things were now clearly separated:

- Designers work on the FLA and then build a SWF to hand to developers.
- Developers use MTASC and the code IDE of their choice to update the SWF with their code and can directly test the modifications they make.

Although these improvements alone would have been helpful to developers, MTASC also uses an improved compiler technology—a language called OCaml—that enables it to compile ActionScript 2 code a lot faster than the Flash IDE compiler. For example, one MTASC user reported the following: "It takes 3–4 seconds to compile more than 300 classes with MTASC, compared to 20–30 seconds with the Macromedia Compiler." That's the reason for the famous MTASC tag line:

> "No more coffee breaks while compiling."

With all these great features, MTASC would have sold well among Flash developers. But it wasn't my or my company's intention to sell MTASC licenses.

MTASC stands for "Motion-Twin ActionScript 2 Compiler," and Motion-Twin is the name of my company. We are based in Bordeaux, France, and we make a living by creating games. We are developers, and we use a lot of open source software such as MySQL, Apache, and PHP. Thanks to this software, we were able to get started without big initial funds, so we wanted to give back to the community what we got for free. That's why MTASC was released as open source software, freely downloadable by everyone at the http://www.mtasc.org website.

MTASC was initially released in October 2004, and then version 1.0 arrived in January 2005, followed by regular releases up to 1.13 in February 2007. During this time, a lot of people started developing great open source ActionScript libraries. There was open source before in the Flash world, but an active community quickly formed around MTASC, which later became the OSFlash.org community because people were not talking anymore about MTASC only but about all the tools and libraries that were becoming available. The thing I could see during 2005–2006 was that having MTASC be open source clearly inspired a lot of people to work on open source software as well. MTASC seemed to play a catalyst role in the evolution of OSFlash, and that was a great experience that continues to this day.

ActionScript 3

In October 2005, MTASC was already quite popular and was getting really stable. Only a few bugs were reported, so releases were getting more spaced apart. Some experimental, nonstandard features were added, such as strict typing and typed arrays, but going further to bring more features to users would mean changing the ActionScript language. This was not possible, since one of MTASC's goals was to keep compatibility with the Flash IDE compiler.

It was at this time that ActionScript 3 was announced.

The immediate question that every MTASC user asked at that time was "Will MTASC support ActionScript 3?" ActionScript 3 was something very different from ActionScript 1 and ActionScript 2; it had a new API, a new language with different features, no backward compatibility, a new virtual machine for faster execution, and so on. Implementing ActionScript 3 support for MTASC would mean rewriting the compiler from scratch. Doing so would be only an attempt to "keep up" with Macromedia. Also, MTASC was a success because it was improving things over the traditional Flash workflow. It was helping developers "scratch their itches." With a new language and a new workflow, who knew what particular itch would need scratching?

Let's look at the points that made MTASC a success and compare them with the new features that ActionScript 3 would bring:

- *Stand-alone command-line compiler*: The ActionScript 3 compiler was also stand-alone.
- *Speed*: The ActionScript 3 compiler was using a new Java-based technology, so there was a good chance that Macromedia (and Adobe later) improved things here too.
- *Free and open source*: Most of the MTASC users were professional Flash users who already owned a Flash IDE license, so they wouldn't save money by using MTASC and would not hesitate to choose the "official" compiler over the open source one if price was its only advantage.

After giving the subject some serious thought, I decided that MTASC should go another way. To innovate even further, more freedom was needed. That's the reason why a new programming language was announced at the OFLA conference in October 2005.

That language would become haXe a few months later.

The birth of haXe

The original goals of haXe were the following:

- Build a language more powerful than ActionScript 2 and ActionScript 3.
- Be able to easily port an ActionScript 2 application to haXe.
- Be able to use this language for Flash 6, 7, 8, and 9.
- Be able to use this language for JavaScript/Ajax.
- Be able to use this language for server-side programming, instead of PHP or Java.

The idea of supporting Flash, JavaScript, and the server in the same language was the most ambitious aspect of the proposal. In a traditional website, developers need to use a lot of different technologies: PHP or another server-side language to access databases and generate HTML, ActionScript to develop the Flash parts of the website, JavaScript to manipulate HTML and forms in the browser, and some kind of XML protocol to communicate between the different components when needed.

The idea of haXe was to be able to write all these parts using one single programming language and to provide transparent communication as part of the standard library. This would trigger a workflow improvement similar to the one MTASC brought about before.

When you are developing several parts of the website, you no longer have to switch between different languages during the development phase. You can have one language, with its standard library, working the same on every platform. If you are developing as part of a team of developers, a single language will improve communication between members. Transparent communications will simplify protocols. And code reuse: the same classes can be compiled at the same time for the server and for the client side, when some data needs to be shared between the two, for example.

Also, for users who didn't want or couldn't make the "big jump" and use haXe for the whole website, haXe needed to bring enough features to improve their workflow. In particular, for Flash users, haXe needed to prove itself to be more useful than alternatives such as MTASC or ActionScript 3.

At the time of this writing, 16 months since the initial proposal was made, all these goals have been fulfilled, beyond all expectations.

haXe for Flash

Covering the three platforms of haXe—Flash, JavaScript, and Neko—would take too much time and goes beyond the scope of this book. This chapter will mostly focus on haXe for the Flash developer. It will introduce the differences between haXe and ActionScript and give a good overview of the haXe features and tools that help Flash developers get their jobs done.

Installing haXe

haXe is available to download from http://haxe.org. An installer is available for each of the main operating systems: Windows, OS X, and Linux. The installer downloads and installs the latest haXe and Neko versions, so it can also be used to upgrade a previous haXe installation when a new version is available.

Once haXe is installed, you are ready to use it and can start writing your first haXe program. The file extension of haXe files is .hx.

haXe IDE

The recommended IDE for haXe is FlashDevelop (http://www.flashdevelop.org). If you already have FlashDevelop 2 installed, then you can install the haxeFD plug-in, which is available at http://haxe.org/haxefd. The upcoming FD3 version will directly support haXe without the need to install a specific plug-in.

The following screenshot shows the FlashDevelop IDE with haXe support, with some autocompletion information.

Sadly, FlashDevelop runs only on Windows right now. But if you are not running Windows, you can also use your favorite editor to edit .hx files. Some support for others editors is available on http://haxe.org. If you don't find any for your favorite editors, try using a syntax mode such as Java or ActionScript 2 for a start. Since there are not so many syntax differences, it should be enough right now.

```
static function mainTransaction(){
    init();
    request = new mtwin.web.Request();
    session = new Session();
    user = if (session.userId == null) new User() els

    user.
         delete              String
    va   description         rl");
    va   email
    va   firstName           ,/]*\/(.*)$/;
    if   getName
         htmlDescription      hed(1).split("/");
         id                   > 0 && request.getPathInf
         insert
    }    lastName
    if   login               i(request.getPathInfoPart(
         level++;
    var handler = new Actions();
    handler.execute(request, level);
    if (template != null){
        var result = executeTemplate();
        sendHeaders();
        Lib.print(result);
    }
    session.close();
}
```

231

Hello, haXe!

The following is a typical "Hello, World" class in haXe/Flash. As you can see, it is similar to a corresponding ActionScript 2 class.

```
class Hello {
    static function main() {
        trace("Hello, haXe ! ");
    }
}
```

Save this class in a Hello.hx file.

Now, you have to compile this class by using haXe so you can get a SWF file. If you are familiar with MTASC or other command-line compilers, you can open a command-line console, go to the directory where the Hello.hx file is saved, and run the following command:

```
haxe -main Hello -swf hello.swf
```

This creates a hello.swf file that, once opened with Flash Player or in a web browser, displays the magic sentence.

HXML files

There is an easier way to use the haXe compiler. First, you have to create an HXML file and put the different command-line arguments inside it, one per line. Here, for example, is the hello.hxml file content:

```
-main Hello
-swf hello.swf
```

Save it into the same directory as your Hello.hx file. If you are on Windows, you can double-click it to start compilation. This will open a console window that will run the haXe compiler. If errors occur, the console will display them and wait for you to press the Enter key. If no error occurs, then the console will close as soon as the compilation is finished.

Double-clicking HXML files is available only for Windows users, but you can run the HXML file from the command line by simply doing this:

```
haxe hello.hxml
```

This results in the same output as the previous command.

Displaying the SWF

Once the compilation is successful, you should have a hello.swf file in your project directory. This is the compiled code that was produced by the haXe compiler. It includes the Hello class as well as the basic haXe library that extends the Flash standard library.

To display the SWF, you can double-click it if you have the stand-alone Flash Player installed, or you can put it into an HTML page such as the following:

```
<htlml>
<head><title>haXe Flash</title></head>
<body bgcolor="#dddddd">
<object classid="clsid:d27cdb6e-ae6d-11cf-96b8-444553540000"
        width="400"
        height="300"
        id="haxe"
        align="middle">
<param name="movie" value="hello.swf"/>
<param name="allowScriptAccess" value="always" />
<param name="quality" value="high" />
<param name="scale" value="noscale" />
<param name="salign" value="lt" />
<param name="bgcolor" value="#ffffff"/>
<embed src="hello.swf"
        bgcolor="#ffffff"
        width="400"
        height="300"
        name="haxe"
        quality="high"
        align="middle"
        scale="noscale"
        allowScriptAccess="always"
        type="application/x-shockwave-flash"
        pluginspage="http://www.macromedia.com/go/getflashplayer"
/>
</object>
</body>
</html>
```

Save this content in the hello.html file, and open it in your web browser. It should display the trace that was done in the Hello.hx file.

haXe trace

Please notice that the trace itself is different from ActionScript. First, the trace is directly displayed on the screen. This is a default behavior, and it can be customized. Also, the trace displays both the file name and the line number where the trace call was made. This gives useful information to the developer to quickly find where the error messages came from.

Now, it's not always easy to have a lot of traces being made on the screen while testing a SWF. For ActionScript 2, several programs exist that capture the traces into a separate window. For haXe, you could also use these programs by redefining the haxe.Log.trace method, but there is already a very good alternative directly available in the haXe standard library: haXe Firebug traces.

To use the haXe Firebug traces, you need to install the following software:

- Firefox, available from http://getfirefox.com
- The Firebug plug-in for Firefox, available from http://getfirebug.com

Once Firebug is installed, restart Firefox and then modify the Hello.hx file with the following content:

```
class Hello {
    static function main() {
        if( haxe.Firebug.detect() )
            haxe.Firebug.redirectTraces();
        trace("Hello haXe !");
    }
}
```

Save and compile again, and open the hello.html file in your browser. You can see the trace by opening the Firebug console with the F12 shortcut or with the menu options View ➤ Firebug. Then navigate to the Console tab, as shown in the following screenshot.

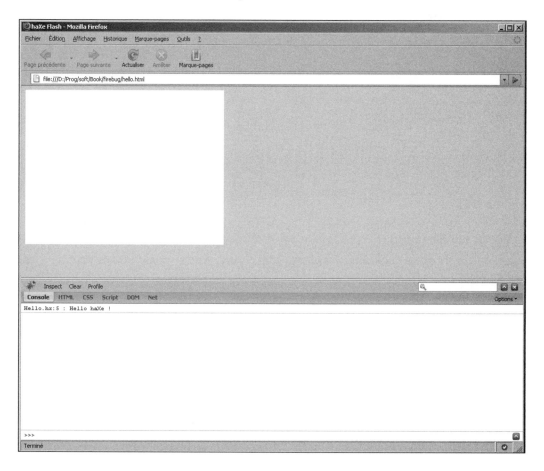

If you want to disable all traces in your program, you can compile with the additional option -trace no in the hello.hxml file.

You have seen so far how to install and set up haXe and how to display traces. You will now learn about the specifics of the haXe language, including what is different and improved compared to ActionScript.

haXe vs. ActionScript

haXe and ActionScript are related. They come from the same family of object-oriented programming languages, and their syntax comes from the C++ language family.

Since the goal of haXe was not to reinvent the wheel, most of the programs you wrote in ActionScript will compile and work the same way in haXe. However, since the language has some differences and makes some improvements over ActionScript, there will always be some changes needed in order to compile your code in haXe.

Syntax differences

I will now cover the differences between ActionScript 2, ActionScript 3, and haXe, starting with a few syntax differences between the languages:

- new: In haXe, class constructors are not named with the name of the class but with the special identifier new. So to declare a simple class, you will do the following in haXe:

```
class Test {
    public function new() {
    }
}
```

- package: In ActionScript 2 and 3, the packages are declared in two ways. haXe adopts the popular Java syntax in order to declare packages. For instance, here's the way to declare the class my.pack.Test:

```
package my.pack;
class Test {
}
```

- for: haXe replaces both ActionScript for and for...in with a single for...in that is a way to *iterate* over any kind of data structure. Here are some examples; we will talk about iterators a bit later:

```
for( elt in ["a","b","c","d"] )
    trace(elt);
for( i in 0...10 )
    trace(i);
```

- switch/break: In haXe, each case in a switch will automatically end with a break, so you can simply write the following:

```
switch( e ) {
case 0: doSomething();
case 1: doSomethingElse();
default: handleError();
}
```

As you can see, these are only small syntax differences between haXe and ActionScript. You will now continue to explore the differences, but this time you'll explore the ones related to basic types.

Basic types differences

The basic types are the ones that are defined as part of the language. There are some differences between ActionScript 2, ActionScript 3, and haXe concerning these basic types that are explained here:

- Int and Float: ActionScript 2 has a single Number numeric type. ActionScript 3 introduced two additional types: int and uint. In haXe, you can use either Int or Float. Here's a small example:

```
var x : Int = 456;
var y : Float = 123.456;
x = y; // error
x = Std.int(y); // works
```

- Dynamic: ActionScript 2 has an Object type that can accept any kind of value, and ActionScript 3 has the * type that can do the same thing. Because of additional types in the haXe type system that you'll see later in this chapter, there is no Object defined in haXe; instead, there is the Dynamic type:

```
var d : Dynamic = "hello";
d = 456;
d = [1,2,3];
```

- Array: Both ActionScript 2 and 3 have a single Array type. Almost all of the time, the content of an Array has the same type, and it has always been a big problem for programmers to remember which type is contained in the Array and to have to cast to the proper type every time the Array is read. To fix this major flaw in the ActionScript languages, haXe uses generics, which can be used in particular with Arrays. For instance, if you use the type Array<String> (reads "array of strings"), your Array will be able to contain only String objects, and every time you read from the Array you'll get back a String (or null). This ensures proper code checking and good documentation. You can still use Array<Dynamic> if you want to store a mix of content in the Array. Here's a short example:

```
var a = new Array<String>();
a.push("hello");
a.push(45); // error
```

In this section, you studied some differences in the way basic types are handled in ActionScript and haXe. I also showed that, thanks to Array generics, haXe code is more comprehensive and safer than the corresponding ActionScript code.

There are still some other changes to study, and then I will start talking about the haXe-specific features that make it such a great language.

API differences

After covering syntax and basic types differences, I'll now discuss the API differences between haXe and ActionScript. First, recall that all the Flash Player APIs available from ActionScript 2 and 3 are available for haXe as well. There is nothing you can do in ActionScript 2/ActionScript 3 that you can't do in haXe.

The only small differences are not the features themselves, but where they are located. In particular, there are no global functions or variables in haXe. The following table shows the different globals in ActionScript and how they are expressed in haXe:

ActionScript 2	ActionScript 3	haXe
_root	N/A	flash.Lib._root
_global	N/A	flash.Lib._global
_level0	MovieClip on stage	flash.Lib.current
trace()	trace()	flash.Lib.trace
e instanceof MyClass	e is MyClass	Std.is(e,MyClass)
(MyClass)e	e as MyClass	cast(e,MyClass)
chr	String.fromCharCode	Std.chr
setInterval/clearInterval	flash.utils.setInterval/clearInterval	see haxe.Timer
escape	encodeURIComponent	StringTools.urlEncode
eval	N/A	flash.Lib.eval
fscommand	fscommand	flash.Lib.fscommand
getTimer	getTimer	flash.Lib.getTimer
getURL	getURL	flash.Lib.getURL
getVersion	N/A	flash.Lib.getVersion
int	int	Std.int
isFinite	isFinite	Math.isFinite
isNaN	isNaN	Math.isNaN
ord	String.charCodeAt(0)	Std.ord
parseFloat	parseFloat	Std.parseFloat
parseInt	parseInt	Std.parseInt

Continued

237

ActionScript 2	ActionScript 3	haXe
print*	N/A	Std.print
random	N/A	Std.random
unescape	decodeURIComponent	StringTools.urlDecode
NaN	NaN	Math.NaN
Infinity	Number.POSITIVE_INFINITY	Math.POSITIVE_INFINITY
-Infinity	Number.NEGATIVE_INFINITY	Math.NEGATIVE_INFINITY
undefined	undefined	null
String()	String()	Std.string

In conclusion, most of these differences are quick to get used to using. It's also not much work to convert an existing ActionScript application to haXe. But at this point you might still wonder why it would be useful to use haXe instead of ActionScript. I'll cover that now and explain the haXe features that make it a very powerful programming language.

haXe features

Writing a compiler is a difficult task to do, but the most difficult part is to convince people to use it. And people have a lot of reasons for not using haXe. Here are a few quotes:

- "ActionScript already works for me."
- "haXe is not official" (that is, made by Adobe).
- "How could something free made by a few guys be better than millions of dollars invested by a big company?"
- "But my client wants the ActionScript source code."
- "What if ActionScript 4 comes? How will haXe keep up with the future?"

All of these are valid points that must be taken into account when explaining haXe to someone who doesn't know about it. One of the best arguments I have is that, even with all these valid points against haXe, a lot of good programmers are still using it. So, there must be a reason for it . . . I'll now explain where haXe makes the difference.

Feature 1: libraries

"Everything that you can do in ActionScript, you can do with haXe as well." This is important to remember. Both the Flash IDE and haXe create SWF files that run on the same Flash Player, so they have the same capabilities.

There is nothing that ActionScript can do that haXe cannot do, but on the other hand, there is nothing that haXe can do that ActionScript cannot do. So, keep in mind that in terms of the Flash API (manipulating movie clips, sound, and video), haXe is equal to ActionScript.

haXe has several kinds of libraries/APIs:

- *The standard APIs (Math, Array, Xml, and so on)*: These are classes that are available on all haXe platforms and work the same everywhere.

- *The Flash APIs (MovieClips, Bitmaps, Sound, and so on)*: These offer everything that Flash Player offers in terms of capabilities.

- *The haXe API*: These are some additional classes that are part of the haXe standard library. Their usage is entirely optional, and they have been added to make the life of the programmer easier. haxe.Firebug is an example of this.

- *Third-party libraries*: There is a tool called haxelib that is part of the haXe distribution that enables everybody to write open source libraries and share them with other developers. There are already more than 50 of these libraries, and each of them can be easily installed on your computer by following the instructions at http://haxe.org/haxelib.

Of course, you don't need to learn from the start how to take advantage of all these possibilities. Most of the projects need to use only the standard and Flash libraries. But when you need some additional facilities, looking first at what is available will save you a lot of time instead of rewriting it by yourself.

Feature 2: interoperability

Of course, a lot of libraries are available in ActionScript as well. Although they are not written in haXe (since both are running on the same Flash Player), it's also possible to reuse existing ActionScript 2 and ActionScript 3 libraries in a haXe program.

In general, what you need to do first is to define some "extern" haXe classes that will enable you to compile a haXe program by using the library API. For example:

```
package mylib;
extern class MyApi {
    public static function foo() : String;
}
```

This enables you to call mylib.MyApi.foo() from your haXe program.

Since some libraries can be quite big, you can automatically generate these extern classes in two ways:

- From a set of ActionScript 2 classes, by using a tool called aheg (http://code.google.com/p/aheg/)
- From a compiled ActionScript 3 library, by using haxe --gen-hx-classes library.swf

Once you've done this, you can use the complete library from haXe just like you would do in ActionScript, except that it's not compiled every time. You will only have to use -swf-lib library.swf in order to integrate it as part of the final SWF.

Feature 3: type inference

In ActionScript, a lot of time is spent by programmers writing obvious things. I'll explain what I mean with the following example:

```
var s : String = "Hello";
```

It's obvious in that case that s is of the type String since you assign it to a String. Here's another example:

```
var h : String = s.substr(0,1);
```

Here, what you know is that s is a String and that the substr method returns a String. Again, it's obvious that h will be a String.

Guessing which type a variable will be depending on what kind of value is assigned to it is called **type inference**. This is entirely done by the haXe compiler, so the programmer no longer needs to write these kinds of obvious types.

Simply writing var obj = new MyObject(); directly assigns the type MyObject to the obj variable.

> *In haXe, most of the time you don't have to write any local variable type. And your code is still strictly typed.*

Feature 4: typed arrays

Strict typing is an important feature for a programming language. It enables you to have an important part of your code checked by the compiler very early and thus removes a lot of testing time from the developer's shoulders.

Also, the more strictly typed your program, the more you can modify it freely, without breaking anything, since if something is not correct in your changes, you will get a compilation error. This does not prevent logic errors, but at least a wide range of errors are avoided by using strict compilation.

But in ActionScript, the most widely used data structure, the Array, is **untyped**. This means it can contain any kind of type. This can be useful in some cases, but in 99 percent of the cases, programmers use arrays containing only a single type. Not being able to express this complete array type leads to a lot of casts needing to be written and breaks the program as soon as you want to change your array content—because of casts, it will compile while still being wrongly typed and hence will be broken.

Although it's not possible with the current Flash Player to enforce that an Array must contain only one kind of type, it's possible to check at compilation that it does. It's called **typed array**, and it's one of haXe's features:

```
class Group {
    public var users : Array<User>; // Array "of" User
}
```

That previous class for the example declares a variable that is an Array containing only instances of the class User. It means that only values typed as User (or subclasses) can be stored into that array, and every time you read the array, the returned type will be User.

Things get even more powerful when combined with type inference:

```
var g = new Group();
var u = g.users[0];
```

In this case, the u variable will be automatically typed as User, since you know that g is a Group and that the users contains instances of the User class.

Typed arrays are very helpful for ensuring that your program is strictly typed.

Please note that although it's not part of this chapter, it's possible to define your own classes as having either one or several type parameters. See the haXe reference manual to learn more about it.

Feature 5: ActionScript 3 generator

To satisfy your clients who need the source code of your project, the haXe compiler includes an option to generate ActionScript 3 code from the corresponding haXe code. You can simply run the following command:

```
haxe -as3 as3_code -main MyMainClass
```

This will generate all the needed .as classes in the as3_code directory. You can then compile with mxmlc by using the following command:

```
mxmlc -output test.swf as3_code/__main__.as
```

This is also a useful feature if you want to develop a library in haXe but use language features such as type inference and typed arrays while still making the ActionScript 3 code available for users who don't use haXe.

Feature 6: speed

haXe improves speed over ActionScript in two domains:

- *At compilation time*: Compiling large programs quickly is an important feature for a compiler. This was one of the reasons for MTASC's success. haXe is based on the same compiler technology; it can then compile large programs faster than the Flash IDE or MXMLC, even while doing additional checking, such as type inference.

- *At runtime*: haXe makes several optimizations that benefit the speed of your program. Let's look at a few of them:

  - *Fast loops*: In ActionScript, you would often use for(var p=0; i<array.length;i++) for browsing the content of an array. You can do the same in haXe by using while, but most of the time you will use the short syntax for(p in array). The main difference with ActionScript is that array.length is evaluated only once, while in haXe it's evaluated for every loop in the script.

241

- *Typed arrays*: In ActionScript 3, access to an array is untyped since the compiler does not know the array content. Because the haXe compiler already has this information, it can directly cast the type as soon as the array is accessed for reading. This leads to a huge performance boost, in particular when doing numerical operations on arrays of numbers.

- *Inlining*: haXe adds an "inline" keyword that can be used in front of static variables and any kind of method. When this variable is used or this method called, its value or body is directly replaced in the calling code, leading to big performance improvements. Refer to the following example:

```
class Inlined {
    static inline var WIDTH = 500;
    var delta : Float;
    public function new(d) {
        this.d = delta;
    }
    public inline function scale( x : Float ) {
        return x * WIDTH + delta;
    }
}

class Test {
    static function main() {
        var inl = new Inlined(10);
        var v = inl.scale(150);
        // will be the same as writing the following :
        var v = 75000 + inl.delta;
    }
}
```

In this example, you can save the cost of a call to a method and a static field access. Since the compiler can also calculate at compile time the result of 150*500, you are also saving a multiplication here.

In conclusion, although using haXe naturally will bring some additional speed (especially in Flash 9 where things can be optimized a lot), it's also possible to use it "inline" to fine-tune your application or library and get the most speed out of it.

Feature 7: independence

"What if ActionScript 4 comes? How will haXe keep up with the future?"

This is often a worry of people learning about haXe. People don't want to be locked into learning a technology that will vanish a few years later.

Let's look at how the Web is evolving. The Web is still very young; it was accessible to the public starting from 1991. And the more it's growing, the more different technologies will be involved.

Flash is a good example of that. It started with ActionScript 1, then ActionScript 2, now ActionScript 3, and surely ActionScript 4, 5, and 6 in the next years. And nothing can guarantee you that the things that you're doing now will be compatible with what will be available in five years. Actually, the only language that can compile to Flash 6, 7, 8, and 9 is not a version of ActionScript but haXe.

In five years from now, Flash might be crushed by Silverlight (although I don't think so) or by another technology.

The whole idea behind haXe is to support the most popular client web platforms, which are currently Flash 6 to 9 and JavaScript. However, the Web will evolve in the upcoming years, and haXe will adapt to it. Its strength is that the language has been designed from the beginning to be able to run on several platforms.

haXe is independent from any technology or company. It's written by developers for developers in order to ensure that every haXe developer will get maximum freedom when choosing the platform on which she wants to build her application.

Feature 8: and much more . . .

It's difficult to list all the advantages of haXe here, so the following is a short list that you can look at more completely in the haXe reference manual:

- *Enums*: You can declare an enum, which is a type that can have a limited set of values with optional parameters, as the following example shows:

```
enum Color {
    Red;
    Green;
    Blue;
    Gray( amount : Float );
}
```

- *Anonymous objects and* typedef: You can declare some anonymous object and strictly type them:

```
typedef User = { name : String, age : Int, male : Bool }
var u = { name : "Nicolas", age : 28, male : true };
```

- *Function types*: You can declare strictly typed function types by listing the arguments and return types:

```
var f : Int -> Int -> Int = function(x,y) return x + y;
trace(f(1,2)); // 3
```

- *Optional arguments*: You can specify that some method arguments are optional:

```
function foo( x : Int, ?y : Int ) {
}
```

- You can define your own iterators for your classes so they can be used with haXe for syntax.
- You can use conditional compilation to define some specific behavior depending on platform or compilation flags:

```
var password;
#if testing
    password = "123456"
#else true
```

```
        password = requestPassword();
#end
// compile with "haxe -D testing" to activate testing flag
```

- You can use getter/setter for variables:

```
class Point {
    public var x(getX,setX) : Int;
    ...
}
```

Summary

haXe includes a carefully chosen set of features that can enhance the type safety of a program, improve the comfort of the programmer, and increase the application's speed while still allowing you to run the same code on different platforms.

haXe is thus independent from current technologies and will continue to support the leading web platforms in the future, with maximal interoperability in mind. Investing time in haXe is rewarding for the programmer, since he's not being locked in to a specific platform.

The future of haXe is guaranteed by the fact that it's open source and used by many professional programmers who are helping to improve it by writing libraries, reporting bugs and fixes, and experimenting with haXe on new platforms that might be the future of the Web. You can learn much more about haXe by visiting the official haXe website at http://haxe.org.

Chapter 10

FUSE AND GOASAP: OPEN SOURCE ANIMATION TOOLS

by Moses Gunesch

Since ActionScript 1.0, animation has consistently been one of the most exciting areas of the open source Flash community. This chapter looks at two open source libraries I've released for coding animation, one for ActionScript 2 and the other for ActionScript 3. Each addresses a wide audience and works as a unifying force in different ways. I started with a top-down approach with Fuse Kit and have since moved toward a more inclusive roots-up strategy with a community initiative called GoASAP. My work is but a small sample from this vibrant corner of ActionScript. This chapter is a tribute to the many others involved, and it's an open invitation for you to join the fun.

Introducing Fuse

Fuse Kit (http://www.mosessupposes.com/Fuse) is an animation-scripting system for ActionScript 2 that uses an interpreter model. It takes a highly condensed list of actions and turns them into animations, as if you'd simply described a timeline in shorthand notation. There are a lot of concrete reference materials for learning Fuse online, and Fuse is somewhat old news these days to many. So instead of a tutorial, this chapter takes a look at the things I think are most valuable about Fuse.

Introducing GoASAP

The Go ActionScript Animation Platform (GoASAP; http://www.goasap.org), also known simply as Go, is a set of ActionScript 3 core classes that make it easy for you to create your own animation tools. For example, it's possible to build a simple working version of Fuse over Go in a few minutes! Go is a potentially fertile breeding ground for all kinds of animation: linear motion (tweens), physics motion, and other completely custom types. Go also aims to provide a thin layer of compatibility between the many systems available today, something from which both authors and users can benefit.

> *A few of my personal Go projects fall into that "other" category: a stop-motion animation player that loads and plays an image series from a ZIP file, as well as a system for playing animation exported from a Maya or 3ds Max timeline with Papervision called Timeline3D. These projects stray from typical linear tweens or physics, and they indicate that the possibilities are wide open. (Motion capture, anyone?)*

Fuse 2: solving ActionScript 2 problems

Fuse Kit hit its stride by its second major release, during the later years of the ActionScript 2 era. It appealed to the peculiar mutant strain of designer-turned-developer that Flash had spawned in its first half decade. Coding for the runtime environment allowed these new programmers to move away from the Flash timeline, but it quickly became apparent that coding animation was fairly involved stuff. The animation utilities passed around that emerging developer community became one of the first real hotbeds of open source sharing in the Flash world.

Open source mash-up

Fuse Kit combines many great ideas from the vibrant global Flash community of that time. These include Zeh Fernando's ActionScript 1 tweening shortcuts from Brazil, Ladislav Zigo's animation engine and custom easing system from Slovakia, a BitmapFilter management tool called FMP from Germany by Danilo Sandner and Bjorn Wibben, and Tatsuo Kato's sequencing and syntax ideas from Japan.

We all know we're indebted to Robert Penner for his easing functions that style animation from *snap* to *swoosh* to *sproing*, originally released under the open source BSD license. But you might not know that as far back as the Flash MX era, Robert also penned a hybrid physics and tweening system—an idea that was ahead of its time and that I am revisiting in GoASAP. Working closely with Adobe's Flash team, Robert continues to contribute groundbreaking animation work. Alex Uhlmann was another forerunner in open source animation; his Animation Package provided a coherent and sophisticated object-oriented approach to animation and vector drawing. Ironically, the majority of the Flash world wasn't quite ready for OO programming at the time, but Alex has now found a place as a major contributor to the world of Adobe Flex. Keith Peters and many others actively contributed to refining the processes of animating with code.

Although Fuse "mashes up" many of these ideas into one coherent package, its code is all its own, and it brought many fresh ideas to the table. Fuse does not entirely conform to or shun object-oriented conventions. It presents a coherent system that is simple enough for designers who have never written a single line of code, but it also can be leveraged for complex tasks by experienced object-oriented coders.

The need for speed in AVM 1

Flash Player 9 introduced a vastly improved ActionScript virtual machine 2 (AVM 2), which allows ActionScript 3 to run many times faster. But in the long, dark days of AVM 1, it was hard to get a SWF to do very much without slowing down and "chugging" during play. Part of this was a code issue. ActionScript 2 was object oriented, but it compiled to the same bytecode as ActionScript 1, so as developers were starting to write full-scale utilities and applications, the player often buckled under heavy lifting. There were some sticky memory-management issues as well, but it was the graphical rendering of animation that hit the hardest. Developer forums bubbled with tips and tricks for making animated content run smoothly. We learned to avoid vector art, switch to low-quality rendering during tough spots, or often simply redesign our projects to try to beat the odds.

A faster engine

Ladislav Zigo's animation utility lmc_tween (based on mc_tween by Zeh Fernando) ran at what seemed like light speed at the time. The magic, it turned out, was a simple concept: by condensing all animations into a single list and then updating them together in sync with the player's built-in pulse, drag is significantly reduced (see Figure 10-1). It works because it compresses all of your program's animation calculations and screen redraws into a tiny sliver of a moment. This allows the player to breathe and catch up on other processes in between, resulting in a fairly significant performance gain.

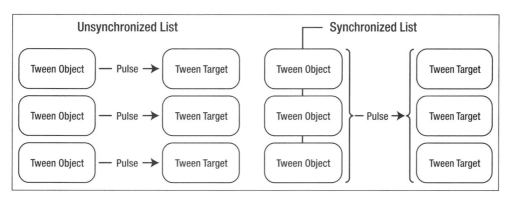

Figure 10-1. Centralizing tweens into a list runs much faster in Flash Player.

This managed tween list architecture was clearly illustrated in a Flash MX class by Nigel Pegg, mx.effects.Tween, still shipped with Flash. (This is a different class from the more familiar mx.transitions.Tween by Robert Penner.) Zigo had drawn from many sources with his engine, but he was the one to clearly demonstrate to the community that this system had an advantage when he published and released the source for an astonishing series of benchmark tests. In an ironic twist characteristic of AVM 1, Zigo's class—a somewhat beastly knot of code—was shown to drastically outperform Penner's clean object-oriented Tween class and many other systems of that time.

The benchmark tests used large visual stacks of lines that stretched gradually across the screen, and they exhibited a gradual cascading-wave effect down the series as they ran (as in Figure 10-2). This was a by-product of the amount of time it took to instantiate the tweens themselves, and it was a striking display of AVM 1's laggy processing.

Figure 10-2. Several thousand line width tweens, all started at once but not staying synchronized as they run.

Zigo's was different, though. Not only did it run significantly faster and smoother than others, but he'd also devised a time-snapping technique that kept the tweens running in a perfectly synced block. For real-world Flash developers, this meant projects with many animations would have a smoother and more even appearance. These benchmarks fostered a minor obsession with animation efficiency in the Flash world, but they also brought to light how much the issue affected real-world authoring for Flash Player.

Reality check

Around that time I released a library called Sequencer that enabled the chaining of animations into **sequences** resembling a complete animation timeline built with code. Sequencer was fully object-oriented and based on Flash's mx.transitions.Tween by Robert Penner. But I was also aware that Zigo had nailed something critical: his system addressed the limitations of AVM 1 directly, and it was easier to use for the real Flash audience of that moment. So, I came up with Fuse: an easier-to-use sequencing system that picked up where Zigo left off and added to it.

This was a bit of a step down from the clean, utopian OO world I'd started living in, back into the muck of AVM 1–optimized spaghetti code, peppered with the usual litany of ActionScript 2 hacks and workarounds. I was willing to make that compromise despite some initial derision for doing so; it was a simple acknowledgment of where Flash was at that time.

The decision paid off. Fuse Kit beat the odds in AVM 1 by offering loads of animation functionality while staying fast and efficient. And thanks to an enlightening conversation I had with Aral Balkan, Fuse 2 was released with an open source MIT license, which opened it up to the whole community.

ZigoEngine: Fuse's animation engine

The ZigoEngine class is a core utility that runs all the dynamic animations in a SWF. It can be used independently of other kit elements. Many newcomers to Fuse Kit ask why there is both a ZigoEngine class and a Fuse utility. The answer is simple: they do different things. ZigoEngine only runs animations, using the synchronized list architecture shown in Figure 10-1. Fuse, on the other hand, is a separate utility that allows you to chain animations into a sequence, like a timeline, and features a special syntax. That is, Fuse runs more than one tween in a row, and ZigoEngine just animates.

Since all it does is animate, ZigoEngine is extremely fast, responsive, and memory efficient, making it the best option for button rollovers and other interactive effects. During play, it generates, manages, and deletes tween objects internally, shielding you from any direct access and thus keeping you clear of ActionScript 2's sticky memory management.

ZigoEngine is amazing in that it can animate just about anything. The following examples provide a snapshot of its usage to illustrate its range, but for more comprehensive examples, you should visit the website and documentation.

```
ZigoEngine.doTween( box_mc,  "_alpha",  0 );
```

This single line of code causes the box MovieClip to fade out. Some animation parameters are omitted for simplicity, so it will adopt defaults like one second with a standard animation style.

You can also very easily animate multiple properties and animation targets at once:

```
ZigoEngine.doTween( [box1_mc,  box2_mc],
                    "_scale, _rotation",
                    [50, 180]);
```

The following example shows a few more features. It runs a two-second brightness effect with a delay of a half second and a callback fired when the tween completes. Callbacks can also be scoped, include arguments, and occur at the tween's start and update as well as at the end.

Here's a color transform animation with a callback:

```
ZigoEngine.doTween( box_mc, "_brightOffset", 100, 2,
                    Strong.easeIn, .5, onBrightComplete);
```

Animating color properties is complex business internally because the red, green, and blue values have to be split out and animated separately. But this only scratches the surface of some of ZigoEngine's complex tween features. It also provides the ability to animate in Bezier curves, like a baseball arcing across the screen. It can be used to animate multiple properties within complex objects, arrays, and matrixes. It can even be used to apply animation to any custom variable within your program.

Another common animation need that entails some complexity is the animation of bitmap filters like blurs and drop shadows. A secondary utility in Fuse Kit called FuseFMP provides this capability (a rewrite of the open source FMP utility from Germany). FuseFMP adds animation properties such as DropShadow_distance that concatenate a shortened filter name with any filter property using an underscore. This allows you to directly target any property of any filter with a single intuitive variable name. As an example of this concatenation, here's the code for an animated horizontal blur:

```
import com.mosesSupposes.fuse.*;
ZigoEngine.register(FuseFMP); // one-time setup
ZigoEngine.doTween( my_mc, "Blur_blurX", 100, 1, "easeInOutQuint" );
```

One of Fuse Kit's innovations is a simple way to indicate you'd like an animation to occur relative to the start position instead of being read as an absolute value. For example, the relative statement "tween 10px to the right" is quite different from its absolute counterpart, "tween to the coordinate x:10 on the stage." Relative positioning is indicated very simply by using a string value instead of a number.

The following shows relative positioning using a string, in other words, "slide 10px up from current position":

```
ZigoEngine.doTween( my_mc, "_y", "-10" );
```

If ZigoEngine lacks a feature you need, you can use the FuseFX system to add your own custom tweens. It works using a registration system, where special tween properties are reserved and associated with custom updater classes. When you run a tween that uses a reserved property, it is recognized and routed to your custom extension. One example extension targeted TextFormat parameters so that font color, font size, letter spacing, and other typographic attributes could be animated.

Here, a FuseFX extension has registered special properties for hue, saturation, and brightness (HSB) color transforms:

```
ZigoEngine.doTween( my_mc, ColorFX.SATURATION, -100 );
```

Beginner options

Beginner options were included in Fuse Kit to help new coders get a head start. The tweening shortcuts popularized by Fernando and Zigo were MovieClip.prototype extensions that are more intuitive for beginners because they operate directly on the animation target instead of in the abstract space of a static function call. Shortcuts were included in Fuse Kit as an optional add-on since they are really a holdover from the ActionScript 1 era.

The following example shows shortcut tweens being chained into a step-by-step sequence using Fuse's "simple syntax" beginner option. (All it really does is intercept tween calls and use them to build an actual Fuse instance in the background.)

```
Fuse.open();
box_mc.rotateTo(180);
box_mc.scaleTo(200);
Fuse.closeAndStart();
```

Stylizing motion

ActionScript animation systems routinely use Robert Penner's easing functions—Quadratic, Exponential, Elastic, Bounce, and others—which now come with Flash and Flex. When installing Fuse using the Extension Manager, a Custom Easing Tool panel is added to the IDE. This is an update of a version originally put out by Zigo. Once installed, it is available under Window ➤ Other Panels ➤ customEasingTool2. The Fuse Extension also adds code hinting and sidebar quick-text to the IDE's Actions panel, plus Help screens.

The Custom Easing Tool panel lets you select and display any standard easing as a graph and lets you watch an animated preview of the motion style. This is a helpful way to quickly familiarize yourself with the standard styles. You can then model and change the easing curve by dragging the control points (see Figure 10-3).

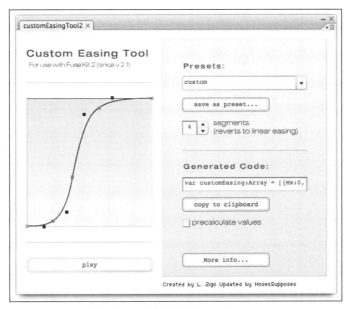

Figure 10-3. Fuse Kit's Custom Easing Tool panel

The panel generates some code, a custom easing array, that can be pasted into your project and used *directly* with ZigoEngine in place of a standard easing function. The following example shows a custom easing array generated by the panel and renamed snapEasing, which can then be used directly in tween calls.

```
import com.mosesSupposes.fuse.*;
ZigoEngine.register(CustomEasing); // once only

var snapEasing:Array = [{Mx:0,My:0,Nx:90,Ny:-6,Px:-34,Py:-75},
  {Mx:56,My:-81,Nx:24,Ny:-228,Px:120,Py:109},{Mx:200, My:-200}];
ZigoEngine.doTween(box_mc, "_x", "200", 1, snapEasing);
```

I consider the Penner easing styles great for production and user interface tweens, but I like to refine and tinker with more significant animations to get them feeling just right. I've personally used the Custom Easing Tool panel many times in my projects. I'm fond of asymmetrical easing like the one shown in Figure 10-3, where the motion starts quickly and then is followed by an elongated out-curve for a smooth and graceful finish.

Fuse: sequencing simplicity

There is an inherent problem with trying to describe animation: no matter how you do it, it's really complex!

Consider this: the Flash IDE's physical timeline interface packs a substantial amount of animation data into a simple graph that makes clear visual sense. But to animate with code, you need to set all of these many parameters for every animation: the target object, end value, duration, easing, and so forth. This sheer volume of information can become overwhelming when describing a whole timeline's worth of layered and overlapped animations.

This is the problem that I attacked head-on when I designed Fuse.

Animation shorthand

My solution was to work on coming up with the ultimate shorthand system, one where looking at the code could be as visually simple as looking at an actual timeline.

Compare the following sequence of Fuse action objects with its plain-English interpretation:

```
{ target:box,
  start_fade:0,
  start_scale:200,
  start_x:"-100",
  delay:.75 },

{ target:box,
  rotation:"-90",
  Blur_blur:10,
  fade:0,
  time:2 }
```

Translation: 1. Position the box 100 pixels to the left of its current location at double its scale, with its visibility off and opacity set to clear; after waiting 3/4 of a second, slide, scale, and fade it back to its initial state. 2. Next, fade the box out while blurring and rotating it 90 degrees counterclockwise over two seconds; then turn its visibility off.

As you can see, the Fuse version fits a lot of information into a small package. In the upcoming section "Smart parsers have more fun," I'll explain some of the details in this example a little more thoroughly. But first, let's look at how Fuses are written and how their code differs from ZigoEngine.

Here's the Fuse version:

```
import com.mosesSupposes.fuse.*;
ZigoEngine.register(Fuse, FuseFMP); // one-time setup

var f:Fuse = new Fuse({ target:box, start_fade:0,
                        start_scale:200, start_x:"-100", delay:.75 },
                      { target:box, rotation:"-90",
                        Blur_blur:10, fade:0, time:2 });
f.start();
```

And here's the same thing without Fuse. FuseFMP and ZigoEngine still manage to keep the code fairly compact, but you can see that a callback is required to create a sequence.

```
import com.mosesSupposes.fuse.*;
ZigoEngine.register(FuseFMP); // one-time setup

box._alpha = 0;
box._visible = false;
FuseFMP.writeFilter(box, "Blur", { blur:0 });
box._xscale = 200;
box._yscale = 200;
box._x -= 100;
ZigoEngine.doTween(box, "_fade, _scale, _x", [100, 100, "100"],
                   1, null, .75, { scope:this, func:doSecondTween});
function doSecondTween():Void {
   ZigoEngine.doTween(box, "_rotation, Blur_blur, _fade",
                      ["-90",10, 0], 2);
}
```

The first obvious advantage of Fuse is its brevity, which becomes only more apparent as a sequence gets longer and more complex. The next clear advantage is its avoidance of using callbacks. Callbacks often add methods to your class, breaking up the parts of an animation and cluttering your code. Using a sequencer utility such as Fuse allows a string of asynchronous actions—actions that play out over time—to be listed in one place, without needing a callback for each further step.

A final advantage visible in this short example is the fuse's legibility when compared to the standard tween calls. In a professional coding environment such as Eclipse, it's usually better to write code as standard method calls so that error checking and code hinting work correctly during the coding process. However, while enumerated objects such as { delay:.75 } clearly spell out each property, returning to a method call later often requires looking up the method's inputs to remind yourself what each argument maps to.

A playable list

Fuse extends the Array class, so it is essentially a playable list of animation actions, each of which is a simple enumerated Object. Fuse actions can fire callbacks or custom events inline, so you don't necessarily need to sequence animation. One common example is to use a Fuse instance to run a program's setup routine by calling an ordered or timed series of commands. But most often a fuse is a blend of animation, callbacks, and events. In the previous example, actions are passed directly to the fuse constructor, but usually it is easier to add each action one by one. To do this, first create a new Fuse instance:

```
var f:Fuse = new Fuse();
```

> Fuse *instances like this are often referred to, somewhat slangily, as **fuses**. In the rest of this chapter, if you read* Fuse, *I am referring to the utility class called* Fuse, *but if you read "a fuse," it means "a* Fuse *instance."*

255

Since Fuse extends Array, adding actions one by one is as simple as using the standard Array method push(). You can also use other Array methods such as splice() to rearrange sequences.

```
f.push({ x:100, time:2, easing:Strong.easeInOut });
```

To run several actions in parallel (so they play at the same time), you can wrap them in another Array:

```
f.push([ { x:"10", delay:.5, time:2, easing:Strong.easeOut },
         { y:"10", time:3, easing:Strong.easeIn } ]);
```

This technique allows you to play any number of simultaneous animations that have different running times, different delays (which staggers them so they don't start at once), or different easing styles. In general, it is that combination—delay, duration, and easing—that defines a single motion, and that motion can be applied to any number of properties on any number of targets. This is why ZigoEngine accepts any number of targets and properties in a single tween call: it is allowing you to apply a single motion—defined by one particular delay-duration-easing combo—to anything you want. A Fuse action object is the same as a tween call: you can pack all the targets and properties that share the same delay-duration-easing combo into one action. But if you want any property to use a different motion, that's when you would break it out into another action object and group the actions using an array.

Here's an example of a simple fuse that uses an Array to group parallel (simultaneous) tweens:

```
import com.mosesSupposes.fuse.*;
ZigoEngine.register( PennerEasing, Fuse, FuseFMP ); // one-time setup

var f:Fuse = new Fuse();
f.target = box;
f.push({ start_x: "-50",
         start_fade:0,
         delay: .25,
         time: .75
       });
f.push([{ x: "200",
          controlY: "-50",
          time: 3,
          ease: "easeInOutBack"
        },
        { Blur_blurX: 20,
          rotation: 10,
          ease: "easeInQuint",
          cycles: 2
        }
       ]);
f.push({ func:trace,  args:"done!" });
f.start();
```

Translation: 1. Start the box faded out with visibility off and 50px to the left; then after a 1/4-second delay, slide it back to its initial position, turn its visibility on, and fade it up over 3/4 of a second. 2. Next, slide the box 200px to the right and make it "hop" up toward a control point that's 50px above it with a "switchback" motion style. While it's hopping and sliding over, make it rock 10 degrees right and blur horizontally; then rock back and unblur by cycling the tween back (the default time is one second, so this back-and-forth animation completes before the slide and makes the target blur the strongest as it's sliding the fastest). 3. Trace the message "done!" to the Output *panel.*

Smart parsers have more fun

As promised in the earlier section "Animation shorthand," I'll now explain in a little more detail how Fuse Kit makes it possible to do so much in such a short snippet of code. First, Fuse supports both the start and end position settings for any animation. (Notice how in the ZigoEngine version earlier, start properties had to be set manually prior to animations.) Start properties are added to Fuse actions using the prefix start_. These properties are set prior to the delay and animation and can also be set prior to starting a whole sequence. This action contains several start properties:

```
{ start_x: "-50", start_fade:0, delay: .25, time: .75 }
```

Translation: Start the box faded out with visibility off and 50px to the left; then after a 1/4-second delay, slide it back to its initial position, turn its visibility on, and fade it up over 3/4 of a second.

One of Fuse's best features, in fact, is its "smart parsing" of start and end properties. This allows you to shorten your shorthand even further by setting either a start or an end *only*, but not necessarily both. In this action, no corresponding end properties are provided, so they are interpreted in various ways. The fade (a ZigoEngine property that combines _visible and _alpha) assumes you mean "fade up to 100" because you started it at 0. The x-slide assumes you mean "start off to the left and return to the start x position" because you did not otherwise specify where to end the animation. Features like this make working with Fuse a lot of fun, because as you test its limits to see how little code you can get away with, you'll find that it fills in missing values in ways that make common sense.

Fuse is also concise when it comes to Bezier curves. Note that the first action in the fuse's second step translated to a "hop" up as it slides right:

```
{ x: "200", controlY: "-50",  time: 3, ease: "easeInOutBack" }
```

Fuse (the logic is actually in ZigoEngine) is able to build a Bezier curve even if only some of the necessary properties are defined. So, you can turn a horizontal x-slide, x:"200", into a hopping motion just by adding a single vertical control point, controlY:"-50". You can freely mix the properties x, y, controlX, and controlY at your leisure, so adding curves is a no-brainer.

Another feature I personally couldn't live without is the ability to use relative-positioning strings for any of these values, including the control points. Trying to figure out where control points should be placed to make a Bezier curve can be maddening, but as you can see here, Fuse lets you declare the control point as "50px above the target's current position." This means you don't even have to know where it is on the stage or do any calculations, and the hop will always look the same even if the target gets moved!

Another great way to shorten Fuse code is to set defaults on the instance, which will be adopted by any action that doesn't uniquely set the same property. In the example, just after the fuse is instantiated, you see the following line:

```
f.target = box;
```

This means that all actions will adopt that target, so you don't have to have a target:box property in each action. You can also specify the default duration, easing, and scope. Callback scoping was much more difficult in ActionScript 2 than it is in ActionScript 3, so this is definitely handy for fuses containing multiple function calls.

Actions can then override any default simply by declaring the property for themselves. In this example, the first action will adopt the Fuse instance's default target box1, which will inch over 100px to the right of its current position. In the second action, only box2 slides over, overriding the default target. The third action uses an array so that both boxes slide over again to the right.

```
var f:Fuse = new Fuse();
f.target = box1;
f.push({ x:"100" });
f.push({ target:box2, x:"100" });
f.push({ target:[box1, box2], x:"100" });
```

The third action could also be written using a special fuse property, addTarget, which adds one or more targets to the default target, keeping things a little simpler:

```
f.push({ addTarget:box2,  x:"100" });
```

Another space-saving Fuse feature makes it easy to reuse actions. In this example, an action is first defined as a variable and then reused in any number of other actions or other fuses. This feature is called **applied actions** because you are basically applying a common action to a new target or set of targets.

```
var fadeOut:Object = { alpha:0, time:.5 };
f.push({ action: fadeOut, target: box1 });
f.push({ action: fadeOut, target: box2 });
```

Much like reusing actions, you can also play any whole fuse sequence from within another fuse. This allows you to reuse whole sequences of actions that otherwise might need to be copied many times. For example, instead of copying and pasting a common set of "outro" actions into many different fuses, you could simply define the shared actions in a single fuse called outroFuse. Any other fuse could then play the outro on its own default targets simply by treating it as an action, like this:

```
f.push( outroFuse );
```

Matching timeline functionality

Code-based sequences have a problem: they can easily become robotic and lose the freedom provided by a timeline. This can be partially addressed by using different delays and durations for the tweens in a group so that they don't all start and end at the same moment. But the typical behavior of any code-based sequencer is that all animations in a group are tallied for completion before the sequence advances forward.

The following fuse has a parallel group followed by a second action:

```
var f:Fuse = new Fuse();
f.target = box;
f.push([ { rotation:90, time: .6 },
         { x:"100", delay:.2, time:1 }
       ]);
f.push({ y: "100", time: 1.2 });
f.start();
```

Here's how this fuse might appear in a timeline, where the top two layers are the grouped rotation/x action and the bottom layer is the second action that animates y.

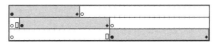

If you think about it, the code is far less flexible than the timeline, because in a timeline you could easily drag the animation on the bottom layer back a few frames so that it overlaps with the first ones, as shown next.

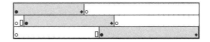

Sequences written with code typically assume that groups of animations need to fully complete before the sequence can step forward. A workaround might be to add the second action into the first group with a long delay, but this not only breaks the list metaphor but it's also very difficult to do in the middle of a longer sequence.

Fuse offers a solution for this issue, a special property called trigger that allows you to specify the moment when the sequence should advance. This creates an overlap where the current action continues to run while the next action has already begun to play.

```
var f:Fuse = new Fuse();
f.target = box;
f.push([ { rotation:90, time: .6 },
          { x:"100", delay:.2, time:1, trigger:.8 } ]);
f.push({ y: "100", time: 1.2 });
f.start();
```

This feature is a lifesaver for animators. It breaks you out of the rigid confines of the list metaphor and allows you to create graceful, natural-looking animation just like you would in the Flash timeline. The trigger property can be a time value as it was in the previous example or a negative time value that is counted back from the end of the current action. If you want the sequence to advance just as one particular animation in a group completes, you can place the trigger property in that action and set it to true. This tags the shorter action to advance the sequence after it completes while longer animations in that group continue to run. (The "trailing" tweens from advanced actions are specially tracked so that the Fuse won't fire its onComplete event until they're done, should they extend beyond the end of the actions list.)

Keepin' it dynamic

Here's another dilemma: you turned to code-driven animation so you'd have more flexibility at runtime, yet you are still being asked to write a *hard-coded sequence* in advance of running it. This presents the same limitations all over again that you faced when using the Flash timeline! The reality of programming for dynamic content is that you might not have access to all the values you need for a sequence, even if you know how it needs to play. For example, maybe you want to write a reusable sequence that will reveal a dynamically loaded image halfway through it using a masking effect, but you don't know what width and height the image will be at sequence creation.

Fuse offers a remarkable feature to address this issue: it actually allows you to run a live lookup on almost any value at runtime as the sequence action executes. You can do this very simply, by setting any value to a getter function that returns the value, instead of a hard-coded number or string.

Fuse can evaluate any value at runtime at the time the action executes:

```
import com.mosesSupposes.fuse.*;
ZigoEngine.register( PennerEasing, Fuse ); // one-time setup
function getRandomX():Number {
  return Math.random()*Stage.width;
}
var f:Fuse = new Fuse();
f.target = box;
f.scope = this;
f.push({ x: getRandomX, ease: "easeOutElastic" });
f.push({ y: function():Number{ return this._ymouse; } });
f.start();
```

This fuse shows two ways runtime evaluation can be written. First, you can define a function in advance and then reference the function in place of a tween value. Here the first action's x property uses this technique, which keeps the Fuse code sleek and makes it easy to reuse the getter function many times. It also keeps the value dynamic, so that if you run the Fuse many times, it will always query for a new random x value, whereas if it had been written as { x: Math.random()*Stage.width }, the random number would have been generated only once at the time the Fuse was created and would remain the same during replays. If you need to get a value only once, you can avoid the hassle of writing a separate function by using an inline function, as in the second action, { y: function():Number{ return this._ymouse; } }. It will animate the box to wherever the mouse is sitting at the moment that action starts in the sequence.

A problem Fuse 2 didn't solve

If you use every feature of the entire Fuse Kit in a single project—ZigoEngine, Fuse, FuseFMP, PennerEasing, CustomEasing, and Shortcuts—it adds around 36KB to your SWF's file size. To reduce this amount, you can compile just the features you need for your project. For example, using ZigoEngine and Fuse adds only about 24KB, less than an average JPEG, which poses no problem for a website project. But even this much is still prohibitive for those pursuing advertising banner projects, which are often strictly capped at very low size limits.

Fortunately, Fuse is only one of many open source animation utilities, and banner builders were able to turn to a project called TweenLite by Jack Doyle (http://blog.greensock.com). That utility is able to perform many basic functions of a tween engine with high efficiency and a tiny 2KB footprint. TweenLite and several similar products continue to provide an excellent solution for that market niche in both ActionScript 2 and ActionScript 3.

Life after Fuse 2: transitioning to ActionScript 3

Many people experience a tortured moment when faced with upgrading to ActionScript 3. If this is you, relax! Take it from me: you have nothing to lose and everything to gain. ActionScript 3 is quite similar to ActionScript 2, and the transition is usually a smooth one. The really distinct changes, such as the new event model, are actually wonderful. Many of the common headaches you've come to live with in ActionScript 2 simply vanish in ActionScript 3, and you'll find that it helps you to write clean, professional-looking code. I also strongly encourage you to set up a professional code editor (addressed elsewhere in Chapters 3 and 4 of this book). Once you make this small transition, you'll find that coding is far more comfortable and vastly more efficient. Finally, if you're still foggy on OO concepts such as inheritance, the migration to ActionScript 3 is the perfect opportunity to take a weekend and study up. These efforts will pay off for you immensely and immediately.

One goal with GoASAP is to make it possible for you to create your own animation tools, ones that fit you the best, instead of having to pick from prefab solutions. My hope is that you, not I, will be the author of Fuse 3—or something even better. If you're moving from Fuse to GoASAP, keep in mind that they are very different systems. But don't be intimidated: as the user base for Go grows, you'll probably start to see more Fuse-like solutions built with it and shared.

Until then, if you're starting to use ActionScript 3 and need a prefab kit to get you through a project, a good alternative to Fuse in ActionScript 3 is Zeh Fernando's Tweener or Jack Doyle's TweenMax. These utilities use an object-literal syntax that should be familiar to Fuse users (although they currently don't support sequencing to the degree that Fuse does). There's no shortage of others, each with their own slightly different approach. Other kits out there may eventually adopt Go into their own code bases since it helps systems play well with each other.

The Go ActionScript animation platform

Coding animation tools has never been easy. This explains the vast divide between the few brave (or foolish!) souls who might attempt such a thing and the rest of the world who are just happy to use these time-savers. What has resulted is a wide variety of creative solutions, none of which is compatible with each other, making the best option simply to pick one for your team and stick with it. Meanwhile, the gap remains wide, and very few developer teams are comfortable venturing out to make an animation library of their own.

GoASAP tries to close this gap by providing an open base system that makes it easy to build your own animation tools in ActionScript 3 for the first time. Instead of a top-down approach like Fuse and other systems, Go takes a roots-up approach that follows from these tenets:

- *Creativity and diversity of animation systems is good*: There is no one-size-fits-all solution because there are many different types of people using such systems.

- *Inefficiency and redundancy are bad; compatibility is good*: One of the problems we're starting to run into is that animation systems don't mix well. When used together, they tend to degrade each other's performance, and although they all contain many common core elements, nothing is shared. It would be far more ideal if you could freely mix animation systems without these problems.

- *More developers doing animation R&D and cross-pollinating their ideas is good*: This does not mean that relying on utilities others create is bad; it simply means that the more people who are able to create and share, the richer the pool of ideas will be.

The ideal solution to these challenges would be a cross-product animation bundle for Flash, Flex, After Effects, and JavaScript written by Adobe (no such thing exists at the time of this writing, although I have brought the proposal to Adobe). This could position Adobe as a leader in scripted animation across the board and would be a far more comprehensive solution than Go, which addresses these issues only in ActionScript 3.

The next best solution at this time is for ActionScript 3 developers to join forces to create a minimal and universal set of core classes that can be shared across various animation systems. If all ActionScript 3 animation systems that could possibly be combined *were* combined, there would not necessarily be very much code shared between them. If you imagine what those few core elements might be, you are essentially picturing what GoASAP attempts to define. But besides that, Go is also a rope bridge spanning the chasm between animation system builders and users. For the first time, it makes it possible for regular ActionScript 3 coders to create in a matter of just a few hours what might otherwise take weeks or months to develop.

GoASAP comes with an open invitation to help refine it. If it doesn't work for you, please help model it into something more truly universal so that everyone's work can be more compatible at a basic level. If you are reading this book as an avid open source consumer but have never open sourced your own work, *now is your chance!* Sharing the tools you make with Go may help countless other developers who might learn from it, get inspired, and eventually share alike. The more, the merrier.

So, what does this core platform look like? Well, to solve the problem of various systems fighting each other with conflicting pulses, Go starts with a pulse engine called GoEngine. Then instead of a rigid framework, Go loosely associates all of the typical elements of animation systems into a collection of options. When used together, these parts interlock tightly, which increases efficiency in a time-based system; however, it is up to you which parts you use. Go also ships with a number of helpful utilities built on these core elements, such as a robust tween base class, a parallel class, and several sequence classes. Using GoASAP, it is eerily easy to re-create Fuse, a basic version of which can be assembled in just a few minutes' work.

DIY developer teams

As I mentioned previously, one of Go's missions is to close the gap and make animation coding feasible on a day-to-day level. This goes beyond you as an individual developer; it also offers a new option for your team. In the past, only the most hard-core developer teams have dared to script their own animation from scratch—often to stunning effect such as with the New York firm Big Spaceship. Usually teams opt for one kit or another and then stick to it, but that too has drawbacks since it is inherently limiting.

The third option that Go offers is a positive balance between these two extremes: a team develops its own animation library that it can continually expand on to meet the unique challenges of each project. But this custom library will remain eminently compatible with the larger community, potentially enhancing your company's image along the way. What your team creates will fit its personal style like a glove, which can only result in a net productivity gain over time as well as a more engaged and empowered approach.

Even teams that usually take a do-it-yourself (DIY) approach can really leverage Go to their advantage, since it provides a coherent core to share and branch from, without putting any limits on the creativity of each individual solution. I was in fact inspired by Big Spaceship and other DIY teams to create a system that would work as well for them as it would for someone who would typically pick a kit solution.

You might worry that your company is simply too busy for such things, but in reality any business will allocate resources where value can be gained. The amount of R&D time your team will need to build its own animation library is significantly reduced by Go, and many companies would very much prefer to have a developer team popularizing original work.

The need for speed in AVM 2

The second ActionScript virtual machine, introduced into Flash Player in conjunction with ActionScript 3, is screamingly fast. Tests show that for animation it may be around five to ten times faster in fact. This is great news, but of course we always want to push the limits. We're now developing with 3D graphics and a full-screen option from the browser, so no matter how fast the player, we still need the most efficient code possible.

The open source tool TweenBencher, distributed with GoASAP, makes it easy to find out how efficient your Go classes are. To test any animation system, you need to first try and "clock" the computer you're. TweenBencher does this by providing a base benchmark: a simple ActionScript 3 animation loop. This script is written to process a tween in the same way a tween engine does with a bare minimum of code (see Figure 10-4).

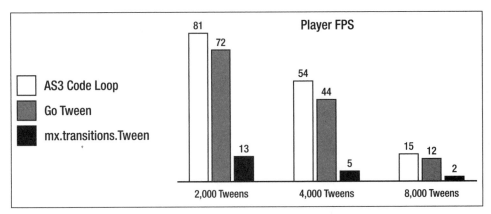

Figure 10-4. A benchmark that compares Go's efficiency to a simple animation code loop

Here you see a comparison showing the ActionScript 3 code loop, a basic tween written using the standard Go base class LinearGo, and the Tween class shipped with Flash. The Flash Tween class differs notably in that it doesn't use a managed tween list. As you can see, the player's frame rate drops significantly when taxed with so many tweens, and this provides a comparative scale.

Go remains very fast, running at 80 percent of the code loop's performance. As you build on Go, your code will lessen its efficiency, so it needs to start out lean and mean. Keep in mind that in a typical project only a handful of tweens would ever be run at once; the benchmark is designed to push the limits of the player and the system. (It's also easy to imagine a particle system or star field with many hundreds of active animations.)

Go addresses the need for speed in several ways. This starts with a highly optimized pulse engine—since at the heart of any animation system is a pulse.

GoEngine: multiple pulses

Go's engine, called GoEngine, is more flexible than most tween engines. It expands on the highly efficient managed tween list model discussed earlier by allowing for *multiple* lists. Instead of picking one pulse for all animation to run on, in Go any animation can specify its own unique pulse rate. GoEngine automatically groups items by pulse to maximize efficiency.

What's the point? Well, let's say you're building a space game. You'll want all of the many enemy ships to share a pulse so that their animation doesn't lag. Since you want these primary animations to run as fast as possible, you should normally leave them at the default ENTER_FRAME pulse rate, which seems to run the smoothest (this is the GoItem.defaultPulseInterval setting). Now, in your ship's cockpit you might have several animated status meters and instrument readouts. Since the gamer's attention won't be as constantly focused on that area, it would be smart to set these secondary animations to a slower pulse. Between 100 and 500 milliseconds should work, depending on the feel you're after. All cockpit readouts should share that slower pulse so their update cycle is also efficient.

This technique will make your game run more smoothly. The processes are divided up neatly, and the less-crucial cockpit animations aren't hitting the player as hard.

GoEngine *is also optimized in another critical area: adding and removing items. Animation items can be packed with complexities of their own, for example, in their setup or shutdown routines, so it's important that the engine doesn't add lags to these processes.* ZigoEngine *did this by using objects for its list instead of arrays, and* GoEngine *carries this further by using the* Dictionary *class. Although arrays perform a touch better in the* for *loop within an update cycle,* Dictionary *classes give far faster access when adding, and especially deleting, entries. That is,* Array.splice() *is much slower than* delete myDictionary[entry].

Less is more

Animation systems can end up layered with complexities—engines often try to manage items in complex ways, items themselves are complex, and so forth. But wait—do you remember the first animation you ever wrote in ActionScript? It was just a few lines of code in a simple loop! Go tries to bring you back around to that level of simplicity by making it possible to add only what you need for any project.

The LinearGo tween base class provides all the standard features commonly included in kits but with a bare minimum of code. This is all-important because as you extend Go with your own functionality, it will necessarily slow things down, so the base classes need to stay as efficient as possible.

As you'll see in the next section, Go's architecture also helps you stay in tight control over exactly which layers of complexity you add to your program.

Go architecture

Go's architecture is very simple. It is built in layers, the lowest of which consists of the GoEngine class; then above that are animation base classes and utilities. The only unique twist is the way that management (across multiple animations) is set up, a defining feature that provides an open format for structuring more complex animation system mechanics.

All that is mandatory to use GoASAP is the lowest layer, core compatibility. The other classes and interfaces are entirely optional.

Remember that Go's classes are not set in stone. Beyond extending them, Go's license gives you permission to modify the actual core classes as well. Just be sure to very clearly notate the changes in the Go classes you modify and put a prominent note in your documentation letting other developers know that they'll need to incorporate those changes instead of using the standard release.

GoASAP is a work in progress, so keep in mind that some details in the following section might have changed since this was written. If Go lacks support for something you need or you find ways to improve its core architecture, please make an effort to participate in discussions and bring these issues to light. Ideally, Go will be a product of its community—so expect changes, and get involved.

Core compatibility layer

GoEngine is the single class considered mandatory for implementing GoASAP. This class imports several interface types:

- IUpdatable: Any object using this interface can add itself to GoEngine to begin receiving updates on whatever pulse it specifies. This is the only requirement for defining an animation item and contains just an update() method and a getter for pulseInterval. Items can then call GoEngine.addItem() and removeItem() to start or stop their pulse.

- IManageable: Any object using this interface can be handled by manager classes.

The following "playable" elements exist at the lowest level of the Go platform. They are not mandatory but can provide important points of commonality:

- GoEvent defines common animation types such as START and COMPLETE. One issue with the many animation systems available today is that they all define very similar events in different packages; GoEvent is designed to be comprehensive and generic.

- IPlayable and PlayableBase work together to define a common set of play controls: start(), stop(), pause(), resume(), and skipTo(). Those controls are defined in IPlayable, while PlayableBase houses a common set of play-state constants such as STOPPED and PLAYING plus a state getter. PlayableBase also extends EventDispatcher since it's often the lowest-level class you extend. These elements sit at the lowest level of the platform since playables can range from an IUpdatable animation item to a general utility, such as a group or a sequence that can be played on its own.

> *Why compatibility? Imagine finding yourself in the middle of a project that requires some unique animation challenges that your standard set of Go-based tools doesn't cover.*
>
> *The approach most common today would be to cram whatever top-to-bottom products can meet these needs into your project, despite any redundancy or loss of efficiency, and then fight through making them work together.*
>
> *Using Go, the picture is brighter. One option would be to hunt down the math formulas that address your particular motion challenges and then use Go to build a few custom classes. But let's say that first you searched around and found several other Go developers had already made the tools you need and released them as open source. Not only will all of these disparate animation classes from various corners of the Web snap together, but they'll coordinate seamlessly in GoEngine's efficient shared update lists. They might also dispatch GoEvent types and use the familiar Go play control methods. If either or both of those developers implemented the IManageable interface, it could mean even tighter coordination within your program, with no extra effort on your part.*

GoItem layer

Go's hierarchy of animation item base classes has been only partially defined at the time of this writing. The branch that is fairly complete is for building tweens (also known as **linear animations** because they have a known start and end). The second branch, physics, is not yet complete, so if physics is your area of expertise, don't hesitate to get involved in helping to define it.

- GoItem: A generic base class for any animation type—tween, physics, or other. This class implements IUpdatable, which makes it compatible with GoEngine. It extends PlayableBase so that it can use play-state constants but leaves the implementation of IPlayable to subclasses. GoItem defines a few conventional properties that can be implemented by any kind of animation: useRounding, meaning snap all animation output values to whole numbers, and useRelative, meaning treat animation inputs as relative, not absolute values. GoItem also includes a debugging feature called timeMultiplier, which can be implemented by subclasses to stretch or compress animation time (LinearGo implements this feature for tweens).

- PhysicsGo is not complete at the time of this writing.

- LinearGo extends GoItem and implements IPlayable. This is a full-featured tween class designed to run fast and be flexible for subclassing (described in the following section).

Utility layer

The Go package includes several common animation utilities as optional extras for grouping or sequencing animation. These make use of the Go platform architecture but actually sit outside it. Typically utilities stand on their own and are used to handle playable items such as tweens—or in some cases, other utilities. A Fuse-syntax parser utility, for example, might generate instances of the utilities listed here:

- PlayableGroup: This playable class wraps a batch of other IPlayable instances and runs them in parallel, using a single set of play controls. Its children can be animation items, other groups, sequences, and so forth, as long as they're playable and dispatch a GoEvent.STOP or COMPLETE when they're done. PlayableGroup dispatches GoEvent.COMPLETE when all its children have finished.

- SequenceBase: The thing that defines a sequence class is what type of SequenceStep it uses for its children. Because ActionScript 3 restricts the overriding of method inputs and return types, this base class defines sequence functionality but allows subclasses to write their own typed methods accepting and returning their actual step type. A SequenceStep is a simple extension of PlayableGroup that dispatches a special SequenceEvent.ADVANCE event when it is complete.

- Sequence: This SequenceBase extension accepts any IPlayable that it wraps in a SequenceStep and then plays its steps one after the next.

- SequenceCA: This sequencer extending SequenceBase uses a special step type, SequenceStepCA. This step has an advance property that can be used to determine exactly when the sequence should step forward, such as after a certain time has elapsed or when a particular child of the step completes. Like Fuse's trigger property discussed earlier, this lets you gracefully overlap and stagger animations like you can in a timeline. You can subclass SequenceAdvance to define a new custom advance type or use one of these options shipped with Go: OnDurationComplete, OnPlayableComplete, OnEventComplete, or OnConditionTrue.

Manager layer

Although GoASAP is designed to be as generic as possible, its management layer differentiates it from any other system available today and is one of its most valuable facets. This layer defines the way that management across animation items is structured. (It is actually part of GoEngine, but I saved it for last since it's a more advanced topic.)

Traditionally, animation systems bake management into their core code base, which increases their functionality but reduces their efficiency. The most typical tween management behavior—provided as an optional class called `OverlapMonitor` in Go—prevents two tweens from trying to handle the same property on the same target at once. But management doesn't stop there; it could also include things like a hit-test manager, a component of a game engine, or a particle-emitter life-cycle manager.

It is not possible for Go as a base platform to know the specifics. So instead, Go provides a decoupled and extensible format for adding system management. By **decoupled**, I mean that managers are left entirely out of the system until they are compiled and activated by the end user. This is done using the command `GoEngine.addManager()`.

Here's how a developer would activate `OverlapMonitor` one time in their program's setup:

```
GoEngine.addManager(new OverlapMonitor());
```

So, you can write as many diverse managers as you want, but it's up to the consumer of your software whether to use any particular manager or to leave it out. For Go system developers, this means total freedom to make managers as specific as you want; for end users it means the freedom to pick and choose or avoid the processing overhead altogether.

The manager layer is simple in its implementation. It consists of a few methods in `GoEngine`, `addManager()`, `removeManager()`, and `getManager()`, plus the following two interfaces:

- `IManager`: Defines a manager with just two methods, `reserve()` and `release()`. `GoEngine` is a "hub" for all active animation items in a program and the repository for user-registered managers. When `IUpdatable` items add themselves to `GoEngine`, if they are of type `IManageable`, the engine passes them over to the `reserve()` method of all registered managers. Similarly, when removed, such items are sent to managers' `release()` method. This way managers get access to all active, manageable animations and can do whatever they please with them. This could be very simple, such as storing a list of items to check for target/property overlap as `OverlapMonitor` does. It could also get complex: a hit-test manager might sniff for a particular interface, add an update callback to each item, and perform some live process to detect collisions.
- `IManageable`: This interface provides a few queries so managers can find out what targets and properties the item is handling and call a `releaseHandling()` method on the item in the case that a conflict is detected.

> Whew! That was a lot of information. In practice, it really isn't such a grind to use Go. In fact, it can be very easy. The most basic way to extend Go in its current form is to create custom tween classes by extending `LinearGo`. That process can be done in just a few steps—I'll show you how in the next section.

Rolling your own animation classes

Using Go, it's possible to create a custom tween class in a matter of minutes. The base tween class `LinearGo` provides all the standard tween settings and functionality, but it leaves the fun of designing the tween to you. It does this by stopping short of defining any particular kind of tween target object or any of the actual properties to be animated.

Using LinearGo by itself

LinearGo is a full-featured tween class. Here's a quick rundown of many of its goodies:

- It has the standard tween properties delay, duration, and easing plus the class settings defaultDelay, defaultDuration, and defaultEasing.

- The useRounding and useRelative options from GoItem. These do nothing on their own but can be implemented in subclasses.

- A repeater instance allows you to cycle the tween's play any number of times.

- Any tween can set its pulseInterval in milliseconds or to GoEngine.ENTER_FRAME.

- A useFrames option that counts updates instead of using seconds, plus getters for timePosition and currentFrame. This is not recommended except for specialty situations—when using seconds, tweens run in real time and won't lag with the player.

- GoEvent types dispatched during play include START, UPDATE, CYCLE, and COMPLETE as well as the user-triggered events STOP, PAUSE, and RESUME. As an alternative to events, you can store and fire one or more callback functions using the addCallback() method.

So if you don't extend LinearGo, what does it animate? It doesn't have any targets or properties! The answer is that it crunches just a single number—stored in its position property (protected: _position), which always starts at 0 and ends at 1, and evaluates to a fraction as the tween runs.

Take a look at this code:

```
var tween: LinearGo = new LinearGo();
tween.addEventListener(GoEvent.UPDATE, moveBox);
tween.start();
function moveBox(event: GoEvent): void {
  boxsprite.x = 50 + (event.target as LinearGo).position * 200;
}
```

This example shows how you can instantiate and use a LinearGo by itself and then listen to its update event and use its position as a multiplier to animate something in your program code.

That technique is fine; there's nothing wrong with it—until you want to reuse the functionality elsewhere in your code, at which point you'd probably end up duplicating the update handler's code into other handlers, which isn't so great. It's nice to know that you can run a LinearGo on its own for custom situations, but by *extending* it you can neatly package the functionality to be quickly reused anywhere, anytime.

> *To create a subclass, you simply use the* extends *keyword. If you're unfamiliar with this technique, you might want to hit the Flash docs or another learning resource on object-oriented programming to brush up. In short, our subclass extends* LinearGo, *which extends* GoItem, *which extends* PlayableBase, *in what is known as an* **inheritance chain** *or* **hierarchy***. Each subclass adopts all of its parent class's methods and properties, almost like a fresh copy that can then be added to or modified by overriding methods. The next example makes use of these OO fundamentals.*

Designing a custom syntax

What I like to do when I start the process of writing a custom class is to write out the syntax the way it should look when it's finished. (That was my approach with Fuse, which was a highly designed syntax.) Today I want a tween that will animate any property on any target. Maybe tomorrow I'll want one that will animate any number of properties, and I can rest easy knowing it will be just as easy to put together, but for now here's how I think my custom tween should look:

```
new PropertyTween(sprite1, "x", 200, 0, 1, Cubic.easeOut, true);
```

My constructor inputs will be the target, property, tween end value, delay, duration, easing, and useRelative value. I'll leave it at that. I want it to be plain and simple. (Be sure to look at LinearGo's documentation so you know all of the options you can include in your constructor.)

Starting the PropertyTween class

Now that I've designed the way my tween will be used, I'm ready to write the constructor and begin writing the tween extension. I'm going to start simply by extending LinearGo and adding a target object, a tween property, and the end value that the tween should animate to:

```
package com.mosesSupposes.go.tutorials
{
  import org.goasap.items.LinearGo;
  public class PropertyTween extends LinearGo {

    public var endVal: Number;

    public function get target(): Object { return _target; }
    public function set target(t: Object):void {
      if (_state==STOPPED)
        _target = t;
    }

    public function get prop() : String { return _prop; }
    public function set prop(prop : String) : void {
```

```
        if (_state==STOPPED)
          _prop = prop;
    }

    protected var _target: Object;
    protected var _prop: String;
    protected var _startVal: Number;
    protected var _changeVal: Number;

    // Constructor inputs can be arranged any way you like.
    public function PropertyTween(target: Object=null,
                                  property: String=null,
                                  endVal: Number=NaN,
                                  delay: Number=NaN,
                                  duration: Number=NaN,
                                  easing: Function=null,
                                  useRelative: Boolean=false ) {
      super(delay, duration, easing, null, null, useRelative);
      this._target = target;
      this._prop = property;
      this.endVal = endVal;
    }
  ...
```

This is not the whole class, just the first part. One of the first things you'll notice about this code is that there's more going on than meets the eye, particularly in the lines that read if (_state==STOPPED), which reference properties from the extended classes.

Reviewing the hierarchy of tween base classes

Let's review the inheritance chain for LinearGo. (You may want to review the earlier "Core compatibility layer" and "GoItem layer" sections that outline these classes.)

```
[a custom tween like PropertyTween] extends LinearGo
  LinearGo extends GoItem implements IPlayable
    GoItem extends PlayableBase implements IUpdatable
      PlayableBase extends EventDispatcher implements IPlayableBase
```

The most relevant information here is at the lowest level, PlayableBase. This class contains a number of public play-state constants: PLAYING, PLAYING_DELAY, PAUSED, and STOPPED. Since this tween extends PlayableBase, it can make a direct internal reference to those constants—they now belong to your custom tween class. PlayableBase also includes a public state getter and a protected _state property, and the base tween class LinearGo keeps it current during play so your class can query its own state at any time. Speaking of the play cycle, LinearGo's play control methods are found in the IPlayable interface: start(), stop(), pause(), resume(), and skipTo(). These standard controls appear in Go's parallel and sequence utilities and any other "playable" class. So to operate your tween, the user will call start() on it.

> *Exploring the GoASAP documentation would be a great idea at this juncture, and here's how to get the most out of it. Navigate to* `PlayableBase` *first, the lowest-level class in the hierarchy chain. It's easy to find because it lives in the topmost directory. Look closely at the header block of that docs page, above the plain-text description— you'll see listings with links for inheritance, implements, and subclasses. Those links will allow you to very quickly navigate the hierarchy listed earlier, and surfing around a little will give you a feel for how the different parts of the Go platform relate. Be sure to scroll down to the methods and properties on each page to get a cursory idea of what's in each class.*

Understanding the hierarchy of classes you're working within is an important part of this learning process, so really take a minute or two to do that now.

Returning to the code for the PropertyTween class, you'll see that it's pretty easy to understand. There are getter/setter properties for your tween target and property, a public variable for the endVal (the numerical value that the property should be tweened to), and a nice simple constructor design.

It's great that LinearGo does not define any of these things for you! Think about how many options there are. For example, if you wanted to write a tween class that supported more than one property, you could change these inputs into a targets:Array and a properties:Array with a corresponding endVals:Array. Or instead of matched arrays, you could provide a single properties:Object input that would parse an enumerated object à la Fuse. A straightforward approach would be to list a set of related properties, such as a SpriteTween with x, scaleX, and alpha properties instead of just a single generic property input. It might make your head spin to think about all the possibilities. There's a lot of room for creativity here.

Writing the guts of the tween class

Now that you've had the fun of designing your tween class, it's time to make it functional. This process involves storing your property's start and change values when the user starts the tween and then applying a simple mathematical formula as the tween updates on its pulse, which is real animation itself.

Here's how the second half of my PropertyTween class will look:

```
...
    override public function start():Boolean {
      if (_target==null || isNaN(endVal) ||
         _target.hasOwnProperty(_prop)==false) {
       return false;
      }
      _startVal = _target[_prop];
      _changeVal = (useRelative ? endVal : endVal - _startVal);
      return (super.start());
    }
```

```
      override protected function onUpdate(type:String): void {
        // the correctValue() call handles useRounding.
        _target[_prop] = correctValue( _startVal + _changeVal * _position );
      }
    }
  }
```

I have overridden two methods of the parent class LinearGo. The start() method is part of the IPlayable interface, and the protected onUpdate() method is an internal callback fired on the tween's pulse from its update() method, called at just the right moment for tween calculations and rendering.

Overriding onUpdate()

You can see the tween being applied in the one line of code in onUpdate(). Within that line you'll see that to calculate the tween's value you need to have a start value and a change value. Those variables are the reason that start() is overridden; they are stored just as the user starts the tween.

Look at the formula itself. Here's the meat of it:

```
  _startVal + _changeVal * _position;
```

This is the magic tween formula that you will use in all your custom tween classes. In plain English, it reads as follows: "start plus a portion of change."

To clarify this a little further, here's a sample of the custom tween, as it will be used:

```
  sprite1.x = 100;
  var t:PropertyTween = new PropertyTween(sprite1, "x", 300);
  t.start();
```

In this example, the start x value is 100, and the end x value is 300. That makes the distance traveled, or change value, 200. So, the formula "start plus a portion of change" will mean "every update, set the sprite's x to its start position (100) plus some percentage of the distance it will travel (200 * _position)." Over time it will travel from its start position of 100 (100 + 0% of 200) to its end position of 300 (100 + 100% of 200). Make sense? This is how, on the tween's pulse, you can position the sprite on its x-axis by knowing simply where it started and how far it needs to travel.

The motion style is automatically factored into the tween by LinearGo, which uses the tween's easing function to factor its _position multiplier, so most of the hard work is already done for you. All you need to do now is trap the start and change values, and *voilà*! You have a functioning tween.

Go conventions: useRounding and useRelative

You might be wondering about the correctValue() call in onUpdate().

The Go platform suggests two conventions (found in GoItem) that are not implemented for you. They have to be written for each custom animation item class, because they directly tie into the "guts" of each custom design, such as the particular data type of a tween value. They are as follows:

- useRounding: Snap all tween output values to whole numbers. This is good for pixel fonts or other situations where exact rendering is critical.

- useRelative: Tween end values should be interpreted as relative to the start position, not as absolutes. In other words, treat them as "from" the start, not "to" the end.

The helper method correctValue() actually takes care of useRounding for you and also corrects any rogue NaN values to 0. A good rule of thumb for writing Go items is to *always* call correctValue() on *any calculated animation values* before applying them to target objects.

The second convention, useRelative, is implemented in the override of start() where the change value is stored. Next I'll cover the steps I took in subclassing start().

> GoItem *has just one* useRelative *property, while any item subclass might have multiple properties. If you've used Fuse, you'll remember that any start or end property can be treated as a relative value individually. But the Go platform doesn't know whether your classes will have one property or multiple properties, so its approach is simply to establish a single convention all items can follow. This does not preclude adding per-property support for relative positioning in your custom item subclasses, but you would need to design and implement that yourself. If you do so, be sure to retain support for the* GoItem *convention: setting* useRelative *once on the instance should make all properties relative.*

Overriding start()

The start() override in my tween class is composed of four statements. I'll walk you through them:

- if (...) return false;: This statement is standard object-oriented boilerplate. If a user tries to start an invalid tween, you reject the call and return false to indicate failure. The order of each element you check is important. First you check whether _target==null, because if it does, trying to access any method or property in it will throw an error. Next you make sure there is a valid numerical end value set using an isNaN() test. Finally, and most important, you use _target.hasOwnProperty(_prop) to be sure that whatever property the user is trying to animate already exists in the target. This is a safe way to ensure that you won't get errors when you try to dynamically set _target[_prop]. In fact, simply trying to access the hasOwnProperty method would have thrown an error if it had been done first and the _target had been null.

- _startVal = _target[_prop];: This is where you trap the tween's start value that will be used in the tween formula in onUpdate(). Since your custom design uses a generic property, you use array brackets to dynamically evaluate it on the target.

- _changeVal = (useRelative ? endVal : endVal - _startVal);: Here is where you implement the second GoItem convention useRelative and trap the tween's change value that you'll need during update. Usually, the change value would be found by subtracting the start value you found in the previous step from the endVal set by the user. In the earlier example I gave, the target was sitting at a start x position of 100 and had set an absolute endVal of 300, and this amounted to *300–100=200*. But if the user has set the tween's useRelative property, it means that 300 would be the change value itself, because they simply mean "move the sprite's x 300 pixels." You'll end up at *100+300=400*, but you don't have to do any further calculations to find _changeVal, since the amount of relative change is still just 300. The ternary statement takes care of that logic in one line of code by simply setting _changeVal to endVal if useRelative is activated or otherwise to the end-minus-start calculation.

- return (super.start());: Finally, you call the start() method of the parent class LinearGo in order to start the tween. Since that method might return false in certain cases, you return its return value instead of just true.

Reviewing what we've done so far

Extending LinearGo to create a custom tween class involves the following steps. I've covered three out of four of these so far.

1. Design the tween target and property types and constructor inputs.
2. Store the tween start and change values in start() and apply them in onUpdate().
3. Implement the GoItem conventions useRounding and useRelative.
4. Optionally, make the tween work with Go managers by implementing IManageable.

Before you look at that last step, let's celebrate the newborn PropertyTween class by giving it a spin around the block!

Using the custom tween

Because of the way I designed my constructor, I can set my target, property, end value, delay, duration, easing function, and useRelative setting all from a single call.

Here's an example of a 1 1/2-second x slide 200px to the right of the sprite's current position (using relative positioning, that is) with a bounce motion style, which will start after a 1/4-second delay:

```
import fl.motion.easing.Bounce;
import com.mosesSupposes.go.tutorials.PropertyTween;

var t: PropertyTween = new PropertyTween(sprite1, "scaleX", 200,
                                        .25, 1.5, Bounce.easeOut, true);
t.start();
```

Setting tween properties

Now remember, LinearGo has a lot of features I'm not using here. Here's another example (without the import statements) where I use the object-oriented nature of this class to first generate the instance and then set each property one by one. Although this approach takes more lines to write, it's visually quite clear, and if you're using an Eclipse-based code editor, it leverages code hinting to great effect.

```
var t: PropertyTween = new PropertyTween(sprite1, "scaleX", 200);
t.delay = .25;
t.duration = 1.5;
t.easing = Bounce.easeOut;
t.useRelative = true;
t.repeater.cycles = 2;
t.repeater.easingOnCycle = Bounce.easeIn;
t.addEventListener(GoEvent.CYCLE, onSlideDone);
t.addEventListener(GoEvent.COMPLETE, onSlideDone);
t.start();
```

I've also set some additional LinearGo options here that I didn't include in my constructor: the tween's repeater instance will now make it cycle forward and then back in a yo-yo motion, mirroring the easing style on its way back. (First the 1/4-second delay will play through, then the sprite will bounce 200px over 1.5 seconds, and then it will immediately reverse direction and do an inverted bounce back to its initial x position.)

Using callbacks and events

The previous example adds several event listeners that link the completion of the first cycle and the completion of all cycles to an event handler called onSlideDone that would need to exist elsewhere in my code. That handler would need to receive an incoming GoEvent parameter and might look something like this:

```
protected function onSlideDone(event: GoEvent):void {
  if (event.type==GoEvent.CYCLE) {
    trace("PropertyTween cycle complete. Starting next cycle...");
    return;
  }
  if (event.type==GoEvent.COMPLETE) {
    var tweenInstance:PropertyTween = (event.target as PropertyTween);
    var tweenTarget:Sprite = tweenInstance.target as Sprite;
    trace("The x slide on" + tweenTarget.toString() + " is complete.");
    trace("Final x position: "+ tweenTarget.x);
  }
}
```

If you prefer using callbacks on your tweens instead of events, you can subscribe any number of callbacks to any of the GoEvent types that LinearGo dispatches using the addCallback() method. In the first line here, the callback will execute at the end of all cycles since the second parameter of addCallback() is the event type, and it will default to GoEvent.COMPLETE if not explicitly set:

```
t.addCallback(function():void{ trace("Done!"); });
t.addCallback(function():void{ trace(sprite1.x); }, GoEvent.UPDATE);
```

Grouping parallel tweens

Go includes several optional utilities that you can use right out of the box. One is PlayableGroup, which enables you to bundle any number of playable items (tweens, other groups, sequences, and so on) into a single playable instance. This way you have easy control to start, stop, or pause the whole batch from one place and listen for a GoEvent.COMPLETE event when the whole batch has finished playing. (If you have used Fuse in the past, this is the same thing as wrapping several action objects in an array.)

The following group starts and runs all the tweens together, but because some tweens have different delays and durations, they will appear to run in a somewhat staggered fashion. The first three of these tweens run on the same target, sprite1, at the same time. My tween class design allowed for only one property to be tweened at once so the parallel group enables me to animate multiple properties at once. However, even if I *had* designed the tween to accept multiple properties, I would still need to run separate tweens in this case, since a tween is by definition defined by its delay-duration-easing combo and those parameters differ here.

```
var g:PlayableGroup = new PlayableGroup();
g.addChild(new PropertyTween(sprite1, "x", 100, 0, 1));
g.addChild(new PropertyTween(sprite1, "y", 100, 1, 2));
g.addChild(new PropertyTween(sprite1, "alpha", 0, 2, 1));
g.addChild(new PropertyTween(sprite2, "x", 100, 0, 1));
g.addEventListener(GoEvent.COMPLETE, onGroupDone);
g.start();
```

Groups store their playable children in an array property called children, and they contain several methods for managing that list including addChild(), removeChild(), getChildByID(), and a generalized state-checker, anyChildHasState(). You can also always access each child directly via the children array.

The PlayableGroup utility features a repeater property similar to that of LinearGo, which allows you to play the group any number of times in a row or indefinitely by setting the repeater's cycles property to Repeater.INFINITE.

Sequencing tweens

GoASAP also includes several out-of-the-box sequence utilities! The first is simply called Sequence and does just what you would expect: runs animations back to back.

```
var s:Sequence = new Sequence();
s.addStep(new PropertyTween(sprite1, "x", 100, 0, 1, null, true));
s.addStep(new PropertyTween(sprite1, "rotation", 360));
s.addStep(new PropertyTween(sprite1, "alpha", 0));
s.addEventListener(GoEvent.COMPLETE, onSequenceDone);
s.start();
```

> *Translation: 1. Slide the Sprite 100px to the right of its current position over one second. 2. Next, spin the sprite around over one second. 3. Finally, fade the sprite out over one second. 4. When the entire sequence is complete, fire an event handler called* onSequenceDone, *not shown here.*

You've probably guessed that sequences have a steps property similar to a group's children property, and if you guessed that it is also an array, you were right. As you pass tweens or any other playable items to the addStep() method (which is similar to the addChild() method of PlayableGroup), sequences automatically wrap them in instances of the SequenceStep class. So earlier, each time I passed a tween instance to the addChild() method, internally that tween was added to an automatically generated SequenceStep, which was then added to the steps array.

```
trace("First step is SequenceStep:"
        + (s.steps[0] is SequenceStep)); // output: true
```

As you can see from this trace statement, even though I passed in a tween instance, it has been converted to a SequenceStep in the sequence.

Adding parallel groups to a sequence

But what is a SequenceStep? The answer is that it's a very simple extension of the PlayableGroup class. (The only difference is that it dispatches a special event on completion, SequenceEvent.ADVANCE, that tells the parent sequence to step forward.) So, since steps are groups, each step in a sequence can contain any number of parallel tweens or any other **playables**—other groups, sequences, or custom IPlayable utilities.

So if I want the rotation and x tweens in my previous example to play at the same time before the fade-out, I could manually create a step with several children before I add it, like this:

```
var s:Sequence = new Sequence();
var step:SequenceStep = new SequenceStep();
step.addChild(new PropertyTween(sprite1, "x", 100, 0, 1, null, true));
step.addChild(new PropertyTween(sprite1, "rotation", 360));
s.addStep(step);
s.addStep(new PropertyTween(sprite1, "alpha", 0));
```

Too complex? Don't fret, there is an easier way! The next version also groups the first two tweens but looks almost exactly like my first sequence example—with one notable difference. (See it?)

```
var s:Sequence = new Sequence();
s.addStep(new PropertyTween(sprite1, "x", 100, 0, 1, null, true));
s.addStep(new PropertyTween(sprite1, "rotation", 360), true);
s.addStep(new PropertyTween(sprite1, "alpha", 0));
s.addEventListener(GoEvent.COMPLETE, onSequenceDone);
s.start();
```

It might not jump out at you, but hidden in the end of the second addStep() call (the rotation tween) is a second parameter: true, passed after the tween. The signature for addStep() looks like this:

```
addStep(item:IPlayable, addToLastStep:Boolean=false):int
```

As you've probably guessed, passing true to that second parameter adds the second tween into the first step, in a group. This saves you the effort of manually instantiating the step and adding children to it first.

Go's Sequence class, like LinearGo and PlayableGroup, also has its own repeater property, so you can set a sequence to play any number of times:

```
s.repeater.cycles = Repeater.INFINITE;
s.start();
```

Here, the sequence will continue to loop until you call stop() on it. You can also cycle specific tweens within a sequence any number of times or cycle any step since steps extend PlayableGroup, resulting in an open, flexible system that can include cycling at any level.

Advanced tween sequencing

Fuse had a special trigger feature to keep code-driven sequences from becoming rigid and robotic (see the earlier section "Matching timeline functionality"). In short, a Fuse trigger makes a step in a sequence advance early—before all of its children have finished playing—which mimics the physical timeline's freedom to overlap the start of a new tween with the ends of previous tweens.

I felt this feature was so important that it needed to be included in GoASAP, but because it adds a significant amount of internal complexity, it is offered as a separate class called SequenceCA. The CA suffix stands for *custom advance*, and Go offers a fully extensible way to create your own criteria for when a step should advance. In SequenceCA, each step is of the type SequenceStepCA, which extends SequenceStep to add an advance property.

This example adds a custom advance to the first step:

```
var s:SequenceCA = new SequenceCA();
s.addStep(new PropertyTween(sprite1, "x", 100, 0, 3));
s.lastStep.advance = new OnDurationComplete(2);
s.addStep(new PropertyTween(sprite1, "rotation", 360, 0, 2));
s.addStep(new PropertyTween(sprite1, "alpha", 0));
s.addEventListener(GoEvent.COMPLETE, onSequenceDone);
s.start();
```

The first step (the x slide) runs for three seconds, but the OnDurationComplete instance set to the step's advance property will force the second action (the spin) to begin after only two seconds have elapsed. The spin lasts for two seconds, meaning that the first two actions of the sequence *overlap* their play for one second. In the Flash timeline, this is similar to having dragged the second tween back so it overlaps with the end of the first tween. It's an important feature for animators because it frees you from needing to wait for all the tweens in a group to finish before you can start the next action, meaning that you can create sequences that are as fluid and graceful as they would be in the timeline.

GoASAP ships with the most common custom advance options: OnDurationComplete (advance after some amount of time has elapsed as in the earlier example), OnPlayableComplete (advance after a particular item in a group has finished playing), OnEventComplete (advance after any arbitrary event in your program is dispatched, such as a load event), and OnConditionTrue (advance when a custom callback returns true). All of these extend the SequenceAdvance base class, which you too can extend to add some new criteria for stepping a sequence forward. This might be entirely specific to the details of a particular project, and that's the beauty of Go. Once you're comfortable with it, you can extend it in any way you need to for any project, constantly branching it out to meet specific challenges.

Making the tween work with managers

The PropertyTween class is nice and simple; it just animates a property of any target object. But what if two tweens were created, perhaps in different parts of a program that are unaware of each other, and both of them tried to tween the same property of the same target object? So far, those tweens would both continue to run at the same time, in direct conflict with each other, which might cause weird visual glitches or disrupt the program's event flow. Normally animation engines (like ZigoEngine, for example) provide some degree of system-level oversight to ensure that the second tween added would automatically stop the first tween. However, that kind of management adds overhead to your program and ends up "baked into" the engine's code as a permanent feature.

> At this time, you may want to return to the earlier "Manager layer" section if you skipped it so that you understand how managers fit into Go's framework. In short, GoASAP provides a way to build managers as stand-alone components that "snap into" GoEngine at runtime, which allows users to add any number of custom managers or exclude all of them to save processing.

One manager shipped with GoASAP called OverlapMonitor performs this task of preventing two tweens from conflicting. But, there's a catch: managers need a way to be able to interact with tweens or other animation items. This is done by implementing the IManageable interface on your tweens, which adds four simple methods. Managers such as OverlapMonitor implement another interface, IManager, which allows users to register them like this in their runtime code:

```
GoEngine.addManager(new OverlapMonitor());
```

This layout keeps things wonderfully optional. First, it allows you to choose whether to bother making your tweens manageable. Then if you do, it still allows the end user of your tweens to pick which managers to use or opt not to use any. The beauty of this is that although you might make your tween manageable so it can be used by OverlapMonitor, someone else might write another custom manager that neither one of us has ever heard of, like some kind of game engine component, and your tween will be ready for that person to use with the new custom manager by simply registering it into the engine. It's an entirely open, entirely extensible system—and luckily for us, making tweens manageable is pretty easy.

Implementing IManageable

> *Keep in mind that Go is still young, and its details may change. Be sure to reference the official GoASAP documentation as you follow this section and any time you implement* IManageable *in the future.*

Implementing IManageable is simple. First, add the `implements` statement to the class declaration:

```
public class PropertyTween extends LinearGo implements IManageable {
```

Next, you need to implement that interface's four methods inside the class body. I usually put this at the bottom of the class with a comment that explains what the methods are for.

```
...
    // IManageable implementation

    public function getActiveTargets(): Array {
      return [ _target ];
    }

    public function getActiveProperties(): Array {
      return [ _prop];
    }

    public function isHandling(properties: Array): Boolean {
      if (state==STOPPED || _prop==null) { return false; }
      if (_target is DisplayObject) { // check for indirect overlap
        if (_prop=="width" && properties.indexOf("scaleX")>-1)
          return true;
        if (_prop=="height" && properties.indexOf("scaleY")>-1)
          return true;
        if (_prop=="scaleX" && properties.indexOf("width")>-1)
          return true;
        if (_prop=="scaleY" && properties.indexOf("height")>-1)
          return true;
      }
      return (properties.indexOf(_prop)>-1); // direct overlap
    }

    public function releaseHandling(...params): void {
      stop();
    }
...
```

The first two methods should report to the manager just the targets and properties that are actively being handled by the tween. (Keep in mind that some tween classes might offer the option of multiple properties, but only some of those might be actively used in a particular play cycle.)

The third method, isHandling(), is key. It should attempt to run an accurate match between the properties passed in and the properties this tween instance is actively handling, and it should return true if any overlap occurs. In many cases, this can be a little bit tricky. Our tween class accepts any type of target object, but in the case of DisplayObject targets, you know that the property width should also check the input array for scaleX, because you wouldn't want two tweens trying to run those properties on the same target at once. The same goes for height and yScale, and you need to check both directions since either the tween or the incoming array might contain either. If your tween actively handles multiple properties, this can get even trickier. The documentation describes these different overlap scenarios in more detail.

The final method, releaseHandling(), provides a way for a manager to request that the animation item stop playing, such as if a conflict has been detected. Usually you simply call stop() from this method.

> *Notes on* releaseHandling *for advanced users: This method is used instead of* stop() *because* IPlayable *is not actually a requirement for animation items, so there may not be any* stop() *method. This method also includes a* ...rest *input to provide flexibility for potentially more complex management behaviors. For example, maybe a future manager will want to release handling on just a specific target or property. That hypothetical behavior is, however, not supported by* OverlapMonitor, *which treats any item as a single animation unit. If you want your Go program to be able to detect overlap and stop individual properties, you could achieve that in several ways. Most simply, only write items that handle one target and property at a time. Or, create a custom manager and add a marker interface to your items that it can sniff for. Or, implement custom behavior in* isHandling() *to remove conflicting properties on the spot and return true only if all properties conflict.*

EllipseTween

There could be no greater way to represent Go as a project than to give a unique example straight out of the community. Go is fairly new, but people are already using it on professional projects. This example runs an elliptical animation and is great for things like carousels. This version is 2D; the author is also building a 3D version for use with Papervision.

The code has been stripped of comments for brevity, but it should look familiar to you after reading the previous sections. You'll see all of the same basic steps involved in the previous tween example, plus the implementation of the IManageable interface.

The Go website links to an open repository called the GoPlayground. You can become a member and share your work with others there, and you'll probably find the official copy of EllipseTween there as a free open source download.

This is `EllipseTween`, a `LinearGo` extension by community member Graeme Asher that animates a clip in a perfect oval path. Although it is simple, Graeme told me that "this is the beauty of Go—you can just write what you need for your project and then expand on that later." If the ellipse calculations in this class look complicated, that's OK: that is the custom portion of Graeme's code. But if you've followed the exercises in this chapter so far, the `LinearGo` structure of the following class should make sense without any further explanation:

```
package com.zaaz.animation {
  import flash.geom.Point;
  import flash.geom.Rectangle;

  import org.goasap.interfaces.IManageable;
  import org.goasap.items.LinearGo;

  public class EllipseTween extends LinearGo implements IManageable
  {
    public var angleTo:Number;
    public var bounds:Rectangle;

    protected var _target:Object;
    protected var _radii:Point;
    protected var _center:Point;
    protected var _startAngle:Number;
    protected var _changeAngle:Number;

    public function EllipseTween(target:Object,
                                 angleTo:Number,
                                 bounds:Rectangle,
                                 duration:Number = NaN,
                                 easing:Function = null,
                                 delay:Number = NaN) {
      super(delay, duration, easing);
      _target = target;
      this.angleTo = angleTo;
      this.bounds = bounds;
    }

    public function get target() : Object {
      return _target;
    }
    public function set target(target : Object) : void {
      if(_state == STOPPED) {
        if (target.hasOwnProperty("x")
            && target.hasOwnProperty("y")) {
          _target = target;
        }
      }
    }
```

```
override public function start() : Boolean {
  if(target == null || isNaN(angleTo) || bounds == null) {
    return false;
  }
  _radii = new Point(bounds.width / 2.0, bounds.height / 2.0);
  _center = _radii.add( new Point(bounds.x, bounds.y) );
  _startAngle = Math.atan2((target.y - _center.y),
                 (target.x - _center.x)) * 180 / Math.PI;
  if(useRelative) {
    _changeAngle = angleTo;
  }
  else {
    _changeAngle = (angleTo - _startAngle) - 90;
  }
  return super.start();
}

override protected function onUpdate(type : String) : void {
  var angle : Number = _startAngle + (_changeAngle * _position);
  var radian : Number = angle * Math.PI / 180.0;
  target.x = super.correctValue(_center.x
                            + _radii.x * Math.cos(radian));
  target.y = super.correctValue(_center.y
                            + _radii.y * Math.sin(radian));
}

// IManageable implementation

public function getActiveTargets() : Array {
  return [_target];
}

public function getActiveProperties() : Array {
  return ["x", "y"];
}

public function isHandling(properties : Array) : Boolean {
  if (state == STOPPED)
    return false;
  return (properties.indexOf("x") > -1
          || properties.indexOf("y") > -1);
}

public function releaseHandling(...params) : void {
  stop();
}
  }
 }
}
```

Testing the Tweens with OverlapMonitor

Here's a class that tests the two tween classes described earlier and shows OverlapMonitor in action. This assumes you followed the section that helps you implement IManageable for PropertyTween. (That interface has to be implemented by both tweens.) You can set a blank FLA's document class to this test class or run it in a Flex ActionScript project.

The test runs an EllipseTween; then, when you click the stage, it runs a PropertyTween on the same target. This allows you to interrupt the elliptical tween during play, resulting in a graceful release of handling as the horizontal tween takes over. To see what happens without OverlapMonitor, comment out the GoEngine.addManager line—now when the tween is interrupted by your click, the tweens will overlap. You'll see strange visual results from this, and because both instances are still active, any events you add for completion will still fire. If your program uses only a few tweens, you could set up a way to call stop() on running tweens before adding a potentially conflicting tween, but OverlapMonitor automates that process for you.

Here is a test class that runs both tweens and tests OverlapMonitor:

```
package {
  import flash.display.Sprite;
  import flash.events.MouseEvent;
  import flash.geom.Rectangle;

  import org.goasap.GoEngine;
  import org.goasap.items.GoItem;
  import org.goasap.managers.OverlapMonitor;

  import com.mosesSupposes.go.tutorials.PropertyTween;
  import com.zaaz.animation.EllipseTween;

  public class TestSomeTweens extends Sprite {

    public var square : Sprite;

    // defines test ellipse bounds
    public var rect : Rectangle = new Rectangle(100, 100, 100, 200);

    public function TestSomeTweens() {
      this.stage.frameRate = 30;
      square = new Sprite();
      square.graphics.beginFill(0xFF3300, 1);
      square.graphics.drawRect(-5, -5, 10, 10);
      addChild(square);

      // draw the path onstage based on the test rect
      this.graphics.lineStyle(0, 0, 0.1);
      this.graphics.drawEllipse(rect.x, rect.y,
                                rect.width, rect.height);
```

285

```
                // place the target on the right edge of the path
                square.x = rect.x + rect.width;
                square.y = rect.y + rect.height / 2;

                // comment out addManager line to see the difference
                GoEngine.addManager(new OverlapMonitor());
                this.stage.addEventListener(MouseEvent.MOUSE_DOWN, onClick);

                // ellipse tween
                var et : EllipseTween;
                et = new EllipseTween(square, 360, rect, 4);
                // relative angleTo - comment out for absolute angleTo
                et.useRelative = true;
                et.start();
            }

            protected function onClick(e : MouseEvent) : void {
                var t : PropertyTween = new PropertyTween(square, "x", 400);
                t.start();
            }
        }
    }
```

When you run this example and click the stage as the ellipse tween plays, you'll see that when the horizontal tween starts, the EllipseTween instance is automatically stopped. OverlapMonitor has successfully prevented the tweens from playing at the same time since both tween classes were manageable.

GoASAP, garbage collection, and memory

Part of the managed list architecture popularized by Zigo involves shielding the user from direct access to tween objects. In the AVM 1 Flash Player (versions 1 through 8), this gave a real advantage because memory was a stickier issue. The player's built-in garbage collection system simply didn't work as well, and the common practice of coding in timeline frames trapped variables and references like flies on flypaper. The event system was also hard to use without clogging memory.

Thankfully, ActionScript 3 and AVM 2 have made massive improvements in this area. We now have tools such as weak references for event listeners and Dictionary objects, which allow the player's garbage collector to sweep away more single-use debris in our code. We can track memory with the System.totalMemory property or use the Flex Debugger, which provides a detailed list of how many objects, method closures, and other potential snags exist in memory.

What this means for animation is that the tightly sealed tween engine model is no longer needed. There's nothing wrong with it, but one could argue that it's overkill. On the other end of the spectrum, Flash's Tween class presented a completely opposite problem. Tween instances are independent manager objects. Since you're the only one who stores any reference to them in your code, tweens that you forget to store in a permanent variable often get garbage collected and stop running midstream! This of course means that later you have to remember to go back and delete those references, so you're back in the ActionScript 2 boat.

GoASAP offers a more open and balanced solution that does not get trapped in either of these extremes. It lets the end user decide whether to store references to tween objects in their code or let them get collected. Either way, the animation will never vanish during play because GoEngine retains a persistent reference to it in its update lists. This means total freedom to generate and start tween objects in your code *with or without* retaining a reference. Retain one if you plan to reuse the tween; otherwise, let it go.

Carrying this even further, you're entirely free to create managed systems with GoASAP if you simply prefer not to have any interaction with tween objects. Build your utilities to work the way you want them to work. For example, in the earlier PropertyTween class, you could add a static call allowing you to start a tween without necessarily retaining a reference to it:

```
public static function go( target: Object,
                           property: String,
                           endVal: Number,
                           delay: Number=NaN,
                           duration: Number=NaN,
                           easing: Function=null,
                           useRelative: Boolean=false ):PropertyTween {
    var tween: PropertyTween = new PropertyTween(target,
                                                 property,
                                                 endVal,
                                                 delay,
                                                 duration,
                                                 easing,
                                                 useRelative);
    tween.start();
    return tween;
}
```

That was easy. The only difference between these inputs and those of the constructor is that target, property, and endVal are mandatory parameters here since otherwise you wouldn't have a tween to start. This simple method provides much of the convenience of a traditional tween engine like ZigoEngine or Tweener. Unlike a full tween engine, there's no static methods allowing you to "look up" the tween in order to pause it or otherwise control it. However, users can easily just store the returned reference to the tween if they need to access it again in their code. Alternatively, you could write a tween-engine-like utility to generate tweens and provide lookups to control them. It's up to you.

You've seen how GoEngine solves the problem of tweens vanishing midstream by retaining a reference to them just during their play cycle. However, some playable objects don't use GoEngine at all, such as a PlayableGroup or Sequence. If you generate and start a sequence but retain no reference to it, you need to ensure it doesn't get garbage collected during play. GoASAP solves this problem with a simple convention.

> IPlayable *objects that do not use* GoEngine *should store a reference to themselves in* PlayableBase._playRetainer *or another static variable when they are started and remove the reference when stopped.*

You can see examples of how this convention is implemented in the PlayableGroup and SequenceBase utility classes that ship with GoASAP. When building playable utilities of your own, be sure to do the same. However, leave it at that—you can easily cause further memory problems if you overmanage things. Be sure to ask yourself at each step of creating a Go utility whether you need to store an internal reference to an item (or to the utility itself) and how you will ensure that the reference is *always* removed at the proper time. This way, your utilities won't end up looking like ActionScript 2 flypaper.

Footprint

Because Go is a fully object-oriented system, its focus is on providing a clear, coherent architecture that you can extend, and thus its file size footprint will vary based on how it is used. It makes no attempt to satisfy strict advertising-banner limits like TweenLite or similar products do, since it is assumed that you'll be using Go within object-oriented programs such as websites or applications. In its current incarnation, GoEngine adds 2KB to your build; adding LinearGo and OverlapMonitor raises the total to about 8KB and includes GoEvent and a number of other classes and interfaces. Using these things plus utilities like PlayableGroup and SequenceCA weighs in at 9KB–13KB.

These sizes are extremely moderate, but again the ultimate total will vary based on your extensions. In stark contrast to many prepackaged APIs, Go brings an open architecture and sophisticated animation functionality to the table but in every way encourages you to add and compile just what you need for any project.

Into the wild: physics, 3D, and beyond

When I was looking for new directions I could take Fuse at the advent of ActionScript 3, I was keenly influenced by people like John Grden (Infrared5) and Josh Hirsch (Big Spaceship) who made me realize that the do-it-yourself contingency was real and growing. They explained that although Fuse was great for the masses, it left out the DIY set with its top-down "kit" approach; it was also not designed for use with the normal workflow in Eclipse and other coding environments that hinge on strict data typing. I was inspired to try to come up with a platform that would support DIY coders in their natural tendency to branch out in new directions, based on the challenges of every new project.

GoASAP is a young project. It offers a lot in the area of linear animation already, provides a coherent architecture for an extensible management layer, and features an efficient central engine. But clearly there's still a long way to go before it lives up to its full potential, most notably in the area of physics animation. It's possible that simply reengineering a few existing physics systems to make use of Go's core compatibility layer would be a good start. But it's also exciting to imagine something like a game engine built with Go that could harness central management to enact seamless switching and mixing of physics and "canned" animation. Ideally I'd like to see a physics system broken into logical layers, just like the linear system is now, making it easier for everyone to roll up their sleeves and get their hands dirty in the same way.

3D is another area that Go can really excel. At the time of this writing, I'm working with the Papervision team to design an animation system for use with exported animations created in Maya or 3D Studio Max. You can already use LinearGo to fabricate all sorts of custom 3D tweens. Since you get to design your tween class's inputs and functionality, you can preset a 3D scene that can be refreshed as the tween updates. If you're already using Papervision, you should be able to package a lot of your loop scripts into a Go class and get them out of your way, while making them easy to reuse in other projects.

Bustin' loose

Part of my personal goal with Go is to erode the artificial barrier between the DIYers and those who simply use prefab kits. In my view, that distinction is a by-product of our Flash roots. Most of us aren't software engineers at heart, and many think they could *never* do things like program animation tools. There's certainly nothing wrong with leveraging the wealth of open source tools out there, but I'd like you to consider taking a little time to *play*.

Back when I was on the cusp of creating Fuse, a chat I had over a beer with designer Matt Owens (of Volume One fame) inspired me to the point of changing the whole direction of my career. I told Matt that I was buried up to my ears in client work and simply could not understand how he found the time to put out so much incredible personal work. He asked me to think about what happens when I have a client who I think is very important; how does that affect other clients? As much as you don't want to or mean to, you end up putting the one client in front of others in little ways. I agreed but didn't entirely see his point, so I asked him to elaborate.

He explained that it's natural to put your clients first and let your own work get pushed down the priority list until you never get to it, or if you do, it's with a sense of resignation and compromise. But the trick is that with a clear decision and the right mind-set, it's equally easy—at least for an hour a day or so—to make *you* your most important client. Not even your most important clients get to cut into this time. With apologies, you have other obligations—but will be back in the saddle ready to work with them in just a few minutes.

This clear vision really blew my mind at the time. It was so simple, and yet Matt was right—I was not giving myself the same level of importance that I so eagerly gave others every day. Soon I was carving out a little of my own time to focus on projects like Fuse and finding it was a lot of fun and that the rest of my work benefited from it too.

More and more, companies like Google are seeing the value of allowing their developers a certain amount of R&D time, which follows the same logic. If you're employed full-time, don't hesitate to bring a proposal to your boss suggesting that with just a few hours of R&D time per week, you and your team will be able to refine and expand on the animation systems you use every day. No matter how busy your company is, it is the same decision for them as it is for an independent contractor like myself—an acknowledgment that carving out and protecting that time can end up vastly improving every other hour put toward client projects.

It might be time to pop a new slot into your calendar and take your phone off the hook for that hour a day. Experimentation is the key to growing your skills. And Go is essentially an open invite to do just that with animation.

So, go and play!

Chapter 11

USING PAPERVISION3D

by Andy Zupko

Papervision3D was originally conceived and developed by Carlos Ulloa in November 2005, inspired by the Joost Korngold session at the Spark conference in Amsterdam. By January 2006, Carlos had developed a fledging class library to transform MovieClips, allowing him to position, rotate, scale, and skew his objects. He used these classes extensively in his personal work and experimentation, and he had fantastic results.

In August 2006, Carlos released a new version of his libraries, now called Papervision, that was fully optimized to use the Flash 8 drawing API. This optimization gave Carlos the ability to use triangle tessellation to add perspective distortion to his projects and create real 3D in Flash. Over the next 10 months, Papervision was developed into 14 classes, and the Papervision 1.0 private beta was released.

Papervision's development sped up dramatically at this point. A new site and blog were created, and Papervision was added to OSFlash.org. John Grden was the first user and contributor to the project. John converted the classes to ActionScript 3, and the huge performance boost made it clear that Papervision had a future in Flash. Hundreds of developers began downloading the code and began contributing to the effort of making a phenomenal open source project.

In early 2007, Ralph Hauwert joined the core team and amazed the community with his technical demos and materials. John Grden also released his X-Wing game, the first of its kind for Flash; soon after, the first commercial sites began appearing.

After spending several months on COLLADA integration, Tim Knip joined the core team in August, and one year after Papervision's initial release, the Papervision 2.0 "Great White" alpha was released. Papervision 2.0 featured a new set of features for developers, including shaders, frustrum culling, COLLADA animation, and multiple viewports.

Shortly after the Great White release, Andy Zupko was formally added to the core team for his work on adding effects to Papervision (among other things), and a new tier of the team was created that focused on noncore tasks and testing.

Currently, Papervision has more than 280 classes dedicated to the core. It has more than 2,500 developers currently signed up on the mailing list, the largest at OSFlash. Papervision's feature set is constantly being expanded and developed, thanks to a great development team and the strong community support behind it.

Who's who

Papervision is constantly being developed, modified, optimized, and tweaked to give it the best developer and user experience possible. Although it is a community effort, Papervision is managed by a dedicated team. The team is divided into two tiers: the core team and the committer team.

The core team

The core team is responsible for all aspects central to the Papervision project: engine quality, releases, team setup, and the overall API. It comprises five members, each with varying responsibilities:

- Carlos Ulloa: Founder and leader of Papervision3D
- John Grden: Component/release manager
- Ralph Hauwert: Engine core/shaders
- Tim Knip: Engine core/DAE/shaders
- Andy Zupko: Effects

The committer team

The committer team is the outer ring dedicated to more specific functionality and noncore tasks:

- Ricardo Cabello: Testing/demos/feature review
- De'Angelo Richardson: Testing/extra features
- Stephen Downs: Flex 2.0 components/effects
- Seb Lee Delisle: Particles/effects
- John Lindquist: Tutorials/documentation

Getting started with Papervision

To begin developing with Papervision, you will need to get your hands on a copy of the source. You can download a stable release of Papervision at http://code.google.com/p/papervision3d/. It includes all the documentation, sample files, and classes you will need to start your first project. In addition to all the stable releases, the Google Code page contains links to the SVN repository, the CS3 component, and the Papervision blog.

SVN

Papervision's Subversion repository is located at http://papervision3d.googlecode.com/svn/trunk/. By using Subversion, you can download the latest working builds of Papervision, as well as revert to older revisions if necessary. To access the Papervision SVN, you will need to download a good SVN client for your operating system, such as TortoiseSVN for Windows (http://tortoisesvn.tigris.org/) or ZigVersion for OS X (http://zigversion.com/).

The repository is structured to have one trunk and multiple branches. The trunk is the most stable build short of downloading a stable release from Google Code. Currently the trunk is not under development because all attention has been turned to developing 2.0. However, it is home to version 1.7 and is quite stable.

Currently there are two branches in the repository: Great White and Effects. Great White is the official 2.0 alpha release of Papervision. It contains the newest changes and is currently under the heaviest development. The Effects branch is almost an exact duplicate of Great White, but it has some small core changes and a slew of additional classes to provide visual pre- and post-render effects to your 3D world. The Effects branch is updated frequently to mirror any changes made in Great White. The two branches will eventually be merged but are currently separated because of the volume of changes currently underway.

It is possible to use the branches for a commercial project, but the developer should be aware that they are constantly being modified and upgraded, and changes may cause conflicts in any projects currently underway. If you want to use one of these branches for a large project, it is a good idea to find a stable revision for your project to fall back on should any updates create conflicts with your code.

The CS3 component

John Grden developed the CS3 component to allow anyone to use Papervision, even if they don't know a single command in ActionScript 3. The component is a visual tool in the Flash CS3 IDE that allows designers and developers to easily add a 3D model to the stage, control their materials, and create a full Papervision world without typing a single line of code. It uses Live Preview, so all changes to the model and camera are visible on the stage at design time, which takes the guesswork out of sizing and positioning 3D models. In addition, the CS3 component and the 3D world it contains are completely accessible via ActionScript, so developers who want to make more complex interactions with their scene have complete power to do so. The component is free and available for download on Papervision's Google Code page. Installing it is easy; just double-click the file, and Adobe Extension Manager should take over and handle the installation. (If it doesn't, you can open the Extension Manager and select the file to install from your hard drive.) If you have Flash open, restart it. Next, open the Components panel (Ctrl+F7), and you will see the component under Papervision3D.

You can also open the component's control panel (Figure 11-1) by selecting Window ➤ Other Panels ➤ PV3D Panel. This panel will allow you to easily select, size, and skin your model directly on the stage.

Figure 11-1. The Flash CS3 component

Explanation of the parts

Before diving into code and trying to explain how to use classes, you will need to understand the core concepts and objects used by Papervision. Four objects are required for every Papervision project: scene, viewport, renderer, and camera. These comprise the what, where, how, and from what point of view of your project.

Scene: the what

The scene is essentially the 3D world in Papervision. It contains all the objects you want to be rendered to the screen. When you add any DisplayObject3D (the standard object type of Papervision), it will be rendered into your viewport. You can position all your elements within the scene the same way you would DisplayObject objects on the stage. By setting the x, y, and z properties of the DisplayObject3D, you can control where your object is set in your 3D world.

Viewport: the where

The viewport is a rectangular region where all 3D content is drawn. It is essentially the window to your 3D world. In Papervision, the viewport is a sprite where all content from the scene is drawn. By default, the viewport is the size of your stage, but it is possible to resize the viewport, as well as have multiple viewports on the screen at the same time. A common use of having two or more viewports is in multiplayer split-screen games, with one viewport for each user. You can also use viewports as materials within other viewports. A rearview mirror in a racing game is a great example of this technique.

Renderer: the how

The renderer is what takes the data from your scene and draws it into your viewport using the camera you specify. The renderer takes all the content from your scene, figures out what it would look like from your camera, and draws it into your viewport.

Camera: from what point of view

The camera is the eye of the user. It is the point of view you want your 3D world to be rendered from. You can manipulate the camera's position and rotation to view your world from any angle. In addition, you can control the zoom and focus of your camera to create different visual effects, as if your world were truly being shot from a digital camera. Like other DisplayObject3D objects, you can move your camera around in your scene using its x, y, and z properties. This gives you the ability to render your scene from any point of view.

Objects in Papervision

Papervision provides a number of DisplayObject3D objects for you to add to your scene. These range from the simple primitives to complex parsers that allow you to import intricate geometry into your 3D world.

Primitives

Papervision has a set of primitive classes included in the core libraries. Primitives are basic geometric shapes that are commonly used in 3D applications. Papervision provides the following primitive objects:

- Cube
- Plane
- Sphere
- Cone
- Cylinder

Although the primitives aren't incredibly complex, with proper texturing they are a lightweight solution to any number of scenarios in Papervision.

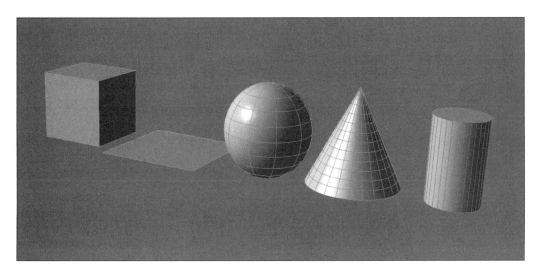

COLLADA

COLLADA is an open standard XML schema used to share 3D data between applications. It was originally developed by Sony with several other collaborators, and it is currently maintained by the Khronos Group. The COLLADA format was chosen as the standard format for Papervision for several reasons. The most important is that most 3D packages are capable of exporting their scenes in the COLLADA format, including 3D Studio Max, Maya, Softimage's XSI, Modo, and even Blender. COLLADA files are also easily parsed, since they are an open XML format and contain all the information that would be useful in a Papervision scene: cameras, lights, geometry, materials, and animations.

The Papervision team has provided the Collada class, which parses the COLLADA file for you and creates a DisplayObject3D with your geometry and materials intact. This gives you the ability to model and texture complex objects in the 3D application of your choice and easily add them to your Papervision project. A new COLLADA parsing class, DAE, is also being developed and is capable of handling many features not supported in the Collada class, including animation and color information.

Figure 11-2 shows a simple spaceship model rendered in Papervision. All geometry, textures, and texture coordinates are parsed from the COLLADA file and entered into a new Collada object. This object can then be added directly into your scene and used like all other objects in Papervision.

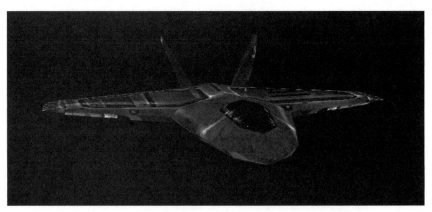

Figure 11-2. A full model parsed from COLLADA and rendered in Papervision

Materials

Papervision gives you the ability to map textures to all your objects in 3D. These textures can be pulled from almost anywhere: the stage, the library, or the file system. All materials are drawn to the screen using the Flash drawing API, which gives the user the ability to map any content to each face of his object. Papervision handles mapping materials correctly to primitives. When importing COLLADA models, you can map your textures in your 3D modeling program, and all the texture coordinates are parsed into your Collada object for you. Different types of materials will allow you to apply different object types as textures in your 3D world.

Color materials

The ColorMaterial object lets you texture your object with a solid color of your choice. They are lightweight and can be used for any number of things, including debugging, shading, or creating transparent faces on your model.

Bitmap materials

BitmapMaterial objects allow you to use either an image or a BitmapData object as your texture. These materials generally remain unchanging, although there is the ability to update the BitmapData in which the material is drawn from.

Movie materials

MovieMaterial objects are similar to bitmap materials, but they can contain any type of DisplayObject in Flash. Moreover, they can be set to be fully animated, so any content that is changing in the MovieClip will be shown while mapped to your 3D object.

Shaded materials

ShadedMaterial objects are new to Papervision 2.0; they give you the ability to dynamically shade your objects. Papervision currently supports four types of shaders: Flat, Gouraud, Phong, and Cell. The Flat and Gouraud shaders provide simple shading across each face. Gouraud is slightly smoother but requires slightly more processing. The Phong shader is the smoothest of the shaders but requires the most processing power. It does, however, give you the ability to use bump mapping on your materials, which adds an extra dimension to your objects. The Cell shader is the slowest of the available shaders but can provide very convincing shading on complex geometry.

Interactivity

One of the great features of Papervision is the ability to interact with your materials as if they were real DisplayObject objects. Remember, even though you can map any material to your object, they are all drawn as bitmap fills. Because of this, you aren't able to capture mouse events on the projected data like you would a regular DisplayObject. Fortunately, John Grden developed the InteractiveSceneManager, which uses a VirtualMouse to dispatch events to your MovieMaterial objects. This allows you to attach buttons, components, or anything else you want, as well as capture mouse events from their 3D projections.

Your first Papervision project

To get started with Papervision, you will complete a short project that will familiarize you with the Papervision API. To follow along with this demo, you will need to have already downloaded the Papervision SVN, have Flash CS3, and have a basic understanding of ActionScript 3.

Setting up Flash

To set up Flash, follow these steps:

1. First, create a new Flash ActionScript 3 document. Select Modify ➤ Document to open the Document Properties dialog box, and set the frame rate to 31 for smooth animation and the stage size to 800×800.

2. Next, you need to include the Papervision libraries for Flash to compile with. You can import these classes by selecting File ➤ Publish Settings ➤ Flash ➤ Settings; the Publish Settings dialog box appears (see Figure 11-3).

3. Click the Browse to Path icon, and select the GreatWhite source directory in your Papervision folder. The path from the root of the Papervision SVN is \branches\GreatWhite\src (Figure 11-4).

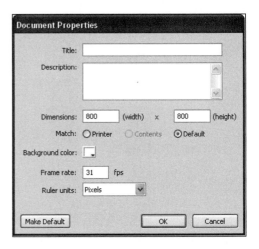

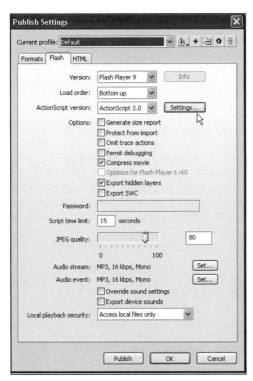

Figure 11-3. Publish Settings dialog box for Flash movie

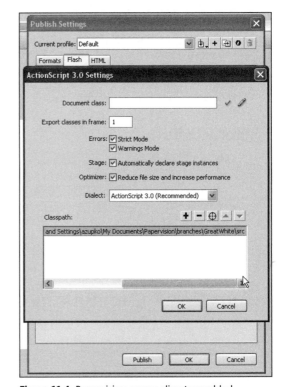

Figure 11-4. Papervision source directory added to classpaths

Creating the asset

Now that Flash is set up, you need to create the texture you want to use for your cube.

1. Start by selecting the Rectangle tool (R) from the toolbar. In the Properties panel, set your line color to black and your line thickness to 0.25. Set your fill color to a light gray, around 0x333333, and set the fill alpha to 40 percent. Now draw a 300X300 rectangle directly on the stage. The size doesn't matter at this point; just try to keep it square to prevent the scale from looking off when the MovieClip is mapped to your cube.

2. Select everything on the stage, and press F8 to open the Convert to Symbol dialog box. Name the MovieClip CubeMaterial. Select the Export for ActionScript and Export in First Frame check boxes. The Class field should automatically populate with CubeMaterial, but if it isn't, enter it now. See Figure 11-3 for a complete view of your properties. This gives Papervision a reference to your material from the Flash library. Remember, you can name your materials anything you want, but you will need to remember these names to be able to reference them from your code.

3. Double-click the CubeMaterial MovieClip in the library to edit it on the stage. Create a new layer called Text. Now select the Text tool (T), and create a new text field in the center of your rectangle. Enter **Hello Papervision** into the new field, and choose a font you like and a size that nearly fills the width of the rectangle—I chose Arial at 38 pt.

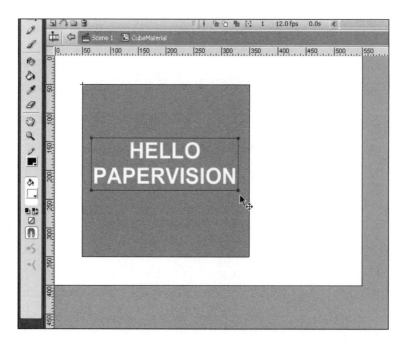

4. Create a new tween with your text layer and add some animation to the text. I chose to apply a glow filter that pulses on and off, but feel free to use any animation you want. The purpose of the animation is simply to show the texture animated while mapped to the cube, so just make sure any animation you add stays within the borders of the background rectangle to prevent any cropping while mapped to the cube.

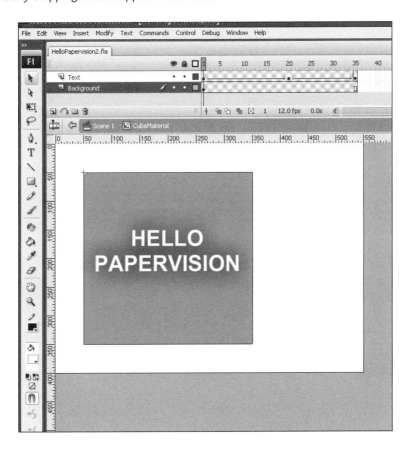

Initializing the scene

To initialize the scene, follow these steps:

1. Return to the root timeline, and delete any content you have on the stage, because this is where your 3D world will be rendered. Next, create a new layer called ActionScript. This is where you will add your code to create a 3D world with Papervision, so open the Actions panel. The first thing you will need to do is import all the classes needed for your project to run:

```
import flash.display.MovieClip;
import flash.display.Sprite;
import flash.events.Event;
import org.papervision3d.cameras.FreeCamera3D;
import org.papervision3d.core.components.as3.utils.ObjectController;
```

```
import org.papervision3d.materials.MovieAssetMaterial;
import org.papervision3d.materials.utils.MaterialsList;
import org.papervision3d.objects.primitives.Cube;
import org.papervision3d.render.BasicRenderEngine;
import org.papervision3d.scenes.Scene3D;
import org.papervision3d.view.Viewport3D;
```

2. Before you can do anything, you need to make sure you have the four required pieces of all Papervision projects:

```
var camera:FreeCamera3D;
var scene:Scene3D;
var renderer:BasicRenderEngine;
var viewport:Viewport3D;
```

Remember, camera is the point of view, scene is all of your 3D "world" data, renderer tells Papervision how to render that world, and viewport is the sprite to which the world is drawn. If you don't have any one of these pieces, you won't be able to render your 3D world.

3. Now you are ready to set up your 3D environment. The first step is to initialize your core classes:

```
camera = new FreeCamera3D(11, 100);
scene = new Scene3D();
renderer = new BasicRenderEngine();

viewport = new Viewport3D(0, 0, true, false);
addChild(viewport);
```

FreeCamera3D is a camera you can point in any direction. By default, it has no rotation and is positioned at (0,0,-1000);. This will let you see any objects that are placed at the origin (0,0,0) without having to worry about any additional positioning. The two parameters you pass into the FreeCamera3D constructor are zoom and focus. I won't cover any of the math in this chapter, but to prevent any perspective distortion, trust me and set the zoom to 11 and focus to 100. This will keep your scene looking natural.

Viewport3D is the sprite container to which you will be drawing all the rendered data. This is the reason you add it to the stage display list. You're passing four parameters into the viewport: width, height, autoScaleToStage, and interactive. autoScaleToStage will automatically size your viewport to fit the stage of your movie, and because you have set this to true, you don't need to specify a width or height in the constructor. interactive allows you to interact with content inside your textures, such as text fields and buttons. Because this demo does not have any interaction of this sort and there is a performance hit when interactivity is enabled, you will simply set it to false.

Adding the cube

Before you can add anything to the 3D world, you need to create some materials to texture your cube:

```
var material:MovieAssetMaterial = new MovieAssetMaterial(
                                    "CubeMaterial", true, true);
material.precise = true;
material.smooth = true;
material.tiled = true;
material.doubleSided = true;
```

A MovieAssetMaterial is a MovieMaterial that pulls its content from the library of your Flash movie. CubeMaterial is the linkage identifier you set to the MovieClip CubeMaterial earlier. You can find this texture in the library of HelloPapervision.fla.

The second parameter passed to MovieAssetMaterial is transparent. Since you have a transparent background, this is set to true so you can see through the cube. The third parameter, animated, is also set to true, since you have animation in your MovieClip and want to see it pulsing on the faces of your cube.

The next properties that are set clean up your texture so it will look good when applied to the cube. Precise tells the material to dynamically tessellate (create triangles) on the face to help eliminate perspective distortion.

By setting smooth to true, the bitmap that your movie is drawn to has smoothing applied, giving a nice antialiased look to your content (Figure 11-5). Since smooth is set to true, you need to enable tiled. The tiled property tells the material to repeat the texture, but in this case, your material is not being scaled down on the face allowing any tiling to be seen—instead, the tiled property is set to help smoothing run faster.

Figure 11-5. No smoothing (top) compared to smoothing (bottom)

Although precision and smoothing do affect performance, you will need to test them on each individual application to find a good balance of quality and speed. Precision will give you speed when your faces are looking toward the camera but will require more processor as faces are at high angles and must be tessellated more. Smoothing will always require more processor, because your content is smoothed every time it is rendered. A way to work around this is to turn smoothing on when an object is close to the camera or has focus so the processing isn't done the entire time your project is running but only when you need it.

The last parameter you set is doubleSided, which tells your material to be drawn on both sides of the face it is applied to. This will allow you to see the back, or inside, of your faces on the cube. When you have doubleSided enabled, you will see the texture as if you really are looking at it from the other side when you are behind it.

Now, follow these steps:

1. Now that the material is set up, you can set it as a texture for your cube. The cube object is set up a little differently than the other primitives, in that you pass a list of materials that will correspond to the appropriate side of the cube. You can create this list with a MaterialsList object. By adding a material with the appropriate name, you can direct to which face it is applied. The cube accepts the following material names: front, back, top, left, bottom, right, and all. Because you don't want to use a different texture for each face, you will set the material name in the list as all. This will apply the texture to every face of the cube.

   ```
   var materialList:MaterialsList = new MaterialsList();
   materialList.addMaterial(material, "all");
   ```

2. Next you can create your cube and pass the MaterialsList through the constructor to tell the cube to use the MovieMaterial object:

   ```
   var cube:Cube = new Cube(materialList, 300, 300, 300);
   scene.addChild(cube);
   ```

   The three parameters after the MaterialsList are height, width, and depth. These set the size of the cube in 3D space. I set all dimensions to be 300 so it will be a perfect cube and small enough for the camera (positioned at (0,0,-1000)) to see. You then add the cube to the scene, which adds it to the 3D world you will be rendering.

3. Next, add some simple control over your cube. You will use the ObjectController class, which was written by John Grden to handle viewing 3D models in the CS3 component. By registering the object with the ObjectController class, whenever you click and drag your mouse, the registered object will rotate as if it were being dragged. You must also register the stage so the ObjectController will have a reference for the mouse.

   ```
   ObjectController.getInstance().registerStage(this.stage);
   ObjectController.getInstance().registerControlObject(cube);
   ```

4. The final step is to set up the project to render the scene every frame of your Flash movie. First, you add an EventListener to catch each ENTER_FRAME event:

   ```
   addEventListener(Event.ENTER_FRAME, tick);
   ```

5. And finally you set up the tick function to handle each event and render your scene:

```
function tick(e:Event):void{

renderer.renderScene(scene, camera, viewport);

}
```

You will notice that to render the scene you use all four of the required core objects. The renderer, a BasicRenderEngine, controls how the scene is rendered. You pass the scene containing your 3D data, the camera you want to use, and the viewport you want your content rendered to as parameters in renderScene. When you call this function, the 3D world will be drawn to the viewport you have added on the stage.

Congratulations! You have just written your first Papervision application! Go ahead and run your project, and you should see a semitransparent cube with glowing text mapped to each side! Click and drag to rotate the cube so you can really see the 3D in action.

And to finish it off, your final code, with necessary imports, should end up something like this:

```
import flash.display.MovieClip;
import flash.display.Sprite;
import flash.events.Event;
import org.papervision3d.cameras.FreeCamera3D;
import org.papervision3d.core.components.as3.utils.ObjectController;
import org.papervision3d.materials.MovieAssetMaterial;
import org.papervision3d.materials.utils.MaterialsList;
import org.papervision3d.objects.primitives.Cube;
import org.papervision3d.render.BasicRenderEngine;
import org.papervision3d.scenes.Scene3D;
import org.papervision3d.view.Viewport3D;
```

```
var camera:FreeCamera3D;
var scene:Scene3D;
var renderer:BasicRenderEngine;
var viewport:Viewport3D;

camera = new FreeCamera3D(11, 100);
scene = new Scene3D();
renderer = new BasicRenderEngine();

viewport = new Viewport3D(0, 0, true, false);
addChild(viewport);


 var material:MovieAssetMaterial = new MovieAssetMaterial("CubeMaterial"
                                                      , true, true);
material.precise = true;
material.smooth = true;
material.tiled = true;
material.doubleSided  =true;

var materialList:MaterialsList = new MaterialsList();
materialList.addMaterial(material, "all");

var cube:Cube = new Cube(materialList, 300, 300, 300);
scene.addChild(cube);

ObjectController.getInstance().registerStage(this.stage);
ObjectController.getInstance().registerControlObject(cube);

addEventListener(Event.ENTER_FRAME, tick);

function tick(e:Event):void{

    renderer.renderScene(scene, camera, viewport);

}
```

Summary

In this chapter, I covered the very basics of Papervision3D. You should have a pretty good understanding of viewports, cameras, scenes, and renderers, as well as some other basic concepts such as materials and primitives. You can now set up a basic Papervision project, add a primitive to your 3D world, and map an animated MovieClip to the sides of it. Although this is a good introduction to Papervision, there is still a lot you can learn about the engine: interactivity, shaders, effects, animation . . . there are a number of directions you can go from here. Fortunately, there are some great resources available to help you learn Papervision:

- Downloadable examples: A number of example files are available in the Papervision SVN. You can find these samples under the trunk in the `examples` folder. The examples do not include complete walk-throughs, but they provide all the code you will need to learn different features of Papervision, including the different materials, interactivity, and COLLADA support.

- Mailing list: There is a mailing list available for developers to ask questions, help others, and share work with at OSFlash.org. The mailing list currently has more than 2,000 members and is very active. You can join the mailing list at `http://osflash.org/mailman/listinfo/Papervision3D_osflash.org`. You can also view transcripts from the mailing list at `http://www.nabble.com`.

- Pv3d.org: John Lindquist started Pv3d.org (`http://www.pv3d.org`) as a grounds-up tutorial site for Papervision 3D. Since its inception, he has done a number of excellent and detailed tutorials that will help you learn many techniques you can use with Papervision. Also, Pv3d.org is becoming the official Papervision tutorial site and will contain even more tutorials and walk-throughs than before.

These are all great resources, and they can really help develop your skills with Papervision3D. Be sure to join the mailing list and let everyone know the cool things you are doing with the engine. The community is what makes Papervision so great, and sharing ideas really drives the engine to be the best 3D option for Flash today.

Chapter 12

INTRODUCING RED5

by Chris Allen and John Grden

Red5 is an open source server written in Java specifically tailored to work with Adobe Flash Player. It supports the TCP socket-based RTMP and the HTTP-based Remoting (AMF) protocol, as well as XML-RPC. Red5 can stream audio and video, either on demand or in a live broadcast scenario using your computer's mic and webcam.

You can use Red5 to develop a variety of applications. Typical uses of Red5 include building video chat applications, multiuser games, and other entertainment-based programs for Flash. Red5 can also conveniently and effectively act as the data tier for rich Internet applications, allowing you to seamlessly connect to external data using either Flash Remoting or RTMP.

So, what are the RTMP protocol and Flash Remoting? When do you use one vs. the other, and how do the two protocols differ? To understand, it helps to look at a bit of background on Internet protocols in general.

The Transmission Control Protocol (TCP) is one of the core protocols that makes the Internet work. It provides an in-order delivery of bytes over the Internet in a stream. A variety of Internet protocols use TCP as a base. These include Simple Mail Transfer Protocol (SMTP), File Transfer Protocol (FTP), Hypertext Transfer Protocol (HTTP), and more. You can think of TCP as a pipe that allows data to flow over it in both directions.

HTTP is a request/response protocol used between a client and a server for transferring data on the World Wide Web. HTTP is built on top of the TCP protocol. Its original purpose was for delivering HTML pages on the Internet, but since then, it has grown to be able to transfer a variety of formats including Action Message Format (AMF). HTTP is by design a stateless protocol, in that one request/response pair doesn't know about others. Once a request has been delivered, the connection between the client and the server is severed.

So, what is AMF, and how does it fit into the picture? Think of AMF like this: it's a binary data format for passing objects to and from Flash Player. You can send these objects over RTMP, which means it's a persistent connection over TCP. Things can flow back and forth over this connection like a pipe that allows stuff to flow in both directions. The things in this case are AMF objects. Most of the examples shipped with Red5 use this method.

With Red5, you can also pass AMF objects over HTTP, meaning it's a call-and-response protocol. Flash connects to the server and says, "Server, give me this object." The server responds, "Here it is," and it hands the AMF object to Flash and closes the connection. With HTTP there's no way for Flash to be passed something by the server without it making a connection again and requesting it. The downside of RTMP is that the connection is always there taking up resources. Passing AMF objects like this over HTTP is called **Flash Remoting**, and likewise, passing AMF objects over a TCP socket is called **Real-Time Messaging Protocol (RTMP)**.

Note that there are quite a few Flash Remoting libraries for various server-side languages. PHPAMF, PyAMF, and Adobe's new open source implementation in Java (called BlazeDS) are just a few examples of these.

Now that you know the difference between the two principal methods of transferring data between Red5 and Flash, which one do you pick? Well, as we already mentioned, RTMP's advantage is that data can be pushed to the Flash client without needing to make a request for it. So, if you need to have data delivered to your client without having to actually request it, you should pick RTMP. Examples of this are chat applications and real-time stock quotes that need to be constantly updated. Streaming video of any type also needs to have an open RTMP connection to work.

In contrast, sometimes you really need only one piece of information at a time, and you know when you need it. Let's say the user has filled out a contact form, and this data needs to be stored on the server. The user would submit the form using a button. In this case, Remoting would be a good choice because there is no need to have data pushed to the client. A simple request of "store this data" and a response of "success" or "failure" are all that is needed. The overhead of keeping an RTMP socket open would be totally overkill in this case.

Red5 also supports RTMPT (the last T stands for Tunneling). In this mode, the Flash client acts in a polling manner, sending multiple HTTP requests over port 80 to simulate a persistent connection. This is useful for getting around firewalls that won't let you stream over ports that RTMP is using.

We will go into more detail about using both Remoting and RTMP in examples in Chapter 13. For now, we'll give you some background on how Red5 came about.

The history of Red5

The Red5 project started on August 31, 2005, when John, fed up with the pricing model for Flash Communication Server, sent an email to the OSFlash list. The subject read "Open source flash communication server: line starts here." Almost immediately he got responses. A team was quickly assembled to reverse engineer the RTMP protocol and get something working as fast as they could.

The two of us teamed together to project manage Red5. Chris focused on the marketing and Java side of things, while John did more of the client side. Luke Hubbard led the architecture of the project. Other Java programmers such as Joachim Bauch and Dominick Accattato soon joined the team. Around the same time, Clause Whalers introduced us to Mick Herres, a talented developer who had previously made great strides in figuring out the RTMP protocol. With his help and the community support surrounding the project, the team was able to, within a month, successfully create an RTMP handshake with a Flash client. Soon after the handshake was established, members of the Red5 team were invited to present at the now-legendary Spark conference in Amsterdam where they demonstrated live video streaming for the first time.

Red5 has come a long way in the past two years. What was once a project for an open source replacement for the Flash Media Server is now so much more. Red5 is a full-featured and stable J2EE server built specifically for the Flash Platform. It is the most powerful and easily modifiable server for Flash today. Support and attention to the server have grown enormously. Demand for presentations on Red5 at Flash conferences around the world is up. FITC in Toronto, Flashforward in Boston, and Flash on the Beach in Brighton, England, are just a few places where Red5 is taking center stage. Magazines such as *Forbes* and *Streaming Media* have mentioned Red5 in articles and interviews, and companies such as Facebook have added exciting new capabilities to their services using Red5. This all ultimately led to the founding of the consulting agency, Infrared5, that focuses on leading Flash technologies built using the Red5 server.

All of this has really pushed the Flash Platform forward and enabled more people to get involved in streaming media with Flash. With the advent of Red5, you saw a huge influx of Flash developers starting to use features of Flash Player they'd never considered touching. This has been a huge boost to the Flash Platform as a whole. Developers can now go to their clients with multiple options, and you have even more developers with NetConnection/NetStream experience pushing Flash as a choice in far more projects than before.

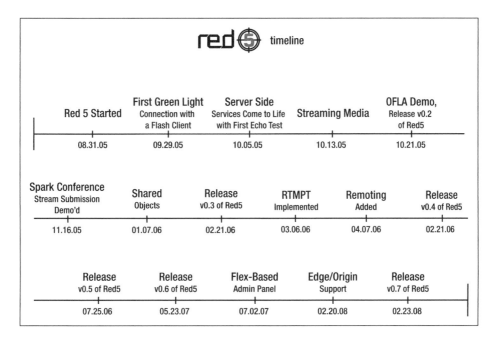

Why the name Red5?

We spent many hours trying to come up with the perfect name. We dreamed up names that ranged from very technical acronyms to single words that didn't really relate. After a day or so of debate, John, being an ardent *Star Wars* geek, suggested Luke Skywalker's call name Red5. The main reasons given were the following:

- It's about "the one" who accomplished the task.
- The Red5 team consists of "mavericks" in their own rights, which is also indicative of Red5 of *Star Wars* fame.
- It is easy to type.
- It is very memorable and appeals to most of the people who would use it.

Whether it's a good name is up for debate, but it is the name that stuck, so rock on!

Installing Red5

Red5 uses some of the latest and greatest open source Java technologies at its core. We use the Spring framework for wiring the application together. We piggyback on the MINA framework for the socket layer of Red5. We ship a stand-alone version that uses the Jetty servlet engine (Jetty, however, can easily be switched out with Tomcat, Resin, or any other J2EE servlet server). There are so many other useful libraries for Java that you can use in Red5 that it would be difficult to cover all of them in this book, and it would be hard to go into much detail on how it's built in these pages. Of course, the code is open to the public, so we encourage you to study how we did things by exploring the code base and asking questions on the mailing lists. Perhaps by doing so you will become one of the next core contributors. The Red5 team would certainly love to have your help.

Red5 runs on any operating system that supports Java 1.5. So, you can run Red5 on nearly any production operating system available, including the following:

- Windows
- Macintosh
- Linux
- Sun

> *The Linux installer is a basic installer and installs Red5 into a default directory. The information contained in this section relates to the Windows and Macintosh installers.*

For this chapter, we'll talk about doing a Windows installation with the Red5 installer. If you are not using Windows, have no fear; the sections and options are generally the same across all operating systems. You can find all the available installers on OSFlash at http://www.osflash.org/red5. You'll find a list of the latest updates at the top of the wiki page for Red5, and as of the writing of this book, we're at version 0.7. However, this setup shows screenshots from the 0.6.2 version, which is similar to 0.7's installer and which contains the same selections for installation.

During the installation, you'll be able to configure the following:

- Red5 application directory
- Red5 webapps directory
- Red5 ports
- Installation options including the option to download application samples and source

> If you have another server or service running on port 1935, 1936, 8088, or 5080, you'll want to either shut those services/applications down or configure Red5 to use other ports. Port configuration is configurable after installation as well.

Simple Windows setup

> Red5 requires Java 1.5 or 1.6 to be installed to run. You'll need to have this installed before continuing with the installation.

First things first: you'll need to download the Red5 installer for your operating system at http://www.osflash.org/red5. In this chapter, we'll go through the Windows setup, so we'll be using the 0.6.3 installer. Follow these steps:

1. After you've shut down any other applications/services running on ports 1935, 1936, 8088, and 5080, launch the installer, and click Next at the opening screen.

2. Red5 is licensed under the LGPL license, and you'll need to accept that to move on.

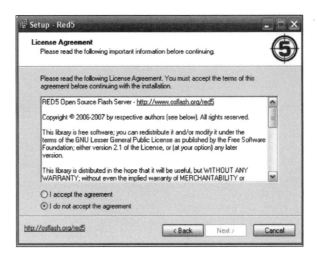

3. Java 1.5 or 1.6 has to be installed for Red5 prior to this installation. If you haven't installed it yet, please refer to the earlier Java installation instructions. Red5's installation will check to see whether you've installed Java and, if so, will attempt to prepopulate the location on this next screen.

> *You can find the latest version of Java for Windows at* http://java.sun.com/javase/downloads/index.jsp.
>
> *For Mac OS X, you can find version 1.5 at* http://www.apple.com/support/downloads/javaformacosx104release6.html *You'll note that Java for Mac OS X is only at 1.5, while the Windows version is at 1.6.*

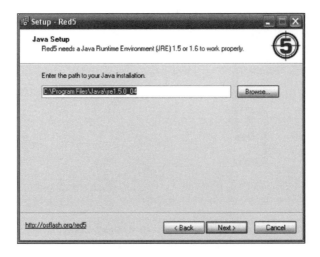

4. Select where you want to have Red5 installed.

> *This is where the* webapps *directory is installed, although you can change the* webapps *location later.*

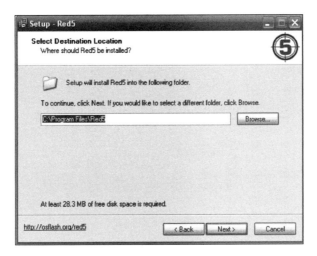

5. You'll now have the opportunity to select the options to install. If this is your first time, you'll probably want to leave the default selections ticked. They include the Java source files as well as the sample Flash applications.

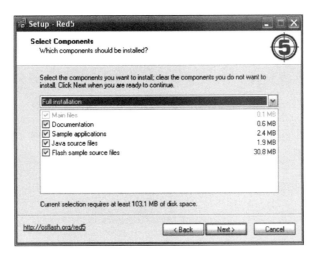

6. With the Windows installation, you get the option of where you want the application icons created.

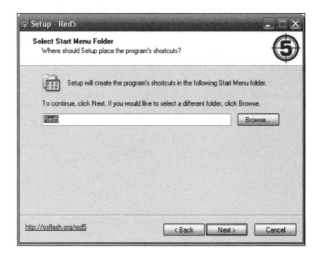

7. This next screen allows you to select whether you want to run Red5 as a service, create a desktop icon, and download sample stream files (FLVs for you to test with). On Windows, running as a service means you register Red5 as an application with Windows and are able to apply user credentials to the application as well as control whether the application starts when the computer is restarted. It also gives you a visual interface in the administration panel that allows you to start, stop, and restart your application.

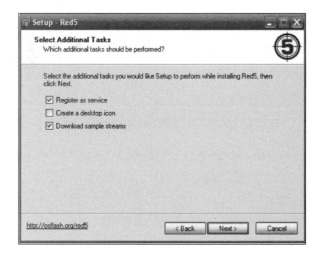

8. At this point, you're ready to select the ports Red5 will use. You can set Red5 to listen on a specific IP/interface or simply provide a port number, and Red5 will listen on that port on all interfaces. The default ports are 1935, 1936, 8088, and 5080. If you want to specify a specific IP address and port, use `<ip>:<port>`. An example is as follows:

```
127.0.0.1:1935
```

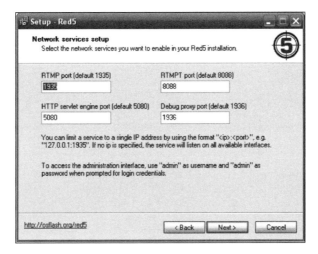

9. Finally, you'll be at the confirmation screen where you can review all of the choices you've made on the previous screens.

10. Clicking Install starts the installation. If you chose to download demo stream (FLV) files, then you'll see the sample FLV content being downloaded during the installation process.

11. When installation is complete, you'll see the final screen that allows you to launch the Red5 service.

Yeah, buddy, that was easy! Now, the first thing you should do, just after starting the service, is to make sure the demo applications work and that the server is, indeed, running.

Checking your installation

To check your installation, open a browser, and go to http://localhost:5080. If you changed the port number for the HTTP servlet engine port in the installation process, you'll want to change the URL to include your specific port number. Next, if Red5 is up and running properly, you should see the Red5 Test Page. If you do not see the page, you'll have to start Red5 manually by clicking the Start RED5 icon in the Start menu in Windows. In Mac OS X, you need to locate the Red5 icon in the applications directory and run it. Then try the previous localhost link again.

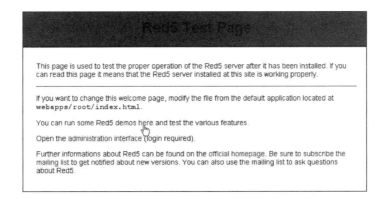

Now, if you'll remember, the webapps folder is where your Red5 applications live by default, and that location is wherever you chose to install Red5. So if you installed Red5 at `C:\Program Files\Red5`, then your webapps would be located at `C:\Program Files\Red5\webapps`. Subsequently, so are the sample source Flash files as well as server files. But we'll get into that later.

Let's get back to the test page and click the link for the demos. On this page you'll find the following links and demos:

- *Ball Demo*: This is a simple shared ball demo that uses shared objects. Be sure to open two of these, because it's a demo about people being able to see one Red5 logo move on both screens when one of the users drags it around.

- *OFLA Demo*: This is a simple video player as shown at the Online Open Source Flash conference. Click Connect, and select a movie from the list box. This is a demo showing how you can pull a list of FLVs from the file system and return that list to a Flash client to be used in a list component.

- *Port Tester*: This is a simple port tester tool that determines which ports Flash Player is able to connect through to the Red5 server. This is a Flex 2 application that runs tests on the various ports on your system. For these demos to work, the most important one is the top Default port (1935 or whatever you may have changed it to).

- *Publisher*: This is a publishing program that can be used to publish, record, and view videos. Open it, and select the Publish tab. Select your webcam device, and click Publish. Then switch back to the View tab, and click Connect in the Settings panel. Then, click Play just below the video area. You should see yourself at this point, which is a published stream from the Publish tab.

- *Simple Chat*: This is a basic chat demo that uses shared objects to send chat messages. Open two of these so that you can actually see the chat back and forth. Click the Connect button, and start typing. Yeah, it's that easy.

- *Simple Broadcaster*: This is a basic live video broadcaster. Open this sample in another tab or window in the browser and then click the Connect button. Be sure to allow Flash Player access to your video cam and mic. Then click the Simple Subscriber link in another tab or window. Click Connect, and you should see your broadcast.

- *Simple Subscriber*: This is a basic live video subscriber to be used with the simple subscriber. See "Simple Broadcaster" in this list.

- *Simple Recorder*: This is a basic live video recorder. Click the Connect to Red5 icon; then click the start record icon (blue), move around (keep your clothes on; this is a family show), and click the stop recording icon (red). Now, you'll have to go to your webapps folder and locate the oflaDemo/streams directory. You should see a new FLV file named red5RecordDemo.flv. You can watch this by importing it into Flash CS3/Flash8, or if you have an FLV viewer, you can load it there.

So far, you've been able to run the sexiest parts of Red5:

- Shared objects
- Video/audio streaming
- Video/audio broadcasting
- Video/audio subscriptions
- Video/audio recording

Yeah, baby! Look at it roll! Cool.

If you thought that was easy, the Mac installation is even easier. In fact, within just a few clicks you're ready to try the samples immediately. In Chapter 13, you'll crack open the simple samples that come with Red5 as well as a sample application setup with Red5, but first let's take a look at how to get Red5 set up for development.

Setting up your development environment

So now that you know how to install Red5 as a stand-alone application, it's important to also know how to set up Red5 for coding Java in Eclipse. Please keep in mind that you can go ahead and use the stand-alone version as described earlier to develop Red5 applications, particularly if you need to write only client-side code for your Red5 application. But when you start delving into some server-side logic, we highly recommend that you set up Eclipse like we are going to show you in the following sections.

Why set up Red5 to run in Eclipse in the first place?

Why go through the trouble of setting all of this up when you have a perfectly good working version of Red5 using the installer? Well, that's an excellent question. Let's see whether we can explain a little better.

First, Eclipse is an excellent tool for both ActionScript and Java development. The tools for writing Java are already built into Eclipse, thus making it fairly simple to get Red5 working within it. You will find that with this setup, coding Java for Red5 is actually quite easy and efficient, and it seamlessly integrates with your ActionScript/Flex projects in the same IDE.

Second, with Red5 running inside Eclipse, you can properly debug your Red5 Java code. Debugging allows you to step through the execution of code in real time. It also allows you to inspect variables, objects, and other properties at runtime. If you have worked with Flex Builder and its debugging capabilities, then you are already familiar with the concept of debugging. This debugging feature of Red5 is extremely powerful and is one of the biggest advantages over Flash Media Server. With Flash Media Server you are stuck simply tracing out things as you go to debug your application, but Red5 is Java based and integrates very well into your development environment, giving you some very powerful tools to make your life as a programmer easier.

Setting up Eclipse for Red5 development

You will need a few things set up before you get started:

- Eclipse needs to be installed: http://www.eclipse.org/downloads/. Installing Eclipse is a relatively painless endeavor, as long as you can deal with the gigantic download. If you aren't sure what features you will need, then we recommend just downloading the Eclipse IDE for Java developers.

- Java 5 or newer needs to be installed. We already talked about how to get Java on your computer when doing the stand-alone Red5 installation. Refer to those steps if you are having trouble or haven't already gotten Java up and running.

Now that you have that out of the way, follow these steps to set up Eclipse for Red5 development:

1. Download the ZIP file. The Red5 team has provided an example Eclipse project to get your environment set up with a working instance of Red5 running in Eclipse. You can find the ZIP file containing the project on the Red5 website at http://osflash.org/red5.

2. Unzip the file. Once you have downloaded the ZIP file, extract the folder to some place on your hard drive.

3. Import the project. The first thing you need to do is open Eclipse. Next open the Java perspective (View ➤ Open Perspective ➤ Java). Then right-click in the Project Explorer, and select New ➤ Java Project.

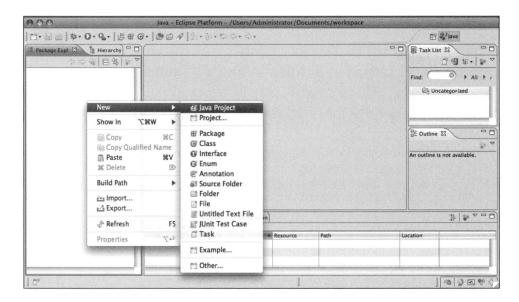

4. All you need to do now is type the name of the project in the Project name **field, and select** Create project from existing source. **Once you have that selected, point to the folder you created when unzipping the project.**

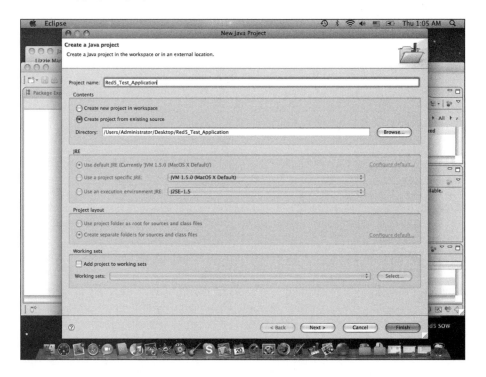

5. Click the Finish button; you should then see the project in your Package Explorer panel like this.

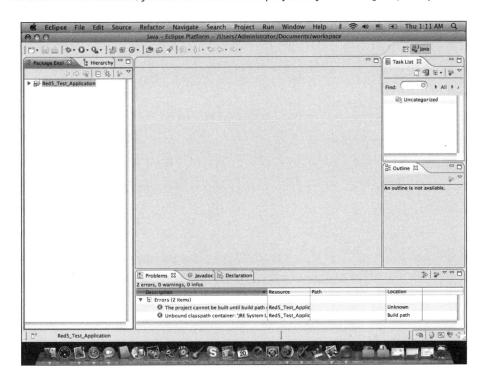

> *If your project shows the following errors in your* Problems *panel:*
>
> ■ The project cannot be built until build path errors are resolved Red5_Test_Application
>
> ■ Unbound classpath container: 'JRE System Library [JVM 1.6]' in project 'Red5_Test_Application'
>
> *then in the* Java *perspective, select the root of the project in the* Package Explorer, *right-click, and select* Properties. *On the next screen, click* Java Build Path. *You then should be able to find the* Libraries *tab. Scroll down, and select* JRE System Library [JVM 1.6]. *Click* Edit, *and select your installed JRE.*
>
> *Basically, if you have those errors, the name you used for the JRE on your system isn't the same as it is on your computer.*

Starting Red5 in Eclipse

In the Package Explorer, select and expand the red5.jar file (under Referenced Libraries), navigate to org ➤ red5 ➤ server, and right-click StandAlone.class. Then select Run As ➤ Java Application. Alternatively, you can select Debug As ➤ Java Application if you have set some breakpoints in your code (more about debugging is available later in this chapter).

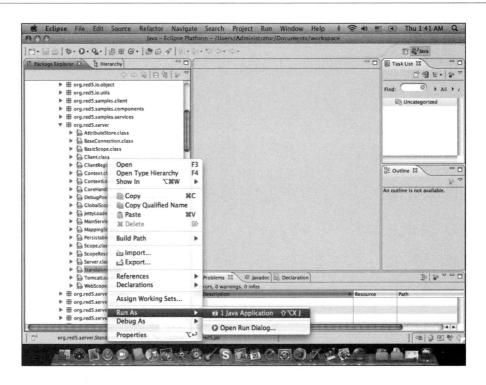

If all went well, you should see the server output a bunch of stuff in the Console panel and eventually write out Startup done in: XXXX ms.

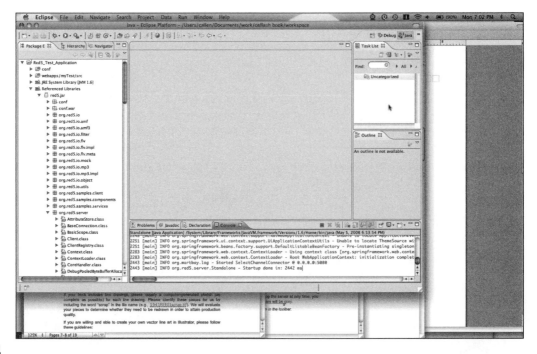

You now have Red5 running inside Eclipse. Congratulations! If you need to stop the server at any time, you can do so by clicking the little red square icon. When Red5 is stopped, the square will be gray.

> *Once stopped, Red5 can be restarted with the little green-and-white button in the toolbar.*

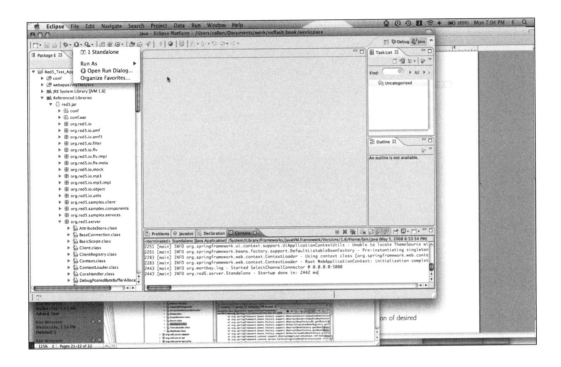

How Red5 web applications are set up

Now that you know how to get Red5 running in Eclipse, you'll look at the sample application that ships with the Red5 example Eclipse project to see how it works. This sample application is called myTest.

Red5 uses the concept of individual applications running within the server; each application doesn't interact with another one. This idea will be familiar to those who have some experience with J2EE servers such as Tomcat or JBoss. The basic way it works is that Red5 is divided into one or more application directories that hold code and configurations specific to that application. Each application in turn has a source directory that contains an entry point or one class that handles the startup and main code access for the application. This entry point class must extend `org.red5.server.adapter.ApplicationAdapter`.

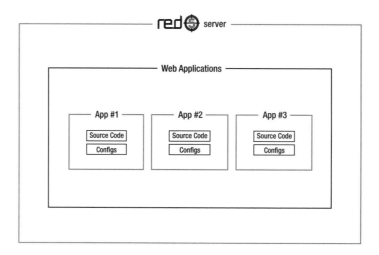

The Red5 application may also contain a streams folder where all recorded streams are stored; FLVs recorded from webcams or microphones sent via a NetStream to this application are stored here.

Directory structure of Red5 applications

Let's take a look at a sample application to see how its directory structure is set up.

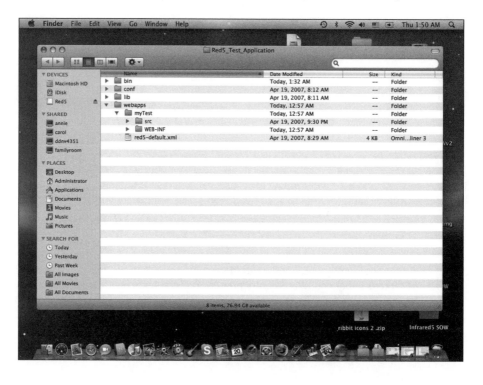

Under the root of this project, you will notice that there is a webapps folder. This is where all Red5 applications are put. In this case, we have only one application called myTest. myTest has a src directory and a WEB-INF directory. The src folder is where the Java source code for this application resides. The WEB-INF directory is where the configuration files for this application are kept.

Source code

In the example application, there is only one class in the src directory. For lack of a better name, we chose the name Application. Open and take a look at the Application.java file by going to the Package Explorer in Eclipse, navigating to webapps/myTest/src, expanding the org.red5.server. webapp.mytest package, and double-clicking Application.java.

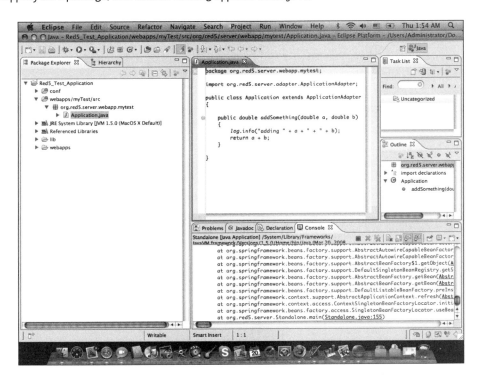

This should open the file in the Java editor in Eclipse. You will see that this is an extremely simple application, and that's the whole point of it. Even if you have never touched a lick of Java, you will have no problem figuring out what's going on here. The class extends org.red5.server.adapter. ApplicationAdapter, and it has one method called addSomething. Believe it or not, all addSomething() does is add two numbers together and return the result. Even your mom could write code like this:

```
package org.red5.server.webapp.mytest;

import org.red5.server.adapter.ApplicationAdapter;
```

```
public class Application extends ApplicationAdapter
{

    public double addSomething(double a, double b)
    {
        log.info("adding " + a + " " + " + b);
        return a + b;
    }

}
```

At this point, you are probably thinking "This is all good, I can see how it works, but how do I trigger this from Flash?" Great question! Let's first just have faith that it works; we'll come back to that a little later. In the next section, you'll learn about those configuration files.

Configuration files

The WEB-INF directory contains four configuration files. Let's go into each one in some detail.

web.xml

This is the standard webapp config file. It allows you to add servlets (used by Flash Remoting HTTP services), context params (used by Spring to modify various settings on the Red5 server), and more. There's not much as a beginning Red5 developer that you should need to modify here. The only thing you will need to change when creating a new application for Red5 is the webAppRootKey value:

```
<context-param>
    <param-name>webAppRootKey</param-name>
    <param-value>/myTest</param-value>
</context-param>
```

This property is what Red5 uses to specify what the RTMP connection string should look like to connect to this application via a NetConnection in Flash. In this case, it's stating that you should use the following: rtmp://myServerName/myTest. We will get to connecting to this from Flash soon.

red5-web.xml

This one holds the application's context. If creating a new application, you will need to specify the entry-point class here like this:

```
<bean id="web.handler"
    class="org.red5.server.webapp.mytest.Application" />
```

The entry-point class is the class that starts off your Red5 application. In this case, the name of our entry-point class is org.red5.server.webapp.mytest.Application. It's the one we've already described that has the addSomething() method.

red5-web.properties

This properties file provides simpler access to properties for red5-web.xml, also read by the Red5 Jetty configuration to set webapp.virtualHosts and webapp.contextPath. Note that if you're deploying in a different servlet engine, you will have to configure these using that servlet engine's config file as well as this file. But for beginners, modifying it here is the easiest, most straightforward way of doing it:

```
webapp.contextPath=/myTest
webapp.virtualHosts=*, localhost, localhost:8088, 127.0.0.1:8088
```

The webapp.contextPath property specifies the remoting address of your application. It is usually set to the same value as your webAppRootKey parameter in web.xml. The reason for this is that you can easily switch between the RTMP and HTTP protocols without changing the path to your application in the NetConnection class. Right now it's set to use http://localhost/myTest.

The webapp.virtualHosts property is used to set the name/names of your server to which Flash will be connecting. In this case, you have it set to use localhost.

log4j.properties

This file is used by Red5 for setting logging levels in your application. Currently, it is set to use the default settings, because there is nothing in it. If you want to change it so that your application displays only critical errors or warnings, for example, you can change that here. But for now, the default log4j settings should be totally fine, because it will give you debug output. For more information on configuring and using log4j, see this web page: http://logging.apache.org/log4j/1.2/manual.html.

> Red5 uses many more configuration files that are out of the scope to cover in this book. We have touched on only the ones you need to alter for an individual Red5 application. For more information on all the configuration files that are used in a Red5 setup, see http://osflash.org/red5/config for details.

Connecting to myTest with Flash

Let's connect to the test application now to see it in action and to get a better understanding of how it all works.

We have put together an FLA file that connects and executes the code in the myTest application. If you open that FLA, you will see that the first frame has a layer called Code, and it contains some ActionScript:

```
flash.events.NetStatusEvent;

// create our responder to pass to Red5 so it knows where
// to return the data
var responder:Responder = new Responder(setValue, null);

// create basic netConnection object
var nc:NetConnection = new NetConnection();
```

```
    // point the NetConnection's scope to this object
    nc.client = this;

    function onBWDone(...rest):void
    {
        // has to be present
    }

    // connect to the local Red5 server
    nc.connect("rtmp://localhost/myTest");

    // add status event listener.  When it's a success, you make the call
    nc.addEventListener(NetStatusEvent.NET_STATUS, handleNetStatus);

    function handleNetStatus(e:NetStatusEvent):void
    {
        trace(e.info.code);
        switch(e.info.code)
        {
            case "NetConnection.Connect.Success":
                nc.call("addSomething," responder, 2, 3);
            break;
        }
    }

    function setValue(obj:Object):void
    {
        trace(obj.toString());
        //txt.text = "";
        txt.text += "\n" + String(obj);
    }
```

As you can see, it's really quite simple. You first create an instance of a Responder, which will handle the results coming from Red5, and then you create an instance of the NetConnection class. Next you connect to the server that is running on localhost. After that, it's just a matter of mapping the NET_STATUS event to the handleNetStatus() function so that you know when the connection has been established. Then it's a matter of calling the method addSomething() and having the result come back from Red5. The result is mapped to the Responder instance, which in turn calls the setValue() function. Inside the setValue() function, the TextField called txt is populated with the result.

Now to test this, you need to make sure that Red5 is running in Eclipse. Return to Eclipse, and make sure it's running now. If so, then all you need to do is press Ctrl/Cmd+Enter in Flash and *voila*! You should see the two numbers added together in the text field. Now that was easy, wasn't it?

Try adding a new method in the Java class, and see whether you can get it to work on your own. We hope this simple example will get you started on creating some more advanced applications in Red5. For now, why not try creating an echo method so that it repeats what you send it? You could try subtraction, multiplication, and so on. Really, the possibilities are limited only by your imagination and your skills at programming. We will be looking at more advanced uses of Red5 in the next chapter, so no worries if you can't think of more exciting things to do at this point.

Debugging Red5 in Eclipse

Now that you have the ability to run Red5 in Eclipse and you have your code in Flash executing the Java code, it is also possible to debug your application in pretty much the same way. To do so, all you need to do is select Debug As ➤ Java Application instead of Run As ➤ Java Application on the StandAlone class.

Give that a try so you can see how it works. Open the Application.java class again, and let's set a breakpoint in this bad boy.

You might be asking, "What the heck is a breakpoint? Why do I need one of those?" It's actually quite simple really. A **breakpoint** is just a way of telling the Java virtual machine to pause its execution of code at this point in your code. Let's say that your application is much more complicated than adding two numbers together and that you were having trouble tracking down why it wasn't working. You can set a breakpoint in the server-side code at the point that's having trouble and check to see that Flash is passing in the right variables or see whether the math that you have in your code is doing the right thing. Once again, this will all make perfect sense if you're a Flex developer, because Flex Builder also offers debugging just like this.

To set a break point, all you need to do is, within the code window, right-click the right side on the line that you want to set the point for and select Toggle Breakpoint; or even simpler, just double-click it.

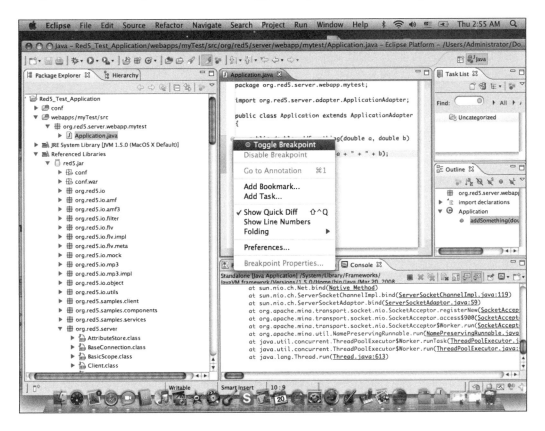

You should then see a little blue dot representing the breakpoint on that line.

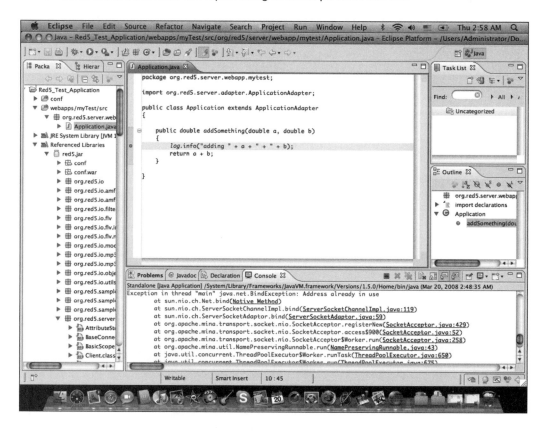

You have now set a breakpoint. We have decided to place the point on the trace that we're doing:

```
log.info("adding " + a + " + " + b);
```

Now if you debug Red5 and this method gets executed, it will stop right here so that you can inspect the application at runtime. So, let's do just that!

First set the breakpoint in the class as we've demonstrated. Next right-click StandAlone.class in the Package Explorer just like you did when running Red5, but this time select Debug As ➤ Java Application.

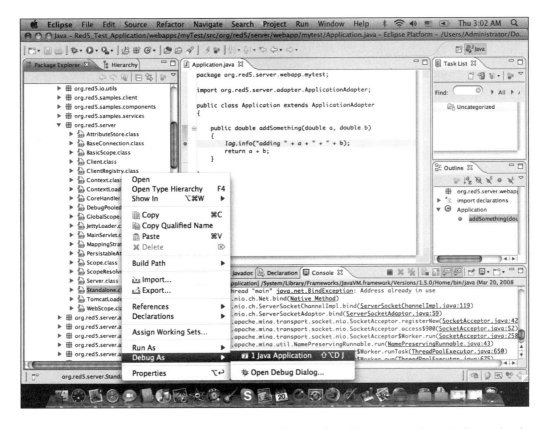

You should see the same type of output you saw before, but this time you have Red5 running in debugging mode. Now try executing the Flash code again to call the addSomething() method.

You will then be promoted to switch to the Debug perspective in Eclipse. Just click Yes.

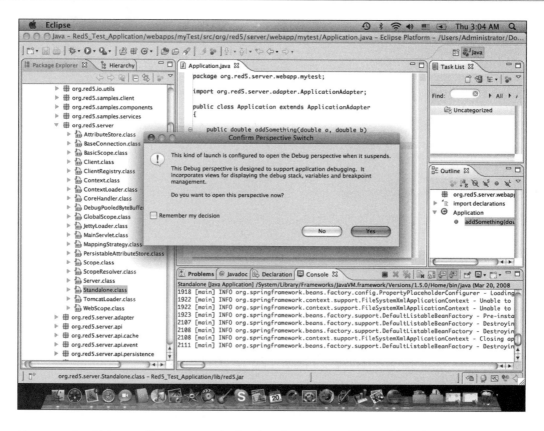

Now you should have a few new panels showing that are specific to debugging. You should see Variables, Breakpoints, Debug, your Console, and the code editor. Let's take a look at the Variables tab to see what it does.

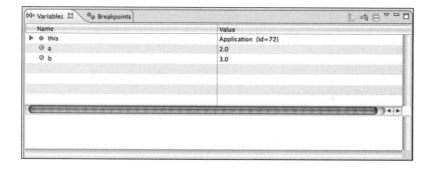

With this panel, you can see the variables being used at any given moment. In this case, you can find the doubles that are being passed in from Flash (2.0 and 3.0).

To get Red5 to proceed, you need to pick one of the controls in the Debug panel. Resume, Suspend, Terminate, Disconnect, Step Into, Step Over, Step Return, and so on, are the controls that allow you to control where to go in your code.

The buttons that you will find most useful are the Step Into, Step Over, Terminate, and Resume buttons. Step Into makes the debugger delve into the code where it is currently stopped, meaning that if you had a line of code like MyObject.doThisStuff();, it would switch to the MyObject class and run through the doThisStuff() method line by line until it returned to the next line where this was called. Step Over would execute MyObject.doThisStuff() but then go to the next line in the current class. Terminate is pretty obvious; it stops the debug session altogether (Red5 won't be running after doing this). Resume will let the application proceed without stepping through the code. It will continue until it hits another breakpoint. If you are curious about what the other buttons do, or how all of this works, play around with it; you certainly won't break anything by doing so. Once again, though, if you are familiar with these features of Flex Builder, you will be right at home and will understand how debugging in Java works right away.

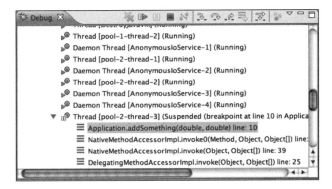

Obviously, debugging this simple of an application isn't that useful, but playing around with it in such a simple example should give you a good idea of how to use debugging when you really need to do so. For more information on debugging Java applications in Eclipse, refer to the help documentation in Eclipse on the subject.

In this chapter, we went over how to get Red5 running as a stand-alone server running on the Windows operating system. You also learned how to get Red5 running inside Eclipse. The Eclipse setup now allows you to delve into developing your own Red5 applications with ease. This setup also allows you to take advantage of debugging and stepping through your code, making it easier to build advanced applications. In addition, you saw some very basic examples of how to code Red5 applications. In the next chapter, you will get a chance to look at some more complex examples using the Red5 server.

Chapter 13

BUILDING SOME RED5 APPS

by John Grden

One of Red5's goals was to bring a Flash server to the Flash masses, and in doing so, we delivered something that does the sexy stuff you'd expect from a streaming server but also has a ton of power in a Java server, and what that brings to the equation is extensibility. Just think about it: Red5 now gives Flash developers an open door to whatever they can attach to a Java server. Imagine being able to talk to hardware devices you normally can't, like MIDI devices! Red5 makes this now possible.

In this chapter, I'll cover the simple sexy stuff that everyone loves to try, and all you'll need is the Flash 8 IDE (or greater) and a running installation of Red5. Then, I'll show you a nice MIDI example with a guitar-teaching tool in which you'll look at the server side for the first time, where you can connect with hardware on a computer that is MIDI capable. And finally, you'll look at a Flex 2/3 example to finish things up. The Eclipse setup is especially nice because of the debugging capabilities that it gives you with Red5. At the time of the writing of this book, this is not possible with Flash Media Server. So, developing your server-side applications becomes far easier because you can use debug tools you're accustomed to when building applications (see Chapter 12 for more details).

Simple samples

The simple samples ship with Red5's installer, and you'll find them in the SWF folder wherever you installed Red5. We've kept them "simple" because of user requests primarily. We found that giving examples in Flash FLA files were far easier for people to appreciate immediately, so we've provided seven samples for your Flash enjoyment. All samples are Action-Script 2/Flash 8 compatible to reach the largest audience possible, but they can be ported to Action-Script 3 very easily if required. Since there is overlap in some of the samples, as far as ActionScript concepts and code are concerned, I'll be covering only some of the samples here.

> *Red5 supports both AMF 1 and AMF 3. AMF stands for Action Message Format, and you can find out more about it at* http://osflash.org/documentation/amf. *In short, AMF allows you to pass primitive Flash objects, such as arrays and objects, from server to SWF, from SWF to server, and from SWF to SWF.*

Before we dive in, it's good to note that the Flash client-side API remains the same as what you'd use with any Flash streaming server technologies, such as Flash Media Server. So, there's already tons of documentation and support for developing applications on the client side. All of the samples I'll cover in this chapter use the same NetConnection object to connect to the locally installed and running Red5 server and the same oflaDemo application:

```
// create basic netConnection object
var nc:NetConnection = new NetConnection();

// connect to the local Red5 server
nc.connect("rtmp://localhost/oflaDemo");
```

> *Why the name oflaDemo? Open Source Flash (OFLA) was an online virtual conference held in the fall of 2005 where I first showed video broadcasting and recording. The name of the app that I used for this demo was named after the conference, and it has stuck ever since.*

Exploring SimpleBallDemo

SimpleBallDemo is the classic demo that shows you the value and use of shared objects and shows you how to synchronize data across Flash clients with a "push" ability. When the shared object on the server is updated, all the clients are notified with the new values associated with that shared object.

What is a shared object? Well, if you're an ActionScripter, then you're familiar with what an object is. Now imagine that object being maintained and available on the server side that all clients have access to read from and write to. When a client changes a value on the shared object, the server notifies and pushes the latest changes to the client. So, that's why it's called a **shared object**. Let's move on.

> *What's the difference between the* SharedObject *that I use to store data on the client's machine (the one that acts like a cookie for Flash) and this* SharedObject *that is used in Red5? Great question! The* SharedObject *that we use with Red5 is often referred to as a remote* SharedObject, *because it is stored remotely on the server instead of on the client's machine. They are both actually the same class; the difference is just in how you use them.*

SimpleBallDemo allows you to open two SWFs (swf1 and swf2, respectively) and then drag the Red5 logo around on swf1 to see it move around on swf2. The idea is that you'll see that when you move the swf1 logo, the coordinates are saved to the shared object, and the server pushes those changes to swf2. swf2 gets notified and then moves the logo to the same X/Y coordinate location. This is one of the first demos we created when Red5 first supported SharedObject.

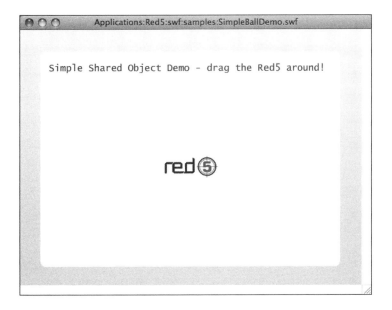

Let's take a look at the code. Note that it's very simple; in fact, the comments should explain everything that's going on here:

```
import mx.utils.Delegate;

// a flag that is switched when we start to drag the log around
var dragging:Boolean = false;

// create basic netConnection object
var nc:NetConnection = new NetConnection();

// connect to the local Red5 server
nc.connect("rtmp://localhost/oflaDemo");
```

```
// create SharedObject - pass the name of the shared object,
 // the netConnection URI ("rtmp://localhost/oflaDemo"),
// and whether or not it's persistent
var so:SharedObject = SharedObject.getRemote("simpleChatDemo",
                                             nc.uri, false);

// set up the onSync events.
// We need to know when someone has added something to the chat
so.onSync = Delegate.create(this, newMovement);

// connect to the SO using the netConnection reference
so.connect(nc);

// drag the logo around
logo.onPress = Delegate.create(this, startMove);
logo.onRelease = Delegate.create(this, stopMove);

// for starting the drag
function startMove():Void
{
    // start dragging the logo
    logo.startDrag();

    // add mouse listener to monitor movements
    dragging = true;
}

// for stopping the drag
function stopMove():Void
{
    // not dragging, set to false
    dragging = false;

    // stop dragging the logo
    stopDrag();
}

function onEnterFrame():Void
{
    // kick out if not dragging
    if(!dragging) return;

    // let everyone know where the logo should move to
    so.data.mousePosition = {x: logo._x, y: logo._y};
}

// this method is called when the data on the shared object is updated
function newMovement(evtObj:Object):Void
{
```

```
            // if we're the ones doing the dragging, return out
            if(dragging) return;
            // we've been notified that there's movement
            logo._x = so.data.mousePosition.x;
            logo._y = so.data.mousePosition.y;
        }
```

By playing with this example, you can quickly see how you can use remote shared objects for so many useful things. How about a text-based chat application or a multiuser game? Later in this chapter, I will show you a Flex example that uses the remote SharedObject for a chat application as well as a Flash-based one. Stay tuned!

Shared objects are an easy way to get started sharing data between users connected to the same Red5 server. A popular use of this is for avatar systems where walking, location, friends lists, and chat are big parts of the application. You can accomplish these types of things, in most cases, without even touching a shred of Java code on the server side. These sample applications are the basis for these types of features!

Exploring SimpleBroadcaster and SimpleRecorder

SimpleBroadcaster is your first endeavor into the video features of Red5. You can do three things with video and Red5 out of the box:

- Stream video
- Record video
- Broadcast live video

SimpleBroadcaster is a simple "broadcaster" for live video streams. You can imagine that this has tons of uses, but probably the most notable are video conferencing and video chat applications. Red5 gives you the ability to broadcast your video camera stream to any client that connects and requests your stream. By the way, this just in . . . that rocks!

Let's take a look at the code, shall we?

```
        import mx.utils.Delegate;

        // create basic netConnection object
        var nc:NetConnection = new NetConnection();

        // connect to the local Red5 server
        nc.connect("rtmp://localhost/oflaDemo");

         // create the netStream object and pass the
         // netConnection object in the constructor
        var ns:NetStream = new NetStream(nc);
```

```
// get references to the camera and mic
var cam:Camera = Camera.get();
var mic:Microphone = Microphone.get();

// set up some simple settings with the cam and mic for quality
setupCameraMic();

// listen for the button clicks
 broadcastButton.addEventListener("click",
                                Delegate.create(this, broadcastClick));
stopButton.addEventListener("click",
                                Delegate.create(this, stopClick));

function broadcastClick():Void
{
    // This FLV is recorded to webapps/oflaDemo/streams/ directory
    // attach cam and mic to the NetStream Object
    ns.attachVideo(cam);
    ns.attachAudio(mic);

     // attach the cam to the videoContainer on stage
     // so we can see ourselves
    videoContainer.attachVideo(cam);

    // publish your cam/mic to red5 for broadcasting
    ns.publish("red5BroadcastDemo", "live");

    // disable the play button
    playButton.enabled = false;

    // enable the stop button
    stopButton.enabled = true;
}

function stopClick():Void
{
    // close the netStream object
    ns.close();

    // clear the videoContainer
    videoContainer.attachVideo(null);
    videoContainer.clear();

    // enable the play button
    playButton.enabled = true;
```

```
        // disable the stop button
        stopButton.enabled = false;
    }

    function setupCameraMic():Void
    {
        // set up cam
        cam = Camera.get();
        // setting dimensions and frame rate
        cam.setMode(320, 240, 30);
        // set to minimum of 70% quality
        cam.setQuality(0,70);

        // set up mic
        mic = Microphone.get();
        mic.setRate(44);
    }
```

Now, again, if you're familiar with ActionScript and the NetConnection/NetStream objects, this will be familiar to you and extremely straightforward. But even if this is all new to you, it should still be easy to follow. Take a look at the broadcastClick() method; this is where the magic happens. The NetStream object is where you attach your Camera and Microphone objects. As soon as you call NetStream.publish(), the input from these devices is sent to your Red5 server and made available as a "live" streaming broadcast.

As you look at the NetStream.publish(name:String[, type:String]) call, you can easily make out what the arguments mean. The first is the name of your stream and is a String value type. This will be the name, or **key**, your clients will use to subscribe to your stream. The second argument is the type of stream you're publishing and is an optional String value. As if it couldn't get any better, to record your stream, you need to change only the second argument in the NetStream.publish() method to record, and Red5 will record your stream: ns.publish("red5BroadcastDemo", "record");.

> Valid values for the type are record, live, and append. record *saves an FLV copy of your session, while* live *(the default value) simply broadcasts your stream to the connected clients.* append *would be used to do just that—add to a currently recorded stream.*

Adobe has really made getting your camera and microphone data very easy with access to static objects called Camera and Microphone:

```
    var cam:Camera = Camera.get();
    var mic:Microphone = Microphone.get();
```

Armed with connections to those devices and Red5, you can create some of the most sophisticated video applications on the Web!

Exploring SimpleSubscriber

Now that you've gone and broadcast a live stream, you'd probably like someone to see it, yes? The SimpleSubscriber demo shows how to do just that, and it's probably just as simple as you're assuming it should be. It makes a NetStream.publish call and passes red5BroadcastDemo as the stream name to which it wants to subscribe.

The important part of the code for this demo is the subscribeClick() method:

```
function subscribeClick():Void
{
    // subscribe to the broadcast
    ns.play("red5BroadcastDemo", -1);

    // disable the play button
    playButton.enabled = false;

    // enable the stop button
    stopButton.enabled = true;
}
```

As you can see, it's very easy to subscribe to a live stream on Red5. The NetStream object gives you a play() method that allows you to pass the name of the stream. While the NetStream object is hooked up to a video object, you'll be able to see the live stream broadcast.

Now, I should probably discuss video quality at this point. You'll see that the broadcaster's quality looks great—that's because it's uncompressed video captured at your computer. You can take control of the quality of video and audio you send, but as always, it's a balancing act of quality vs. performance and lag. I won't go into too much detail about the uses of these properties and best practices, but I will cover what each does in some detail here.

The following is the code for the broadcaster since that's where the quality is controlled from. You'll notice a method at the very bottom of the broadcaster code called setupCameraMic.

```
function setupCameraMic():Void
{
    // set up cam
    cam = Camera.get();
    // setting dimensions and frame rate
    cam.setMode(320, 240, 30);
    // set to minimum of 70% quality
    cam.setQuality(0,70);

    // set up mic
    mic = Microphone.get();
    mic.setRate(44);
}
```

First, look at Camera.setMode() and its four arguments:

- Width:int: The default is 160. This is the requested capture width of video.
- Height:int: The default is 120. This is the requested capture height of video.
- fps (frames per second): Number: The default is 15. This is the requested rate, measured per second, that you want the camera to capture video. I have it at 30 in the demo, which is very optimistic! You should start out with the default, and if you feel you really need to raise it, then make the adjustment. Otherwise, you're better off letting Flash Player manage this with the favorArea setting. Again, this really depends on your application's requirements.
- favorArea:Boolean: The default is true. If the camera of the broadcasting client doesn't support the specified width, height, and frames per second (fps), then these settings are manipulated to whatever the camera will support. Otherwise, when this is set to true, the width and height will be maintained at the expense of dropping the frame rate. If set to false, the frame rate will be favored.

All three of these parameters are very important and can have a huge impact on your application's performance. A bigger resolution means more data, as does a higher frame rate. You have to find a balance that suits your application and gives you the quality you want at the bandwidth you can afford.

Next, Camera.setQuality() has two arguments:

- bandwidth:int: The default is 16384. This is the bytes per second the application will allow in terms of bandwidth. A setting of 0 means Flash Player will maintain the bandwidth necessary to achieve the quality you want.
- quality:int: The default is 0. A setting between 1 and 100 will determine the amount of compression to apply to each frame that is captured. A setting of 0 means that the quality can vary based on the bandwidth requirement.

345

With `Camera.setQuality`, I set bandwidth to 0 and quality to 70. I'm telling Flash Player to maintain quality and use whatever bandwidth is necessary to do so. This might be what you'd do for an application that runs on a LAN only or locally to the user's computer if you want high-quality recordings or broadcasts.

The last one is `Microphone.setRate()`, which lets you pass an int value of 5, 8, 11, 22, or 44, which is in KHz. The default value is 8KHz if your sound card supports it. Otherwise, it's bumped up to 11KHz by Flash Player. For most situations where speech is the type of sound passed, 8KHz or 11KHz will do just fine. If you require more fidelity, then try 22KHz or 44KHz, but as always, this means more bandwidth.

> For more information on other methods and properties of the `Camera` and `Microphone` objects, refer to the Flash or Flex help files.

Creating simple chat using SoSend

In *SoSend*, *So* means `SharedObject`, and *Send* refers to the method in which you'll send and receive messages from the Red5 server. This is different from the simple chat client that uses `SharedObjects` and simply changes a property on the `SharedObject` to push a new message to the clients (see the earlier SimpleBall sample). This demo sends and receives messages from Red5 and other users by calling a method on the server side via `SharedObject`.

Confused? Let's take a look at the code; it's really pretty straightforward:

```
import mx.utils.Delegate;

// create basic netConnection object
var nc:NetConnection = new NetConnection();

// connect to the local Red5 server
nc.connect("rtmp://localhost/oflaDemo");

 // create StoredObject - pass the name of the shared object,
 // the netConnection URI ("rtmp://localhost/oflaDemo"),
 // and whether or not it's persistent
var so:SharedObject = SharedObject.getRemote➡
("simpleChatDemo", nc.uri, false);

// set up the handler for the new messages
// and delegate them to a local function
// this method will be called from the server when so.send is called.
so.newMessage = Delegate.create(this, newMessageHandler);

// connect to the SO using the netConnection reference
so.connect(nc);

// listen for the send button clicks
send.addEventListener("click", Delegate.create(this, sendMessage));

// add a listener for key events
Key.addListener(this);


function sendMessage():Void
{

    // send via call to method on all the shared objects
    // this will be reflected back down to clients by the server
    so.send("newMessage", message.text);

    // clear text input
    message.text = "";
}

function onKeyUp():Void
{
    if(Key.getCode() == 13 && message.length > 0)
    {
        // if ENTER was hit and there's a message to send,
        // call sendMessage()
        sendMessage();
    }
}
```

```
function newMessageHandler(newChat:String):Void
{
    // return if newChat is null
    if(newChat == null) return;

    // show in chat
    history.text += newChat + "\n";

    // scroll the chat window
    history.vPosition = history.maxVPosition;
}
```

Two methods make this application work: sendMessage() and newMessageHandler(). To send a new chat message, all you have to do is call so.send(nameOfServerMethod:String, newMessage:String), and the message will be pushed out to all clients connected to this application. In this sample, that equates to so.send("newMessage", message.text). At this point, you might be wondering where this newMessage method is defined—is it on the server side or client side? It's actually defined on the client side. When you set this on the client side, it tells Red5 to create it on the server. You can see that I've defined the newMessage method on the SharedObject and created a handler for it in this one line:

```
so.newMessage = Delegate.create(this, newMessageHandler);
```

Now, any client that connects to this SharedObject using this code will have created a handler for this method and will receive the new message from any of the clients that call it. On the receiving client's side, newMessageHandler is called with a new chat message (String value) and—bingo!—you're up and running.

This technique is nice in that you don't have to listen for sync events on the SharedObject; you just define a method and a method handler, and it works like all the other methods in your class.

Exploring SimpleStreamPlayer

Through all of these demos you can see a common thread: the NetStream object. The SimpleStream-Player demo looks just like all of the other samples using video and the NetStream object. The only thing you have to do is pick out some killer FLV videos and put them into the streams folder of any web application of Red5. So if you look in the oflaDemo application in webapps that ships with Red5, you'll see a streams folder. You're in business!

If the code gets any easier, I'll be out of a job:

```
// create basic netConnection object
var nc:NetConnection = new NetConnection();

// connect to the local Red5 server
nc.connect("rtmp://localhost/oflaDemo");

 // create the netStream object and pass the
 // netConnection object in the constructor
var ns:NetStream = new NetStream(nc);

// attach the netStream object to the video object
videoContainer.attachVideo(ns);

// listen for the button click
playButton.addEventListener("click", this);

function click():Void
{
    // called via the "Play" button
     // simply call play on the netStream object,
     // and pass the name of the FLV.
    // This FLV is sitting in webapps/oflaDemo/streams/ directory
    ns.play("yourFLVFileNameHere.flv");
}
```

NetStream.play() requires you to send the name of the FLV you want to play back. This is the same as when you played back a live stream or set the name of a stream you wanted to record. When playing back an existing FLV, the .flv extension is optional and not necessary.

Well, that's a good overview of the code included in the simple samples in the Red5 installation package. We've covered the following:

- Using remote shared objects
- Using methods on shared objects
- Broadcasting live video
- Subscribing to a live broadcast
- Recording a broadcast
- Playing streams

- Working with Camera and Microphone objects
- Working with NetConnection and NetStream objects

At this point, you should be armed with enough information to get you on your way to creating rich applications using Red5 as your server choice. You've seen with the simple samples how easy it is to get up and running using the Flash IDE, and in the next section, you'll learn how to use Flex Builder with ActionScript 3 and Red5.

Being a guitar hero

For this next sample, I'll cover the basics of receiving MIDI data using Red5 as the conduit, if you will, for Flash. I've created an application called GuitarPlayerPro, which is an AIR/Flex 3 application using Papervision3D, Flex 3, AIR, and Red5 to create a unique guitar-teaching tool. Here's what it looks like in action:

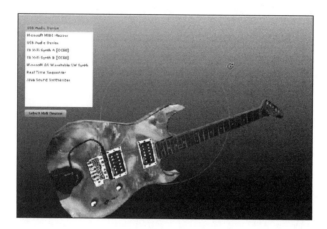

The trick, obviously, is receiving MIDI data. Flash Player does not have a way to receive MIDI information, but Red5 does, and you can use Red5 to listen and talk to any MIDI device connected to your computer. So, how does the MIDI information get to and from Flash? Let's take a look.

Since you have a NetConnection object that allows you to use RTMP to send data, why not make that data MIDI data, right? That's exactly what I did. Red5 comes with the same MIDI application I've been using for the GuitarPlayerPro application and allows you to receive a list of all MIDI in/out devices as well as receive and send MIDI information. In GuitarPlayerPro, I used that MIDI information to light up the neck of a 3D guitar (which happens to be a 3D model of my actual guitar) to show players *how* to play the guitar from whatever point of view works best for them—either from above the guitar in the way they look at their own guitar or from a traditional view as if they were sitting in a room with a teacher looking at their guitar.

I'll cover how to get the two MIDI device lists from Red5 so that you can choose which in and out devices you want to listen to, and then I'll cover the MIDI packet that comes through and what information you can use from it.

Getting a list of MIDI devices

The following is a screenshot of the Red5 Midi Connection Panel window I've created for show and to allow me to select in and out MIDI devices. All you have to do is select one device from both lists and then click the Select Midi Device button. This will pass the two selections to Red5, and at that point, if they are valid device names, Red5 will set itself up to deal with these two selections.

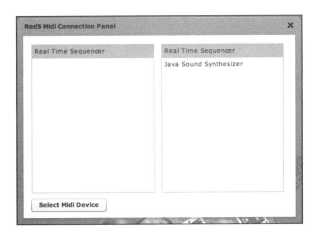

The MXML for this custom component is very basic, as you can see next, and I've done the typical code-behind with a base class called MidiDeviceControlPanelClass. You'll notice that there are two List controls in the form that are bound to two public properties in a singleton class called MidiConnector:

    deviceListIn
    deviceListOut

As you can guess, when these two properties are then initialized with data, the List components are automatically updated. All you have to do is make those two properties public and bindable, and you're in business!

```
<?xml version="1.0" encoding="utf-8"?>
<custom:MidiDeviceControlPanelClass
    xmlns:custom="com.rockonflash.midi.controls.*"
    xmlns:mx="http://www.adobe.com/2006/mxml" width="468" height="340"
    creationComplete="init()"
    showCloseButton="true"
    close="closeme();"
    title="Red5 Midi Connection Panel">
    <mx:Script>
        <![CDATA[
            import com.rockonflash.midi.guitarplayerpro.➥
net.MidiConnector;
        ]]>
    </mx:Script>
    <mx:Canvas width="100%" height="100%">
```

```
            <mx:List labelField="label" x="10" y="10"➡
width="208" height="245"
                id="deviceList_in"
                dataProvider="{MidiConnector.getInstance()➡
.deviceListIn}">
        </mx:List>
        <mx:List labelField="label" x="230" y="10"➡
 width="208" height="245"
                id="deviceList_out"
                dataProvider="{MidiConnector.getInstance()➡
.deviceListOut}">
        </mx:List>
        <mx:Button x="9" y="264" label="Select Midi Device"
                id="selectMidiDeviceButton"/>
    </mx:Canvas>
</custom:MidiDeviceControlPanelClass>
MidiDeviceControlPanelClass:
package com.rockonflash.midi.controls
{
    import com.rockonflash.midi.guitarplayerpro.net.MidiConnector;

    import flash.events.MouseEvent;

    import mx.containers.TitleWindow;
    import mx.controls.Button;
    import mx.controls.List;

    public class MidiDeviceControlPanelClass extends TitleWindow
    {
        public var deviceList_in                :List
        public var deviceList_out               :List
        public var selectMidiDeviceButton       :Button;

        public function init():void
        {
            selectMidiDeviceButton.addEventListener(
                MouseEvent.CLICK,
                handleSelectMidiDevice
            );
        }

        public function closeme():void
        {
            visible = false;
        }

        private function handleSelectMidiDevice(e:MouseEvent):void
        {
            MidiConnector.getInstance().setMidiDevice
```

```
                    (
                        deviceList_in.selectedItem.data,
                        deviceList_out.selectedItem.data
                    );
                }
            }
        }
```

Now let's check out the code for the singleton. This isn't going to be an exhaustive exercise in single-tons or code practices, but I will mention that a **singleton** is a single instance of an object. It's ideal for classes that deal with managing data, but you don't necessarily want to create a static class. For this application, it made perfect sense to use a singleton because it deals with managing MIDI data as well as being the conduit for MIDI interaction with Red5. That's why I called it MidiConnector.

The first thing to notice is that deviceListIn and deviceListOut are setters. You do this so that you can take the raw array of names returned and push them into an array filled with objects that have two properties: label and data. This is because List components can accept arrays whose members are objects with these two properties. Without any additional code, you'll see the list of devices populate the List controls in the control panel.

```
[Bindable (event="updateDataListIn")]
public function set deviceListIn(data:Array):void
{
    _deviceListIn = [];
     for(var i:Number=0;i<data.length;i++)
     _deviceListIn.push({label:data[i], data:data[i]});
    dispatchEvent(new Event("updateDataListIn"));
}
[Bindable (event="updateDataListIn")]
public function get deviceListIn():Array
{
    return _deviceListIn;
}


[Bindable (event="updateDataListOut")]
public function set deviceListOut(data:Array):void
{
    _deviceListOut = [];
     for(var i:Number=0;i<data.length;i++)
     _deviceListOut.push({label:data[i], data:data[i]});
    dispatchEvent(new Event("updateDataListOut"));
}
[Bindable (event="updateDataListOut")]
public function get deviceListOut():Array
{
    return _deviceListOut;
}

private var _deviceListIn                    :Array;
private var _deviceListOut                   :Array;
```

So, now you have two List components filled with MIDI in and out devices. What happens next? You need to let Red5 know which two devices you want to use. To do that, you call the setMidiDevice() method and pass in two arguments. The first argument is the MIDI in device, and the second is the MIDI out (both are String value types):

```
public function setMidiDevice(midiDeviceIn:String,
                              midiDeviceOut:String):void
{
    nc.call("connectToMidi", null, midiDeviceIn, midiDeviceOut);
}
```

If you have Red5 running on OS X or Windows in a command prompt, you'll see something like the following in the output, which doesn't look very professional but is a simple message that lets you know "it worked!"

```
[INFO] 2008-02-10 15:41:01,919 pool-3-thread-11:
( org.red5.demos.midi.Application.connectToMidi )
It worked!
```

Duuude, you're about to rock! Right now, you're ready to receive and send MIDI signals via RTMP! It's fast, it's easy, and, hey, it's fun!

Receiving MIDI messages

In this section, you'll learn how to receive MIDI messages. When Red5 receives a MIDI message, it passes it on by calling a midi method on the client. The client has to create a method called midi() within the scope set by the client property of the NetConnection object. This means that when you create the NetConnection object, you set its client property to the class you're currently in:

```
public var nc:NetConnection = new NetConnection();

// in the constructor:
nc.client = this
// Then, define the midi method like you see here and you're in business!
public function midi(time:Number, data:Array):void
{
    dispatchEvent(new MidiDeviceEvent(MIDI_MESSAGE, data));
}
// The midi() method receives 2 arguments:
time:Number
data:Array
```

The time property is *when* the note was received at Red5's end essentially. This might be useful in some other application, but for the GuitarPlayerPro application, it really wasn't necessary. The data array is where the magic happens as you can imagine. There are three indexes to the array, and here's how they break down:

- octave/string hit [Number]: On a guitar doing MIDI, this means "which string was hit." Its value is a Number type and ranges from 107–112 (a low E string would be 107, while a high E would be 112).
- note value [Number]: The actual note played.
- velocity value [Number]: How hard the player hit the note.

On an application that's not using a musical instrument, Velocity as well as Octave might be pointless, but Note is usually what you're after in nearly all situations. And at this point, you're receiving messages from whatever device is generating the MIDI data!

The next step is simple, but to be complete, let's take a look at sending MIDI messages rather than just receiving them!

Sending MIDI messages

I created a demo last year that involved Wii remotes, drums rendered in Papervision3D, and a Roland drum module. I used Red5 to send MIDI notes to the Roland sound module to trigger the realistic drum sounds. This was a *much* faster solution than trying to have Flash Player play MP3s of the sounds of the drums. I was able to play the drums like an electronic drum kit with this setup.

Sending MIDI messages is as simple as this bit of code:

```
public function sendMidiMessage(note:Number, velocity:Number):void
{
    // 144 = NOTE_ON
    // n = note (any valid midi note)
    // 0-128 = velocity
     nc.call("sendMidiShortMessage3",
         new Responder(handleMidiSendResponse),
         144, note, velocity, 0);
}

public function handleMidiSendResponse(e:Object):void
{
    trace("handleMidiSendResponse", e);
}
```

In this code, you create a method called sendMidiMessage, and you pass it note and velocity. To send the message to Red5 to pass along to the Roland drum module, you use NetConnection.call(). The first argument is a String value of the name of the method to call on the server side, and the second argument is the response handler. You have to define a response handler, or you'll receive runtime errors. The next three arguments are "note on" (144), the note itself, and then velocity. That's all you need! So for the drum demo, all I did was calculate some velocity value based on how hard I swung the Wii remote and pass that to Red5. This ended up being very fast and responsive, which was ideal for a drum demo. That's it! The code for getting MIDI messages in and out of Flash using Red5 is pretty basic, and it's fast.

As promised, here's the entire code for MidiConnector.as, which includes all of the previous code samples. Again, this is a singleton with two bindable properties: deviceListIn and deviceListOut.

```
package com.rockonflash.midi.guitarplayerpro.net
{
    import flash.events.EventDispatcher;
    import flash.events.IEventDispatcher;

    import flash.net.NetConnection;
    import com.blitzagency.xray.logger.XrayLog;
    import flash.events.NetStatusEvent;
    import flash.net.ObjectEncoding;

    import flash.net.Responder;
    import com.rockonflash.midi.guitarplayerpro.events.MidiDeviceEvent;
    import flash.events.Event;

    public class MidiConnector extends EventDispatcher
    {
        public static var NEW_MIDI_DEVICES:String = "newMidiDevices";
        public static var URI:String = "rtmp://localhost/midiDemo";
        public static var MIDI_MESSAGE:String = "midiMessage";
        public static var NEW_MIDI_DEVICE_SELECTED:➡
String = "newMidiDeviceSelected";

        private static var _instance:MidiConnector = null;
        public static function getInstance():MidiConnector
        {
            if(_instance == null) _instance = new MidiConnector();
            return _instance;
        }

        public var nc:NetConnection = new NetConnection();

        [Bindable (event="updateDataListIn")]
        public function set deviceListIn(data:Array):void
        {
            _deviceListIn = [];
            for(var i:Number=0;i<data.length;i++)
                _deviceListIn.push({label:data[i], data:data[i]});
            dispatchEvent(new Event("updateDataListIn"));
        }
        [Bindable (event="updateDataListIn")]
        public function get deviceListIn():Array
        {
            return _deviceListIn;
        }
```

```
[Bindable (event="updateDataListOut")]
public function set deviceListOut(data:Array):void
{
    _deviceListOut = [];
    log.debug("DEVICES OUT", data);
    for(var i:Number=0;i<data.length;i++)
        _deviceListOut.push({label:data[i], data:data[i]});
    dispatchEvent(new Event("updateDataListOut"));
}
[Bindable (event="updateDataListOut")]
public function get deviceListOut():Array
{
    return _deviceListOut;
}

private var _deviceListIn:Array;
private var _deviceListOut:Array;
private var log:XrayLog = new XrayLog();

public function MidiConnector(target:IEventDispatcher=null)
{
    super(target);
    NetConnection.defaultObjectEncoding = ObjectEncoding.AMF0;
}

public function doConnection():void
{
    NetConnection.defaultObjectEncoding = ObjectEncoding.AMF0;
    nc.client = this;
    nc.addEventListener(NetStatusEvent.NET_STATUS, ➡
netStatusHandler);

    nc.connect(URI);
}

public function setMidiDevice(midiDeviceIn:String, ➡
midiDeviceOut:String):void
{
    nc.call("connectToMidi", null, ➡
midiDeviceIn, midiDeviceOut);
    dispatchEvent(new Event(NEW_MIDI_DEVICE_SELECTED));
}

private function updateMidiInDeviceList(data:Array):void
{
    deviceListIn = data;
}
```

357

```
        private function updateMidiOutDeviceList(data:Array):void
        {
            deviceListOut = data;
        }

        public function sendMidiMessage(note:Number, ➥
velocity:Number):void
        {
            //[144, 128, 128], 0
            // 144 = NOTE_ON
            // 128 = note
            // 128 = velocity
            nc.call("sendMidiShortMessage3", ➥
new Responder(handleMidiSendResponse), 144, note, velocity, 0);
        }

        public function handleMidiSendResponse(e:Object):void
        {
            log.debug("handleMidiSendResponse", e);
        }

        public function midi(time:Number, data:Array):void
        {
            //log.debug("midi received", data);
            dispatchEvent(new MidiDeviceEvent(MIDI_MESSAGE, data));
        }

        private function netStatusHandler(e:NetStatusEvent):void
        {
            log.debug("netstatus", e.info);

            switch(e.info.code)
            {
                case "NetConnection.Connect.Success":
                    log.error("netConnection Success");
                    nc.call("getMidiInDeviceNames",
                        new Responder(updateMidiInDeviceList));
                    nc.call("getMidiOutDeviceNames",
                        new Responder(updateMidiOutDeviceList));
                break;

                case "NetConnection.Connect.Failed":
                    log.error("netConnection failed");
                break;
            }
        }
    }
}
```

Flexing your Red5 muscles

I didn't want to leave you without a Flex example using ActionScript 3, so here's a demo that Chris Allen has been using very successfully when he speaks at conferences and gives an overview of what Red5 is capable of. A big thanks to Dominick Accattato for putting this Flex sample together; it has been a great learning tool for so many people.

This sample is really a refresher of the simple samples in that it covers live video broadcasting and subscription as well as chat via SharedObjects. The main difference here is that it's using ActionScript 3 with AMF 3 and is a very nice look at how easy it is to develop for Red5 using Flex Builder.

> You can find this demo as well as the presentation notes at Chris's blog: http://blog.ff9900.org/?p=38.

Let's look at the main application .mxml file, which is called FITC2007_Streaming.mxml. For simplicity, it's not using a code-behind, and the ActionScript is right in there in the script tags. Again, this is meant to be a quick sample and easy to understand rather than showing you proper Flex class and component creation and organization. The three components you'll be looking at all have their code within Script tags in the MXML itself as well.

In the following code, you just need to focus on the two main methods for this demo: onCreationComplete and onNetStatus.

onCreationComplete is called when the application has finished creating its visual assets and is now ready to start doing work. The first thing that happens is that you connect to Red5 through a singleton called ConnectionManager. It has one method you'll use called connect() in which you pass the URI address to which you want to connect the client. ConnectionManager also has one other method called getConnection(), and its job is to simply return the NetConnection object for use with any and all components that might need to use the NetConnection reference.

The next method is onNetStatus, and here you're interested in the NetConnection.Connect.Success message. Once you receive that notice, you can go ahead and connect the three components for use with this application. Each of these components has a conn property, and you set it directly on the instances.

```
FITC2007_streaming.mxml:

<mx:Script>
<![CDATA[
    import mx.controls.Alert;
    import com.ir5.fitc.conference.net.ConnectionManager;
    import mx.events.FlexEvent;

    // private variables
    private var connectionManager:ConnectionManager;
    private var conn:NetConnection;
```

```
public function onCreationComplete(event:FlexEvent) : void
{
    trace("event: " + event);
    /*
    NetConnection.defaultObjectEncoding = ObjectEncoding.AMF0;
    SharedObject.defaultObjectEncoding = ObjectEncoding.AMF0;
    */
    connectionManager = ConnectionManager.getInstance();

    connectionManager.connect("rtmp://localhost/myTest");

     connectionManager.addEventListener(NetStatusEvent.NET_STATUS,
                                          onNetStatus);

}

public function onNetStatus(event:NetStatusEvent) : void
{
    trace("event: " + event);

    if(event.info.code == "NetConnection.Connect.Success")
    {
        conn = connectionManager.getConnection();
        this.videoPlayer.conn = conn;
        this.videoBroadcaster.conn = conn;
        this.chat.conn = conn;
    }
    else
    {
        mx.controls.Alert.show("Error", "Error");
    }
}
]]>
</mx:Script>
```

The previous code block is the main application MXML, and its main job is to simply create the connection to Red5 as soon as it loads. If it loads successfully, it then sets the conn property for the videoPlayer, videoBroadcaster, and chat modules. At this point, all three modules will be able to communicate with Red5 via this one NetConnection object. I think it's worth mentioning that you can use one NetConnection for multiple uses.

VideoBroadcaster.mxml

VideoBroadcaster.mxml is identical to the SimpleBroadcaster.mxml sample. When the broadcast button is clicked, the component attaches the camera to the NetStream object and then calls NetStream.publish() with a string ID and a second argument that tells Red5 what to do with the streaming video it's receiving, which in this case is live, which means other clients can watch the stream.

```
public function broadcast(event:Event) : void
{
    trace("event: " + event);

    // guard against null
    if(conn == null) return;

    cam = Camera.getCamera();
    video.attachCamera(cam);

     // create the netStream object and pass the netConnection
     // object in the constructor
    ns = new NetStream(conn);

    ns.attachCamera(cam);
    ns.publish(this.streamName.text, "live");
}
```

VideoPlayer.mxml

VideoPlayer.mxml is identical to SimpleSubscriber.mxml as well. All it does is simply attach the NetStream object to the video container, call NetStream.play(), and pass the name of the live broadcast along to Red5. That's it!

```
public function connect(event:Event) : void
{
    trace("event: " + event);

     // create the netStream object and pass the netConnection
     // object in the constructor
    var ns:NetStream = new NetStream(conn);

    video = new Video();
    video.attachNetStream(ns);
    video.width = 320;
    video.height = 240;
    ns.play(streamName.text);

    var comp:UIComponent = new UIComponent();
    comp.addChild(video);
    comp.width = 320;
    comp.height = 240;
    this.vBox2.addChild(comp);

}
```

Chat.mxml

Chat.mxml is the final of the three components for this Flex sample application, and it's a little more complicated, but not by much. I really wanted to show you the onSync events that are possible when you use a remote shared object with Red5 and you update properties of the data object. The onSync event has a changeList array, and each object in the array has a code property. You check that code property for success and change codes so that you know it's safe to add the chat to the output window. If either of those codes comes through, you simply access the actual data via the so.data[list[i].name] object reference. You pass that to the output window, and now you've just added a chat to the output.

```
public function onConnected(conn:NetConnection) : void
{
    trace("conn: " + conn);

    // guard against null
    if(conn == null) return;

    // Set up remoteSharedObject stuff
    so = SharedObject.getRemote("chat", conn.uri);
    so.connect(conn);
    so.addEventListener(SyncEvent.SYNC, onSync);
}

public function onSync(event:SyncEvent) : void
{
    trace("event: " + event);

    var list:Array = event.changeList;
    trace("event.changeList.length: " + event.changeList.length);

    for(var i:Number=0; i<list.length; i++){
        switch(list[i].code) {
            case "clear":
                trace("list[" + i + "].code: " + list[i].code);
                break;
            case "success":
                trace("list[" + i + "].code: " + list[i].code);
                output.text += so.data[(list[i].name)];
                break;
            case "reject":
                trace("list[" + i + "].code: " + list[i].code);
                break;
            case "change":
                trace("list[" + i + "].code: " + list[i].code);
                output.text += so.data[(list[i].name)];
                break;
            case "delete":
                trace("list[" + i + "].code: " + list[i].code);
```

```
                    break;
                }
            }
        }
```

The SyncEvent object will return five possible codes in a changeList array:

- clear: This means either that you have successfully connected to a remote shared object that is not persistent on the server or the client or that all the properties of the object have been deleted—for example, when the client and server copies of the object are so far out of sync that Flash Player resynchronizes the client object with the server object. In the latter case, SyncEvent.SYNC is dispatched, and the code value is set to change.

- success: If you have changed a property on SharedObject, this means the client changed the shared object successfully.

- reject: This means the client tried unsuccessfully to change the object; instead, another client changed the object.

- change: If another user changes SharedObject or the server resynchronizes, you will receive this event.

- delete: This means an attribute was deleted.

As a side note, if you want to delete the SharedObject reference from the client in hopes of reconnecting, the help files will tell you to use SharedObject.clear(). I recommend you use this call and then set the SharedObject reference to null:

```
public function destroy():void
{
    sharedObject.clear();
    sharedObject = null;
}
```

This completely destroys the SharedObject reference and avoids any problems with re-creating the reference to a new SharedObject. Without it, you may encounter issues with reconnecting to the remote SharedObject.

Links and more

At this point, you've been exposed to the sexiest parts of Red5, but that's just the beginning! I covered video broadcasting and subscriptions, you learned about shared objects and simple chat modules, and you took a decent look at how to communicate with MIDI devices via Red5. You can take these examples and use them right out of the box to get started on your masterpiece application! What was important here was that you got a taste of what you can possibly do with Red5 and start thinking outside of the normal bounds of Flash as a client.

If you're a Java developer reading this, you probably can't wait to try a few hundred ideas and sink your teeth right into the server-side API! If you're a Flash/Flex developer, you're probably amazed at how easy and fast it is to get up and running with some very powerful functionality. Either way, Red5 is an essential addition to anyone's arsenal of tools and technologies.

Getting involved in the community is what has made Red5 such a successful project and application. People who are passionate about this type of technology have really kept the project on track and made it one of the best around for providing these types of server solutions for the Flash Platform. In the following links, you will find the e-mail list for the general Red5 users as well as the Red5 developers list. The developers list exists for more technical questions about the code base, while the general list is more for discussion on how Red5 is used.

Here are some links for more information about the content covered in this chapter:

- http://www.osflash.org/red5: General Red5 page on OSFlash.org
- http://osflash.org/mailman/listinfo/red5_osflash.org: General mailing list
- http://osflash.org/mailman/listinfo/red5developers_osflash.org: Developers mailing list
- http://www.joachim-bauch.de/tutorials/red5/: Tutorials by Joachim Bauch
- http://www.shocksites.com: Forums for Red5
- http://dl.fancycode.com/red5/api/: Red5 docs (updated nightly)
- http://jira.red5.org/confluence/dashboard.action: Red5 wiki
- http://blog.ff9900.org: Chris Allen's (of Infrared5) personal blog

INDEX